Dictionary of SCIENTIFIC AND TECHNICAL TERMS ENGLISH - FRENCH FRENCH - ENGLISH FOR STUDENTS AND EVERYONE ELSE

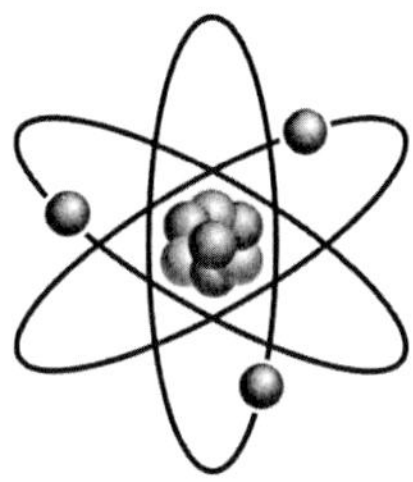

DICTIONNAIRE DES TERMES SCIENTIFIQUES ET TECHNIQUES ANGLAIS – FRANCAIS FRANCAIS - ANGLAIS

A l'intention des élèves de la section européenne et les classes STI2D

OUSSAMA SAYADI
PHYSICS AND CHEMISTRY TEACHER

Dictionary of SCIENTIFIC AND TECHNICAL TERMS

ENGLISH-FRENCH
FRENCH-ENGLISH
FOR STUDENTS AND EVERYONE ELSE

Dictionnaire des
Termes techniques et scientifiques
Anglais – Français
Français - Anglais
A l'intention des élèves
de la section européenne
et les classes STI2D

LES ÉDITIONS DU NET
22 rue Édouard Nieuport 92150 Suresnes

To my mother
Yomn Tizani

ISBN : 978-2-312-01315-2

The dictionary includes scientific terms in:

Physics
Chemistry
Mathematics
Computer Science
Renewable Energy
Laboratory glassware
Physics instruments

Dictionnaire de
Termes techniques et scientifiques
Anglais – Français
Français - Anglais
A l'intention des élèves
De la section européenne
Et les classes STI2D

If it was given to me to see a little further than others, it is because I was standing on the shoulders of giants.

S'il m'a été donné de voir un peu plus loin que les autres, c'est parce que j'étais monté sur les épaules de géants.

Isaac Newton

That's one small step for man,
one giant leap for mankind.

C'est un petit pas pour l'homme,
un bond de géant pour l'humanité.

Neil Armstrong

Special thanks to
my friends and colleagues:

Magali RENOU
Mathematics teacher

Stéphane VANDEWYNCKELE
Antoine Despres
Physics and chemistry teachers

Yomn Al-Kaissi
Goldsmith University of London

Zeid Wehbe
Financial support

For their interest in my work
for stimulating questions, remarks, proof reading and advice

How to use this dictionary

The dictionary is divided into two main sections:

- English – French and
- French – English.

In the dictionary seven parts that provide simplified information about physical and chemical science, sustainable developments and renewable energy, mathematics and computer sciences.

At the end of each section, tables are followed by comprehensive index and illustrations.

Comment utiliser le dictionnaire

Le dictionnaire est divisé en deux parties:

- Anglais – Français et
- Français – Anglais.

Le dictionnaire comporte sept chapitres donnant des informations simplifiées dans les domaines de la physique, la chimie, le développement durable, l'énergie renouvelable, les mathématiques et l'informatique. A la fin de chaque chapitre, on trouve des tableaux et des illustrations explicatives.

Sommaire

ENGLISH – FRENCH

PART 1

PHYSICS – PHYSIQUE

Physics is the science of Nature in
the broadest sense.
Physicists study the behavior and
interactions of matter and radiation.
The laws of physics are generally expressed
as mathematical relations.
These laws represent an attempt to establish the relation-
ships between different
experimental data.

La physique est la science de la nature dans
le sens le plus large.
Les physiciens étudient lc comportement et les interactions
de la matière
et le rayonnement.
Les lois de la physique sont généralement exprimées par
des relations mathématiques.
Ces lois représentent une tentative d'établir les rapports
entre les différentes
données expérimentales.

A

Aberration: aberration

- **When all the rays from a point object are not focused at a single image point, Gauss conditions are not respected, the resulting blurring of the image is called aberration.**
- **Lorsque les rayonnements provenant d'un objet ne sont pas focalisés en un point, les conditions de Gauss ne sont pas respectées, l'image floue obtenue est appelée aberration.**

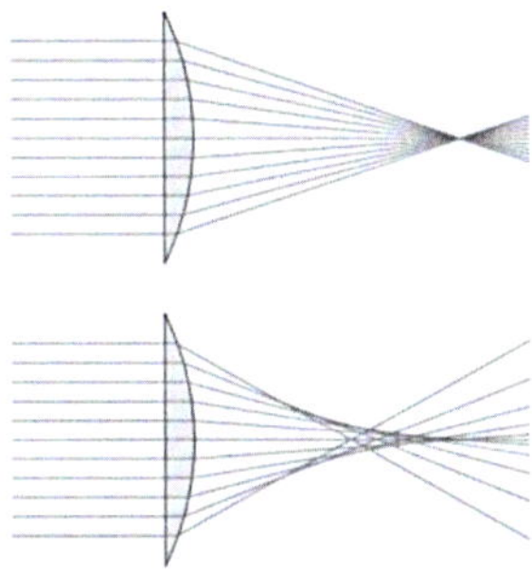

Absolute pressure: pression absolue

- **Is the measured pressure relative to vacuum.**
- **C'est la pression mesurée par rapport au vide.**

Absolute zero: zéro absolue

- **Is the lowest temperature that could exist in the Universe. It is defined as 0K on the Kelvin scale and as −273.15 °C on the Celsius scale.**
- **C'est la température la plus basse qui puisse exister dans l'Univers. Elle vaut -273,15 °C à l'échelle Celsius ou 0K à l'échelle Kelvin.**

Absorbed dose: dose absorbée

Absorption Line: raie d'absorption (raie de Fraunhoffer)

- **A dark line at a particular wavelength of a spectrum, formed when a cool, tenuous gas between a hot radiating source and the observer absorbs electromagnetic radiation of that wavelength.**
- **Une raie sombre observée sur le spectre d'une lumière traversant un gaz à basse température. La longueur d'onde de cette raie dépend de la composition chimique du gaz.**

Absorbance: absorbance

- **Logarithm of the ratio of incident to transmitted radiant power through a solution.**
- **L'absorbance traduit l'aptitude d'une solution à absorber une radiation considérée.**

Acoustic wave: onde acoustique

- **Acoustics is a branch of physics whose purpose is the study of sounds and mechanical waves. It uses wave phenomena and mechanical vibration.**
- **L'acoustique est une branche de la physique dont l'objet est l'étude des sons et des ondes mécaniques. Elle fait appel aux phénomènes ondulatoires et à la mécanique vibratoire.**

AC/DC: AC/DC

- **The description AC/DC refers to equipment designed to be operate on either alternating current AC or direct current DC.**
- **La désignation AC/DC est indiquée sur les appareils électriques fonctionnant en courant alternatif AC ou en courants continus DC.**

Acceleration: accélération

- **Is the rate of change of velocity over taken time. In SI units, acceleration is measured in meters per second squared ($m.s^{-2}$).**
- **C'est la variation par unité de temps de la vitesse divisée par le temps, son unité dans le SI est le $m.s^{-2}$.**

Accommodation: accommodation

- **Is the process by which the vertebrate eye changes optical power to maintain a clear image (focus) on an object as its distance changes.**

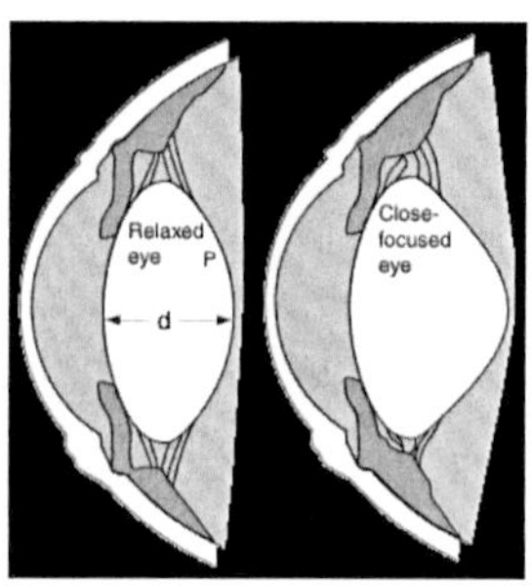

- **C'est le processus des modifications oculaires adaptatives permettant d'assurer la netteté des images pour des distances différentes de vision.**

Action and reaction: action et réaction

- **Every action is accompanied by a reaction of equal magnitude but opposite direction.**
- **Pour chaque action il se produit une réaction opposée et égale entre deux corps.**

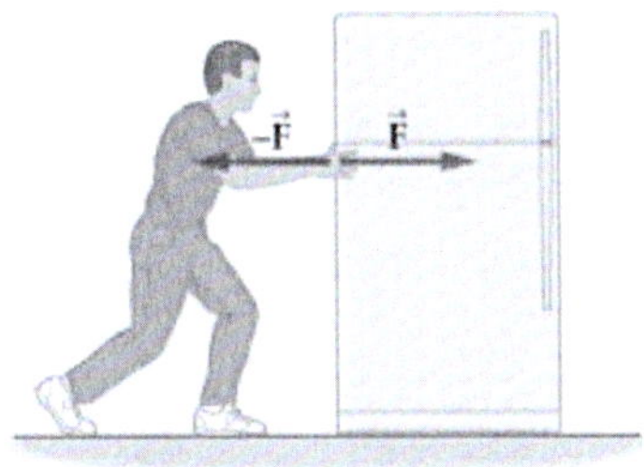

Activity: activité

- **In chemical thermodynamics, activity (symbol a) is a measure of the effective concentration of a species in a mixture.**
- **In nuclear physics, the nuclear activity is the velocity of disintegration of a radioactive material. Its unity in SI is Bq (one disintegration per second).**
- **L'activité chimique (symbole a) d'une espèce chimique correspond à la concentration active de cette espèce.**
- **En physique nucléaire, l'activité d'une source radioactive est la vitesse de désintégration du matériau radioactif. L'unité dans le SI est le becquerel (Bq), une désintégration par seconde.**

Adjust: régler

- **Adjust a measurement apparatus.**
- **Régler un appareil de mesure.**

Aerodynamics: aérodynamiques

- **Is a branch of dynamics concerned with studying the motion of air, particularly when it interacts with a moving object.**

- **C’est une branche de la dynamique des fluides qui porte principalement sur la compréhension et l'analyse des écoulements d'air et son interaction avec les objets en mouvement.**

Aerodynamic drag force: force de résistance aérodynamique

- **When a solid moves through a fluid, an aerodynamic drag force opposes the displacement. It depends on the fluid, but also the geometric characteristics of the moving solid.**
- $F_{res} = 1/2\rho_a.S.C_x.v^2$

  F_{res} : aerodynamic drag force (N)

  ρ_a: fluid density ($kg.m^{-3}$)

  S: cross-section area of the solid (m^2)

  C_x: dimensionless coefficient of drag reflecting the aerodynamics of the solid

  v: speed of the solid ($m.s^{-1}$)
- **Lorsqu'un solide se déplace dans un fluide, une force de résistance aérodynamique s'oppose au déplacement. Elle dépend du fluide, mais aussi des caractéristiques géométriques du solide en mouvement.**
- $F_{rés} = 1/2\rho_a.S.C_x.v^2$

  $F_{rés}$: force of résistance aérodynamique (N)

  ρ_a: masse volumique du fluide ($kg.m^{-3}$)

  S: section frontale du solide (m^2)

  C_x: coefficient reflétant l’aérodynamisme du solide

  v: vitesse du solide ($m.s^{-1}$)

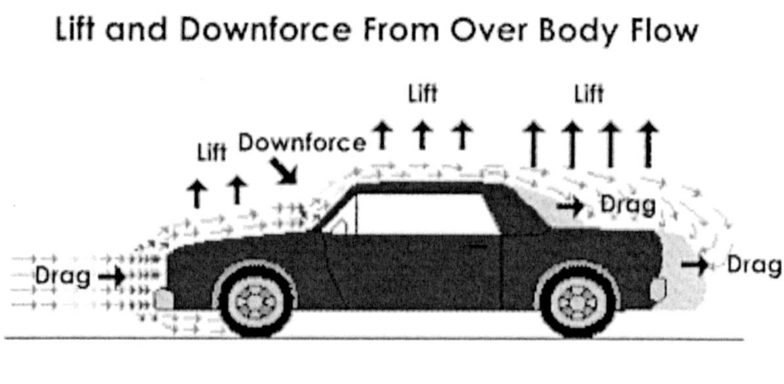

Alpha decay: décroissance alpha

- **Is a type of radioactive decay in which an atomic nucleus X emits an alpha particle and becomes an atomic nucleus Y.**
- **C'est une forme de désintégration radioactive où un noyau atomique X émet une particule alpha et se transforme en un noyau Y.**

Alpha rays: radiations alpha

- **Are the least penetrating, and can be stopped by a layer of skin or a sheet of paper, discovered by Rutherford in 1899.**
- **Ce sont des radiations peu pénétrantes découvertes par Rutherford en 1899, la peau ou une feuille peut l'arrêter.**

Alternating current and voltage: courant et tension alternatif

- **In alternating current and voltage (AC) the movement of electric charge periodically reverses direction. In direct current and voltage (DC), the flow of electric charge is only in one direction.**
- **En courant et en tension alternative (AC), les charges électriques changent de sens de façon périodique. En courant et tension continus (DC), les charges se déplacent dans une seule direction.**

AM/FM: AM/FM

- **Amplitude modulation/frequency modulation.**
- **Modulation d'amplitude/modulation de fréquence.**

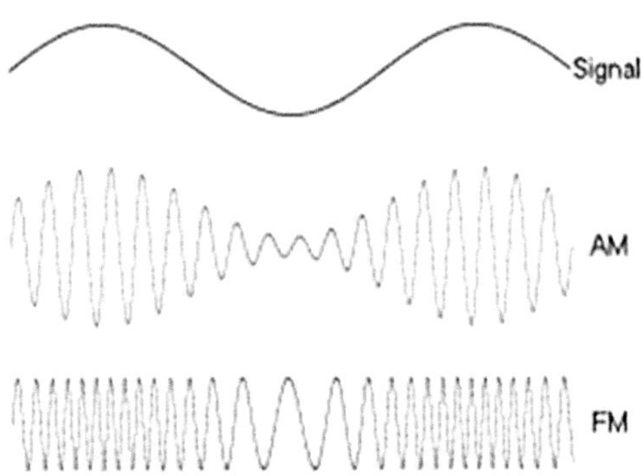

Ammeters: ampèremètre

- **Is an instrument used to measure the current flow in the circuit; it is always connected in series with a circuit.**

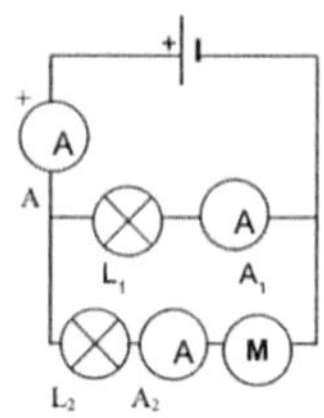

- **C'est un appareil utilisé pour mesurer l'intensité du courant électrique dans un circuit, il se branche in série.**

Amorphous solide: matière amorphe

- **In part of the older literature, the term has been used synonymously with glass. Nowadays, "amorphous solid" is considered to be the overarching concept, and "glass" the more special case: Glass liquids are amorphous solids.**
- **C'est un composé dans lequel les atomes ne respectent aucun ordre à moyenne et grande distance, ce qui le distingue des composés cristallisés. Les verres, les élastomères et les liquides sont des composés amorphes.**

Ampere: Ampère

- **SI base unit for the electric current (symbol A).**
- **Unité de l'intensité du courant électrique dans le SI.**

Amplifier: amplificateur

- **Is an electronic device for increasing the power of a signal.**
- **C'est un dispositif électronique qui augmente la puissance d'un signal.**

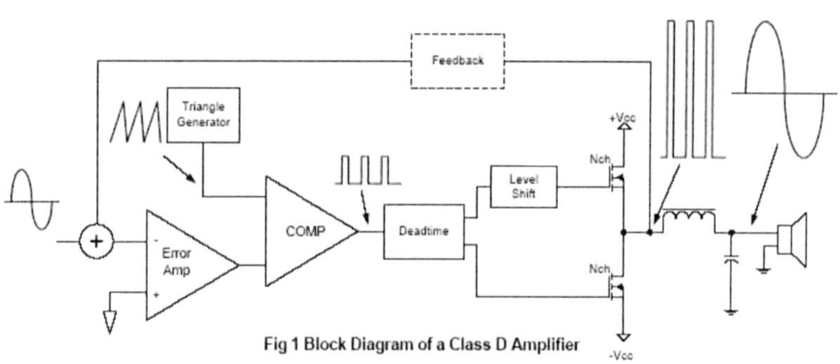

Fig 1 Block Diagram of a Class D Amplifier

Amplitude: amplitude

- **Is the maximum displacement of a particle from its equilibrium position.**
- **C'est le déplacement maximal d'une particule de sa position d'équilibre pour une onde mécanique.**

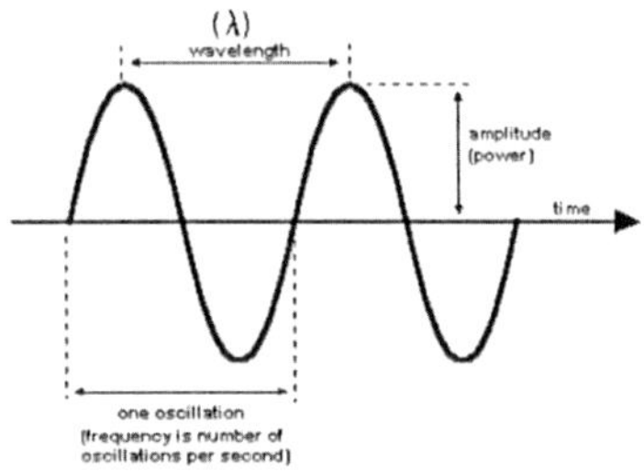

Analog signal: signal analogique

- **Transmit information in the form of continuous variation of a physical quantity.**

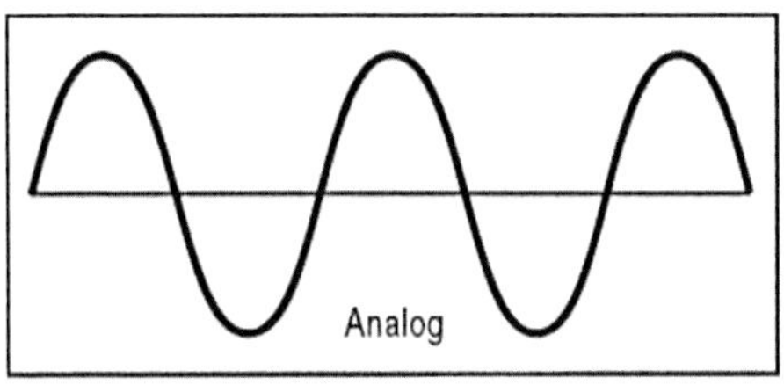

- **Transmet des informations sous la forme de variation continues d'une grandeur physique.**

Anemometer: anémomètre

- **Is a device for measuring wind speed used in wind turbines.**
- **C'est un appareil permettant de mesurer la vitesse du vent, utilisé dans les éoliennes.**

Angle swept: angle balayé

Angstrom (ångström): Angstrom

- **Is a unit of length equal to 10^{-10} m.**

- **Its symbol is the Swedish letter Å.**
- **An Ångstrom is on the order of the size of an atom.**
- **C'est une unité de longueur égale à 10^{-10} m.**
- **Son symbole est la lettre suédoise Å.**
- **Un Ångstrom est de l'ordre de la taille d'un atome.**

Angular acceleration: accélération angulaire
- **Is the rate of change of angular velocity over time.**
- **In SI units, it's measured in radians per second squared (rad.s^{-2}).**
- **C'est le rapport de la variation de la vitesse angulaire sur le temps correspondant.**
- **L'unité dans le SI est radian par seconde au carré (rad.s^{-2}).**

Angular displacement: déplacement angulaire
- **Is the angle through which a point has been rotated in a specified sense about a specified axis.**
- **C'est un angle correspondant à arc de cercle.**

Angular frequency (angular speed): fréquence angulaire
- **Is the magnitude of the vector quantity angular velocity.**
- $\omega = 2\pi/T = 2\pi f$

  where

  $\omega = d\theta/dt$ **is the angular frequency or angular speed (rad.s^{-1})**

  T is the period (s)

  f **is the ordinary frequency (Hertz)**

  $d\theta$ **is the angle (radian)**
- **C'est une mesure de la vitesse de rotation.**
- $\omega = 2\pi/T = 2\pi f$

  Avec
- $\omega = d\theta/dt$ **la fréquence angulaire ou vitesse angulaire (rad.s^{-1})**
- **T est la période de rotation (en s)**
- f **est la fréquence (en Hertz).**
- $d\theta$ **est l'angle (en radian)**

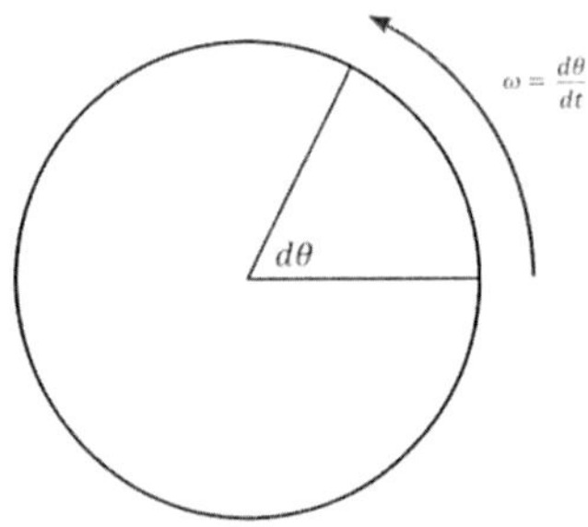

Angular velocity: vitesse angulaire

Antenna: antenne

- **Is an electrical device which couples waves in free space to an electrical current used by a receiver or transmitter.**
- **C'est un dispositif permettant d'émettre grâce à un émetteur ou de capter grâce à un récepteur les ondes électromagnétiques.**

Anti-reflective film: film antireflet

- **Is a type of optical coating applied to the surface of lenses and other optical devices to reduce reflection.**
- **C'est une couche qui augmente la transmission de la lumière et réduit les reflets parasites au sein du verre.**

Arc Degree: degré d'arc

- **A unit of angular measure in which there are 360 arc degrees in a full circle.**
- **Unité de mesure angulaire, un cercle contient 360 degrés d'arc.**

Arc Minute: minute d'arc

- **Abbreviated arcmin.**
- **A unit of angular measure in which there are 60 arc minutes in 1 arc degree.**
- **Abréviation arcmin.**
- **Unité de mesure angulaire, 1 degré d'arc contient 60 arcmin.**

Arc Second: seconde d'arc

- **Abbreviated arcsec.**
- **A unit of angular measure in which there are 60 arc seconds in 1 arc minute and therefore 3600 arc seconds in 1 arc degree.**
- **One arc second is equal to about 725 km on the Sun.**
- **Abréviation arcsec.**

- **Unité de mesure angulaire, 1 arcmin contient 60 arcsec et par conséquence 3600 arcsec dans 1 degré d'arc.**

Archimedes' screw: vis d'Archimède

- **Is a machine historically used for transferring water from a low-lying body of water into irrigation ditches.**
- **C'est une machine utilisée historiquement pour pomper de l'eau vers des canaux d'irrigations.**

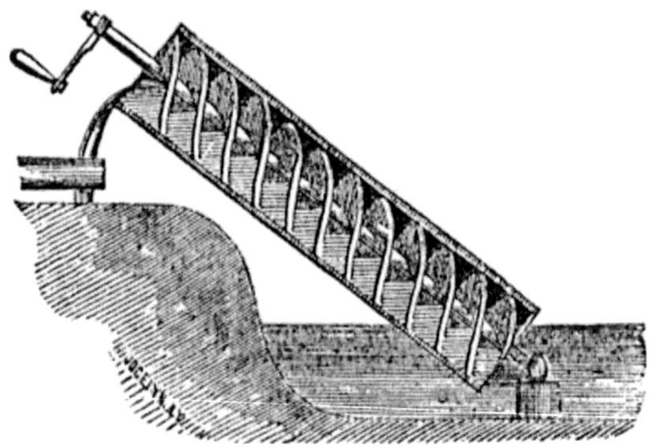

Archimedes' principle: principe d'Archimède

- **Any object, wholly or partially immersed in a fluid, is buoyed up by a force equal to the weight of the fluid displaced by the object.**
- **Tout corps immergé dans un fluide, est soumis de la part de celui-ci à une force verticale orientée vers le haut. Sa valeur est égale au poids du volume du fluide déplacé par le corps immergé.**

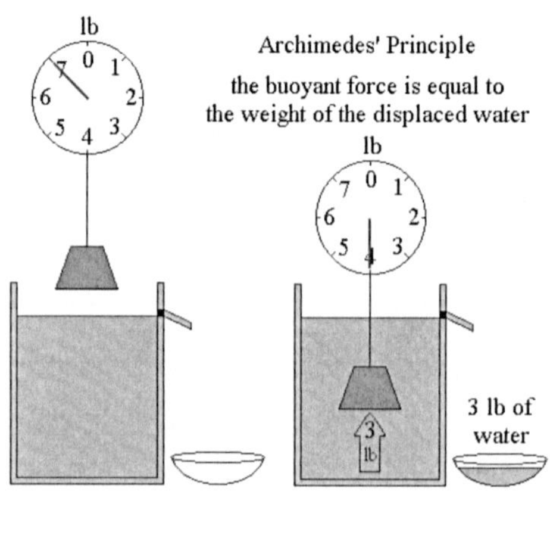

Asteroid: astéroïde

- **A rocky space object that can be a few feet wide to several hundred miles wide. Most asteroids in our solar system orbit in a belt between Mars and Jupiter.**
- **C'est une pierre rocheuse qui a une dimension variable de quelques mètres à plusieurs centaines de kilomètres. La plupart des astéroïdes de notre système solaire gravitent dans une ceinture entre Mars et Jupiter.**

L'astéroïde Lutetia

Astigmatism: astigmatisme

- **Is an optical defect in which vision is blurred due to the inability of the optics of the eye to focus a point object into a sharp focused image on the retina.**
- **C'est un défaut des systèmes optiques qui ne donnent pas d'un point une image ponctuelle, mais une image étalée à cause de l'incapacité de l'œil de focaliser l'image sur la rétine.**

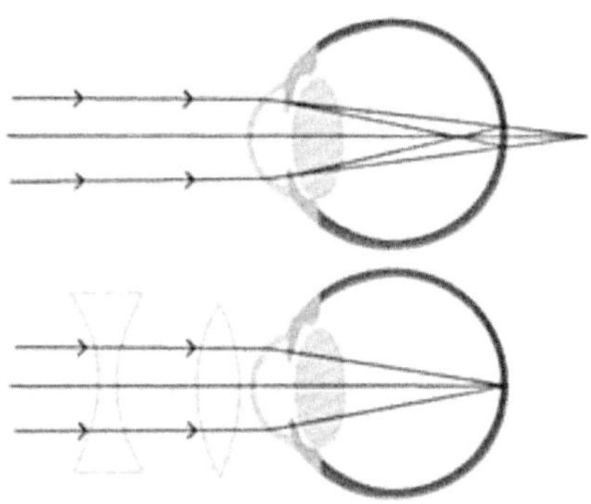

Astronomer: astronome

- **Scientist who observes and studies planets, stars, and galaxies.**
- **C'est un scientifique qui observe et étudie les planètes, les étoiles et les galaxies.**

Astronomical unit (A.U): unité astronomique (U.A.)

- **Is the average distance between the Earth and the Sun which is equal to 150,000,000 kilometers.**
- **C'est la distance moyenne entre la Terre et le Soleil, qui est égale à 150.10^6 kilomètres.**

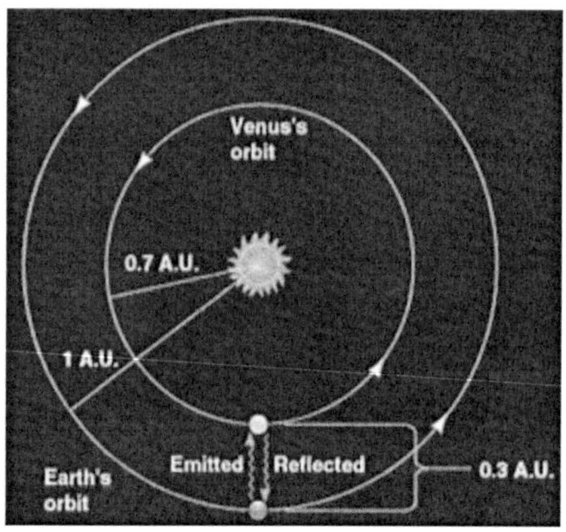

Astrophysics: astrophysique

- **Is the branch of astronomy that deals with the physics of the Universe.**
- **C'est une branche interdisciplinaire de l'astronomie qui concerne principalement la physique et l'étude des propriétés des objets de l'univers.**

Asynchronous (induction) motor: moteur asynchrone

- **An induction or asynchronous motor is an AC motor in which all electromagnetic energy is transferred by inductive coupling from a primary winding to a secondary winding, the two windings being separated by an air gap. In three-phase induction motors, that are inherently self-starting, energy transfer is usually from the stator to either a wound rotor or a short-circuited squirrel cage rotor.**
- **La machine asynchrone, connue également sous le terme anglo-saxon de machine à induction, est une machine électrique à courant électrique alternatif sans connexion entre le stator et le rotor.**

Les machines possédant un rotor « en cage d'écureuil » sont aussi connues sous le nom de machines à cage ou machines à cage d'écureuil. Le terme asynchrone provient du fait que la vitesse de rotation du rotor de ces machines n'est pas exactement déterminée par la fréquence des courants qui traversent leur stator.

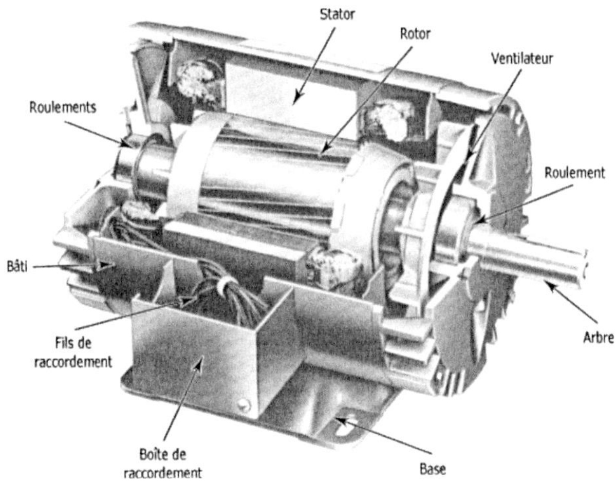

Atmosphere (atm): atmosphére (atm)

- **Unit of pressure (atm).**
- **Unité de pression (atm).**

Atmospheric pressure: pression atmosphérique

- **Is the force per unit area exerted against a surface by the weight of air above that surface in the Earth's atmosphere.**
- **C'est la pression par unité de surface qu'exerce le mélange gazeux constituant l'atmosphère considérée.**

Apparatus: appareil

- **Instrument of measurement.**
- **Instrument de mesure.**

Atmosphere: atmosphère

- **Is an envelope of gases surrounding the Earth. It shields us from the UV coming from the Sun and contains the air we breathe. Without it life would not exist.**

- **C'est une enveloppe de gaz qui entoure la Terre. Il nous protège des rayonnements UV provenant du soleil et contient l'air que nous respirons. Sans elle, la vie n'existerait pas.**

Atomic clock: horologe atomique

- **Is used as primary standards for international time distribution services, to control the frequency of television broadcasts, and in global navigation satellite systems such as GPS.**
- **Utilisé pour le maintien du Temps Atomique International (TAI) et la distribution du Temps universel coordonné, qui sont les échelles de temps de référence. Ils sont également employés dans les technologies de positionnement géographique GPS.**

Atomic masse unit: unité de mass atomique

- **Is a unit that is used for indicating mass on an atomic or molecular scale. It is defined as one twelfth of the rest mass of an unbound atom of carbon 12 and has a value of $1.66054.10^{-27}$kg.**
- **Its symbol is (u).**
- **C'est une unité de mesure standard utilisée pour mesurer la masse des atomes et des molécules. Elle est définie comme 1/12 de la masse d'un atome du carbone 12. Elle vaut approximativement $1,66054 \times 10^{-27}$ kg.**
- **Son symbole est (u).**

Audible sounds: son audible

- **Are sound waves with a range of frequency between 20 Hz and 20 kHz.**
- **Ce sont des ondes sonores dans la gamme de fréquence allant de 20 Hz à 20 kHz.**

Audibility threshold: seuil d'audibilité

- **Is the minimum sound level of a pure tone that an average ear with normal hearing.**
- **C'est le niveau sonore minimal d'un son pur que l'oreille moyenne peut entendre.**

Aurora: aurore

- **A display of colored light given off by collisions between charged particles trapped in a planet's magnetic fields and atoms of atmospheric gases near the planet's magnetic poles. Aurora is visible on**

Earth as the aurora borealis or northern lights and the aurora australis or southern lights.

- **C'est une lumière colorée émise par les collisions entre les particules chargées piégées dans des champs magnétiques d'une planète et des atomes de gaz atmosphériques à proximité des pôles magnétiques de la planète. L'aurore est visible sur la terre comme les aurores boréales ou les aurores australes ou les lumières du Sud.**

Average acceleration: accélération moyenne

Average power: puissance moyenne

Avogadro's constant: constant d'Avogadro

- **Fundamental physical constant, representing the molar number of entities N_A=6.022.10^{23}mol^{-1} (Avogadro's number).**
- **Valeur fondamentale qui représente le nombre d'entités élémentaires dans une mole, N_A=6.022.10^{23}mol^{-1} (Nombre d'Avogadro).**

Axis: axe

- **An imaginary straight line around which an object spins.**
- **C'est une ligne imaginaire autour duquel un objet tourne.**

B

Band pass filter: filtre passe-bande

- **Is a filter only allowing a band or frequency range between a low cutoff frequency and a high cutoff frequency of the filter.**
- **C'est un filtre ne laissant passer qu'une bande ou intervalle de fréquences compris entre une fréquence de coupure basse et une fréquence de coupure haute du filtre.**

Bar: bar

- **Unit of pressure.**
- **Unité de pression.**

Barometer: baromètre

- **Instrument for pressure measurement. Indicates the state of the weather: stormy, rain, change, fair and dry.**
- **Instrument pour mesurer la pression. Indique l'état de la météo : tempête, pluie, changement, beau et sec.**

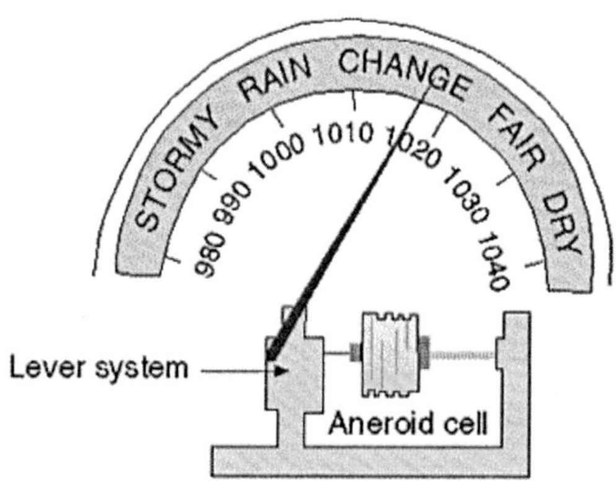

Battery: pile, batterie

- **Is one or more electrochemical cells that convert stored chemical energy into electrical energy.**
- **C'est un dispositif électrochimique qui transforme l'énergie chimique en énergie électrique.**

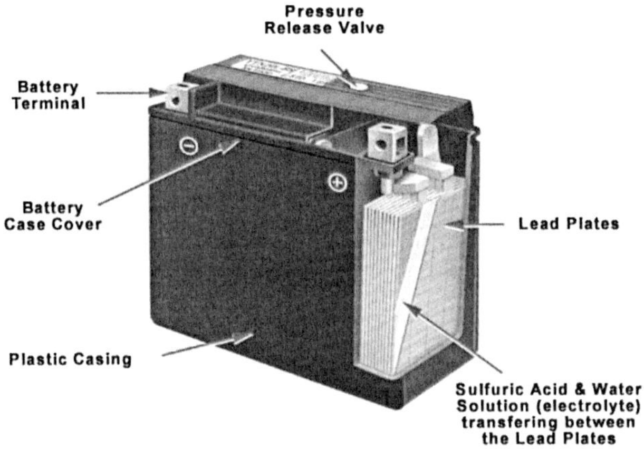

Bearing: roulement

- **Is a device to allow constrained relative motion between two or more parts, typically rotational.**
- **Ce sont des organes utilisés en construction mécanique pour supporter et guider, en rotation, des arbres de transmission.**

Bearing tube: tube de roulement à palier

Becquerel: Becquerel

- **Unit of radioactivity.**
- **Unité de la radioactivité.**

Beta radiation: radiation bêta

- **Are determined to have a greater power than alpha particles, able to penetrate up to one to two centimeters of water or human flesh or by a sheet of aluminum a few millimeters thick, discovered by Rutherford in 1899.**
- **Ce sont des radiations plus pénétrantes que les radiations alpha, découvertes par Rutherford, ils peuvent être arrêtés par un centimètre ou deux centimètres d'eau ou une feuille d'aluminium de plusieurs millimètres.**

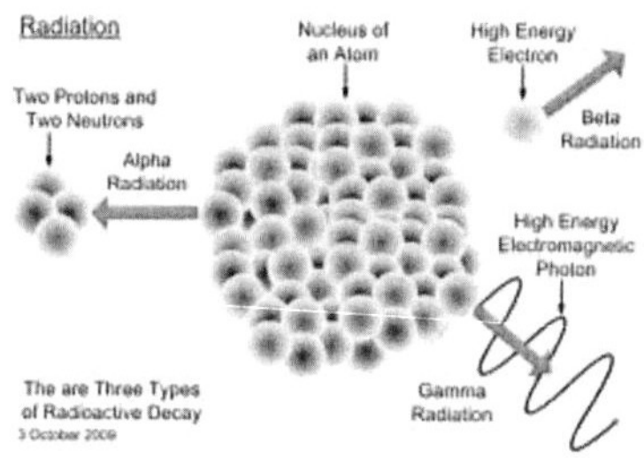

Black Hole: Trou Noir

- **A region of space that has so much mass concentrated in it that there is no way for a nearby object or electromagnetic rays to escape its gravitational pull.**
- **C'est une région de l'espace où des étoiles qui s'effondrent sur elles même, empêchant tout objet ou rayonnement électromagnétique de s'échapper.**

Blade: pale d'une éolienne

- **Is a part of wind turbine.**
- **C'est une partie d'une éolienne entrainée par le vent.**

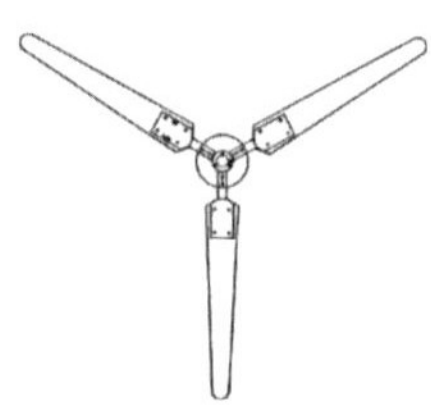

Big bang theory: théorie de Big bang
- **Is a cosmological theory of the early development of the universe.**
- **C'est une théorie cosmologique qui décrit l'évolution et le début de l'Univers.**

Big Crunch: Big Crunch
- **Is one possible scenario for the ultimate fate of the universe, in which the metric expansion of space eventually reverses and the universe collapses, ultimately ending as a black hole singularity.**
- **C'est un scénario possible du destin de l'Univers. Il désigne l'effondrement de l'univers à la fin d'une phase de contraction symétrique de la phase d'expansion faisant suite au Big Bang. C'est donc en quelque sorte un « Big Bang à l'envers ».**

Binding energy: énergie de liaison
- **Is the mechanical energy required to disassemble a whole into separate parts.**
- **C'est l'énergie mécanique nécessaire pour séparer deux parties liées entre elles.**

Black body: corps noir
- **Is an idealized physical body that absorbs all incident electromagnetic radiation. Its temperature changes with its emission spectrum (Wien's Law).**
- **C'est un corps qui absorbe tous les rayonnements électromagnétique. Sa température évolue avec son spectre d'émission (Loi de Wien).**

BLDC (brushless DC motor): moteur à courant continu sans balais
- **This motor doesn't contain rotational collectors and then no brushes. BLDC motor requires a microprocessor-controlled system to control coils in the stator. Brushless motors are widely used in industrial engineering field especially in servo-mechanism for a manufacturing process.**
- **They are used in fans for cooling computers and to outfit the electric bikes. They are found in model airplanes.**
- **C'est un moteur qui ne contient aucun collecteur tournant et donc pas de balais. Un système électronique de commande est nécessaire pour assurer la commutation du courant dans les enroulements statoriques. Les moteurs brushless sont largement utilisés dans l'industrie, en particulier dans les servomécanismes des machines-outils et dans le domaine de la robotique.**

- **Ils sont utilisés dans les ventilateurs assurant le refroidissement des ordinateurs et ils équipent également les vélos à assistance électrique. On les retrouve dans le domaine l'aéromodélisme.**

Boyle's law: loi de Boyle-Mariotte
- **Describes the relationship between the pressure and volume of a gas at constant temperature.**
- **Equation formula P.V = n.R.T**
- **Elle relie la pression et le volume d'un gaz à température constante.**
- **Formule P.V = n.R.T**

Brittle (ness): fragile, fragilité
- **A material is brittle if, when subjected to stress, it breaks without significant deformation.**
- **Un matériau est fragile lorsqu'on lui impose des contraintes mécaniques il se fracture.**

Brownian motion: mouvement Brownien
- **Is the presumably random drifting of particles suspended in a liquid or the mathematical model used to describe such random movements, which is often called a particle theory.**
- **C'est une description mathématique du mouvement aléatoire des particules immergées dans un fluide, cette description est appelée théorie de particules.**

Bulb: ampoule

Bullets: balls
- **Is a projectile propelled by a firearm.**
- **C'est un projectile propulsé par une arme.**

C

Calibration: étalonnage

- **Is a comparison between measurements.**
- **C'est une procédure permettant d'obtenir le même résultat de plusieurs appareils à partir de la même situation initiale.**

Capacitance (C): capacité (C)

- **Capacitance is the ability of a body to store an electrical charge. Any body or structure that is capable of being charged, either with static electricity or by an electric current, exhibits capacitance. A common form of energy storage device is a parallel-plate capacitor. In a parallel plate capacitor, capacitance is directly proportional to the surface area of the conductor plates and inversely proportional to the separation distance between the plates. If the charges on the plates are +q and −q, and U gives the voltage between the plates, then the capacitance C is given by $C=q/U$.**
- **The SI unit is the farad (F).**
- **La capacité représente la quantité de charge électrique stockée pour un potentiel électrique donné. Elle est définie comme étant la somme des charges électriques d'un élément divisée par le potentiel de cet élément $C=q/U$.**
- **L'unité est le farad (F).**

Capacitor: condensateur

- **Is a device for storing electric charge.**
- **C'est un dispositif pour emmagasiner la charge électrique.**

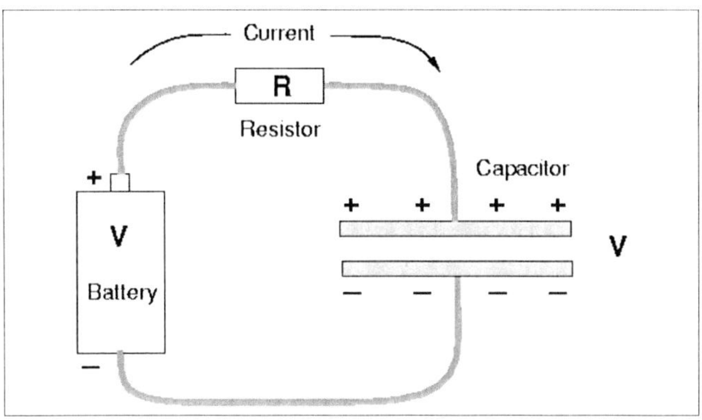

Carrier wave: onde porteuse

- An electromagnetic wave that can be modulated, as in frequency, amplitude, or phase, to transmit informations, or other signals.
- Onde dont la fréquence et l'amplitude sont constantes et propres à l'émetteur, utilisée comme support pour les signaux électromagnétiques.

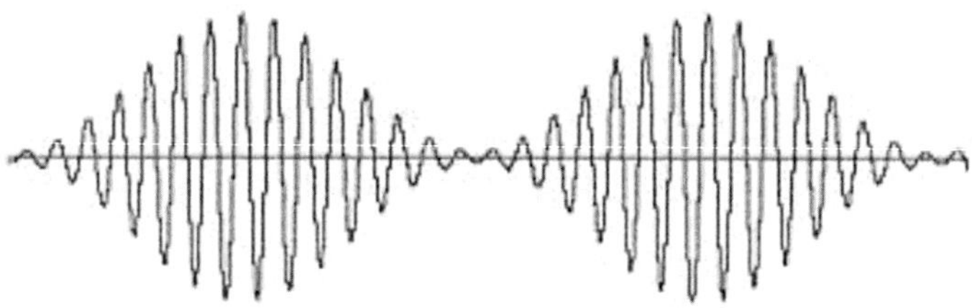

CCD: CCD
- Charge Coupled Device. A semiconductor light detector which converts light (UV, visible or IR) to electrical impulses. Such detectors are used by a number of the instruments on satellites.
- Capteur photographique. C'est un composant électronique photosensible servant de convertir un rayonnement électromagnétique (UV, visible ou IR) en un signal électrique. Il est utilisé dans les satellites.

Celerity: célérité
- Used to indicate the velocity of light.
- Ce vocabulaire est utilisé pour désigner la vitesse de la propagation de la lumière.

CELIAS: CELIAS
- Charge, Element, and Isotope Analysis System. Instrument aboard satellites which analyzes the constituents of the solar wind.
- Système d'analyse des charges, éléments et isotopes. Instrument utilisé dans les satellites pour analyser les constituants du vent solaire.

Celsius temperature scale: échelle de température en célsius
- Abbreviated °C.
- A unit of temperature.
- Zero degree Celsius is equal to 273 K (Kelvin).
- Water freezes at 0 °C and boils at 100 °C (at S.T.P.

Standard conditions of temperature and pressure).
- **Degrees Fahrenheit = Degrees Celsius x(9/5) +32.**
- **Symbolisé °C.**
- **Unité de mesure de la température.**
- **Zéro dégrée Celsius est égale à 273 K (Kelvin).**
- **La température de congélation de l'eau est égale 0 °C et l'ébullition est égale à 100 °C (dans les C.N.T.P. Conditions Normale de Température et de Pression).**
- **Dégrées Fahrenheit = Dégrées Celsius x (9/5) +32.**

Centigrade temperature scale: échelle centigrade de température
- **Is a scale and unit of measurement for temperature before 1948.**
- **C'est l'unité de l'échelle de température avant 1948.**

Centimeter-Gram-Second (CGS): Centimètre-Gramme-Seconde CGS
- **Abbreviated cm-g-s. The system of measurement that uses these units for distance, mass, and time.**
- **Système utilisant les unités de distance, masse et le temps. Symbolisé par cm-g-s.**

Centre of gravity: centre de gravité
- **Is the point where the action of the gravity forces is applied.**
- **C'est le point où est appliquée la force résultante associée à l'ensemble des forces qui agissent sur tous les points qui constituent un système.**

Centre of mass: barycentre
- **The center of mass or mass center is the mean location of all the mass in a system.**
- **C'est une notion physique et mécanique, elle désigne le point où devrait être concentrée toute la masse du système.**

Centrifugal force: force centrifuge
- **Represents the effects of inertia that arise in connection with rotation and which are experienced as an outward force away from the center of rotation.**
- **C'est l'effet ressenti dû aux mouvements de rotation et se traduit par une tendance à éloigner les corps du centre de rotation.**

Chain reaction: réaction en chaine

- Is a sequence of reactions where a reactive product causes additional reactions to take place.
- C'est une réaction dans laquelle un des agents nécessaires à la réaction est produit lui-même par la réaction, causant des réactions additionnelles et successives.

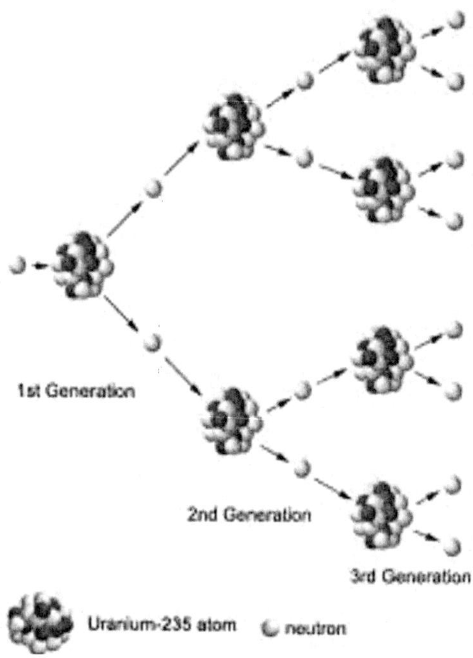

Charles' law: loi de Charles

- Is an experimental gas law which describes how gases tend to expand when heated, described a century earlier by the French Guillaume Amontons.
- C'est une loi expérimentale décrivant le comportement des gaz lorsqu'ils sont chauffés. Commentée un siècle auparavant par le français Guillaume Amontons.

Chromosphere: chromosphere

- The layer of the solar atmosphere that is located above the photosphere and beneath the transition region and the corona. The chromosphere is hotter than the photosphere but not as hot as the corona.

- **C'est la basse atmosphère du Soleil. C'est une fine couche rose de gaz, transparente pour la lumière visible, située entre la photosphère et la couronne solaire. Elle est plus chaude que la photosphère mais moins chaude que la couronne solaire.**

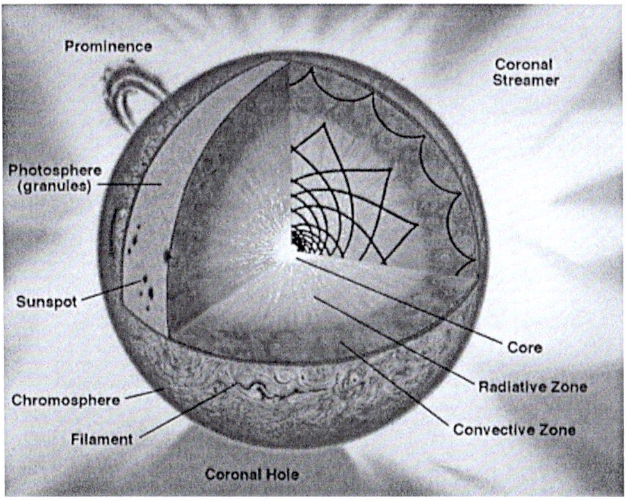

Circuit breaker: disjoncteur
- **Is an operated electrical switch used to protect an electrical circuit from damage caused by overload or short circuit.**
- **C'est interrupteur électrique utilisé pour protéger un circuit électrique de dommage causé par un défaut électrique (surintensité).**

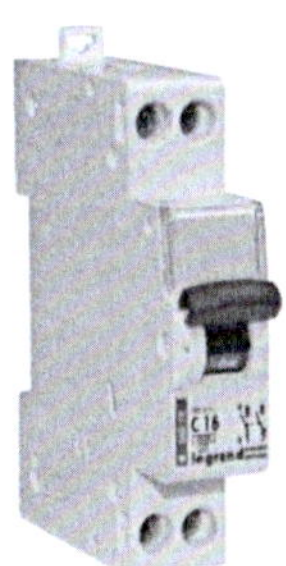

Circular motion: mouvement circulaire
- **Is the rotation along a circle or a circular orbit.**
- **C'est la trajectoire décrivant un cercle.**

Coal: charbon

- Is a combustible black or brownish-black sedimentary rock coal is composed primarily of carbon along with variable quantities of other elements, chiefly hydrogen, with smaller quantities of sulfur, oxygen and nitrogen.
- C'est un combustible noir ou marron formé à partir de la dégradation de la matière organique des végétaux. Le charbon est composé de carbone, hydrogène, soufre et d'azote.

Coherence: cohérence

- In physics, coherence is a property of waves that enables stationary interference.
- En physique, c'est l'ensemble des propriétés de corrélation d'un système ondulatoire.

Coil (solenoid): bobine

- Is a circular wire found on some electrical transformers, inductors, all of which are sets of wire coils.
- C'est un fil en forme circulaire qu'on trouve dans les transformateurs et les bobines.

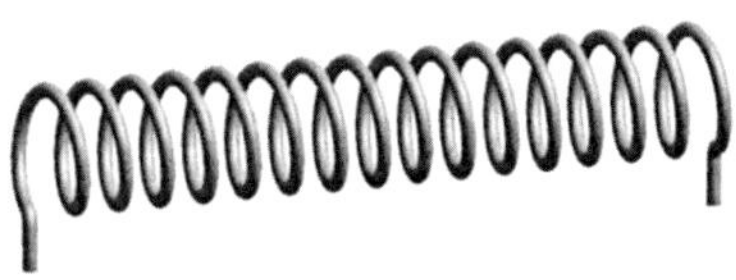

Compass: boussole

- Is made up of a magnetic needle indicating the north.
- Une aiguille aimantée qui indique le nord.

Composite materials: matériaux composites

- Naturally occurring materials made from two or more constituent materials with significantly different physical or chemical properties.
- C'est un assemblage d'au moins deux matériaux. L'assemblage obtenu possède des propriétés physico-chimiques différentes que les matériaux seuls.

Compression: compressibilité

- Is a term used in connection with longitudinal wave and refers to the region where the particles of the medium are 'bunched up'.

- Ce terme en rapport avec les ondes longitudinales, désigne la région ou les particules du milieu sont 'comprimées'.

Conduction (see heat conduction): conduction

Conduction band: bande de conduction

Conductors: conducteurs
- Is a material which contains movable electric charges.
- C'est un matériau qui laisse passer des charges électriques.

Conservation of energy: conservation de l'énergie
- Energy can never be created nor destroyed; it's only ever converted from one form to another.
- L'énergie ne peut pas être créée ni détruite. Elle peut être convertie d'une forme en une autre.

Constellation: constellation
- Is a collection of stars or galaxies that form a recognizable group as viewed from Earth.
- C'est une collection d'étoiles ou de galaxies visibles et reconnaissables de la Terre.

Continuous spectrum: spectre continu
- A radiation in which all wavelengths is present.
- C'est une radiation dans laquelle toutes les longueurs d'onde sont présentes.

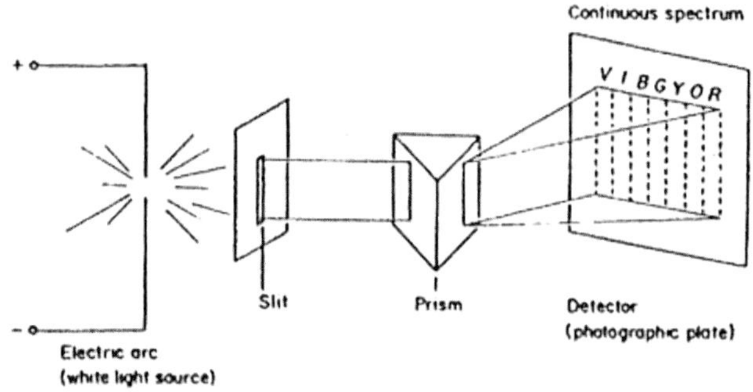

Convection (see heat conduction): convection

Converter DC-AC : convertisseur DC-AC

- **Is a device changing DC current into AC current**
- **C'est un dispositif qui transforme le courant continu en courant alternatif**

Core: Cœur solaire

- **In solar astronomy, the innermost part of the Sun, where energy is generated by nuclear reactions.**
- **En astronomie solaire, c'est la partie centrale du soleil ou les réactions nucléaires sont générées.**

Corona: corona, couronne

- **The outermost layer of the solar atmosphere. The corona consists of a highly rarefied gas with a temperature greater than one million Kelvin. It is visible to the naked eye during a solar eclipse.**
- **C'est la couche extérieure de l'atmosphère solaire. La corona contient des gaz extrêmement raréfiés où la température atteint un million de kelvin. Elle est visible lors des éclipses solaires.**

Coronagraph: Coronagraphe

- **Telescope for observing the corona. Often contains an occulting disk which covers the disk of the Sun so that the corona may be more easily observed.**
- **C'est un télescope qui sert à observer la couronne solaire. Il contient un disque central occultant le soleil pour mieux observer la corona.**

Coronal Hole: tache solaire

- **An area of the corona which appears dark in X-rays and ultraviolet light. They are usually located at the poles of the Sun, but can occur other places as well.**
- **Ce sont des taches sombres qui apparaissent dans la couronne solaire visible dans les rayonnements Ultraviolets et les rayons-X. Souvent visible dans les pôles solaires.**

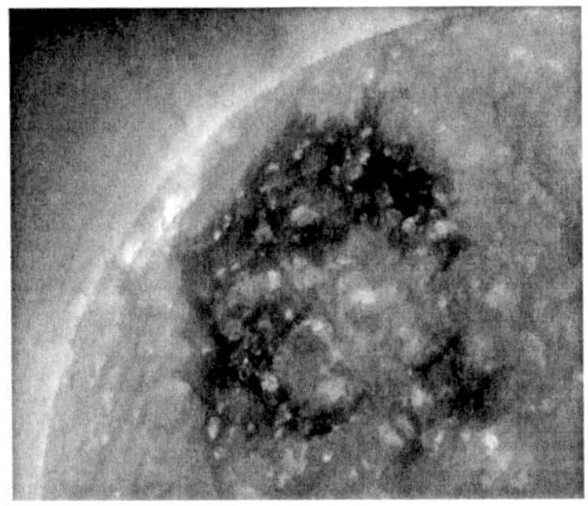

Coronal Mass Ejection: éjection de la masse coronale

- **A huge magnetic bubble of plasma that erupts from the Sun's corona and travels through space at high speed.**
- **C'est une éruption de la couronne solaire d'une énorme bulle magnétique de plasma qui voyage à travers l'espace à très grande vitesse.**

Coronal Streamer: flux coronal

- **Large scale magnetic structures observed in the Sun's corona.**
- **Une large structure magnétique observée dans la couronne solaire.**

Cosmic Ray: rayonnement cosmique

- **High energy charged particles traveling through interstellar space at nearly the velocity of light.**
- **Particules chargées d'une très grande énergie voyageant à travers l'espace interstellaire à une vitesse proche de celle de la lumière.**

Cosmodetector: cosmodétecteur

- **The cosmodétecteur is a detector of cosmic muons particles. It is composed of four parts:**
  1. **Rackets scintillator: detects the possible passage of muons.**
  2. **The photomultiplier (PM) amplifies the signal detected by the scintillator.**
  3. **The electronic parts: converts the received output of the AM analog signal into a digital signal and discriminates the signal too weak (set by the experimenter.**
  4. **Software.**
- **To this material is added to the loan two scintillators:**
  1. **One to measure the lifetime of the muon**
  2. **For the second measurement from the muon.**

- **Le cosmodétecteur est un détecteur de muons cosmiques. Il est composé de 4 parties :**
  1- **Les raquettes de scintillateur : détecte le passage éventuel des muons.**
  2- **Le photomultiplicateur (PM) : amplifie le signal détecté par le scintillateur.**
  3- **La partie électronique : transforme le signal analogique reçu à la sortie du PM en signal numérique et discrimine les signaux trop faibles (fixé par l'expérimentateur.**
  4- **Le logiciel.**
- **A ce matériel s'ajoute l'empreinte de deux scintillateurs:**
  1- **L'un pour mesurer la durée de vie du muon.**
  2- **Le deuxième pour mesure la provenance des muons.**

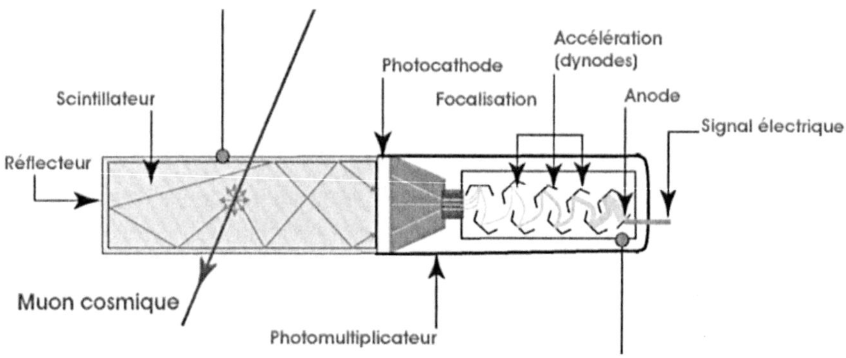

- **Les muons sont détectés par la lumière qu'ils induisent dans les lattes de scintillateur plastique.**
- **Le photomultiplicateur permet de transformer la lumière en signal électrique et de l'amplifier.**
- **La photocathode réagit par effet photo-électrique à l'arrivée d'un photon et émet des élecrons.**
- **Ces électrons sont accélérés et collectés grâce à une haute tension électrique (env. 2kV) appliquée à la cathode, aux dynodes et à l'anode.**
- **Les électrons se multiplient à chaque dynode.**
- **Les électrons sont ensuite collectés sur l'anode et créent un signal électrique.**

COSTEP: AEPHT

- **Comprehensive Suprathermal and Energetic Particle Analyzer. Instrument aboard satellites which analyzes high energy particles in the solar wind.**

- **Analyseur d'énergie de particule et de la très haute température. C'est instrument utilisé par les satellites qui analysent la haute énergie des particules dans le vent solaire.**

Coulomb: Coulomb (C)

- **Is the charge transported by a steady current of one ampere in one second,**
- **Symbol C.**
- **Is the SI derived unit of electric charge.**
- **Q=I.t**
- **1 C = 1 s.A**
- **C'est la quantité d'électricité traversant une section d'un conducteur parcouru par un courant d'intensité de 1 ampère pendant 1 seconde.**
- **Symbole C.**
- **C'est l'unité de la charge électrique dans le SI.**
- **Q=I.t**
- **1 C = 1 s.A**

Coulomb's Law: loi de Coulomb

- **Is a law describing the electrostatic interaction between electrically charged particles.**
- **C'est une loi qui décrit l'interaction électrostatique entre charges électriques.**

Couple of forces: couple de forces

Crater: cratère

- **A hole caused by an object hitting the surface of a planet or a moon.**
- **Un trou creusé par un objet heurtant la surface d'une planète ou d'une lune.**

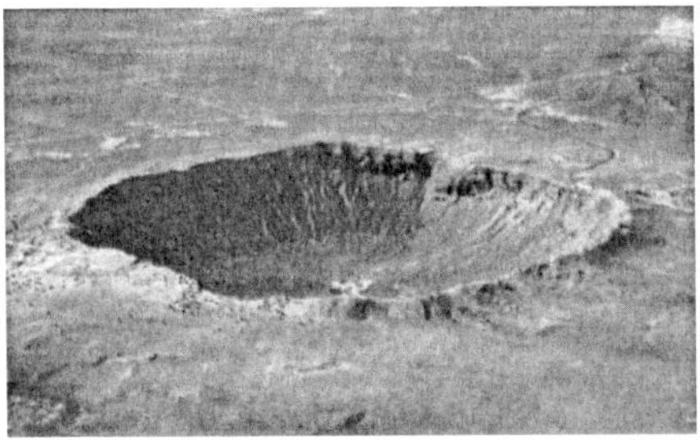

Crest: Crête

- **A crest is a term coined from water waves and refers to the maximum height of the wave.**
- **C'est un terme qui désigne le point maximal d'une onde.**

Curie temperature: température de Curie

- **A magnet will lose its magnetism if heated above the Curie temperature. There are various Curie temperatures in function of different substances.**
- **Un aimant perd son magnétisme s'il est chauffé au-delà de la température de Curie. La température de Curie varie en fonction des métaux.**

Current: courant

- **Is the flow of electrons round the circuit.**
- **I=Q/t**

  I: current (A)

  Q: charge flowing (C)

  t: time taken (s)
- **C'est le flux d'électrons dans un circuit électrique.**
- **I=Q/t**

  I: intensité du courant (A)

  Q: charges écoulés (C)

  t: temps écoulé (s)

Cut-off frequency: fréquence de coupure

Cut-off threshold: seuil de coupure

D

Dalton's Law of partial pressure: loi de Dalton de pression partielle

- **States that the total pressure exerted by a gaseous mixture is equal to the sum of the partial pressures of each individual component in a gas mixture.**
- **C'est une loi qui énonce que dans le cas de gaz parfaits, la pression totale exercée par un mélange est égale à la somme des pressions partielles des constituants.**

Damped harmonic motion: amortissement du mouvement oscillatoire

- **In real oscillators friction, or damping, slows the motion of the system.**
- **C'est un phénomène de ralentissement du mouvement oscillatoire à cause du frottement.**

Damping: amortissement

- **In physics, damping is any effect that tends to reduce the amplitude of oscillations in an oscillatory system. In mechanics, friction is one such damping effect.**
- **En physique, l'amortissement est l'effet engendré par l'entrée d'un système, qui tend à s'opposer aux variations de la sortie du système. Le frottement peut amortir.**

Dark matter: matière noire

- **Is a mysterious invisible substance that makes around 85 per cent of all the matter in the Universe.**
- **C'est matière mystérieuse invisible qui constitue approximativement 85 pour cent de toute la matière de l'Univers.**

De Broglie wavelength (matter wave): longueur d'onde de De Broglie

- **The De Broglie equations relate the wavelength λ and frequency ν to the momentum p, respectively as:**

$$p=h/\lambda=h.\nu/c$$

Where λ is the wavelength of the particle
h is Planck's constant of the particle,
p is the momentum of the particle,

c is the light celerity.

- **En physique, l'hypothèse de De Broglie est l'affirmation que toute matière est dotée d'une onde associée: ceci donne lieu à la dualité onde-particule. La longueur d'onde et la quantité de mouvement d'une particule sont reliées par l'équation:**

$$p=h/\lambda=h.\nu/c$$

Avec λ est la longueur d'onde de la particule,

h est la constante de Planck de la particule,

p est la quantité de mouvement de la particule,

c est la célérité de la lumière.

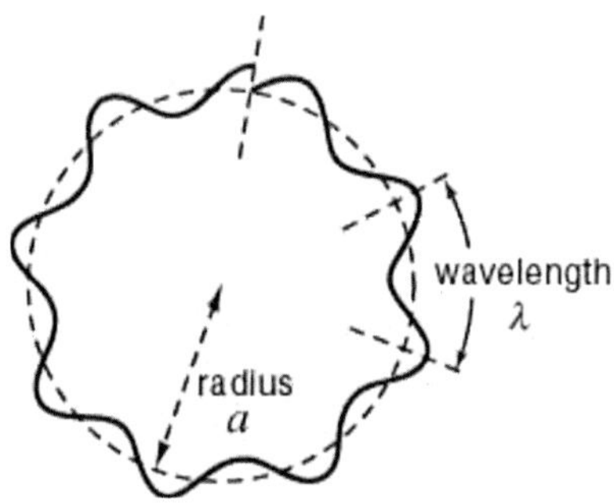

Decibel: décibel

- **Unity of measurement of sound power (dB). Doubling the power of the sound adds 3 dB to its rating. Thus a sound of 15 dB is twice as loud as a sound of 12 dB.**
- **Unite de la mesure de la puissance sonore (dB). Chaque fois on double la puissance sonore on rajoute 3 dB. Ainsi un bruit de 15 dB est deux fois plus fort qu'un son de 12 dB.**

Density (relative density Rd): densité

- **Is the ratio of the density (mass of a unit volume) of a substance to the density of a given reference material, it's given by the relation:**
- $Rd_{substance}=\rho_{substance}/\rho_{reference}$
- **C'est le rapport de la masse volumique d'une substance par rapport à une masse volumique de référence, la relation qui lie ces grandeurs:**

- $d_{substance} = \rho_{substance} / \rho_{référence}$

Derived quantity: quantité dérivée
- **Is a physical quantity which is not a base quantity in SI.**
- **C'est une quantité physique qui n'est pas dans le SI.**

Derived unity: unité dérivée
- **Is a physical unity which is not a base unity in SI.**
- **C'est une unité qui n'est pas dans le SI.**

Destructive interference: interférence destructive
- **Means that two or more waves meeting at a point oppose one another at all times and have zero resultant.**
- **Lorsque deux ondes ou plus dans des directions opposées se rencontrent en un point et que leur résultante est nul.**

Detector: détecteur

Device: dispositif
- **In physics, a device is an instrument used for measuring or an electrical component.**
- **En physique, un dispositif peut être un appareil de mesure ou un circuit électrique.**

Diamagnetic: diamagnétique
- **Are weakly magnetized substances by a surrounding magnetic field.**
- **Ce sont des matériaux faiblement aimantable par un champ magnétique.**

Differential pressure: pression différentielle
- **Is the measured pressure relative to a reference selected pressure.**
- $P_{diff} = P_1 - P_2$
- **Est la pression mesurée par rapport à une pression de référence choisie.**

Diffraction: diffraction
- **Is the spreading out of a beam of waves outside the boundaries set by straight line motion.**
- **C'est la dispersion de l'énergie d'une onde après avoir rencontrée un fil ou une fente très fine de même ordre de grandeur que la longueur d'onde.**

Diffraction at a single slit: diffraction à travers une fente

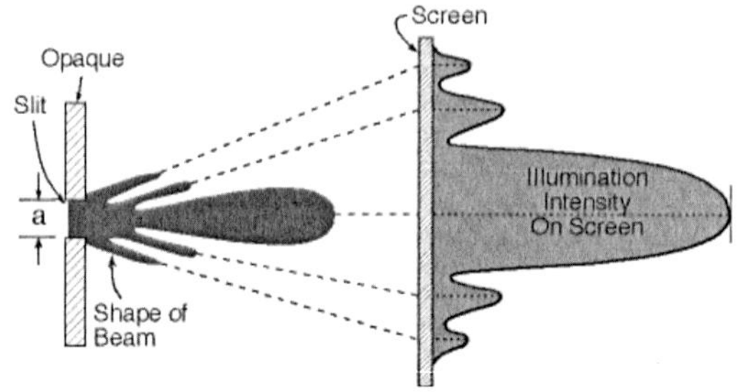

Diffraction at a small circular hole: diffraction à travers un trou circulaire

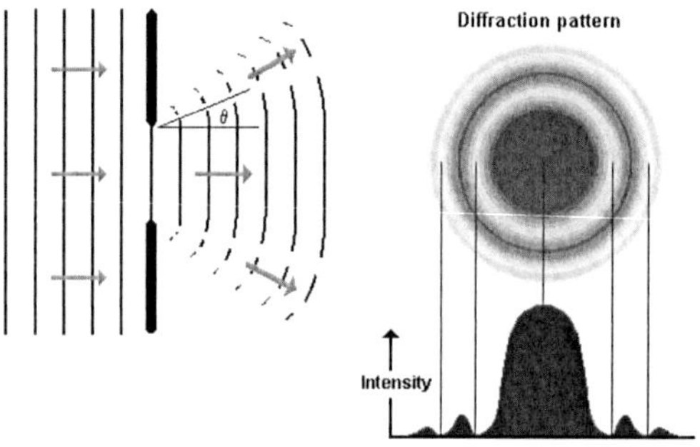

Digital Analog Converter: Convertisseur Analogique Numérique

- **Is a device that converts analog signals into digital signals.**
- **Converting analog to digital is to provide the means for a perfect reproduction of sound or images. The analog in music, is the conversion of sound waves into electric signals.Technic, which is a source of diverse losses or defects. Scanning comprises encoding information (audio, visual or graphical) of a series of binary numbers (o and 1), then to be decoded.**
- **C'est un dispositif qui convertit un signal analogique en un numérique signal.**
- **Passer de l'analogique au numérique, c'est se donner les moyens d'une reproduction parfaite du son ou de l'image. L'analogique en matière de musique, c'est la conversion des ondes sonores en signaux électriques.Technique qui est source de diverse déperditions ou défauts. La numérisation consiste à coder l'information (sonore, visuelle ou graphique) en une succession de nombres binaires (o et 1), puis à la décoder.**

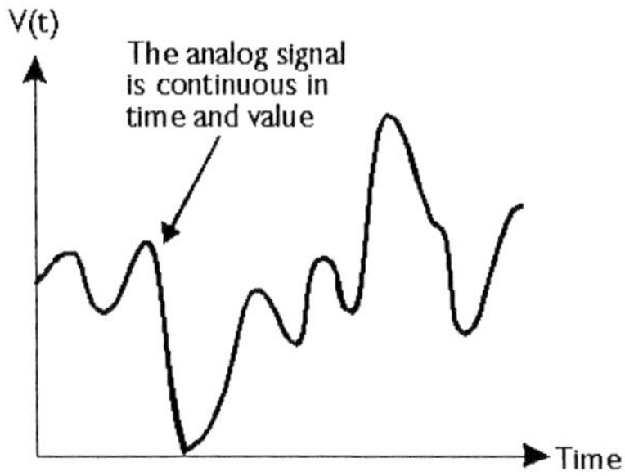

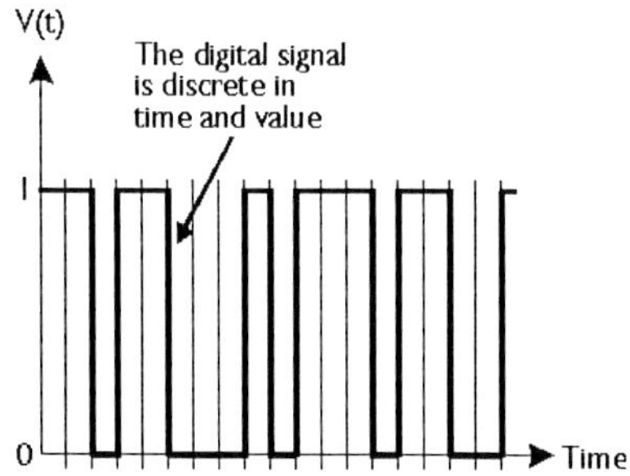

Digital signal: signal numérique

- **Transmits information in the form of discrete values.**

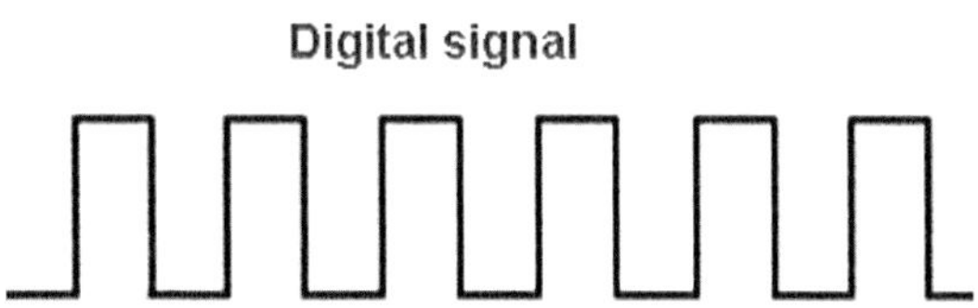

- **Transmet des informations sous la forme de valeurs discrètes.**

Diode: diode

- **An electrical component which conducts current in one direction but not the other.**
- **C'est un composant électrique qui laisse passer le courant dans un seul sens.**

Direct current (DC) moteur: moteur à courant continu

Dispersion of light: dispersion de la lumière

- **Is the separation of a beam of light into its component wavelengths or colors**
- **C'est la séparation d'un rayonnement lumineux en ses longueurs d'onde ou les couleurs qui les composent.**

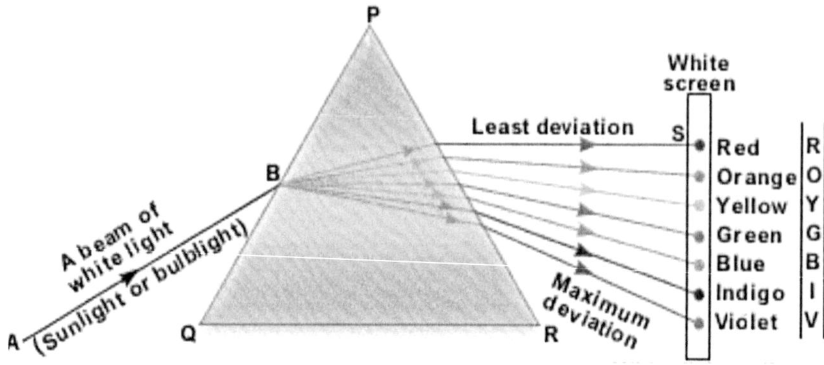

Displacement: déplacement

- **Defines the position of one point with reference to another point.**
- **Définie la position d'un point par rapport à un autre.**

Distance travelled: distance parcourue

- **Is measured along the travel path. The path may be curved or straight.**
- **C'est la mesure le long d'un parcours entre points, indépendamment de la nature du parcours.**

Disturbance: bruit, parasite

- **Is an undesirable signal that alters the transmission of a signal.**
- **Perturbations diverses indésirable qui modifient un signal lors de sa transmission.**

Doppler Effect: effet Doppler

- **The Doppler effect is the change in the frequency of a sound due to the person listening moving relative to the source of the sound. If you move towards a source (or stand still and it moves towards you) the pitch, or frequency of the sound, increases. Likewise, if you move away from the source, the pitch of the sound decreases and it sounds lower. This can be easily noticed in the pitch of an ambulance siren as it gets closer, passes you and then moves away.**
- **The Doppler effect is used in medicine to study blood flow. It can tell you if blood is moving towards or away from the probe.**
- **L'effet Doppler est la variation de la fréquence d'un bruit dû à la personne qui écoute par rapport au déplacement de la source du**

bruit. Si vous vous déplacez vers une source (ou restez immobile et la source se déplace vers vous) la hauteur, ou la fréquence du son, augmente. De même, si vous vous éloignez de la source, la hauteur du son diminue et il semble plus faible. Cela peut être facilement remarqué dans le cas d'une sirène d'ambulance lorqu'elle se rapproche, ensuite elle s'éloigne.

L'effet Doppler est utilisé en médecine pour étudier le flux sanguin. Il peut vous dire si le sang s'approche ou s'éloigne de la sonde.

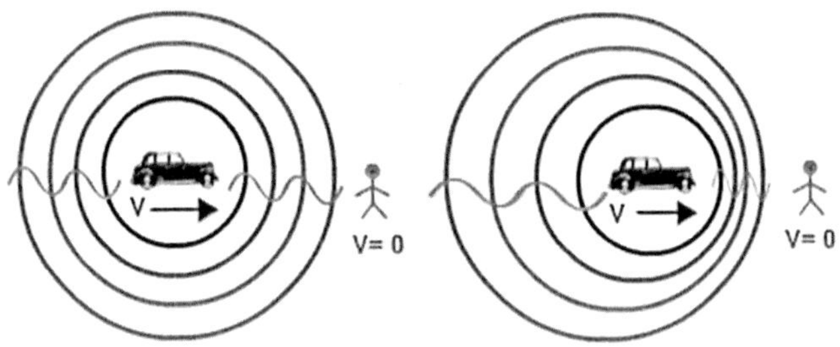

Source at rest Source in motion

Drag: force de frottement
- **Refers to forces that oppose the relative motion of an object.**
- **C'est la force qui s'oppose au mouvement d'un corps.**

Drift speed: vitesse moyenne des particules
- **Is the average velocity that a particle, such as an electron, attains due to an electric field.**
- **C'est la vitesse moyenne qu'une particule peut atteindre. Cas d'un électron sous l'effet d'un champ électrique.**

Ductility: ductilité
- **Is a solid material's ability to deform under tensile stress.**
- **C'est la capacité d'un matériau à se déformer sans se rompre.**

E

Earth connection: prise de Terre

Earthquake: tremblement de terre
- **Earthquakes occur when a sudden release of energy in the Earth's crust shakes the ground by generating seismic waves.**
- **Les tremblements de terre se produisent quand une libération soudaine d'énergie dans la croûte de la terre fissure le sol en générant des ondes sismiques.**

Efficiency (machines) : rendement
- **Efficiency = (USEFUL Energy OUTPUT)/(TOTAL Energy INPUT)**
- **Rendement = (Energie UTILE)/(Energie ABSORBEE)**

Einstein's photoelectric equation: équation photoélectrique d'Einstein
- **According to Plank's quantum theory, light is emitted from a source in the forms of bundles of energy called photons. Energy of each photon is $E=h\nu$. Einstein made use of this theory to explain how photo electric emission takes place.**
- **According to Einstein, when photons of energy $E=h\nu$ fall on a metal surface, they transfer their energy to the electrons of metal. When the energy of photon is larger than the minimum energy required by the electrons to leave the metal surface, the emission of electrons take place instantaneously.**
- **Selon la théorie quantique de Planck, la lumière est émise par une source sous la forme de faisceaux de d'énergie appelé photons. L'énergie de chaque photon est $E = h\nu$. Einstein a fait usage de cette théorie pour expliquer comment l'émission photoélectrique a lieu.**
- **Selon Einstein, lorsque les photons d'énergie $E=h\nu$ chutent sur une surface métallique, ils transfèrent leur énergie aux électrons du métal. Lorsque l'énergie de photon est supérieure à l'énergie minimum requis par les électrons pour quitter la surface métallique, l'émission d'électrons a lieu instantanément.**

Elastic limit: limite d'élasticité
- **The maximum stress which can be applied to an elastic specimen without causing a permanent change in the dimension of the specimen.**
- **C'est le maximum de contrainte qu'on peut appliquer sur un matériau élastique sans le déformer.**

Elastic strain energy: énergie de tension élastique
- **Is the energy stored in a material under stress.**
- **C'est l'énergie stockée dans un matériau sous contrainte.**

Elasticity: élasticité
- **Is the ability of a material to recover its original shape or size once a deforming stress has been removed.**
- **C'est la capacité d'un matériau de trouver sa forme originale après avoir subi une contrainte.**

Electric charge: charge électrique
- **Is a fundamental property of matter.**
- **Electric charge = electric current x time**
- **Its unit is Coulomb (C) in the SI**
- **C'est une propriété fondamentale de la matière.**
- **Charge électrique = courant électrique x temps.**
- **Son unité dans le SI est le Coulomb (C)**

Electric current: courant électrique
- **Is a flow of electric charge (electrons) through a conductor**
- **C'est un déplacement d'ensemble de porteurs de charge électrique, généralement des électrons, au sein d'un matériau conducteur**

Electric circuit: circuit électrique
- **Is a complete loop of conducting material which includes a current source and a current detector**
- **C'est un circuit fermé contenant des matériaux conducteurs, un générateur et des appareils de mesures**

Electric field: champ électrique
- **Is a region in which a force would act on an electric charge.**
- **Région dans laquelle une charge électrique est soumise à une force.**

Electric motor: moteur électrique
- **Is a machine which transforms electrical energy into mechanical energy.**
- **C'est une machine qui transforme l'énergie électrique en énergie mécanique.**

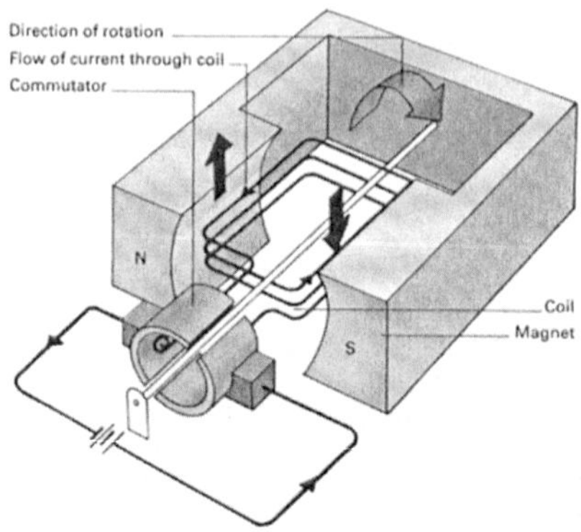

Electric potential: potentiel électrique (tension)

- **Is the electric potential difference U between two points equals the work done per unit charge bringing a very small positive charge from one point to the other (U=W/Q).**
- **C'est la différence de potentiel U entre deux points égale au travail effectué pour amener une charge positive d'un point à l'autre (U=W/Q).**

Electrical power: puissance électrique

- **Is the rate of supply of electrical energy or the rate of dissipation of electrical energy.**
- **Energie électrique échangée par unité de temps.**

Electrocardiogram (ECG) : Electrocardiogramme

- **If a patient complains of chest pains or shortness of breath it is important to check that their heart is working properly. The heart is a muscle made up of four chambers which contract to push blood and around the body. The messages that tell the muscle to contract are electrical signals, and by measuring these signals we can see if there is anything wrong with the heart. To take an ECG, three electrodes are placed on the surface of the skin: one on the right arm, one on the left arm, and one on the left leg. These contacts are connected to a machine called an electrocardiograph. This draws lines on graph paper showing the electric potential between each electrode over time.**

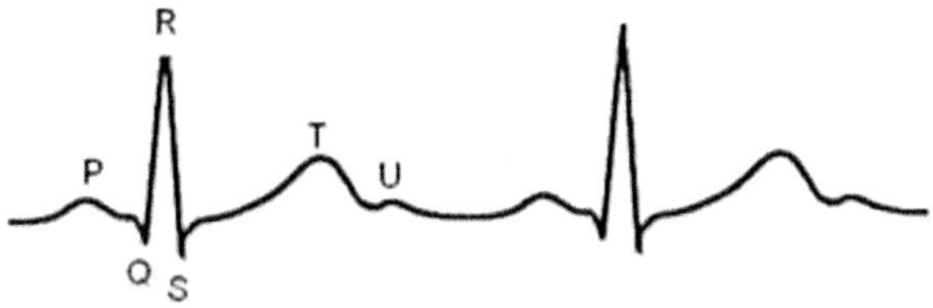

- **Si un patient se plaint de douleurs à la poitrine ou d'essoufflement, il est important de vérifier que le cœur fonctionne correctement. Le cœur est un muscle constitué de quatre chambres qui se contractent pour pousser le sang dans le corps. Les messages qui commandent la contraction musculaire sont des signaux électriques, et par la mesure de ces signaux nous pouvons voir s'il y a quelque chose qui ne fonctionne pas correctement dans le coeur. Pour prendre un ECG, trois électrodes sont placées sur la surface de la peau: l'une sur le bras droit, un sur le bras gauche, et l'autre sur la jambe gauche. Ces contacts sont reliés à une machine appelée un électrocardiographe. Des traces sur du papier graphique montrant le potentiel électrique entre chaque électrode au fil du temps.**

Electromagnetic converter: convertisseur électromagnétique

Electromagnetic induction: induction électromagnétique
- **Electromagnetic induction is the production of an electric current across a conductor moving through a magnetic field.**
- **E=Blv**
- **Which E is the induced e.m.f. and l is the wire length and B is the magnetic field at a speed v.**
- **L'induction électromagnétique est la production d'un courant électrique à travers un conducteur placé dans un champ électrique.**
- **E=Blv**
- **Ou E est la f.e.m induite, l est la longuer du fil et B est le champ magnètique à la vitesse v.**

Electromagnetic spectrum: spectre électromagnétique

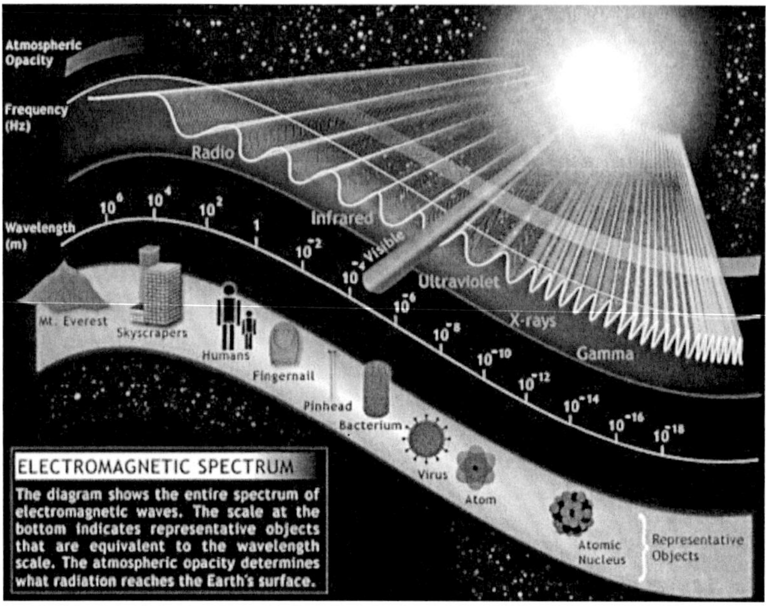

Electromagnetic waves: onde électromagnétique

- **Are transverse waves (the disturbance acts perpenduclarly to the direction of propagation) can propagate in a vacuum.**
- **Ce sont des ondes transversales (la perturbation est perpendiculaire à la direction de la propagation) et elles se propagent dans le vide.**

Electromotive force (e.m.f): force électromotrice f.é.m.

- **Is a voltage generated by a battery or by a magnetic force measured in volts.**
- **C'est un voltage généré par une batterie ou par une force magnétique mesuré en volts.**

Electron: électron

- **Is a subatomic particle carrying a negative electric charge e^-=-1.6x10^{-19}C.**
- **C'est une particule élémentaire. Elle possède une charge électrique élémentaire de signe négatif e^-=-1,6x10^{-19}C.**

Electron volt: électronvolt

Electrostatics: électrostatique

Electrolysis: électrolyse

- **Is a method of using a direct electric current (DC) to drive an otherwise non-spontaneous chemical reaction.**
- **C'est une méthode qui permet de déclencher des réactions chimique non spontanées grâce à un courant électrique continu.**

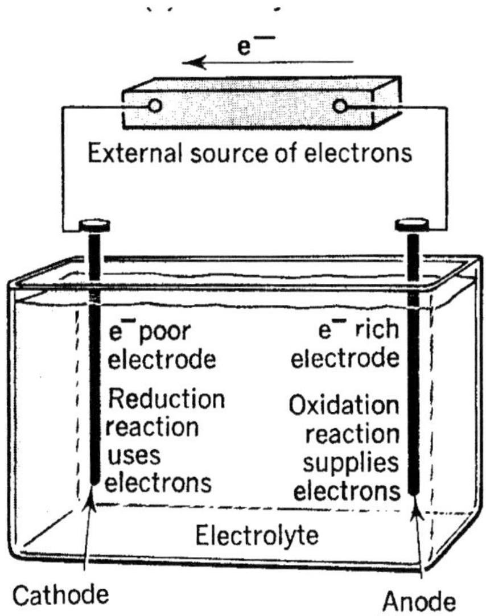

Electrolytes: électrolytes

- **Are liquids which contain charges which can move freely.**
- **Ce sont des liquides dans lesquels des charges peuvent se déplacer librement.**

Elementary charge: charge élémentaire

- **Electromagnetic fundamental physical constant equal to the charge of a proton and used as atomic unit of charge, $e=1{,}602176.10^{-19}C$**
- **C'est la quantité de charge électrique portée par un électron, $e=1{,}602176.10^{-19}C$**

Elusive force: force insaisissable

- **Gravity is an elusive force**
- **La gravité est une force insaisissable**

Emission spectrum: spectre d'émission

Endoscopy: endoscopie

- **Is a way of looking inside the human body through a narrow, flexible scope. It is mostly used to diagnose problems in the oesophagus, stomach and intestines, including ulcers, bleeding atumours. If something suspicious is seen, a biopsy (a small sample of tissue) can be taken and examined later by a pathologist to see what it is. Typically optical fibres are used to transfer light to the end of the endoscope and a miniature video camera records the image.They have a biopsy channel (along which tissue can be taken or other surgical instruments can be passed) and water pipe for washing the field of view clear.**
- **Laparoscopy is an extension of this technique where the scope is used to look inside the abdomen and pelvis through a small cut, or incision.**
- **C'est une façon de regarder à l'intérieur du corps humain à travers un champ d'application restreint, flexible. Elle est principalement utilisée pour diagnostiquer des problèmes de l'œsophage, de l'estomac et des intestins, y compris les ulcères, le saignement d'atumours. Si quelque chose de suspect est vu, une biopsie (un petit échantillon de tissu) peut être prélevé et examiné plus tard par un pathologiste pour voir ce que c'est. Typiquement des fibres optiques sont utilisés pour transférer la lumière à la fin de l'endoscope et une caméra vidéo miniature enregistre l'image. Ils ont un canal de biopsie (le long de laquelle le tissu peut être pris ou autres instruments chirurgicaux peut être transmis) et une tuyau d'eau pour laver le champ de vision et voir clair.**
- **La laparoscopie est une extension de cette technique dont la portée est utilisé pour regarder à l'intérieur de l'abdomen et du bassin par une petite ouverture ou incision.**

Energy: énergie

- **Is the ability to do work. An object or substance has energy if it can move or if it can generate heat, sound, or electricity. Energy can be converted from one form to another, but it can never be destroyed.**
- **Grandeur permettant d'effectuer un travail. Un objet ou une substance a de l'énergie si elle peut se déplacer ou si elle peut générer de la chaleur, du son, ou de l'électricité. L'énergie peut être convertie d'une forme à une autre, mais ne peut jamais être détruite.**

Energy balance: bilan d'énergie

Energy chain: chaîne d'énergie

Energy converter: convertisseur d’énergie

Energy efficiency: performance énergétique

Energy exchanges: échanges d’énergie

Energy flux: flux énergétique

- **Light quantity emited by a source**
- **ϕ_E=W/t**

  ϕ_E: energy flux in watts (W)

  W: luminous energy radiated by the source in joule (J)

  t: time taken in second (s)
- **Quantité de lumière émise par une source**
- **ϕ_E=W/t**

  ϕ_E: flux énergétique en watts (W)

  W: énergie lumineuse rayonnée par la source en joule (J)

  t: durée en second (s)

Energy level: niveau d’énergie

- **It is a measurable quantity used in quantum mechanics. The energy of an atom can only take discrete values. These energy levels are characteristic of the atoms of the same chemical element. Only quantum mechanics allows us to interpret these phenomena.**

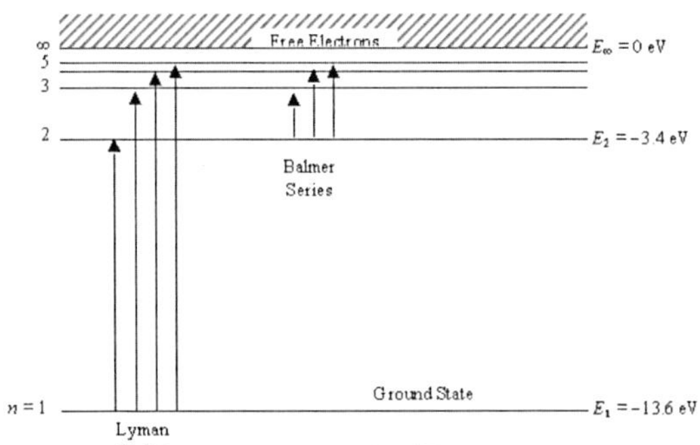

Hydrogen Energy Level Diagram

- **C’est une quantité mesurable utilisée en mécanique quantique. L’énergie d’un atome ne peut prendre que des valeurs discrètes. Ces niveaux énergétiques sont caractéristiques des atomes d’un**

même élément chimique. Seule la mécanique quantique permet d'interpréter ces phénomènes.

Energie noire: black energy
- **Is a strange, unexplained phenomena that is causing the expansion of the universe to accelerate.**
- **C'est un étrange et inexplicable phénomène qui est à l'origine de l'accélération de l'expansion de l'Univers.**

Energy sources: source d'énergie

Energy transfer: transfert d'énergie

Energy cycle: cycle d'énergie

Engine: moteur
- **Are machines which convert energy into mechanical work to power vehicles, to drive other machines or to generate electricity.**
- **Ce sont des machines qui convertissent l'énergie en travail mécanique pour alimenter des véhicules, à faire fonctionner d'autres machines ou à produire de l'électricité.**

Equation: équation

Equation of rotational motion: équation d'un mouvement circulaire
Equation of straight line motion: équation d'un mouvement linéaire

Equivalent dose: dose équivalente

Error : erreur

Escape speed: vitesse d'échappement

Etch: graver

Evaporation and cooling: évaporation et refroidissement

Exchange particles: échange de particules

Excitation: excitation

Exothermic transformation: transformation exothermique

Experiments: expériences

Exponential decay: décroissance exponentielle

Exponential law of radioactive decay: loi de décroissance exponentielle de radioactivité

Extention cord: câble de liaison, rallonge

Extrasolar planet: exoplanète
- **Is a planet outside the Solar System, and orbits around another star than the Sun.**
- **C'est une planète en dehors de système solaire, elle orbite autour d'une étoile autre que le soleil.**

Engine: moteur, engin
- **An engine or motor is a machine designed to convert energy into useful mechanical motion.**
- **C'est une machine qui convertit l'énergie en mouvement mécanique utile.**

Eye surgery: chirurgie des yeux
- **Laser eye surgery can be used to correct long or short sight, and astigmatism (distorted vision).**
- **La chirurgie oculaire au laser peut être utilisée pour corriger une longue ou une courte vue, et l'astigmatisme (vision déformée).**

F

Farad: Farad

- **Unit of the capacity of a capacitor.**
- **Unité de la capacité d'un condensateur.**

Faraday's Law: loi de faraday

Ferrites: ferrites

Ferromagnetism: ferromagnétisme

Field: champ

Field lines (electric): spectre d'un champ électrique

Field lines (magnetic): spectre d'un champ magnétique, ligne de champ

Filament lamp: filament d'une lampe

Finite energy sources: sources d'énergie finies

Fire extinguisher: extincteur

Fissile: fissile

- **The nucleus can undergo a fission reaction.**
- **Le noyau peut subir une réaction de fission.**

Fission reaction: réaction de fission

- **Is the splitting up of a large nucleus triggered by the absorption of a neutron. This reaction is used to produce**
- **Energy.**
- **C'est le fractionnement d'un noyau déclenché par l'absorption d'un neutron. Cette réaction est utilisée pour produire de l'énergie.**

Fissile materials: matériaux fissiles

Fission: fission

Fixed point: point fixe

Fleming's left hand rule: règle de la main droite de Fleming
- **Tells you which way the electromagnetic force acts**
- **Cette règle indique la direction dans laquelle la force électromagnétique agit**
- **L'index indique la direction du champ magnétique**
- **Le majeur indique la direction du courant électrique**
- **Le pouce indique la direction de la force électromagnétique**
- **The first finger points the direction of the Magnetic Field 'B'**
- **The second finer points the direction of the Current 'I'**
- **The thumb points direction of Electromagnetic Force 'F'.**

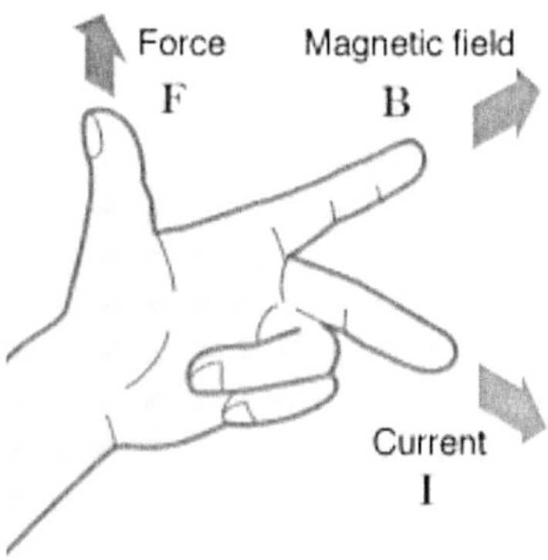

Flexibility: flexibilité

Flotation: flottaison

Flow: écoulement

Flowmeter: débitmètre
- **A device used in physics to measure the flow of a liquid.**
- **Un instrument utilisé en physique pour mesurer le débit d'écoulement d'un liquide.**

Flow speed or flow velocity: vitesse d'écoulement

- **$v = D_v/S$, flow speed of a liquid in meter per second (m/s)**
- **D_v: volumetric flowrate of the liquid in meters cubes per second ($m^3.s^{-1}$)**
- **S: cross-section of the pipe in meters squares (m^2)**
- **$v = D_v/S$, vitesse d'écoulement du liquide en mètres par seconde ($m.s^{-1}$)**
- **D_v: débit volumique du liquide en mètres cubes par seconde ($m^3.s^{-1}$)**
- **S: section droite de la canalisation en mètres carrés (m^2)**

Fluid matter: matière fluide

Foil: feuille

Force: force

Fossil fuels: carburant fossile

Fracture: cassure, fracture

Frame of reference: referential
- **A frame of reference in physics, is a solid benchmark against which we study the motion of a point.**
- **Le référentiel est le solide de référence par rapport auquel on étudie le mouvement d'un point.**

Free fall: chute libre
- **A body is said to be falling freely when, left on its own, it falls under the only action of its weight.**
- **Un corps est en chute libre, lorsqu'il tombe sous le seul effet de son poids.**

Frequency: fréquence
- **Is the number of oscillations made per second by a particle**
- **$F = 1/T$ in Hertz (Hz)**
- **T in second (s)**
- **C'est le nombre de fois qu'un phénomène périodique se reproduit par unité de temps**
- **$F = 1/T$ en Hertz (Hz)**
- **T en seconde (s)**

Fundamental interactions: interactions élémentaires

- **In particle physics, fundamental interactions (sometimes called interactive forces) are the ways that elementary particles interact with one another.**
  - **a- The gravitational interaction: holds the planets in their orbits around the Sun.**
  - **b- The electromagnétic interaction: binds the negatively charged electrons to the positiveley charged nucleus in the atom.**
  - **c- The strong interaction: binds together protons and neutrons in the nucleus of atoms.**
  - **d- The weak interaction: allows radioactive decay of nuclear particles.**
- **En physique de particules, les interactions élémentaires correspondent à la façon comment les particules s'interagissent entre elles.**
  - **a- Interaction gravitationnelle: maintient les planèts dans leurs orbites autour du soleil.**
  - **b- Interaction électromagnétique: maintient la cohésion entre les électrons chargés négativement et le noyau chargé positivement au sein de l'atome.**
  - **c- Interaction forte: maintient la cohésion entre les protons et les neutrons dans le noyau de l'atome.**
  - **d- Interaction faible: permet la décroissance radioactive des particules nucléaires.**

Friction: frottement

- **Is the force resisting the relative motion of solid surfaces, fluid layers, and/or material elements sliding against each other.**
- **Ce sont des interactions qui s'opposent à la persistance d'un mouvement relatif entre deux systèmes en contact.**

Fuel rod (uranium): bar combustible (uranium)

Fundamental particules: particules fondamentales

Fuse: fusible

Fusion (see thermonuclear fusion): fusion

G

Galaxy: galaxy

- **Is an enormous group of stars.**
- **Our galaxy called Milky Way contains billions of stars.**
- **C'est une vaste collections d'étoiles.**
- **Notre galaxy La Voie Lactée contient des milliards d'étoiles.**

Gamma decay: décroissance gamma

Gamma radiation: radiation gamma

- **They have the greatest penetrating power of the three types of radiation (alpha, beta and gamma), able to pass through a human body, a meter of concrete and many centimeters of lead.**
- **Ce sont les radiations les plus pénétrantes des trois types de radiations (alpha, beta et gamma), ils sont capables de passer à travers le corps humain, un mètre de béton et plusieurs centimètres de plomb.**

Gas: gaz

Gas discharge lamp: lampe à décharge à gaz

Gauge pressure: jauge pour mesurer la différence de pression entre l'intérieur d'une bouteille et l'extérieur

General gas equation: équation générale des gaz parfait

Generator: générateur

Geothermal energy: énergie géothermique

Glass bell jar: cloche sous vide
- **A device used to prove that sound can travel through vacuum.**
- **Un dispositif utilisé pour montrer que le son ne se propage pas dans le vide**

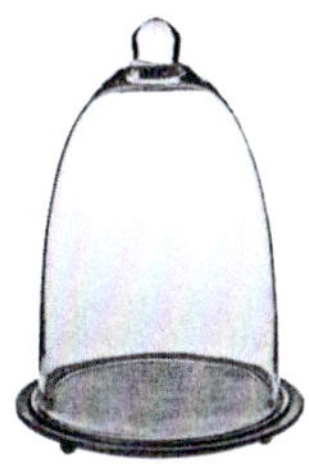

Glass fibres: fibres de verre

Glasses: lunettes

Gluons: gluons (particule)

Gradient: gradient (grad)

Granulometry (particle size): granulométrie
- **The laser granulometry or particle size allows the measurement of the particle size of unknown dimension (0.05 to 900µm). It is therefore particularly suitable for polymer suspensions, to any type of mineral powder. This technique is based on the diffraction of light. When a laser beam illuminates a particle, we can observe diffraction fringes. The intensity of the diffracted radiation and the diffraction angle depend on the particle size.**
- **By illuminating a slit width by a monochromatic laser source of λ perpendicular to the plane of the gap wavelength, is observed on a screen a diffraction pattern. The diffraction spots are evenly distributed on either side of the central spot. A measurement of the width L of the central diffraction spot used to deduce the slot width by the relationship:**

a = 2 λ D / L

- **La granulométrie laser permet la mesure de la taille de particules de dimension inconnue (comprise entre 0,05 et 900µm). Elle convient donc particulièrement aux suspensions de polymères, à tout type de poudres minérales. C'est une technique basée sur la diffraction de la lumière. Lorsqu'un faisceau laser éclaire une particule, on peut observer des franges de diffraction. L'intensité du rayonnement diffracté et l'angle de diffraction sont fonction de la taille des particules.**
- **En éclairant une fente de largeur a par une source laser monochromatique de longueur d'onde λ, perpendiculaire au plan de la fente, on observe sur un écran une figure de diffraction. Les taches de diffraction sont réparties régulièrement de part et d'autre de la tache centrale. Une mesure de la largeur L de la tache centrale de diffraction permet de déduire la largeur de la fente par la relation:**

a = 2 λ D / L

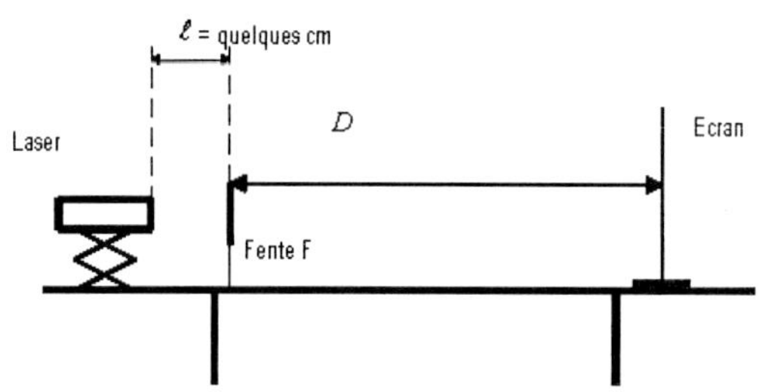

Graph: graphe

Gravimeter: gravimètre

- **Is an instrument used for measuring the local gravitational field of the Earth.**
- **C'est un instrument utilisé pour mesurer le champ gravitationnel local (champ de pesanteur) de la Terre.**

Gravitation: gravitation

- **Gravitation, or gravity, is a natural phenomenon by which physical bodies attract with a force proportional to their mass.**
- **La gravitation est le phénomène d'interaction physique qui cause l'attraction réciproque des corps massifs entre eux, sous l'effet de leur masse.**

Gravitational constant: constante gravitationnelle

Gravitational field strength: intensité du champ gravitationnel

Gravitational potential (radial fields): potentiel gravitationnel (champ radial)

Ground wire: fil de terre

H

Hadrons: hadrons (particules)

Half-life: demi-vie

Hall Effect: effet Hall

Hall probe: sonde à effet Hall
- A divice used for measuring the magnetic field.
- Instrument pour mesurer le champ magnétique.

Hard iron: fer dur
- Used in the construction of magnets
- Utilisé pour la fabrication des aimants

Hard magnets: aimant permanent
- Permanent magnets
- Aimant permanent

Hardness: dureté

Heat: chaleur

Heat capacity: capacité calorifique

Heat conduction: transfert de chaleur par conduction
- Is the process where vibrating particles pass on their extra kinetic energy to neighboring particles without matter displacement.
- C'est le processus de transfert d'énergie cinétique par la vibration des particules de proche en proche sans déplacement de matière.

Heat convection: transfert de chaleur par convection
- Convection occurs when the more energetic particles move from the hotter region to the colder region (liquid or gas) and take their heat energy with them with matter displacement.

- **C'est un mode de transfert de particules énergétiques de la zone chaude vers la zone froide (liquide ou gaz) par déplacement de matière.**

Heat radiation: transfert de chaleur par radiation

- **Heat radiation can travel through vacuum like the solar energy and Infra-Red radiation emitted by hot bodies.**
- **La chaleur par radiation peut voyager dans le vide comme la chaleur provenant de soleil et le rayonnement infrarouge émis par tout corps chaud.**

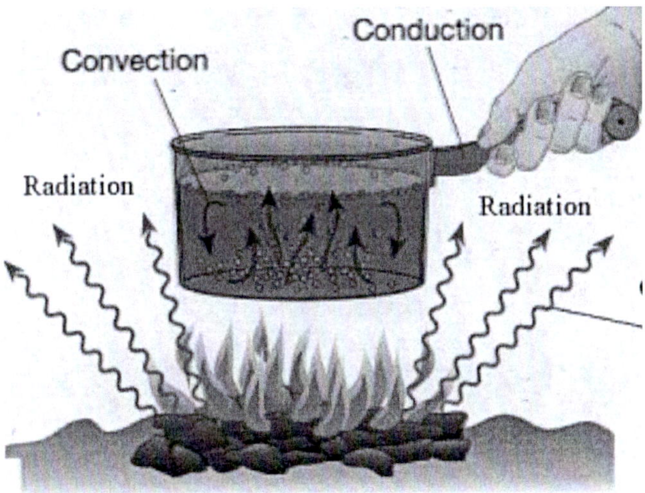

Heat engine: machine à chaleur

- **Is a system that performs the conversion of heat or thermal energy to mechanical work.**
- **C'est une machine qui convertit la chaleur ou l'énergie thermique en énergie mécanique.**

Heat pump: pompe à chaleur

- **Is a machine or device that diverts heat from one location at a lower temperature to another location at a higher temperature using me-**

chanical work. Refrigerators and freezers, air conditioners are examples of heat pump.
- C’est un dispositif thermodynamique permettant de transférer la chaleur du milieu le plus froid vers le milieu le plus chaud. Le réfrigérateur ou le climatiseur sont des pompes à chaleur.

Heat transfer: transfert de chaleur par conduction, convection ou par radiation.
- Is a discipline that concerns the exchange of thermal energy from one physical system to another.
- Echange thermique d’un système physique vers à un autre.

Heat capacity: capacité thermique
- Is the measurable physical quantity that characterizes the amount of heat required to change a substance's temperature by a given amount. In the International System of Units (SI), heat capacity is expressed in units of Joule(s) per kelvin (J/K).
- C’est une grandeur permettant de quantifier la possibilité qu'a un corps d'absorber ou restituer de l'énergie par échange thermique au cours d'une transformation pendant laquelle sa température varie. Elle s'exprime en joule/kelvin (J/K).

Heating value: pouvoir calorifique

Helical spring (coil spring): ressort hélicoïdal
- Is a mechanical device, which is typically used to store energy and subsequently release it, to absorb shock, or to maintain a force between contacting surfaces. They are made of an elastic material formed into the shape of a helix which returns to its natural length when unloaded.
- C’est un dispositif mécanique qui libère une énergie stockée, il absorbe les chocs et il sert à maintenir une force entre deux surfaces. Il est sous forme d’hélice, et il revient à sa forme initiale une fois non sollicité.

Henry (H): Henry (H)
- The SI unit for self-inductance.
- Unité de l’inductance dans le SI.

Higgs boson: boson de Higgs

- **The Higgs boson is the keystone of the fundamental structure of matter. This particle gives mass to all other particles in our universe. Without the Higgs boson, the particles will never encounter, they couldn't create protons and neutrons, which together with electrons, form the matter.**
- **Le boson de Higgs est la clef de voûte de la structure fondamentale de la matière. Cette particule donne leur masse à toutes les autres particules de notre Univers. Sans le boson de Higgs, les particules ne se rencontreraient jamais, elles ne pourraient créer des protons et neutrons, qui, combinés aux électrons, forment la matière.**

High pass-filter : filtre passe-haut

High voltage : haute tension

High-voltage transmission : réseaux électriques
- **Is the bulk transfer of electrical energy, from generating power plants to substations located near population centers.**
- **C'est un ensemble d'infrastructures permettant d'acheminer l'énergie électrique des centres de production vers les consommateurs d'électricité.**

Higher frequency waves: ondes à haute fréquence
- **They have more energy, and it's the energy of a wave that does the damage**
- **Ce sont les ondes les plus énergétiques et elles causent le plus de dégâts**

Hinge: charnière
- **Is a type of bearing that connects two solid objects, typically allowing only a limited angle of rotation between them**
- **C'est un élément de mécanisme fonctionnant selon le principe d'une liaison pivot**

Homogeneity: homogène
- **A material that is homogeneous is uniform in composition or characters.**
- **Un matériau est homogène si sa composition est uniforme.**

Horseshoe magnet: aimant en forme de fer à cheval

Hooke's law: Loi de Hooke
- **States that the stress is proportional to strain.**
- **La déformation est proportionnelle aux contraintes.**

Hourglass: sablier
- **Is a sand glass called sand timer or egg timer, measures the passage of a few minutes or an hour of time.**
- **C'est un instrument qui permet de mesurer un intervalle de temps (minutes ou heures) par écoulement de sable.**

Housing: habitat

Hubble's law: Loi de Hubble
- **States that speed of recession "v" of a galaxy from another is proportional to their distance apart "d".**
- **The constant of proportionality H=v/d**
- **La vitesse de récession d'une galaxie par rapport à une autre est proportionnelle à la distance qui les sépare.**

Hurricane: ouragan

Hydrogen atom: atome d'hydrogène
- **First element of periodic table. It contains one proton and one electron.**
- **Première élément de la table de classification périodique des éléments. Il contient un proton et un électron.**

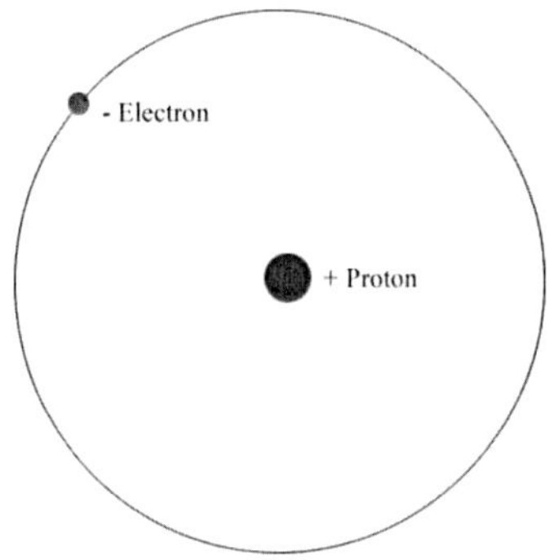
- Electron
+ Proton

I

Ice point: point de congélation

- **Is a physical process that results in the phase change of a water from a liquid to a solid, 0°C (273.15 K) at STP.**
- **C'est le passage de l'état liquide à l'état solide de l'eau, 0°C (273.15 K) dans les C.N.T.P.**

Ideal gas equation: Equation des gaz parfaits

- **$pV = nRT = (m/M)RT$**

  Where:

  - p is gas pressure in Pascal's (Pa)

  - V is the volume of gas in cubic meters (m^3)

  - m is the mass of gas in kilograms (kg)

  - M is the molar mass in kilograms per mole ($kg.mol^{-1}$)

  - n is the amount of gas in moles (mol)

  - R is the molar gas constant whose magnitude is $8.31 J.K^{-1}.mol^{-1}$

  - T is the gas temperature in kelvins (K).

  Avec:

  - p est la pression du gaz en pascals (Pa)

  - V est le volume du gaz en mètres cube (m^3)

  - m est le masse du gaz en kilogramme (kg)

  - M est la masse molaire en kilogramme par mole ($kg.mol^{-1}$)

  - n est la quantité de matière du gaz en moles (mol)

  - R est la constante du gaz dont la valeur est égale à $8.31 J.K^{-1}.mol^{-1}$

  - T est la température du gaz en kelvins (K).

Illuminance: éclairement

- **$E = \phi/S$**

  E: éclairement (lux)

  ϕ: flux lumineux de la source en lumens (lm)

  S: surface éclairée (m)

- **$E = \phi/S$**

E: illuminance (lux)

ϕ: luminous flux of the source in lumens (lm)

S: illuminated surface (m)

Impulse: impulsion

- **When a tennis ball is struck with a racket, the force on the ball changes magnitude rapidly.**
- **Moment où la force change rapidement, exemple : lorsqu'une balle de tennis est frappée par une raquette.**

Incandescent light bulb (lamp): lampe à incandescence

Incident (see reflaction): incident

Induced e.m.f. (electromagnetic force): f.e.m. force éléctro-magnétique induite

- **An e.m.f. generated in a conductor by changing magnetic flux.**
- **Force électromagnétique produite par une variation d'un flux magnétique.**

Inductance: inductance (L)

- **Is a constant related to an inductor of an electrical circuit, denoted L.**
- **The SI unit is Henry (H).**
- **C'est une grandeur liée à la bobine, symbolisée par L.**
- **Son unité dans le SI est le Henry (H).**

Inductive reactance: réactance inductive

- **X_L is proportional to the signal frequency f and the inductance L of an inductor, $X_L = 2\pi fL$.**
- **X_L est proportionnel à la fréquence et l'inductance L d'une bobine, $X_L = 2\pi fL$ (impédance).**

Inelastic collision: collision non élastique

- **Collision without conservation of kinetic energy.**
- **Collision sans conservation de l'énergie cinétique.**

Infra-red (IR): infrarouge (IR)

- Is an electromagnetic radiation with a wavelength longer than that of visible light, measured from the nominal edge of visible red light at 790 nanometers, and extending to 100 micrometers
- C'est une onde électromagnétique de longueur supérieure à celle de la lumière rouge et elle est comprise entre 790 nm et approximativement 100 micromètres

Infrasound: infra son
- Are sound waves with a range of frequency under 20 Hz.
- Ce sont des ondes sonores inaudibles par les humains dont la gamme de fréquence est en dessous de 20 Hz.

Insulators: isolant
- Electrical insulators
- Isolant électrique

Intereference: interférence
- Is the consequence of superposition of two or more waves that meet at one point in space.
- Phénomène observé lorsque deux ondes ou plus se superposent en un point de l'espace.

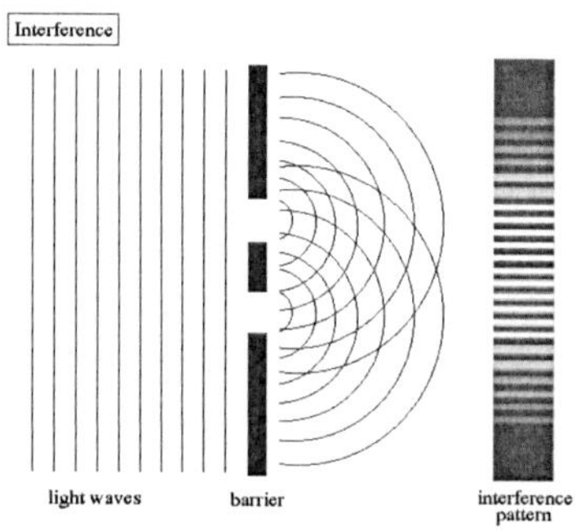

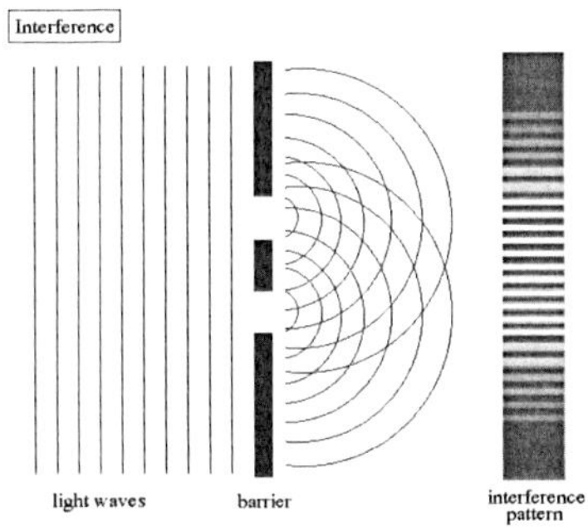

Internal energy: énergie interne

- **The total sum of the kinetic and potential energies of all individual molecules which go to make up an object.**
- **Somme totale de l'énergie cinétique et l'énergie potentielle des molécules qui composent un objet.**

Internal resistance: résistance interne

- **Is the resistance to current flow in an electrical power source**
- **C'est la résistance au courant électrique dans un fil conducteur.**

Ionic bond: liaison ionique

- **Is an attachment between the atoms in a molecule in which electrons from an atom of one element are transferred to the atom of a second element**
- **C'est une liaison entre des atomes de deux molécules dans lesquelles il y a transfert d'électrons.**

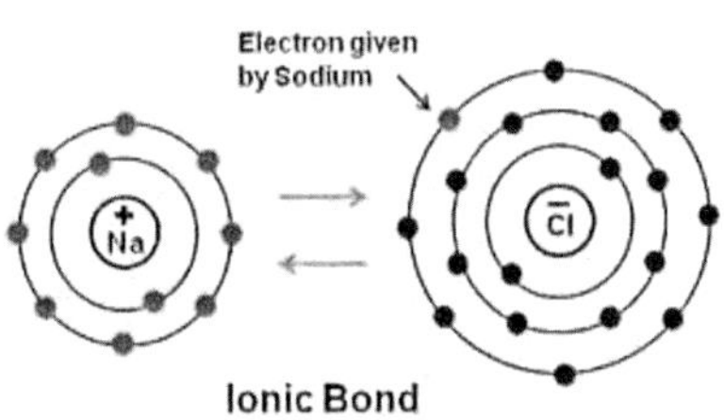

Ionisation: ionisation

- **Is the process by which an atom receives enough energy to lose at least one electron.**
- **C'est l'énergie nécessaire pour qu'un atome perde au moins un électron.**

Ionizing radiation: rayonnement ionisant
- Kind of radiation which ionizes a gas put in its path.
- Radiation qui ionise un gaz.

IR (Infrared): IR (Infrarouge)
- Electromagnetic wavelengths from 700 nm up to about 1mm.
- Longueur d'ondes de 700 nm jusque 1mm.

Isothermal changes: changement isothermique
- Changement at constant temperature
- Changement à température constante.

Isotope: isotope
- A nuclide with the same atomic number as another nuclide but with a different mass number.
- Deux noyaux de même nombre atomique (proton) mais de nombres de masse (nucléons) différents.

Insulation: isolation

International Atomic Time (TAI): Temps Atomique International (TAI)
- The International Atomic Time (TAI from French) is a time scale based on the use of atomic clocks that define the second. The second is defined as the time period equal to 9192631770 a period of the radiation corresponding to the transition between the two hyperfine levels of the quantum ground state of the cesium 133 atom. TAI is obtained due to the running average of more than 300 atomic clocks.
- Le TAI est une échelle de temps base sur l'usage d'horloges atomiques qui définissent la seconde. La seconde est définie comme la durée égale à 9192631770 fois une période de la radiation correspondant à la transition entre les 2 niveaux quantiques hyperfins de l'état fondamental de l'atome de césium 133. Le TAI est obtenu grâce à la moyenne de la marche de plus de 300 horloges atomiques.

Inverter dc-ac: onduleur
- Is an electrical device that converts direct current DC to alternating current AC.
- C'est convertisseur électrique à partir d'une source d'énergie électrique continue DC en courant alternatif AC.

J

Joule: Joule

- **Unit of energy in the SI unit, its symbol is J.**
- **A 100 watt light bulb converts 100 joules of electrical energy per second into heat and light.**
- **Unité de l'énergie dans le SI, symbole J.**
- **Une ampoule de 100 watt convertie 100 joules d'énergie électrique par seconde en chaleur et en lumière.**

Joule's effect: effet Joule

- **Is a physical law expressing the relationship between the heat generated by the current flowing through a conductor.**
- **C'est une loi physique permettant de donner la relation entre chaleur dissipée par l'effet d'un courant électrique dans un matériau conducteur.**

K

Kelvin: Kelvin

- **Unit of temperature in the SI unit, its symbol is K**
- **Unité de la température dans le SI.**

Kilogram: kilogramme

- **Is the mass of a cylinder in platinium-iridium deposited at the Internationam Office of Weight and Measures at Sèvres.**
- **C'est la masse d'un cylindre en platine-iridium déposé au Bureau International du Poids et de Mesure à Sèvres.**

Kilowatt-hour: kilowattheure

- **The energy transferred from a source which delivers energy for one hour at a constant rate of a thousand watts. It has the symbol kWh and equals 3.6 MJ.**
- **C'est l'énergie transmise pendant une heure. Son symbole est le kWh et elle vaut 3,6 MJ.**

Kinetic energy: énergie cinétique

- **Is the energy possessed by a mass "m", by reason of its motion of velocity "v".**
- **The symbol is E_k**
- **The SI unit is the joule (J).**
- **The equation of the kinetic energy is: $E_k=½mv^2$.**
- **C'est l'énergie que possède une masse "m" lorsqu'elle se déplace à une vitesse "v".**
- **Son symbole est E_c**
- **Son unité dans le SI est le joule (J)**
- **L'équation de l'énergie cinétique est : $E_c=½\ mv^2$.**

Kepler's laws: Lois de Kepler

- **Are the three laws discovered by keeper :**
  - **a- The first law: A planet moves round the sun along an elliptical path with the sun at one focus of the ellipse.**
  - **b- The second law: The straight line joining a planet to the sun sweeps out equal areas in equal times.**
  - **c- The third law: The ratio of the square of a planet's orbital period T to the cube the radius of its orbital path is the same for all planets:**

$$T^2/R^3 = (4\pi^2)/(G.M_s)$$

Where M_s is the mass of the Earth and G is the gravitational constant

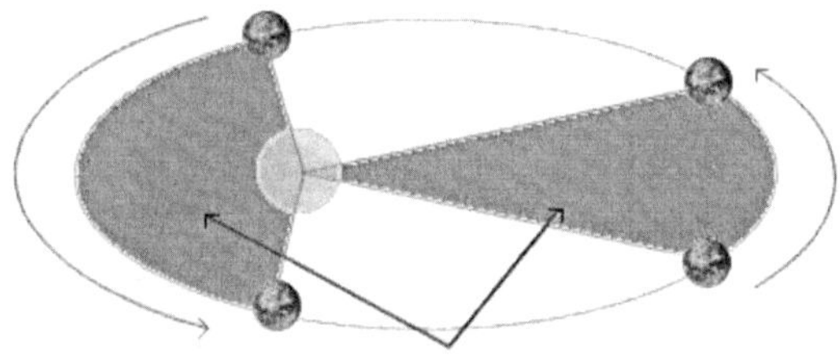

Sweeping out equal area in equal time

- **Ce sont les trois lois découvertes par Kepler:**
  - a- **Première loi: Dans un référentiel héliocentrique, la trajectoire du centre d'inertie des planètes est une ellipse dont le soleil occupe l'un des foyers.**
  - b- **Deuxième loi: Le segment de droite reliant le Soleil à la planète balaie des aires égales pendant des durées égales.**
  - c- **Troisième loi: Pour toutes les planètes, le rapport entre le carré de la période de révolution T et le cube du demi-grand axe de l'ellipse est le même. Ainsi, pour une trajectoire circulaire de rayon R:**

$$T^2/R^3 = (4\pi^2)/(G.M_s)$$

où M_s est la masse du Soleil et G est la constant universelle.

Kirchhoff's laws: lois de Kirchhoff

- **Are the two laws:**
  - a- **Kirchhoff's first law: States that the sum of all currents flowing towards a junction of a number of conductors equals the sum of the currents leaving the junction.**
  - b- **Kirchhoff's second law: States that the directed sum of the electrical potential differences around any closed circuit is zero.**
- **Ce sont les deux lois de Kirchhoff:**
  - a- **Loi des nœuds: La somme algébrique des intensités des courants qui entrent par un nœud est égale à la somme des intensités des courants qui en sortent.**
  - b- **Loi des mailles: La somme algébrique des différences de potentiel le long de la maille (circuit fermé) est nulle.**

Knot: nœud

- **Is a unit of speed equal to one nautical mile.**
- **It's defined as 1.852 km/ hour.**
- **C'est une unité marine de la vitesse.**
- **Un nœud est égal 1,852 km/heure.**

L

Laser (Light Amplification by Stimulated Emission of Radiation): laser

- **Is a device that emits light through a process of optical amplification based on the stimulated emission of photon.**
- **C'est un appareil émettant de la lumière amplifiée par émission stimulée.**

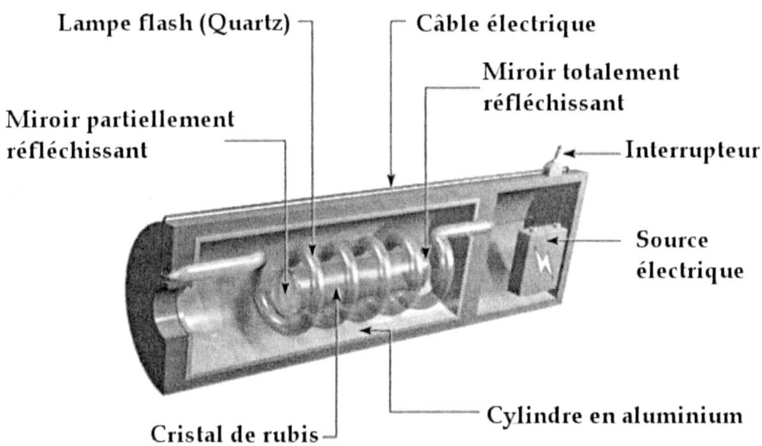

Lead screen: écran de plomb

Length: longueur

- **It is the property of a line.**
- **The SI unit is the meter.**
- **The symbol is "m".**
- **L'unité est le mètre 'm'.**

Lens: lentilles

- **Is an optical device**
- **The main lenses are convergent and divergent.**
- **C'est un objet utilisé en optique**
- **Les principales lentilles sont convergentes et divergentes.**

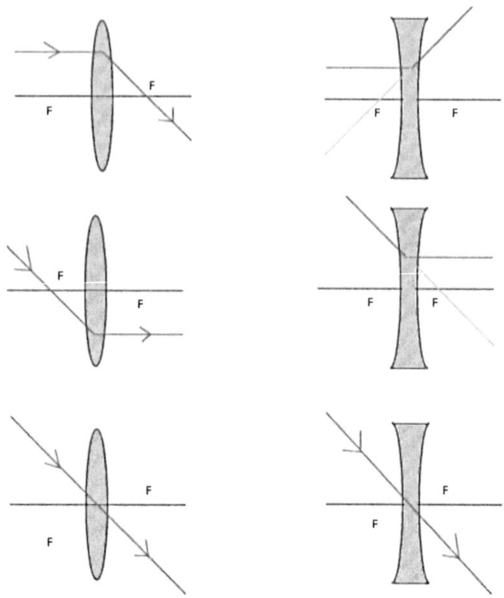

Lightning: foudre

Light year: année lumière

- **Is the distance travelled by the light during one year.**
- **1 ly = $9.46x10^{12}$ km.**
- **The light travels at about 300,000 km/s (186,000 miles/s).**
- **C'est la distance parcourue par la lumière en un an.**
- **1 année lumière = $9.46x10^{12}$ km.**
- **La lumière parcours 300000 km/s (186000 miles/s).**

Linear polarization: polarisation linéaire

Logic gate: porte logique

Logitudinal waves: ondes longitudinales

- **In longitudinal waves the vibrations are along the same direction as the wave is travelling (compression and rarefaction).**
- **La perturbation provoquée est parallèle à la direction de propagation de l'onde (compression et dépression).**

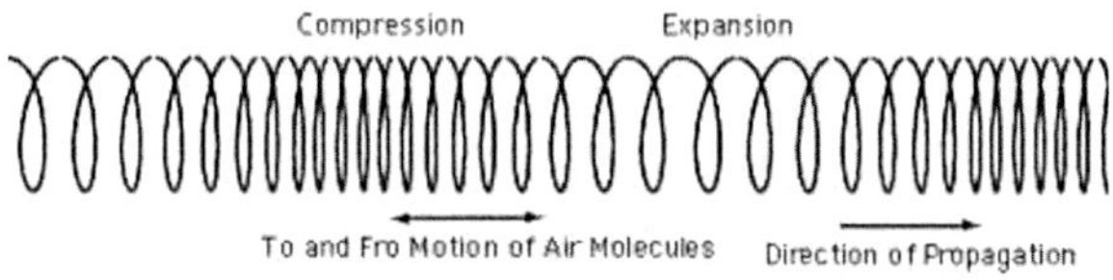

Low pass-filter: filtre passe-bas

Low voltage: basse tension

Luminous flux: flux lumineux

M

Mach number: nombre de Mach

- **Is the speed of an object moving through air, or any other fluid substance, divided by the speed of sound.**

  It's commonly used to represent the speed of an object when it is traveling close to or above the speed of sound

  $M_a = U/a$

  Where "M_a" is the Mach number

  "U" is the relative velocity of the source to the medium

  And "a" is the speed of sound in the medium.

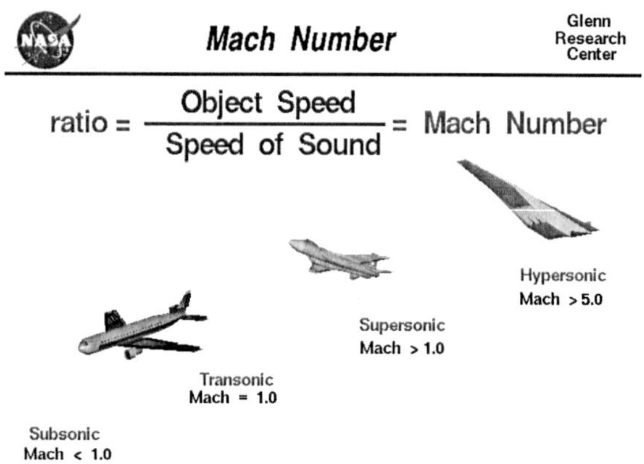

- **C'est un nombre sans dimension, noté M_a, qui exprime le rapport de la vitesse d'un objet au repos dans un fluide sur la vitesse du son dans ce même fluide**

  $M_a = U/a$

  où

  «M_a » est le nombre de Mach

  « U » est la vitesse de l'objet (par rapport à son environnement)

  « a » est la vitesse de propagation ou célérité du son dans l'environnement considéré.

Machine: machine

- **Is a device which turns one type of energy into another**

- **C'est un dispositif qui transforme l'énergie d'une forme à une autre.**

Magnet: aimant

- **Is a material that produces a magnetic field.**
- **C'est une matière ou objet qui produit un champ magnétique.**

Magnetic field: champ magnétique

- **Is a mathematical description of the magnetic influence of an electric current and magnetic materials.**
- **C'est un modèle mathématique qui décrit l'influence magnétique d'un courant électrique et des matériaux magnétiques.**

Magnetic flux: flux magnétique

- **A measure of the total amount of magnetic field passing through a given area.**
- **$\Phi = BAN\cos\theta$**
- **Where Φ is the magnetic flux and B is the magnetic field passing through the coil area A at an angle θ of N turns.**
- **Où Φ est le flux magnétique, B est le champ magnétique passant à travers une bobine de surface A avec angle θ de N spires.**

Magnetic force: force magnétique

- **The force produced by a magnetic field on a magnet, an electric current or a moving charge.**
- **$F = BIl\sin\alpha$**
- **Where F is the magnetic force and I is the current at an angle α to a magnetic field B and l is the length over which the current flows in the field.**
- **La force produite par un champ magnétique sur un aimant, un courant électrique ou une charge on movement.**
- **Où F est force magnétique et I est l'intensité du courant électrique à un angle α avec le champ magnétique B et l la longueur ou le courant circule dans le champ.**

Magnetized needle: aiguille aimantée

Magnetic resonance imaging (MRI): imagerie par résonnance magnétique (IRM)

- Is a medical imaging technique used in radiology to visualize detailed internal structures.
- C'est une technique d'imagerie médicale permettant d'obtenir des vues 2D ou 3D de l'intérieur du corps avec une résolution relativement élevée.

Magnetic spectrum: spectre magnétique

Magnetic stirrers: agitateur magnétique

- Used in chemistry lab to ensure the homogenization of a medium.
- C'est instrument utilisé en chimie ayant pour but d'assurer l'homogénéisation d'un milieu.

Magnification: grandissement

- Is the process of enlarging something only in appearance, not in physical size.
- C'est un processus d'agrandissement d'un objet (dans les apparences) grâce à une lentille (loupe).

Magnifying glass (hand lens, magnifier): loupe

- Is a lens which is used to produce a magnified image of an object
- C'est une lentille qui grandit l'image d'un objet

Manometer: manomètre

- An instrument used to measure the pressure.
- Instrument de mesure de la pression.

Maser (Microwave Amplification by Stimulated Emission Radiation): Maser

- Is a device that produces coherent electromagnetic waves through amplification by stimulated emission.
- C'est un dispositif permettant d'émettre un faisceau cohérent de micro-ondes par émission stimulée.

Masse flowrate: débit massique

- $D_m = m/t$, masse flow rate of a liquid in kilogram per second ($kg.s^{-1}$)
- m: liquid mass in kilogram (kg)
- t: flow time in seconds (s)
- $D_m = m/t$, débit massique du liquide en kilogrammes par seconde ($kg.s^{-1}$)
- m: masse de liquide en kilogrammes (kg)

- **t: durée de l'écoulement en seconde (s)**

Matter waves (De Broglie wavelength): voire longueur d'onde De Broglie

Mean speed: vitesse moyenne
Mechanical energy: énergie mécanique

Medical imaging: imagerie médicale

Microchip: puce électronique
- **Is a tiny electronic circuit on a semiconductor wafer.**

- **Est un circuit électronique minuscule sur une plaquette de semi-conducteur.**

Milky way: la voie lactée
- **Is the home galaxy of the Solar System**
- **C'est le nom de la galaxie dans laquelle se situe le Système solaire**

Microwaves: micro-ondes (hyperfréquences)
- **Are electromagnetic waves with wavelengths ranging from one millimeter to one meter, or equivalently, with frequencies between 300 GHz and 30 MHz.**
- **Ce sont des ondes électromagnétiques de longueurs d'onde intermédiaire entre un millimètre et un mètre, de fréquences correspondantes à 300 GHz et 30 MHz.**

Modulation: modulation
- **Is the process of impressing the information to be transmitted upon the higher frequency radio or telephone carrier wave.**
- **Variation d'une caractéristique d'un signal comportant l'info par la fréquence d'une onde porteuse.**

Momentum: quantité de mouvement

- **Is a physical quantity that allows doing calculations about what happens when moving bodies collide.**
- **Momentum = mass x velocity**
- **p = mv (kg.m.s^{-1})**
- **C'est une grandeur physique qui permet de faire des calculs sur ce qui se passe quand les corps en mouvement se heurtent.**
- **Quantité de mouvement = masse x vitesse**
- **p =mv (kg.m.s^{-1})**

Momentum of inertia: moment d'inertie

Momentum of a force: moment d'une force

Motion: mouvement

- **The motion of an object describes the displacement, velocity and acceleration, the distance of a moving object.**
- **Le mouvement d'un objet décrit son déplacement, sa vitesse, son acceleration et la distance parcourue dépuis l'origine.**

N

National grid: réseaux d'électricité

- **Is the network of pylons and cables which covers the whole country.**
- **C'est un réseau de pylônes et de câbles électriques qui couvre le pays.**

Neutrino: neutrino

- **Is an elementary particle that usually travels close to the speed of light, is electrically neutral, and is able to pass through ordinary matter almost unaffected**
- **C'est une particule élémentaire, qui se déplace à une vitesse proche de celle de la lumière, elle est électriquement neutre et capable de traverser la matière sans l'affecter**

Nebula: nebuleuse

- **Is a large amount of gas and dust particles and are considered to be the birth places of the stars**
- **C'est un amas de gaz et de poussières considéré comme un lieu de naissance d'étoiles**

Newton's Laws: Lois de Newton

1- **First Law:**

In a Galilean's frame of reference, so long as the forces on an object are all *balanced*, then it'll just *stay still*, or else if it's already moving it'll just carry on at the *same velocity* so long as the forces are all *balanced*:

$$\sum \vec{F} = \vec{0} \;\; (\frac{d\vec{V}}{dt} = \vec{0} \text{ then } \vec{V} = \overrightarrow{cst})$$

2- Second Law:

In a Galilean's frame of reference, if there is an unbalanced force, then the object will accelerate in that direction. The size of the acceleration is decided by the formula:

$$\sum \vec{F} = m\,\vec{a}$$

3- Third Law:

If object A *exerts a force* on object B then object B exerts *the exact opposite force* on object A:

$$\vec{F}_{A/B} = -\vec{F}_{B/A}$$

1- Première loi ou principe d'inertie:

Dans un référentiel galiléen, lorsqu'un solide est soumis à des forces qui se compensent (solide pseudo-isolé), le vecteur vitesse de son centre d'inertie ne varie pas: si la somme des forces est nulle, alors la vitesse est constante :

$$\sum \vec{F} = \vec{0} \;\; (\frac{d\vec{V}}{dt} = \vec{0} \text{ donc } \vec{V} = \overrightarrow{cst})$$

2- Deuxième loi:

Dans un référentiel galiléen, la somme des forces extérieures appliquées à un solide est égale au produit de la masse du solide par l'accélération de son centre d'inertie :

$$\sum \vec{F} = m\,\vec{a}$$

3- Troisième loi ou principe des actions réciproques:

Lorsqu'un corps A exerce sur un corps B une action mécanique modélisée par une force, alors le corps B exerce sur le corps A une force opposée et égale :

$$\vec{F}_{A/B} = -\vec{F}_{B/A}$$

Node: nœud

Noise: bruit
- **Various disturbances that affect a signal during transmission.**
- **Perturbations diverses qui modifient un signal lors de sa transmission.**

Nuclear decay: radioactivité
- **Is a natural process by which an atomic nucleus of an unstable atom loses energy by emitting ionizing particles.**
- **C'est un phénomène naturel au cours duquel des noyaux atomiques instables se transforment spontanément en dégageant de l'énergie sous forme de rayonnements divers.**

Nuclear power: puissance nucléaire
- **C'est l'utilisation de la fission nucléaire pour produire de la chaleur et de l'énergie électrique**
- **Is the use of sustained nuclear fission to generate heat and do useful work**

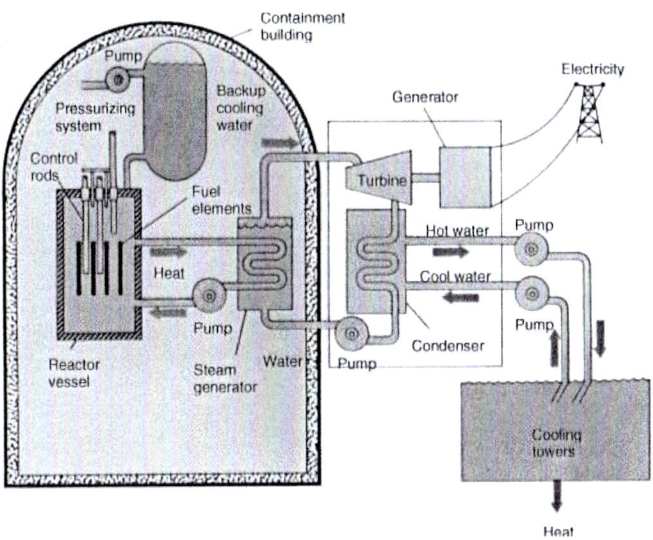

Nuclear fission: fission nucléaire
- **Is a nuclear reaction in which the nucleus of an atom splits into smaller part sand releasing a tremendous amount of energy.**

- Lorsqu'un neutron percute le noyau de certains isotopes lourds, il existe une probabilité que le noyau impacté se scinde en deux noyaux plus légers en dégageant une énorme quantité d'énergie.

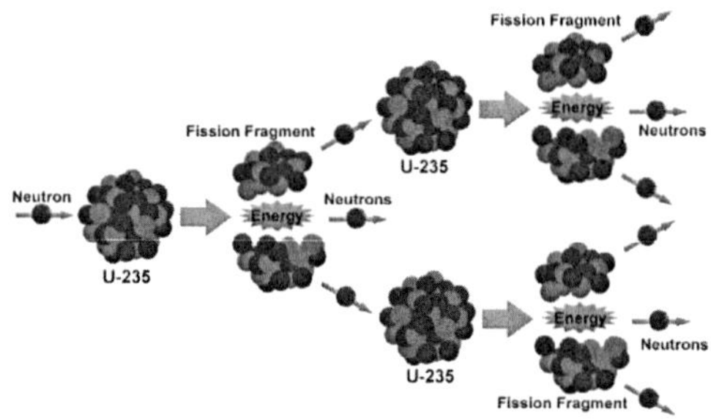

Nuclear fusion: fusion nucléaire

- Is the process by which two or more atomic nuclei join or to merge together to form a single heavier nucleus. Energy is given out.
- La fusion nucléaire est une réaction où deux noyaux atomiques s'assemblent pour former un noyau plus lourd. Une quantité d'énergie est dégagée.

Nuclear magnetic resonance: résonance magnétique nucléaire

- Nuclear magnetic resonance (NMR) is a physical phenomenon in which magnetic nuclei in a magnetic field absorb and re-emit electromagnetic radiation. NMR is used in advanced medical imaging techniques, such as in magnetic resonance imaging (MRI).
- La résonance magnétique nucléaire (RMN) désigne une propriété de certains noyaux atomiques possédant un spin nucléaire placés dans un champ magnétique. Lorsqu'ils sont soumis à un rayonnement électromagnétique (radiofréquence), les noyaux atomiques peuvent absorber l'énergie du rayonnement puis la relâcher lors de la relaxation. L'utilisation la plus connue dans le grand public est l'imagerie par résonance magnétique nucléaire (IRM).

Nuclear medicine: médecine nucléaire

Nuclear reactions: réactions nucléaires

Nucleus: noyau

- Is the very dense region consisting of nucleons (protons and neutrons) at the center of an atom.

- **Désigne la région située au centre d'un atome constituée de protons et de neutrons.**

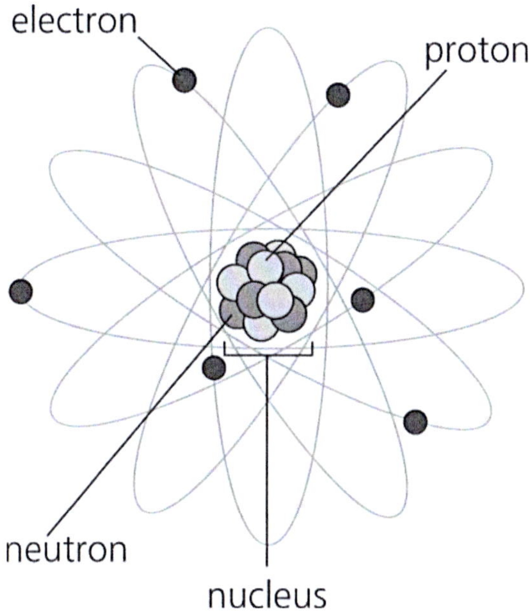

O

Ohm's law: loi d'Ohm

- **Is the relation between the current through a conductor and the potential difference, U=RI.**
- **C'est une loi physique permettant de relier l'intensité du courant électrique traversant un dipôle électrique à la tension à ses bornes, U=RI.**

Operating point: point de fonctionnement

Optical fibre: fibre optique

- **Is a flexible, transparent fiber made of very pure glass that acts as a waveguide between the two ends of the fiber.**
- **C'est un fil en verre flexible très fin qui a la propriété de conduire la lumière et sert dans les transmissions de données.**

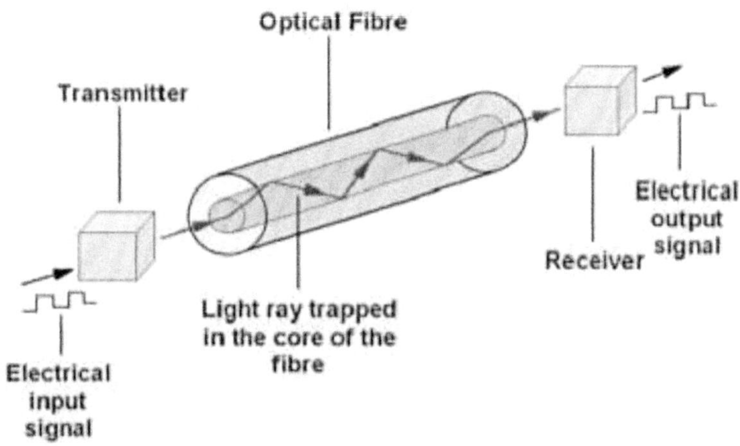

Optical pumping: pompage optique

- **That is the Principle on which the Laser works; it is the process of reversing the relationship between the population of high-level and low-level energy of electrons, atoms or molecules, because they are predominantly in the state of lowest energy. Optical pumping allows the realization of the phenomenon of stimulated emission.**

- **The laser acts as an amplifier of light by *stimulated Emission* based on optical pumping.**

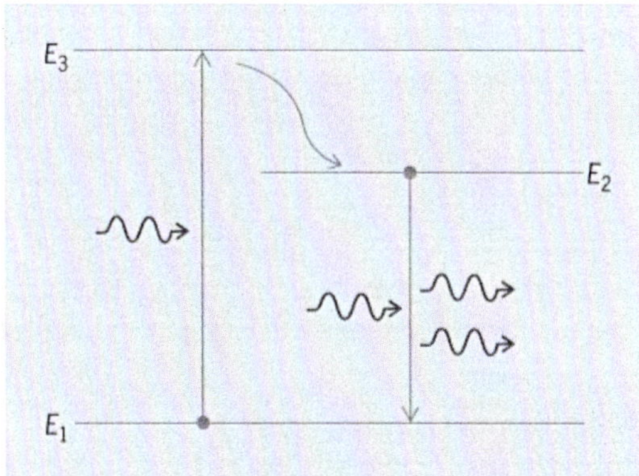

- **A first atom is energized from an electric current. By de-energized, the first atom releases a photon (amount of energy) will strike another atom. The other atom will excite and release a photon in turn. This photon has the same frequency and the same wavelength as the first. Both photons will collide with other atoms and so on. These photons then bounce mirrors opposite the tube to gain more energy (more photons) that allows them to pass through the semi-reflective mirror and produce a light beam.**
- **C'est le Principe sur lequel le Laser fonctionne, il s'agit d'inverser le rapport entre les populations hautes et basses énergie des électrons, atomes ou molécules car ils sont majoritairement dans l'état de plus basse énergie. Le pompage optique permet la réalisation du phénomène *d'émission stimulée*.**

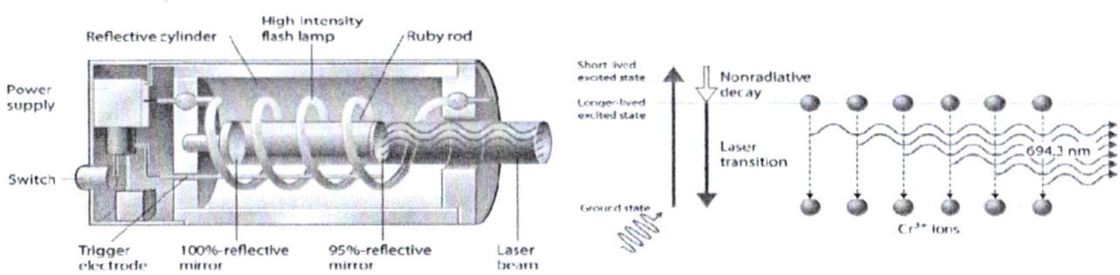

- **Le Laser fonctionne comme un amplificateur de lumière par émission stimulée basé sur le Principe de pompage optique.**
- **Un premier atome est excité à partir d'un courant électrique. En se désexcitant, ce premier atome libère un photon (une quantité**

d'énergie) qui va percuter un autre atome. L'autre atome va s'exciter puis libérer un photon à son tour. Ce photon aura la même fréquence et la même fréquence et la même longueur d'onde que le premier. Les deux photons vont percuter d'autres atomes et ainsi de suite. Ces photons rebondissent ensuite sur les miroirs opposés du tube pour acquérir une plus grande énergie (plus de photons) ce qui leurs permet de passer à travers le miroir semi-réfléchissant et produire un faisceau lumineux.

Optical resolution: résolution optique
- **Describes the ability of an imaging system to resolve detail.**
- **C'est la capacité de montrer les détails d'une image.**

Orbital motion: mouvement orbital
- **An orbit is the gravitationally curved path of an object around a point in space.**
- **Une orbite est la trajectoire que dessine dans l'espace un corps autour d'un autre corps sous l'effet de la gravitation.**

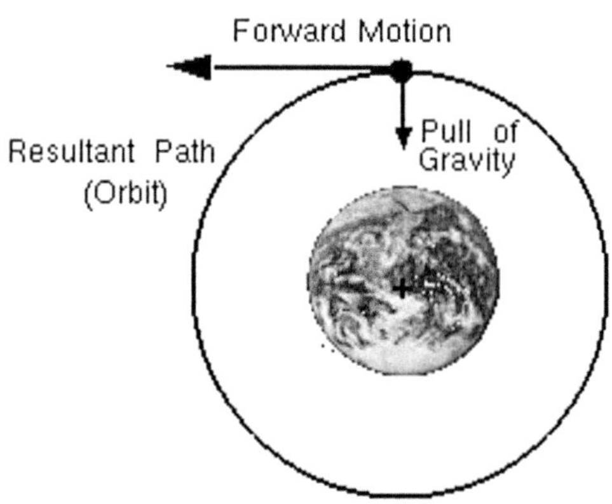

Overcurrent: surtension

Overlap: s'imbriquer, chevauchement

P

Passband: bande passante

- **Is the width of a band of frequency $f_{max} - f_{min}$, measured in Hertz.**
- **C'est la largeur, mesurée en Hertz, d'une plage de fréquence $f_{max} - f_{min}$ (fréquence de coupure).**

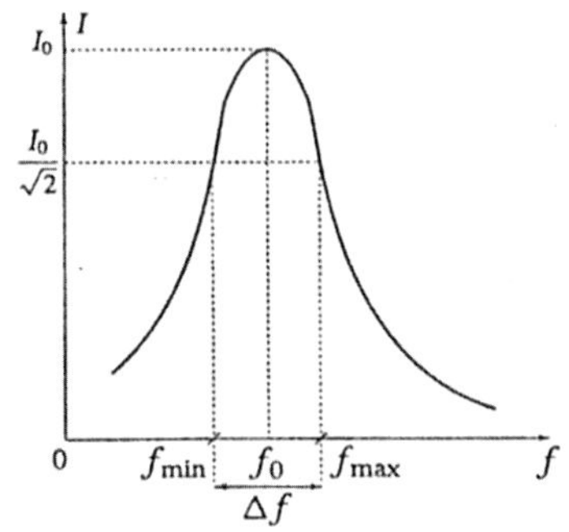

Pendulum: pendule

- **A pendulum is a weight (or bob) suspended from a pivot so that it can swing freely. When a pendulum is displaced sideways from its resting equilibrium position, it is subject to a restoring force due to gravity that will accelerate it back toward the equilibrium position.**
- **Un pendule est un poids (ou bob) suspendu à un pivot de manière à pouvoir osciller librement. Quand un pendule est déplacé latéralement à partir de sa position d'équilibre au repos, il est soumis à une force de rappel due à la gravité qui va accélérer le retour vers la position d'équilibre.**

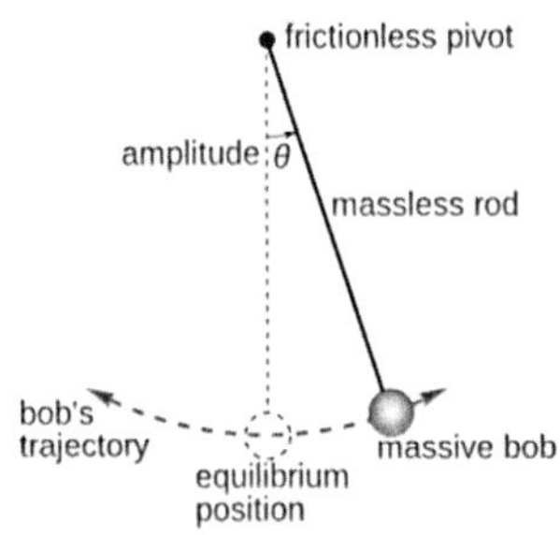

Period: période

- **Is the time that it takes a particle to make one complete oscillation.**
- **C'est le temps nécessaire pour qu'une onde fasse une oscillation complète.**

Photoelectric effect: l'effet photoélectrique

- **When a metal is subjected to in the light of a given wavelength (Ultra-violet), electrons are released from the surface of the metal. This experience demonstrated by Heinrich Hertz in 1887 proves that light has a particle nature.**
- **This phenomenon has been explained by Albert Einstein in 1905. He postulated that a light beam is composed of particles carrying a quantum of energy, called later ''photon'' by Gilbert Lewis in 1926.**

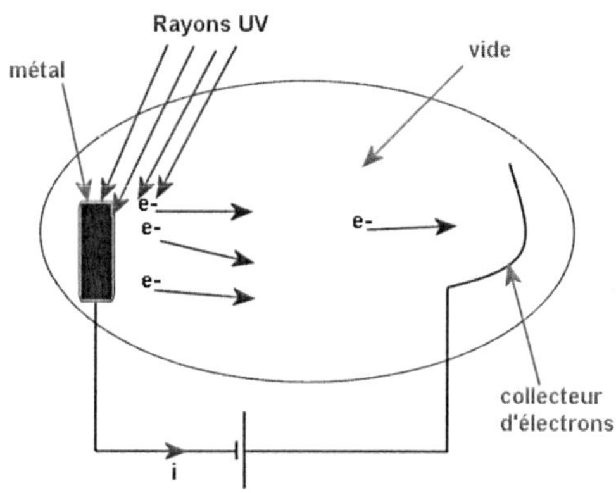

- **Lorsqu'un métal est sous soumis à la lumière de longueur d'onde donnée (rayonnement ultraviolet), des électrons sont arrachés de sa surface. Cette expérience mise en évidence par Heinrich Hertz en 1887 prouve que la lumière présente une nature corpusculaire.**
- **Cet effet a été expliqué par Albert Einstein en 1905, il postule qu'un rayonnement est constitué de particules transportant des quanta d'énergie. Cette particule a été nommé ''photon'' par Gilbert Lewis en 1926.**

Photon (energy quantum): photon (quanta d'énergie)

- **It's a quantum object (neither wave nor particle, charge less and massless) whose behavior is described by quantum mechanics. Mathematical function called a wave function is associated with this** quantum object. This complex function is used to calculate the probability of finding the quantum object at a given location. For this reason quantum phenomena present a probabilistic aspect highlighted by the experience of Thomas Young (Young's slits) and Augustin Fresnel.

- C'est un objet quantique (ni onde ni particule de masse nulle et sans charge) dont le comportement est décrit par la mécanique quantique. Une fonction mathématique appelé fonction d'onde, est associé à cet objet quantique. Cette fonction complexe permet de calculer la probabilité de trouver l'objet quantique à un endroit donné. Pour cette raison les phénomènes quantiques présentent un aspect probabiliste mise en évidence par l'expérience de Thomas Young (fentes d'Young) et Augustin Fresnel.

Pitch of a sound: hauteur d'un son

- The pitch of a sound (whether it is high or low) depends on its frequency or wavelength. Long waves have a lower frequency and pitch than short waves.
- La hauteur d'un son (qu'elle soit haute ou basse) dépend de sa fréquence ou de sa longueur d'onde. Ondes longues ont une fréquence et une hauteur inférieure que les ondes courtes.

Planck's constant: constante de Planck

- A fundamental constant of nature with a value of $6.626x10^{-34}$ joules.seconde that lies at the heart of quantum physics. Planck's constant is responsible for quantising energy and other physical quantities in atomic realm.
- C'est une constante fondamentale de la nature d'une valeur égale à $6{,}626x10^{-34}$ joules.seconde. cette constante se trouve au cœur de la physique quantique. La constante de Planck est responsable de la quantification de l'énergie et d'autres grandeurs physiques dans le domaine atomique.

Planet: planète

- Planets are the largest objects that circle around stars. They may be rocky, like the Earth, or made mostly of gas and liquid, like Jupiter.
- Les planètes sont les plus gros objets qui font le tour autour des étoiles. Elles peuvent être rocheuses, comme la Terre, ou faits principalement de gaz et de liquide, comme Jupiter.

Plug: fiche, prise (électrique)

Plug in (out): brancher, (débrancher)

Potential energy: énergie potentielle

- **Is the energy stored in a body or in a system due to its position in a force field. It is potentially refundable to the solid form of kinetic energy.**
- **C'est l'énergie stockée dans corps ou un système à cause de sa position, dans un champ de forces. Elle est potentiellement restituable au solide sous forme d'énergie cinétique.**

Potential energy of gravity: énergie potentielle de pesanteur

- E_p=m.g.h
  - E_p: potential energy of gravity (J)
  - m: solid mass (kg)
  - h: height of the center of inertia of the solid (m)
- E_p=m.g.h
  - E_p: énergie potentielle de pesanteur (J)
  - m: masse du solide (kg)
  - h: hauteur du centre d'inertie du solide (m)

Potential energy (elastic) of a spring: énergie potentielle élastique d'un ressort

- $E_p = 1/2\ k.x^2$
  - E_p: elastic potential energy of a spring (J)
  - k: stiffness constant ($N.m^{-1}$)
  - x: extension or compression of the spring (m)
- $E_p = 1/2\ k.x^2$
  - E_p: énergie potentielle élastique d'un ressort (J)
  - k: constant de raideur ($N.m^{-1}$)
  - x: allongement ou compression du ressort (m)

Power electronics: électronique de puissance

- **Is the application of solid-state electronics for the control and conversion of electric power.**
- **C'est l'une des branches de l'électrotechnique, elle concerne les dispositifs permettant de changer la forme de l'énergie électrique.**

Power supply: alimentation électrique

- **Is a device that supplies electrical energy.**
- **C'est dispositif qui alimente un circuit en énergie électrique.**

Pressure: pression

- **Is the value of the pressing force exerted by surface unit.**
- **P = F/S**
- **P: pressure (Pascal :Pa), F : force (Newton :N), S : area (square meter :m^2)**
- **Est la valeur de la force pressante exercée par unité de surface.**
- **P = F/S**
- **P: pression (Pascal: Pa), F : force (Newton: N) et S : surface (mètres carrés: m^2)**

Pressure reducing valve: réducteur de pression (détendeur)

- **Is a device that is installed on a water service either in a commercial or residential building in order to reduce the buildings water pressure from 8 bars to 2.5 bars.**
- **C'est un dispositif industriel ou domestique qui sert à réduire la pression de l'eau de 8 bars à 2,5 bars.**

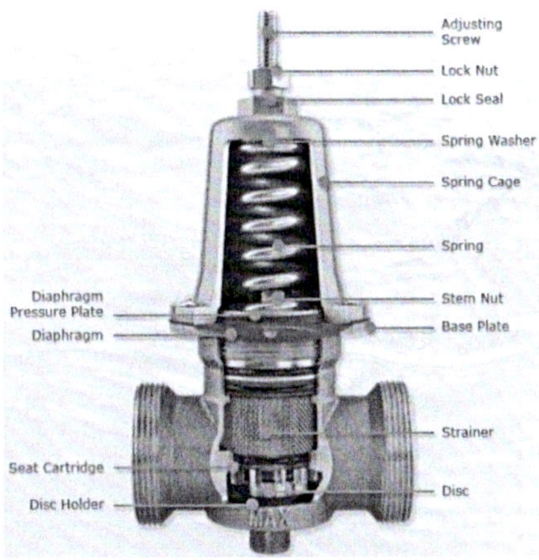

Protection shield: écran de protection

Pulley: poulie

- **Mechanism composed of a wheel on an axle or shaft that may have a groove between two flanges around its circumference. A rope, cable, belt or chain usually runs over the wheel and inside the groove.**

- **Mécanisme composé d'une roue sur un axe ou arbre qui peut avoir une rainure entre deux brides autour de sa circonférence. Une corde, un câble, courroie ou une chaîne s'étend généralement sur la roue et l'intérieur de la rainure.**

Pulsars: Pulsars

- **Is an electromagnetic radiations (radio frequencies) emitted by rotating neutron stars.**
- **Ce sont des étoiles rotatives de neutrons qui émettent des radiations électromagnétiques (souvent sous forme de radio fréquences).**

Q

Quantum (from ''Latin'' means indivisible quantity): quantum (du ''latin'' quanta qui signifie une quantité indivisible)

- **A term introduced at the beginning of the twentieth century to describe the indivisible packets of energy that an oscillator could emit or absorb. Quantum or quantized, can be applied to any physical property of a microphysical system or object that is discontinuous, that can change only by discrete units. Photon is a quantum of electromagnetic radiation with a fixed amount of energy.**
- **Terme introduit au début de vingtième siècle pour décrire les paquets indivisibles d'énergie qu'un oscillateur pourrait émettre ou absorber. Quantum ou quantifiée, peut être appliquée à n'importe quelle propriété physique d'un système microphysique ou l'objet qui est discontinue peut changer uniquement par des unités discrètes. Un photon est un quantum de radiation électromagnétique portant une énergie constante.**

Quantum mechanics: mécanique quantique

- **Quantum mechanics, also known as quantum physics or quantum theory, is a branch of physics providing a mathematical description of the dual particle-like and wave-like behavior and interaction of matter and energy.**
- **La mécanique quantique est la branche de la physique qui a pour but d'étudier et de décrire les phénomènes fondamentaux à l'œuvre dans les systèmes physiques, plus particulièrement à l'échelle atomique et subatomique.**

Quantum field theory: théorie quantique des champs

- **It is the natural and quantic language of particle physics and condensed matter physics.**
- **C'est la nature et le langage quantiques des particules physiques et des problèmes condensés physique.**

Quark: quark

- **A quark is an elementary particle and a fundamental constituent of matter.**
- **Les quarks sont les constituants élémentaires de la matière.**

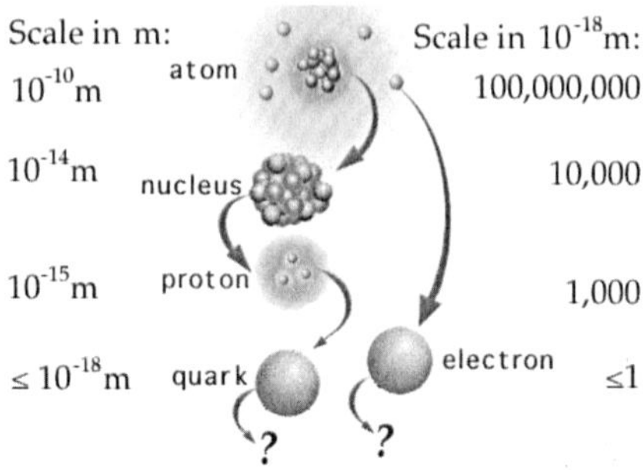

Quasar: quasar

- **Is a very energetic and distant active galactic nucleus. Quasars are among the most luminous objects in the universe.**
- **C'est une galaxie lointaine et très énergétique avec un noyau galactique actif. Ce sont les objets les plus lumineux de l'univers.**

R

Radar and sonar: radar et sonar
- **Radar, which is short for Radio Detection And Ranging.**
- **Sonar, meaning Sound Navigation And Ranging.**
- **They are systems that locate objects. They work by sending out waves, detecting echoes from objects and measuring the distance in between.**
- **Radar sends out a narrow pulse of radio waves.**
- **Sonar sends out a pulse of high-pitched sound, known as ultrasound.**
- **Ce sont des systèmes qui localisent les objets. Ils fonctionnent en émettant des ondes et en détectant les échos réfléchis permettant ainsi de mesurer la distance qui les sépare.**
- **Le radar émet une salve d'ondes radios.**
- **Le sonar émet une pulsation de son aigu, appelé ultrasons.**

Radiation: rayonnement
- **Is a process in which energetic particles or waves travel through a medium or space.**
- **C'est un processus d'émission ou de transmission d'énergie dans un milieu.**

Radiation energy: énergie de rayonnement

Radiation protection: radioprotection

Radio: radio
- **Is an invention we can use to send and receive information through the air and even deep into space without connecting wires.**
- **C'est une invention que nous pouvons utiliser pour envoyer et recevoir des informations par le biais de l'air et même en profondeur dans l'espace sans fils de connexion.**

Radio waves and microwaves : ondes radio et micro-ondes
- **Radio waves and microwaves are two types of electromagnetic waves.**

Electromagnetic waves, which we will call EM waves, like all waves transport energy but can, do so through a vacuum. Sound waves and ocean waves require matter to transport energy but EM

waves can do so without the presence of matter. Because of this, satellites can use radars to work on projects outside of the Earth's atmosphere and on other planets. EM waves travel at a constant speed through a vacuum called the speed of light abbreviated by the letter "c" (299,792,458 meters per second).

- Les ondes radio et les micro-ondes sont deux types d'ondes électromagnétiques.

  Les ondes électromagnétiques, que nous appellerons ondes EM, comme toutes les ondes, elles transportent de l'énergie, mais peuvent le faire dans le vide. Les ondes sonores et les vagues de l'océan exigent la présence de la matière pour transporter de l'énergie, mais les ondes électromagnétiques peuvent le faire sans la présence de la matière. Pour cette raison, les satellites peuvent utiliser les radars pour communiquer en dehors de l'atmosphère de la Terre et d'autres planètes. Les ondes électromagnétiques se déplacent à une vitesse constante dans le vide égale à la vitesse de la lumière en abrégé par la lettre "c" (299792458 mètres par seconde).

Radioactive decay: désintégration, décroissance radioactive

Radioactive-carbon dating: datation par le carbone 14

- Is a radiometric dating method that uses the naturally occurring radioisotope carbon 14 (^{14}C) to estimate the age of carbon-bearing.
- C'est une méthode de datation radiométrique basée sur la mesure de l'activité radiologique du carbone 14 (^{14}C) contenu dans de la matière organique dont on souhaite connaître l'âge absolu.

Radioactivity: radioactivité

- Is a natural process by which an atomic nucleus of an unstable atom loses energy by emitting ionizing particles like α, β, γ.
- C'est un phénomène physique naturel au cours duquel des noyaux atomiques instables, se transforment spontanément en dégageant de rayonnements divers de type α, β, γ.

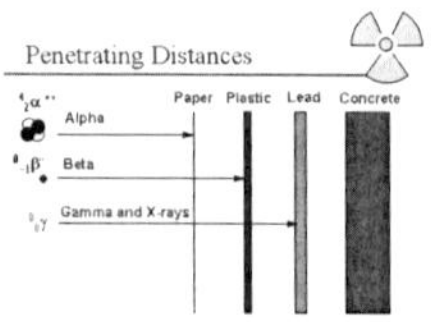

Radio Detection And Ranging (RADAR): détection et détermination de distance par ondes radio

Radiography: radiographie

Radio waves: ondes radio
- **Is a type of electromagnetic radiation with wavelengths from one meter to ten kilometers.**
- **Ce sont des ondes électromagnétiques de longueurs d'ondes de un mètre jusque dix kilomètres.**

Rainbow: arc en ciel
- **Is a meteorological phenomenon that appears as a multicolored arc.**
- **C'est une dispersion de la lumière par l'air humide.**

Random error: erreur aléatoire

Rarefaction: détente (décompression)
- **A term used in connection with longitudinal waves and refers to the region where the particles of the medium are 'stretched out'.**
- **Ce terme en rapport avec les ondes longitudinales qui désigne la région ou les particules de milieu sont détendues 'allongées'.**

Ray (beam): rayon (faisceau)

Receiver: récepteur

Rechargeable battery: accumulateur électrique
- **Is a group of one or more electrochemical cells.**
- **C'est un groupe de cellules électrochimiques.**

Rectilinear movement: mouvement de translation rectiligne

Red: rouge
- **Is a colors in the wavelength range of roughly 630–740nm**
- **C'est une couleur de longueur d'onde correspondante à 630-740nm**

Red Giants: giants rouges

- Stars considerably larger than our Sun and have a much lower surface temperature than our Sun.
- Ce sont des étoiles beaucoup plus grande que le Soleil et d'une température plus faible.

Relative pressure: pression relative

- Is the measured pressure relative to the atmospheric pressure.
- $P_{rel} = P_{abs} - P_{atm}$
- P_{abs} : absolute pressure, P_{atm} : atmospheric pressure
- Est la pression mesurée par rapport à la pression atmosphérique.
- $P_{rel} = P_{abs} - P_{atm}$
- P_{abs} : pression absolue, P_{atm} : pression atmosphérique

Reflection: réflexion

- Is the change in direction of a wave front at an interface between two different media
- C'est un changement de direction d'un front d'onde à la surface séparant deux milieux

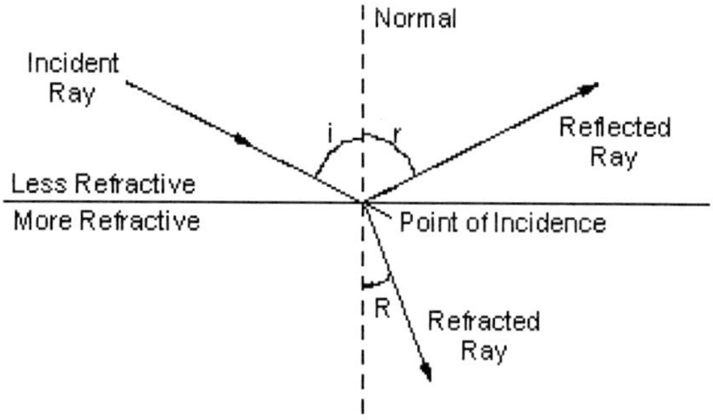

Refraction: réfraction

- Is the change in direction of a wave due to the change of medium
- C'est un phénomène de déviation d'une onde lorsque sa vitesse change entre deux milieux.

Refrigerators: réfrigérateur

- Is a cooling apparatus
- C'est un appareil qui sert à refroidir

Relative permeability: perméabilité relative

- Is the ability of a material to support the formation of a magnetic field within itself.

- **Caractérise la faculté d'un matériau à modifier un champ magnétique.**

Relativity: relativité

- **General relativity or the general theory of relativity is the geometric theory of gravitation published by Albert Einstein in 1916. It is the current description of gravitation in modern physics which is explained as a distortion of space-time. General relativity generalizes special relativity and Newton's law of universal gravitation.**
- **La relativité générale publié par Einstein en 1916, fondée sur le principe de covariance générale qui étend le principe de relativité aux référentiels non-inertiels, est une théorie relativiste de la gravitation, c'est-à-dire qu'elle décrit l'influence sur le mouvement des astres de la présence de matière et plus généralement d'énergie, et cette théorie est expliqué par la distortion de l'espace-temps en tenant compte des principes de la relativité restreinte. La relativité générale englobe et supplante la théorie de la gravitation universelle d'Isaac Newton qui en représente la limite aux petites vitesses.**
- **Special relativity: is the physical theory of measurement in inertial frames of reference proposed in 1905 by Albert Einstein.**

  This theory is based on two postulates:

  a- **Postulate 1: The laws of physics are expressed in the same way in all Galilean frames.**

  b- **Postulate 2: The speed of propagation of light in vacuum is independent of the motion of the light source and is invariant in any change of Galilean frame.**

  c- **Consequence, there is a maximum speed equal to the speed of light c in vacuum, which cannot be exceeded by any signal carrying information, nor any particle. It can be achieved only by massless particles such as photons.**
- **Relativité restreinte: est la théorie formelle élaborée par Albert Einstein en 1905 en vue de tirer toutes les conséquences physiques de la relativité galiléenne et du principe que la vitesse de la lumière dans le vide a la même valeur dans tous les référentiels inertiels.**

  Cette théorie repose sur deux postulats:

  a- **Postulat 1: Les lois de la physique s'expriment de la même façon dans tous les référentiels galiléens.**

  b- **Postulat 2: La vitesse de propagation de la lumière dans le vide est indépendante du mouvement de la source lumineuse et elle est invariante dans tout changement de référentiel galiléen.**

  c- **Conséquence: il existe une vitesse limite, égale à la célérité c de la lumière dans le vide, qui ne peut être dépassée par aucun signal transportant une information, ni aucune particule. Elle ne** peut être atteinte que par les particules de masse nulle comme les photons.

Requirements: exigences

Reservoir: réservoir

Resistance: résistance
- Is anything in the circuit which slows the flow down.
- N'importe quel élément qui réduit le flux.

Residue: résidu
- Matter remaining after completion of a chemical or physical process, such as evaporation, combustion, distillation, or filtration.
- Reste de matière après avoir effectué un processus chimique ou physique, comme l'évaporation, combustion, distillation ou filtration.

Robot: robot (automate)
- Is a machine designed to imitate human actions. It can perform a range of tasks that are often too dangerous or monotonous for a human to do.
- Est une machine conçue pour imiter les actions humaines. Il peut effectuer une série de tâches qui sont souvent trop dangereux ou trop monotone pour un être humain à faire.

Rover: voiture lunaire
- Vehicles designed to explore the surface of celestial bodies (moon, planets, etc.).
- Véhicules destinés à explorer la surface des corps célestes (lune, planets, etc.)

Rugged: robuste

S

Satellite: satellite

- **Satellites are objects that move in orbit around other objects of greater mass. A satellite may be natural, like the Moon, or artificial, like an orbiting spacecraft.**
- **Les satellites sont des objets qui se déplacent en orbite autour d'autres objets de plus grande masse. Un satellite peut être naturel, comme la Lune, ou artificiel, comme un vaisseau spatial en orbite.**

Sample: échantillon

Sampling: échantillonnage

Scan: scintigraphie

Scattering: dispersion ou diffusion

- **The deflection of one particle by another.**
- **La déviation d'une particule par une autre.**

Schrödinger equation: équation de Schrödinger

- **The fundamental equation of the wave mechanics version of quantum mechanics that governs the behavior of a particle or the evolution of a physical system by encoding how its wave function varies with time.**

$$\frac{\hbar^2}{2m}\nabla^2\Psi + V\Psi = \frac{i\hbar\partial}{\partial t}\Psi$$

- **C'est la version de l'équation fondamentale de la mécanique d'onde dans le domaine de la mécanique quantique qui régit le comportement d'une particule ou l'évolution d'un système physique en expliquant la façon dont la fonction d'onde varie avec le temps.**

Screw: vis

- **Is a type of fastener characterized by a helical ridge, known as an external thread or just thread, wrapped around a cylinder.**

- **C'est un organe mécanique, comportant une tige de section circulaire, avec sur sa périphérie un filetage forme générée par le balayage d'une section le long d'une hélice.**

Seismology: seismologie
- **Seismology is the study of earthquakes and seismic waves that move through and around the earth.**

Seismologist: seismologiste
- **Is a scientist who studies earthquakes and seismic waves.**

Seismic waves: ondes sismiques
- **Are the waves of energy caused by the sudden breaking of rock within the earth or an explosion. They are the energy that travels through the earth and is recorded on seismographs.**
- **Types of Seismic Waves**
- **There are several different kinds of seismic waves, and they all move in different ways. The two main types of waves are body waves and surface waves. Body waves can travel through the earth's inner layers, but surface waves can only move along the surface of the planet like ripples on water. Earthquakes radiate seismic energy as both body and surface waves.**

1- **Body Waves: Traveling through the interior of the earth, body waves arrive before the surface waves emitted by an earthquake. These waves are of a higher frequency than surface waves.**
   a- **P Waves: The first kind of body wave is the P wave or primary wave. This is the fastest kind of seismic wave, and, consequently, the first to 'arrive' at a seismic station. The P wave can move through solid rock and fluids, like water or the liquid layers of the earth. It pushes and pulls the rock it moves through just like sound waves push and pull the air. Have you ever heard a big clap of thunder and heard the windows rattle at the same time? The windows rattle because the sound waves were pushing and pulling on the window glass much like P waves push and pull on rock. Sometimes animals can hear the P waves of an earthquake. Dogs, for instance, commonly begin barking hysterically just before an earthquake 'hits' (or more specifically, before the surface waves arrive). Usually people can only feel the bump and rattle of these waves.**

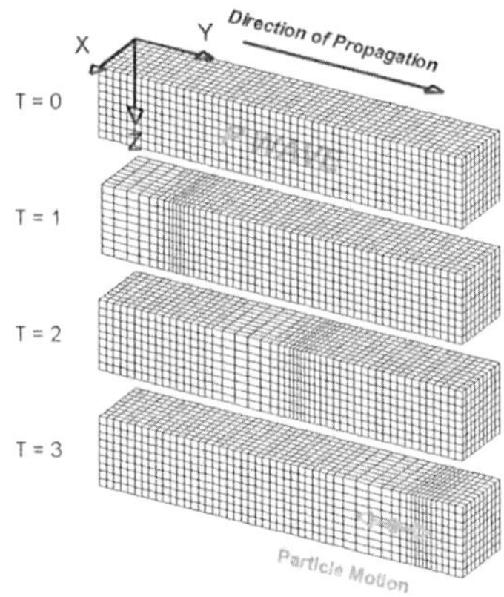

P waves are also known as compressional waves, because of the pushing and pulling they do. Subjected to a P wave, particles move in the same direction that the the wave is moving in, which is the direction that the energy is traveling in, and is sometimes called the 'direction of wave propagation'.

b- S Waves: The second type of body wave is the S wave or secondary wave, which is the second wave you feel in an earthquake. An S wave is slower than a P wave and can only move through solid rock, not through any liquid medium. It is this property of S waves that led seismologists to conclude that the Earth's outer core is a liquid. S waves move rock particles up and down, or side-to-side perpindicular to the direction that the wave is traveling in (the direction of wave propagation).

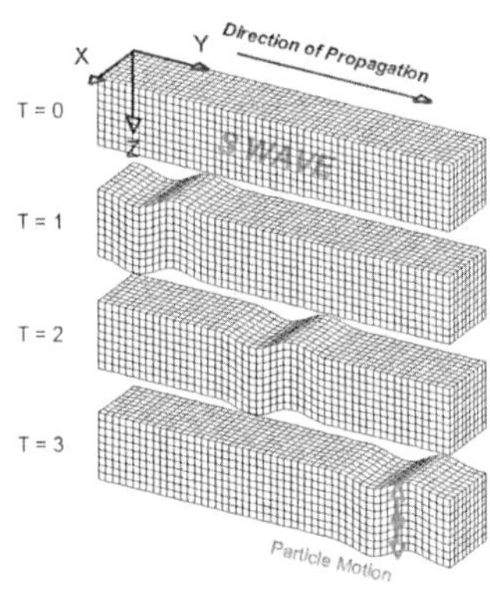

2- Surface Waves: Travelling only through the crust, surface waves are of a lower frequency than body waves, and are easily distinguished on a seismogram as a result. Though they arrive after body waves, it is surface waves that are almost enitrely responsible for the damage and destruction associated with earthquakes. This damage and the strength of the surface waves are reduced in deeper earthquakes.

a- Love Waves: The first kind of surface wave is called a Love wave, named after A.E.H. Love, a British mathematician who worked out the mathematical model for this kind of wave in 1911. It's the fastest surface wave and moves the ground from side-to-side. Confined to the surface of the crust, Love waves produce entirely horizontal motion.

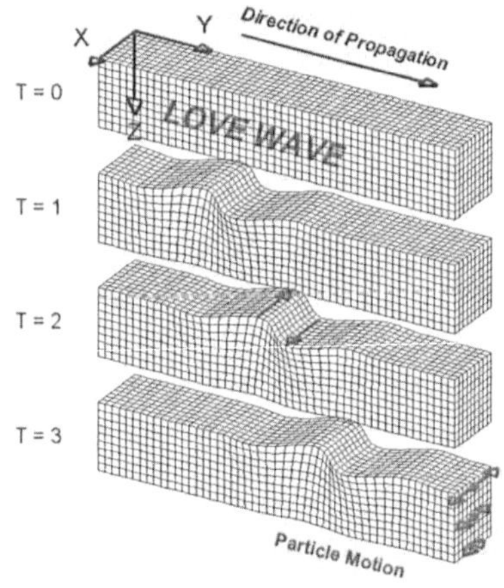

b- Rayleigh Waves: The other kind of surface wave is the Rayleigh wave, named for John William Strutt, Lord Rayleigh, who mathematically predicted the existence of this kind of wave in 1885. A Rayleigh wave rolls along the ground just like a wave rolls across a lake or an ocean. Because it rolls, it moves the ground up and down, and side-to-side in the same direction that the wave is moving. Most of the shaking felt from an earthquake is due to the Rayleigh wave, which can be much larger than the other waves.

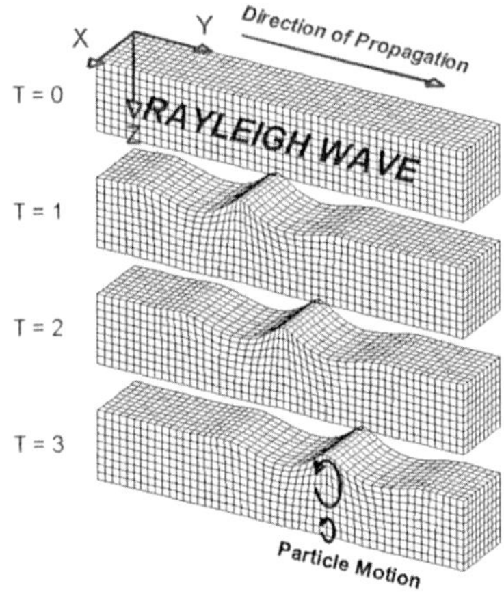

- Ce sont des ondes d'une énergie produite lors d'une rupture brusque des roches dans la terre ou d'une explosion. Ce sont les énergies qui voyagent à travers la terre et enregistrées par les sismographes.
- Types d'ondes sismiques
- Il existe plusieurs types d'ondes sismiques, et ils se déplacent tous de différentes façons. Les deux principaux types d'ondes sont les ondes de volume et les ondes de surface. Les ondes de volume peuvent voyager à travers les couches internes de la terre, mais des ondes de surface ne peuvent se déplacer que le long de la surface de la planète comme des rides sur l'eau. Les tremblements de terre émettent de l'énergie sismique à la fois les ondes de volume et des ondes de surface.
  1- Les ondes de volume: se propagent à travers l'intérieur de la terre, des ondes de volume arrivent avant les ondes de surface émises par un tremblement de terre. Ces ondes sont d'une fréquence supérieure à celle des ondes de surface.
    a- Ondes P: Le premier type d'onde de volume est l'onde P ou l'onde primaire. C'est le type d'onde le plus rapide des ondes sismiques, et, par conséquent, le premier à «arriver» à une station sismique. L'onde P peut se déplacer à travers la roche solide et des fluides, comme l'eau ou les couches liquides de la terre. Il pousse et tire la roche, il se déplace à travers tout comme des ondes sonores à pousser et tirer l'air.

    Les ondes P sont également connues comme des ondes de compression, en raison de la poussée et de traction qu'ils font. Soumis à une onde P, les particules se déplacent dans la même direction que le l'onde se déplace dans ce qui est le sens de ce que l'énergie se déplace dans, et est parfois appelée "direction de propagation de l'onde".

b- Ondes S: Le deuxième type d'onde de volume est l'onde S ou l'onde secondaire, qui est la deuxième onde vous sentez dans un tremblement de terre. Une onde S est plus lente qu'une onde P et ne peut se déplacer dans la roche, et non par un milieu liquide. C'est cette propriété d'onde S qui a conduit les sismologues à conclure que le noyau externe de la Terre est un liquide. Les ondes S déplacent les particules de roches de haut en bas, ou perpendiculaire à la direction de propagation de l'onde.

2- Les ondes de surface: se propagent seulement à travers la croûte terrestre, les ondes de surface sont d'une fréquence inférieure aux ondes de volume, et elles sont faciles à distinguer sur un sismogramme. Bien qu'elles arrivent après les ondes de volume, ces ondes de surface sont presque entièrement responsables des dommages et destructions associées aux tremblements de terre.

a- Onde Love: Le premier type d'ondes de surface est appelé une onde de Love, nommé d'après AEH Love, un mathématicien britannique qui a travaillé sur le modèle mathématique pour ce type d'onde en 1911. C'est l'onde de surface la plus rapide et déplace le sol de côté à côté. Confiné à la surface de la croûte terrestre, les ondes Love produisent des mouvements totalement horizontal.

b- Ondes de Rayleigh: L'autre type d'ondes de surface est l'onde de Rayleigh, du nom de John William Strutt, Lord Rayleigh, qui a prédit mathématiquement l'existence de ce type d'onde en 1885. Une onde de Rayleigh roule sur le sol comme une vague roule sur un lac ou un océan. Parce qu'il roule, il se déplace au sol de haut en bas et d'un côté à côté dans la même direction de déplacement de l'onde. La plupart du tremblement de terre ressenti est due à l'onde de Rayleigh, qui peut être beaucoup plus grande que les autres ondes.

Sequence of firing: séquence de mise à feu

Semiconductor: semi-conducteur

- Is a material with electrical conductivity due to electron flow intermediate in magnitude between that of a conductor and an insulator.

- **Un semi-conducteur est un matériau qui a les caractéristiques électriques d'un isolant, mais peut être conducteur par rapport à l'énergie (tension électrique, &clairement, chauffage, etc….).**

Sensitivity: sensibilité

Sensor: capteur
- **Is a device that measures a physical quantity and converts it into a signal which can be read by an observer or by an instrument.**
- **C'est un dispositif transformant l'état d'une grandeur physique observée en une grandeur utilisable.**

SI system (International System): système international SI
- **The General Conference on Weights and Measures, held in Paris during October 1960, decided to establish a practical system of units, known as International System (abbreviated SI). This contains the following six basic units:**
  1- **The meter, unit of length.**
  2- **The kilogram, unit of mass.**
  3- **The second, unit of time.**
  4- **The ampere, unit of intensity of electric current.**
  5- **The Kelvin, unit of temperature.**
  6- **The candela, unit of luminous intensity.**
- **Lors de la Conférence Générale du Poids et de Mesure tenu en octobre 1960 à Paris, une décision a été prise pour établir un système partique d'unité, connu comme le Système International (abrégé SI). Ce système contient les six unités de base:**
  1- **Le metre, unité de longueur.**
  2- **Le kilogramme, unité de masse.**
  3- **La seconde, unité du temps.**
  4- **L'ampère, unité de l'intensité du courant électrique.**
  5- **Le Kelvin, unité de température.**
  6- **La candela, unité de l'intensité lumineuse.**

Shear modulus: module de cisaillement
- **Is defined as the ratio of shear stress to the shear strain, denoted by G.**
- **C'est une grandeur physique propre à chaque matériau et qui caractérise les déformations causées par des efforts de cisaillement, noté G.**

Short circuit: court-circuit

- **Is an abnormal low-resistance connection between two nodes of an electrical circuit that are meant to be at different voltages.**
- **C'est la mise en connexion de deux points d'un circuit électrique entre lesquels, il existe une faible résistance.**

Significant figures: chiffres significatif

- **A significant figure is the one which appears in the number expressing a measurement, excluding the zeros which precede the first figure different from zero.**
- **Un chiffre significatif est celui qui apparaît dans le nombre exprimant une mesure, en excluant les zéros qui précèdent le premier chiffre différent de zéro.**

Signal: signal

- **Physical variable that transmits information.**
- **Grandeur physique qui transmet de l'information.**

Seismograph: sismographe

- **Seismographs locate the origin of earthquakes and measure their force.**
- **Les sismographes localisent l'origine d'un tremblement de terre et mesure son intensité.**

Slipping: glissement

- **Slipping '*s*' is the rotation rate of the magnetic field, relative to the rotor, divided by the absolute rotation rate of the stator magnetic field.**
- $s = (n_s - n)/n_s$

  s: slipping

  n_s**: absolute rotation rate of the stator magnetic field (rpm)**

  n: rotation rate of the rotor (rpm)
- **Le glissement 'g' correspond à l'écart de vitesse de rotation d'une machine asynchrone par rapport à la vitesse de rotation de son champ statorique.**
- $g = (n_s - n)/n_s$

  g: glissement

  n_s**: fréquence de rotation du champ magnétique (**$tr.min^{-1}$**)**

  n: fréquence de rotation du rotor ($tr.min^{-1}$**)**

Slip rings: bagues collectrices
- **Are rings of copper used in generators.**
- **Ce sont des bagues en cuivre utilisées dans les générateurs électriques.**

Slope: pente

Slots: trous (encoches)

Spacecraft: vaisseau spatial
- **There are three main types of spacecraft: artificial satellites, unmanned probes and manned spacecrafts. All require powerful rockets to lift them into space.**
- **Il existe trois principaux types de véhicules spatiaux: satellites artificiels, des sondes sans pilote et des vaisseaux spatiaux habités. Tous exigent de puissantes fusées pour les soulever dans l'espace.**

Spectral lines: raie spectrale
- **The pattern of coulored lines of light on a black background is called an emission spectrum. A series of black lines on a coloured back ground is called an absorption spectrum (Fraunhofer lines).**
- **Splitting the light into a spectrum reveals the chemical elements that make up stars. The different elements are indicated by dark absorption lines.**
- **Le motif de lignes colorés de lumière sur un fond noir est appelé spectre d'émission. Une série de lignes noires sur un fond coloré en arrière-plan est appelé un spectre d'absorption (spectre de Fraunhofer).**
- **Le fractionnement de la lumière en un spectre révèle les éléments chimiques qui composent les étoiles. Les différents éléments sont indiqués par des lignes d'absorption sombres.**

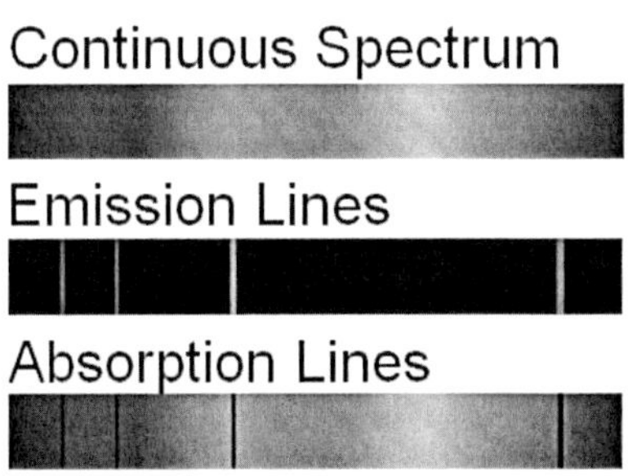

Spectroscopy: spectroscopie

- The field of physics concerned with analyzing and studying absorption and emission spectra.
- It is the interaction between electromagnetic radiations and matter.
- C'est un domaine de la physique concerné par l'analyse et l'étude des spectres d'absorption et d'émission.
- C'est l'interaction entre les rayonnements électromagnètiques et la matière.

Speed of light: vitesse de la lumière

Speedometer: indicateur de vitesse

- Is a gauge that measures and displays the instantaneous speed of a land vehicle.
- C'est instrument qui mesure la vitesse instantanée d'un véhicule.

Spike: pic

- Voltage spike.
- Pic de tension.

Star: étoile

- Stars are large balls of hot gas that produce light and heat through nuclear reactions. Our Sun is an average yellow star.
- Most stars contain two main gases – hydrogen and helium.
- Les étoiles sont de grosses boules de gaz chaud qui produisent de la lumière et de chaleur par des réactions nucléaires. Notre Soleil est une étoile moyenne jaune.
- La plupart d'étoiles contienent deux principaux gaz – hydrogène et hélium.

Steady speed: vitesse uniform

- Forces must be in balance.
- La somme de forces est nulle.

Steel: acier
- Steel is an alloy that consists mostly of iron and has a carbon content between 0.2% and 3% by weight, depending on the grade.
- L'acier est un alliage métallique utilisé dans les domaines de la construction métallique et de la construction mécanique. Il est constitué d'au moins deux éléments, majoritairement le fer puis le carbone dans des proportions comprises entre 0,2 % et 3 % en masse.

Stepper motor: moteur pas à pas

Stimulated emission (see optiacl pumping): émission stimulée

Stopwatch (chronometer): chronomètre
- Is a handheld timepiece used to measure the amount of time elapsed.
- C'est un instrument permettant de mesurer la durée d'un événement.

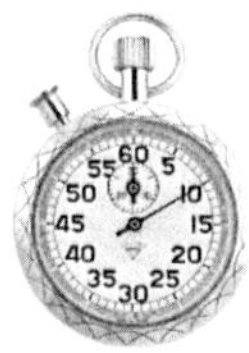

Stone corner: pierre angulaire

Strength of gravity (g): intensité de la pesanteur (g)
- On Earth g is equal to 9,8 N/kg, g depend of planet's size.
- Sur Terre g est égale à 9,8 N/kg, g dépend de la taille de la planète.

String theory: théorie des cordes
- String theory is an active research theory in particle physics that attempts to reconcile quantum mechanics and general relativity.
- La théorie des cordes est l'une des voies envisagées pour régler une des questions majeures de la physique théorique: fournir une description de la gravité quantique c'est-à-dire l'unification de la mécanique quantique et de la théorie de la relativité générale.

Socket: prise de courant (douille d'une ampoule)

Soddy's laws: lois de Soddy

- **During a nuclear reaction the number of protons and the number of nucleons are conserved.**
- **Pendant une réaction nucléaire le nombre des protons et les nucléons se conservent.**

$$^{A}_{Z}X \rightarrow\ ^{A-4}_{Z-2}Y +\ ^{4}_{2}He$$

Solar cell: cellule photovoltaïque

- **Also called photovoltaic cell or photoelectric cell is a solid state electrical device that converts the energy of light directly into electricity by the photovoltaic effect.**
- **Une cellule photovoltaïque est un composant électronique qui produit de l'électricité grâce à l'effet photovoltaïque.**

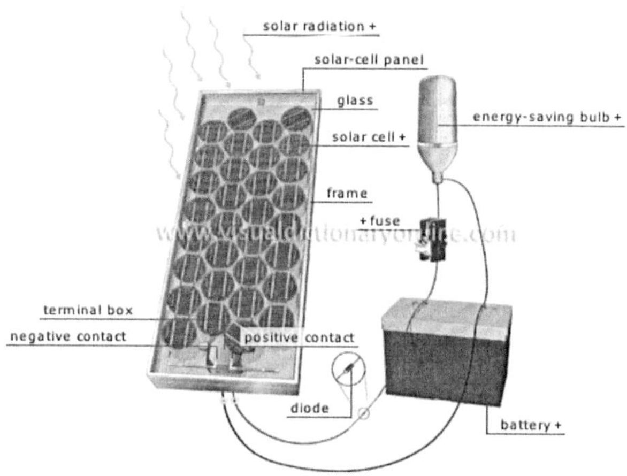

Solar energy: énergie solaire

Solar panels: panneaux solaire

Solar power: puissance (énergie) solaire

- **Solar power harnesses the energy in the Sun's rays. It is a non-polluting source of energy that will not run out until the Sun dies, billions of years in the future.**

- **L'énergie solaire exploite l'énergie contenue dans les rayons du soleil. C'est une source non polluante d'énergie qui ne s'épuiseront pas avant que le soleil meurt, des milliards d'années dans le futur.**

Solar powered charger: chargeur solaire
- **Is a solar cell used for rechargeable batteries.**
- **C'est une cellule photovoltaïque utilisée pour charger les piles rechargeables.**

Solar system: système solaire
- **Our solar system is made up of the Sun and the objects that orbit it. These include the nine planets and their moons, as well as asteroids, comets and meteors.**
- **Notre système solaire est composé du Soleil et des objets qu'ils tournent autour. Il s'agit notamment des neuf planètes et leurs lunes, ainsi que les astéroïdes, les comètes et les météores.**

Soft iron: fer doux
- **Used in the construction of transformers.**
- **Utilisé dans la construction des transformateurs.**

Soft magnets: aimant temporaire
- **Temporary magnets**
- **Aimant temporaire**

SONAR (SOund Navigation And Ranging): SONAR
- **Ultrasound waves used to detect and estimate the range of submerged objects.**
- **Ondes ultrasons utilisés pour détecter et estimer les objets submergés.**

Sound: son

- **Is a form of energy that can be heard. It is caused by vibration and travels in waves through solids, liquids and gases.**
- **C'est une forme d'énergie qui peut être entendu. Elle est causée par les vibrations et se déplace par vagues à travers les solides, les liquides et les gaz.**

Sound level: niveau sonore

Sound level meter: sonomètre

Sound intensity: intensité sonore

- **Characterizes the volume**
- **$I=P/S$**

  I: intensity in watt per meter square ($W.m^{-2}$)

  P: power in watts (W)

  S: surface in meters square (m^2)

- **Caractérise le volume sonore**
- **$I=P/S$**

  I: intensité en watt par mètre carré ($W.m^{-2}$)

  P: puissance en watts (W)

  S: surface en mètres carré (m^2)

Sound waves: ondes sonore

- **Are mechanical waves because they need a medium to propagate. They are longitudinal (the disturbance acts parallel to the direction of propagation); they cannot propagate in the vacuum.**

- Ce sont des ondes mécaniques car elles ont besoin d'un milieu naturel pour se propager. Elles sont longitudinales (la perturbation de l'onde est parallèle à la direction de la propagation) ; elles ne se propagent pas dans le vide.

Space probes: sondes spatiale

Splitting up: fractionnement

Spring: resort
- A spring is an elastic object used to store mechanical energy
- Un ressort est une pièce mécanique qui utilise les propriétés élastiques de certains matériaux pour absorber de l'énergie mécanique

Spring constant: constante de raideur
- Is a constant related to a coil spring, symbol k, it's unite is $N.m^{-1}$
- C'est une constante liée à un ressort, noté k, son unité est $N.m^{-1}$

Spring scale (dynamometer): dynamomètre
- Is simply a spring fixed at one end with which we can measure forces.
- C'est un appareil qui mesure des forces.

Sprocket: pignon, roué dentée
- Profiled wheel with teeth that meshes with a chain or other perforated or indented material.
- Une roue dentée qui entraine une courroie.

Supernovae: Supernova
- Is an enormous shock wave due to a star colossal explosion

- **C'est une énorme onde de choc dû à une explosion colossale d'étoile**

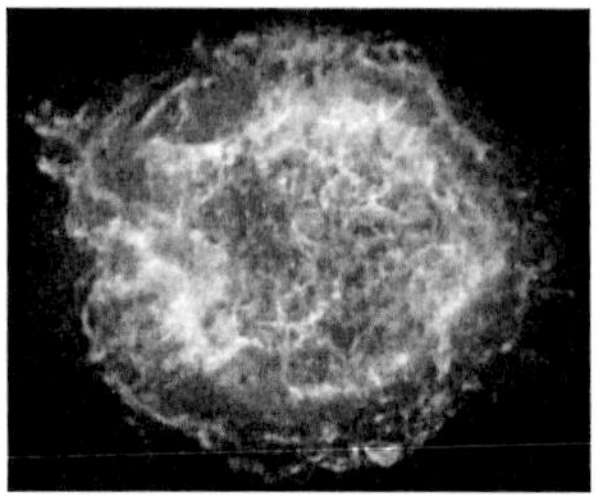

Sun: soleil
- **The Sun is the closest star to Earth. It is a globe of hot gas, mostly hydrogen, and lies at the center of our solar system.**
- **Le Soleil est l'étoile la plus proche de la Terre. Il s'agit d'un globe de gaz chaud, principalement de l'hydrogène, et se trouve au centre de notre système solaire.**

Sundial: cadran solaire
- **Is a device that measures time by the position of the Sun.**
- **C'est un instrument qui mesure le temps en fonction de la position du soleil.**

Sun energy: énergie solaire
- **Is the energy derived directly from the Sun.**
- **C'est l'énergie dérivée de soleil.**

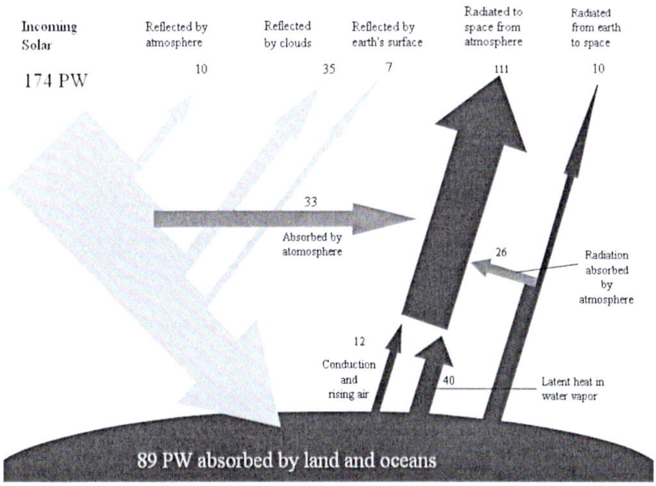

Surface of emission: surface d'émission

Switch: interrupteur

Switch on (off): allumer, éteindre

Synchronous motor: moteur synchrone

Synchronous speed: vitesse de synchronisme

Systematic error: erreur systématique

T

Target: cible, obgectif, but.

Technology: technologie

- **Technology is the practical use of knowledge to construct things, to make work easier and to make our lives more comfortable. It is also used to cure diseases.**
- **La technologie est l'utilisation pratique des connaissances pour construire des choses, pour rendre le travail plus facile et pour rendre nos vies plus à l'aise. Elle est également utilisé pour guérir des maladies.**

Telecommunication: télécommunication

- **Is the transmission of words, sounds, images or data over long distances as electronic or electromagnetic signals.**
- **C'est la transmission de mots, de sons, d'images ou de données sur de longues distances sous forme de signaux électroniques ou électromagnétiques.**

Telephone: téléphone

- **Telephones are instruments for communicating over long distances. They send speech to another location as electric currents, laser light or radio waves.**
- **Les téléphones sont des instruments pour communiquer sur de longues distances. Ils envoient la parole à un autre endroit comme les courants électriques, la lumière laser ou les ondes radios.**

Telescope: télescope

- **Telescopes are instruments for studying objects that are far away. Astronomers use various kinds of telescope to find out more about stars and planets.**
- **Les télescopes sont des instruments pour étudier des objets éloignés. Les astronomes utilisent divers types de télescopes pour en savoir plus sur les étoiles et les planètes.**

Television: télévision

- **Television (TV) is the transmission of pictures and sound from one place to another. It is one of the most important means of mass communication in the world.**

- **Télévision (TV) est la transmission d'images et de sons d'un endroit à l'autre. Il est l'un des moyens les plus importants de la communication de masse dans le monde.**

Temperature: température

- **Is a scalar quantity that gives an indication of the degree of hotness or coldness of a body.**
- **Temperature can be transmitted by three ways: convection, conduction and by radiation.**
- **C'est une grandeur qui indique le degré de chaleur d'un corps.**
- **La température peut être transmise de trois façon : par convection, par conduction et par radiation.**

Terminal velocity: vitesse limite

- **Is the maximum speed can be reached by a car or free-falling objects.**
- **C'est la vitesse maximale qu'une voiture ou un objet en chute libre peut atteindre.**

Thermal conductivity: conductivité thermique

Thermal energy: énergie thermique

Thermal solar sensor: capteur solaire thermique

Thermodynamics laws: les lois thermodynamiques

- **The zeroth law - establishes the existence of thermal equilibrium and allows temperature to be defined.**
- **The first law (conservation of energy)-establishes that work and heat are both perfectly good ways of increasing the internal energy of an object.**
- **The second law - the entropy of the universe can never decrease.**
- **The third law – objects can never be cooled down to absolute zero.**
- **La loi zéro - établit l'existence de l'équilibre thermique et permet de définir la température.**
- **La première loi (conservation de l'énergie) - prévoit que le travail et la chaleur sont les deux façons parfaits d'augmenter l'énergie interne d'un objet.**
- **La deuxième loi - l'entropie de l'univers ne peut jamais diminuer.**
- **La troisième loi - les objets ne peuvent jamais être refroidis jusque zéro absolu.**

Thermography: thermographie

Thermonuclear Fusion: fusion thermonucléaire

- **The combination of atomic nuclei at high temperatures to form more massive nuclei with the simultaneous release of energy. Thermonuclear fusion is the power source at the core of the Sun. Controlled thermonuclear fusion reactors, when successfully implemented, could become an attractive source of power on the Earth.**
- **La combinaison de deux noyaux à haute température pour former un noyau plus massif en relâchant de l'énergie. La fusion thermonucléaire est la source de l'énergie qui se forme au cœur de Soleil. Des études sont en cours pour contrôler et fabriquer des réacteurs thermonucléaire qui pourrait être une source d'énergie de future.**

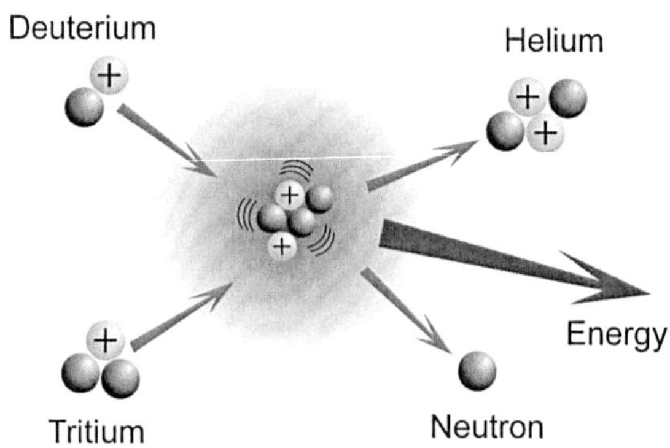

Thin lens formula: formule de conjugaison

- **Is the mathematical relation between object distance and its image with respect to a lens.**
- **C'est une formule mathématique reliant la position d'un objet à celle de son image par un système optique.**

Thrust: poussée

Time: temps

- **We use time to track the passing of days, in hours, minutes and seconds. In addition to natural units of time, people have invented other ways to measure it.**

- **Nous utilisons le temps pour suivre le passage des jours, en heures, minutes et secondes. En plus des unités naturelles du temps, les humains ont inventé d'autres façons de le mesurer.**

Tool: outil
- **Is a device that can be used to produce an item or achieve a task.**
- **C'est instrument qui est utilisé pour fabriquer un produit ou pour effectuer une tache.**

Torque: couple (d'un moteur)
- **Torque is the turning moment caused by a system of two or more forces that tend to cause rotation.**
- **T = k.I**

  T : torque (N.m)

  K : electromechanic constant ($N.m.A^{-1}$)

  I : electric current (A)
- **Le couple est le moment de rotation provoqué par un système de deux ou plusieurs forces qui provoquent une rotation.**
- **T = k.I**

  T: couple (N.m)

  K: constante électromécanique ($N.m.A^{-1}$)

  I: intensité (A)

Tornado: tornade

TRACE: TRACE
- **Transition Region and Coronal Explorer, a satellite name launched by NASA in 1998. TRACE observes the Sun's atmosphere in ultraviolet wavelengths.**
- **C'est un satellite lancé par la NASA en 1998 qui a pour objectif d'explorer la couronne solaire.**

Transition Region: Région de transition
- **Area of the Sun's atmosphere with temperatures between those of the chromosphere and the corona, 20,000 - 1,000,000 K.**
- **C'est une zone de l'atmosphère solaire qui se situe entre la chromosphère et la couronne dont la température varie entre 20000 et 1000000 K.**

Track: suivre

Transducers: transducteurs

- **A device that converts energy from one form to another.**
- **C'est un dispositif qui convertit l'énergie d'une forme à une autre.**

Transformer: transformateur

- **Is a device that transfers electrical energy from one circuit to another through inductively coupled conductors, the transformer's coils.**
- **To increase the voltage, we need a step-up transformer.**
- **To decrease the voltage, we need a step-down transformer.**
- **Transformers only work on AC, this is the main reason why mains electricity is AC.**
- **C'est un convertisseur d'énergie électrique d'un circuit électrique à un autre par un couple de bobines inductives.**
- **Pour augmenter la tension électrique, on utilise un transformateur élévateur de tension.**
- **Pour diminuer la tension électrique, on utilise un transformateur abaisseur de tension.**
- **Les transformateurs ne fonctionnent qu'en AC, c'est la raison pour laquelle l'électricité est principalement en AC.**

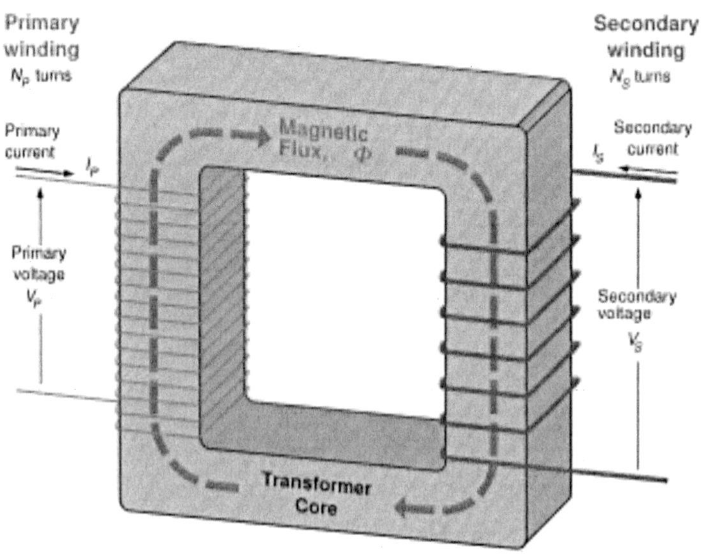

Transformer equation: équation de transformateur

- **Primary Coil Voltage / Secondary Voltage = Number of turns on Primary Coil / Number of turns on Secondary**
- **$V_p / V_s = N_p / N_s$**
- **Tension Primaire / Tension Secondaire = Nombre de spires au Primaire / Nombre de spires au Secondaire**

Transmission coefficient: coefficient de transmission

Transverse waves: ondes transversale

- **In transverse waves the vibration is perpendicular to the direction of travel of the wave.**
- **La perturbation provoquée est perpendiculaire à la direction de propagation de l'onde.**

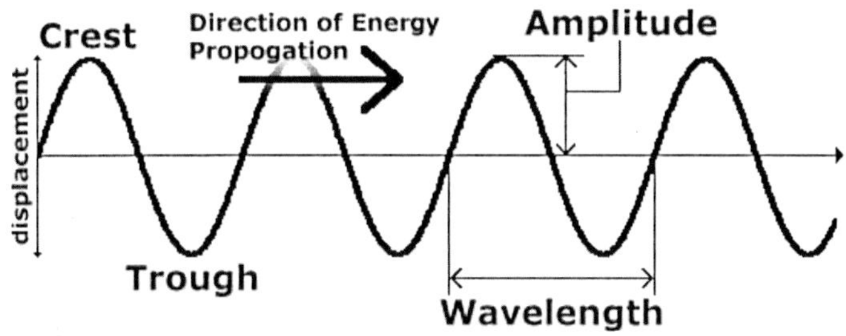

Trough: cuvette

- **A term coined from water waves referring to the lowest point of the wave.**
- **C'est terme qui désigne le point minimum d'une onde.**

Tunnel effect : effet tunnel

- **Sometimes quantum particles can go through walls, as if an invisible tunnel opened up before them! Imagine throwing an electron against a wall. If the wall is thick, the electron bounces back, which seems normal. But the electron is a quantum particle and also behaves like a wave. If the wall is very thin, the electron may be found on both sides of the wall, which means it can sometimes go through the wall. This is called the tunnel effect, one of the main effects at the base of Nano-sciences.**
- **Une particule quantique peut parfois traverser les murs, comme si un tunnel invisible s'ouvrait à elle ! Imaginons un électron lancé**

contre un mur. Si le mur est épais, l'électron rebondit, ce qui paraît normal. Mais l'électron est quantique et se comporte comme une onde. Si le mur est très fin, l'électron peut se retrouver des deux côtés du mur à la fois, ce qui parfois lui permet de passer au travers. C'est l'effet tunnel, un des effets au cœur des nanosciences.

Turning point: tournant
- **Newton's law of gravity is a turning point in classic physics history.**
- **La loi de Newton sur la gravité est un tournant dans l'histoire de la physique classique.**

U

Ultrasonography: échographie

Ultrasound: ultrason

- **Ultrasound from 20000 Hz to several billion hertz can be produced by ultrasound transducers (a device that converts energy from one form to another) using mechanical electromagnetic and thermal energy.**
- **Bats can produce frequencies from 50 kHz to 200 kHz.**
- **Les ultrasons correspondent aux fréquences au-delà de 20000 Hz produits par des transducteurs (un dispositif qui convertit l'énergie d'une forme à une autre) qui utilisent une énergie thermique et électromagnétique.**
- **Les chauves-souris peuvent produire des fréquences allant de 50 kHz à 200 kHz.**

Utrasound transducer: transducteur ultrason

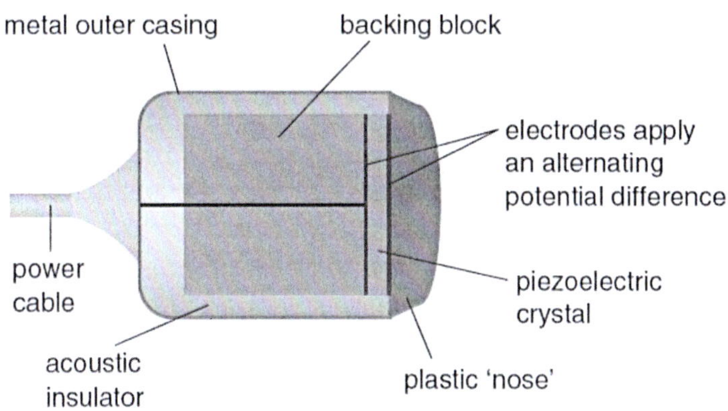

Ultrasound imaging: échographie (imagerie par ultrason)

- **Ultrasound uses sound waves with frequencies between 1 and 10MHz to look inside the body. These frequencies are too high to be heard by humans. The ultrasound waves, like all waves, can be re-**

flected, refracted or transmitted at boundaries. It is the reflections, or echoes, which are used to produce ultrasound images.
- L'échographie utilise des ondes sonores à des fréquences comprises entre 1 et 10 MHz pour voir l'intérieur du corps. Ces fréquences sont trop élevées pour être entendu par les humains. Les ondes ultrasonores, comme toutes les ondes, peuvent être réfléchie, réfractée ou transmise. Ce sont les reflets ou les échos, qui sont utilisées pour produire des images ultrasonores.

Ultraviolet light: lumière ultraviolet
- Is electromagnetic radiation with a wavelength shorter than that of visible light, in the range 10 nm to 400 nm.
- C'est la radiation électromagnétique d'une longueur d'onde en dessous de celle de domaine visible, entre 10 nm et 400 nm.

Uninterruptible power supply: alimentation sans interruption
- Is an electrical apparatus that provides emergency power to a load when the input power source fails.
- C'est un dispositif de l'électronique de puissance qui permet de fournir à un système électrique une alimentation électrique stable lorsqu'un il y a une coupure de secteur.

Upstream: amont

Upthrust: soulèvement
- Is the force that pushes an object up and makes it seem to lose weight in a fluid. The upthrust (Archimedes' principle) keeps ships afloat.

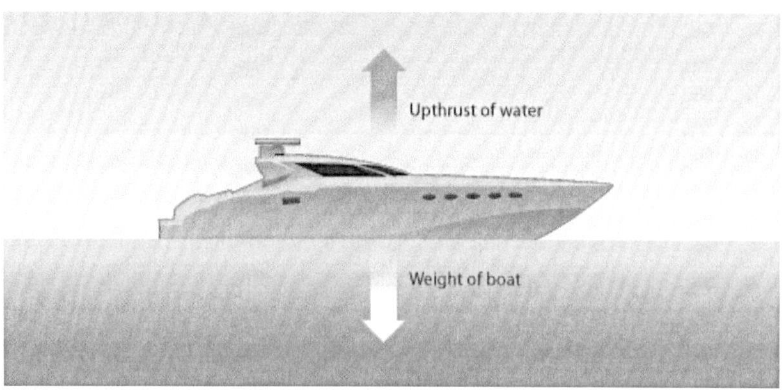

- **C’est la force qui pousse un objet vers le haut et donne l'impression de perdre du poids dans un fluide. La force de soulèvement (poussée d’Archimède) garde les navires à flot.**

Universal Time: temps universel
- **Abbreviated UT. The same as Greenwich Mean Time (GMT) in England. US Eastern Standard Time (EST) is five hours earlier than Universal Time.**
- **Abréviation UT. C’est le temps qui prend Greenwich en Angleterre comme référence (GMT). Aux Etats-Unis le temps EST est 5 heures plutôt que le temps universel.**

UVCS: SCUV
- **Ultraviolet Coronagraph Spectrometer. An ultraviolet spectrometer aboard satellites.**
- **C’est un spectromètre installé dans les satellites pour mesurer les rayonnements ultraviolet.**

V

Vacuum: vide

Vacuum cleaner: aspirateur

- **Is a device that uses an air pump to create a partial vacuum to suck up dust.**
- **C'est un appareil électroménager muni d'une pompe à air créant une dépression qui provoque l'aspiration de poussière.**

Vacuum pump: pompe à vide

- **Is a device that removes gas molecules from a sealed volume. It was invented by Otto von Guericke in 1650.**
- **C'est un outil qui permet d'extraire un gaz dans une enceinte. Inventé par Otto von Guericke en 1650.**

Vacuum energy: énergie du vide

- **Is an underlying background energy that exists in space even when the space is devoid of matter (free space).**
- **C'est l'énergie sombre qu'on trouve dans l'espace malgré l'absence de la matière.**

Valence band: bande de valence

Velocity: vitesse

- **The speed of an object in a given direction.**
- **C'est la vitesse d'un objet dans une direction donnée.**

Vergence: vergence

- **The vergence of a light bundle in optics is the reciprocal of the distance between the point of focus and a reference plane. It is measured in diopters ($1\ \delta = 1\ m^{-1}$).**
- **En optique géométrique, la vergence est une grandeur qui sert à caractériser les propriétés de focalisation d'un système. Elle est homogène à l'inverse d'une longueur et s'exprime en dioptrie ($1\ \delta = 1\ m^{-1}$).**

Visible range: domaine visible

Voltage: voltage

- **Is the driving force that pushes the current round.**
- **C'est une force qui pousse le courant dans un circuit.**

Voltmeter: voltmètre

- **Is an instrument used to measure the potential difference between two points of a conductor; it is always connected across a device in parallel.**

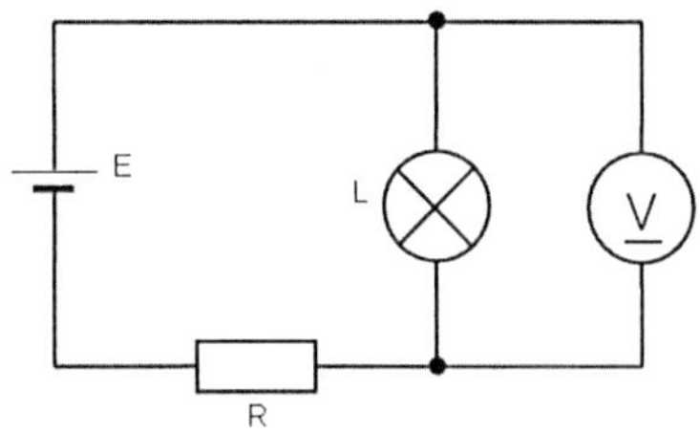

- **C'est appareil utilisé pour mesurer la différence de potentiel aux bornes d'un conducteur, il se branche in parallèle.**

Volumetric flowrate: débit volumique

- **$D_v = V/t$, volumetric flow rate of a liquid in meter cubes per second ($m^3.s^{-1}$)**
- **V: volume de liquide en mètres cubes (m^3)**
- **t: durée de l'écoulement en seconde (s)**
- **$D_v = V/t$, débit volumique du liquide en mètres cubes par seconde ($m^3.s^{-1}$)**
- **V: liquid volume in meter cube (m^3)**
- **t: flow time in seconds (s)**

W

Wall clock: horologe
- **Is an instrument used to indicate time.**
- **C'est un instrument qui indique le temps.**

Water clock (clypsydra): clepsydre
- **Is any timepiece in which time is measured by the regulated flow of liquid.**
- **C'est une horloge à eau, fonctionnant sur le principe d'écoulement d'eau.**

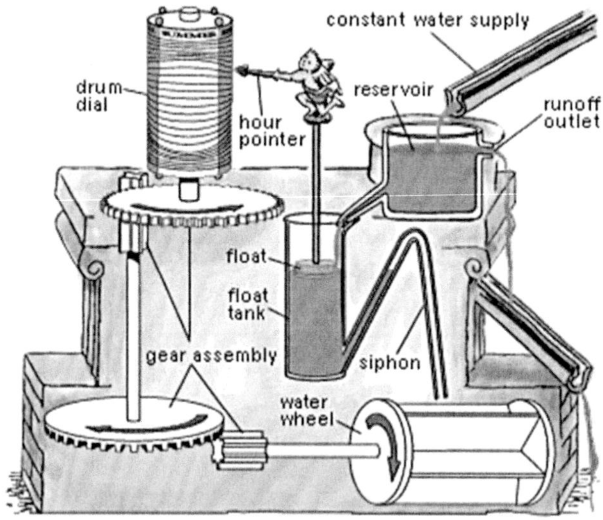

Warps and curves (general relativity): déformation et courbes (relativité générale)
- **Is a part of the current description of gravitation in modern physics, published by Albert Einstein in 1916.**
- **C'est une partie de l'explication actuelle du phénomène de gravité publiée par Albert Einstein en 1916.**

Washer or hardeware: rondelle
- **Is a thin plate (typically disk-shaped) with a hole in the middle. It is normally used to distribute the load of a threaded fastener, such as a screw or nut.**

- **En mécanique, une rondelle est un disque mince avec un trou, habituellement au centre. Elle est utilisée pour supporter la pression d'une vis.**

Wasted energy: énergie perdue
- **Is the lost energy often as heat.**
- **C'est l'énergie dissipée par effet joule.**

Water waves: vagues
- **Are surface waves that occur on the free surface of oceans and seas. They usually result from the wind blowing over a vast enough stretch of fluid surface.**
- **Lorsque le vent souffle sur la surface d'un océan, d'une mer ou d'un lac, il crée une agitation sous la forme d'une succession de vagues.**

Watt: watt
- **A rate of energy transfer of one joule per second**
- **Symbol (W)**
- **C'est l'énergie transmise d'un joule par second**
- **Symbole (W)**

Wattmeter: watttemètre
- **A device for measuring electrical power.**
- **Un instrument de mesure de la puissance électrique.**

Wave: onde
- **Is a disturbance that travels from one point to another carrying energy without any flow of materials.**
- **C'est une perturbation qui se déplace d'un point à un autre transportant de l'énergie mais sans transport de matière.**

Wavelength: longueur d'onde
- **Is the distance along a medium between two successive particles that have the same displacement or the distance from crest to crest (peak to peak) or trough to trough of an electromagnetic wave.**
- **C'est une grandeur physique, homogène à une longueur, utilisée pour caractériser des phénomènes périodiques.**

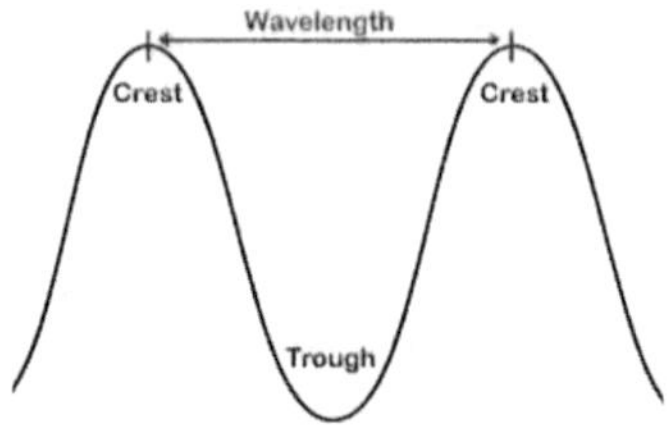

Wavemeter: ondemètre

- **Is a device for the measurement of radio frequency energy at different frequencies.**
- **Appareil servant à mesurer la longueur d'onde d'une émission radioélectrique, ou à régler un poste émetteur ou récepteur sur une longueur d'onde déterminée.**

Wave-particle duality: dualité onde-particule

- **Postulates that all particles: electrons, photons, matter and radiation exhibit both wave and particle properties. The experience demonstrated by Heinrich Hertz in 1887 proves that light has a particle nature. The experience of Thomas Young (Young's slits) and Augustin Fresnel demonstrated in 1800 proves that light has a wave nature.**
- **Louis De Broglie in 1923 describes the light and generally the electromagnetic waves as a flux of photons behaving as wave and particle at the same time.**
- **C'est un postulat selon lequel toutes les particules: électrons, photons, matières et les radiations présentent simultanément des propriétés d'ondes et de particules. L'expérience d'Heinrich Hertz en 1887 a démontré que la lumière a une nature corpusculaire. L'expérience de Thomas Young (fentes de Young) et Augustin Fresnel a démontré en 1800 que la lumière a une nature ondulatoire.**
- **Louis De Broglie en 1923, décrit la lumière et généralement les ondes électromagnétiques comme un flux de photons se comportant à la fois comme une onde et comme une particule.**
- **La dualité onde-particule conduit à associer une onde de longueur d'onde λ à toute particule, matérielle ou non, de quantité de mouvement de valeur p telle que :**

$$P = h/\lambda = h.\nu/c \text{ car } \lambda = c/\nu$$

Avec h la constante de Planck : $h=6,63x10^{-34}$ J.s
La longueur d'onde λ exprimée en mètre
La célérité de la lumière $c=3.10^8$ $m.s^{-1}$
Et la quantité du mouvement p exprimée en $kg.m.s^{-1}$

- **L'énergie transportée par un photon est :**

$$\xi=h.\nu$$

Avec h la constante de Planck : $h=6,63x10^{-34}$ J.s
La fréquence ν de l'onde exprimée en Hertz (Hz)
Et l'énergie ξ exprimée en Joule (J).

- **The De Broglie equations relate the wavelength λ and frequency ν to the momentum p, respectively as:**

$$p=h/\lambda=h.\nu/c \text{ hence } \lambda=c/\nu$$

Where λ is the wavelength of the particle
h is Planck's constant of the particle,
p is the momentum of the particle,
c is the light celerity.

- **Energy carried by photon is equal to:**

$$\xi=h.\nu$$

Where ξ is the energy in Joule,
h is Planck's constant of the particle,
ν is the wave frequency of the particle in Hertz.

Wave speed: vitesse d'onde

- **Is the speed with which energy is carried in the medium by the wave; it depends on the nature and properties of the medium.**
- **Est la vitesse avec laquelle l'énergie est portée dans le milieu par la vague, elle dépend de la nature et les propriétés du milieu.**

Wavefront: front d'onde

- **Is the wave propagating in straight-line, a line of points having the same phase.**

- **C'est un ensemble de points se propageant en line et en phase.**

Wear out: s'user

Weber: Weber
- **The SI unit of magnetic flux.**
- **C'est l'unité du flux magnètique dans le SI.**

Weight: poids
- **Is the force acting on a mass due to the gravitational field in which it is placed**
- **The SI unit is the newton (N).**
- **C'est la force agissant sur une masse à cause de la force gravitationnelle**
- **Unité dans le SI est le newton (N)**

Weightless: sans poids
- **Means the absence of the force exerted by the Gravity.**
- **Absence de la force exercée par la gravité.**

Weightlessness: impesanteur
- **Formally means the condition of zero gravitational force like astronomer in the space or a constant speed falling body.**
- **C'est l'état d'un corps dans lequel l'ensemble des forces gravitationnelles et inertielles auxquelles il est soumis sont nuls, comme un astronome dans l'espace ou un corps en chute libre à vitesse constante.**

Wein's law: loi de Wein
- **Is a law of physics used to describe the spectrum of thermal radiation (frequently called the blackbody function).**
- **Elle caractérise la dépendance du rayonnement du corps noir à la longueur d'onde.**

Wind power: énergie éolienne
- **Wind power uses the power of the wind to turn machinery or generate electricity. It is a renewable, non-polluting source of energy.**
- **L'énergie éolienne utilise la puissance du vent pour tourner une machine ou produire de l'électricité. C'est une ressource renouvelable, non polluante d'énergie.**

Wire: fil conducteur
- **Is a metal in the form of a thread**
- **C'est un métal en forme d'un fil**

Wiring: câblage
- **Electrical wiring in general refers to insulated conductors used to carry electricity, and associated devices.**
- **Câblage, en électricité, est un fil électrique qui sert à conduire le courant électrique et relier les différents dipôles.**

Word equation: équation sous forme de mot
- **An equation in which the mathematical symbols are replaced by the names of the variables they correspond to.**
- **Lorsque les symboles mathématiques dans une équation sont remplacés par des mots correspondants.**

Work: travail
- **Is the amount of energy transferred to an object when it is moved by a force applied to it by different object.**
- **The symbol for work is W.**
- **The SI unit is the $N.m^{-1}$**
- **C'est la quantité d'énergie transmise à un corps lorsqu'il se déplace à cause d'une force qui lui est appliqué.**
- **Son symbole est W.**
- **L'unité est le $N.m^{-1}$**
- **$W = F \times d$**

Work function: travail d'extraction

- **The minimum energy that must be given to an electron to liberate it from the surface of a metal, in the photoelectric effect.**
- **C'est l'énergie minimale que l'on doit fournir pour extraire un électron de la surface d'un métal, c'est l'effet photoélectrique.**

White dwarf: naine blanche

- **A star which has used up its nuclear fuel and collapsed to a very small size.**
- **Une étoile qui a épuisée son énergie nucléaire et s'est effondrée sur elle-même.**

White light: lumière blanche

- **Visible light that includes all colors and, therefore, all visible wavelengths.**
- **Lumière visible contenant toute les couleurs et par conséquence les longueurs d'onde visible.**

X

X-member: traverse cruciforme, croisillon

X-ray analysis: examen radiographique

X-ray apparatus: appareil radiographique

X-ray photogrph: radiogramme, radiographie

X-ray therapy: radiothérapie

X-ray radiography: imagerie par rayon X
- **Is one of the most commonly used methods of diagnosis. It can be used to examine broken or fractured bones, teeth, the digestive system, the lungs and to detect breast cancer.**
- **C'est l'une des méthodes les plus couramment utilisées de diagnostic. Il peut être utilisé pour examiner des os cassés ou fracturés, les dents, le système digestif, les poumons et pour détecter le cancer du sein.**

X- rays: rayon X
- **Is a form of electromagnetic radiation. X-rays have a wavelength in the range of 5 picometers to 10 nanometers, corresponding to frequencies in the range 3×10^{16} Hz to 3×10^{19} Hz.**
- **C'est une forme de rayonnement électromagnétique à haute fréquence dont la longueur d'onde est comprise approximativement entre 5 picomètres et 10 nanomètres, ce qui correspond à des fréquences de 3×10^{16} Hz to 3×10^{19} Hz.**

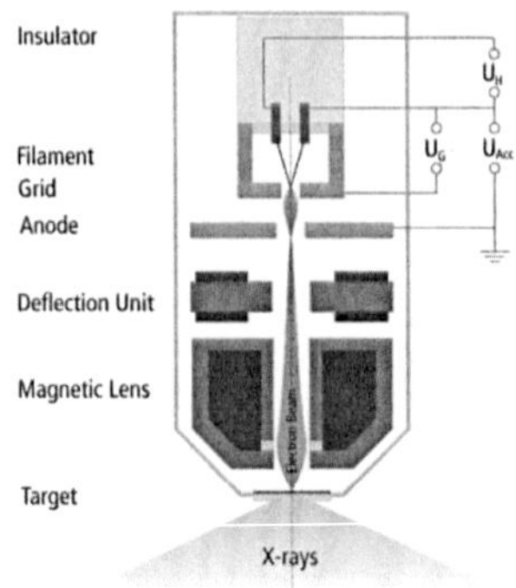
Insulator
Filament
Grid
Anode
Deflection Unit
Magnetic Lens
Target
X-rays
U_H
U_G
U_{Acc}
Electron Beam

Y

Yaw: pivoter: embarder

Yaw system: system de guidage, giration
- **The yaw system of wind turbines is the component responsible for the orientation of the wind turbine rotor towards the wind.**
- **C'est dispositif de guidage utilisé dans les éoliennes pour les orienter dans la direction du vent.**

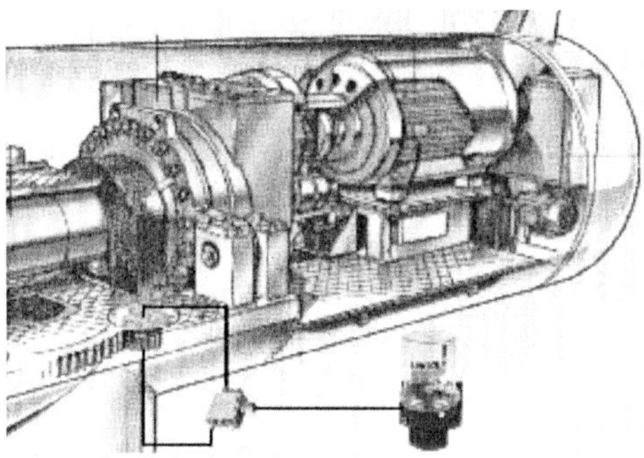

Yield: rendement
- **The ratio of the useful power to the absorbed power.**
- **La rapport de la puissance utile sur la puissance absorbée.**

Yield capacity: productivité

Yield load: charge limite d'élasticité

Yield point: limite élastique
- **The point beyond which a further small increase in tensile stress produces a large increase in strain. Beyond this point, the material may extend a great deal more before it breaks.**
- **Le point au-delà duquel une légère augmentation de la contrainte de traction produit une forte augmentation de tension. Au-delà de ce point, le matériau peut s'étendre davantage avant qu'il ne casse.**

Yield strength: limite de résistance

Yield stress: contrainte à la rupture

Yoke: fourche, cadran

Yoke bolt: boulon d'articulation

Yoke piece: culasse

Young's fringes: franges de Young
- **The bright and the dark bands seen as a result of constructive and destructive interference of light in Young's double slit experiment.**
- **Les bandes lumineuses et les bandes sombres observées à la suite d'une interférence constructive et destructive de la lumière dans l'expérience de la double fente de Young.**

Young's modulus: module de Young, module d'élasticité
- **A measure of the stiffness of a stretched rod or wire under tension or compression. It is equal to the stress of the wire or rod divided by the longitudinal strain.**
- **Une mesure de la rigidité d'une tige étirée ou d'un fil sous tension ou en compression. Elle est égale à la tension du fil ou de la tige divisée par la contrainte longitudinale.**

Z

Zee frame: cadre en Z

Zeeman Effect: effet Zeeman

- **A splitting of spectral lines in response to a magnetic field. It is used to measure magnetic field strengths on the Sun and on other astronomical objects.**
- **Lignes spectrales à fractionnement en réponse à un champ magnétique. Il est utilisé pour mesurer les forces du champ magnétique du Soleil et sur d'autres objets astronomiques.**

Zener diode: diode de Zener

Zenith: zénith

Zerk fitting: raccord de graissage

Zero adjustement: réglage à zéro

Zero datum: référence zéro

Zero field: champ nul

Zero-gravity: apesanteur, gravité zéro

Zero level: niveau zéro

Zero load: charge à vide

Zero-point energy: énergie zéro

- **Is the lowest possible energy that a quantum mechanical physical system may have; it is the energy of its ground state.**
- **C'est l'énergie la plus basse qu'un système physique peut avoir.**

Zero reset: remise à zéro

Zero state: état de repos

Zinc: zinc

Zinc foil: feuille de zinc

Zinc plating: galvanisation au zinc

Zip code: code postal

Zip fastener: fermeture éclair

Zipped: compacté

Zooming: agrandissement

Z-section: section en Z

Appendices

PHYSICS INSTRUMENTS
INSTRUMENTS DE MESURE EN PHYSIQUE

Battery tester	**Testeur de batterie**	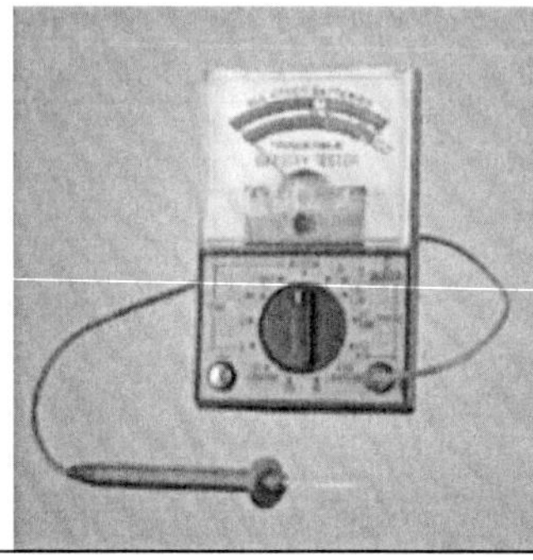
Conductivityme-ter	**Conductimètre**	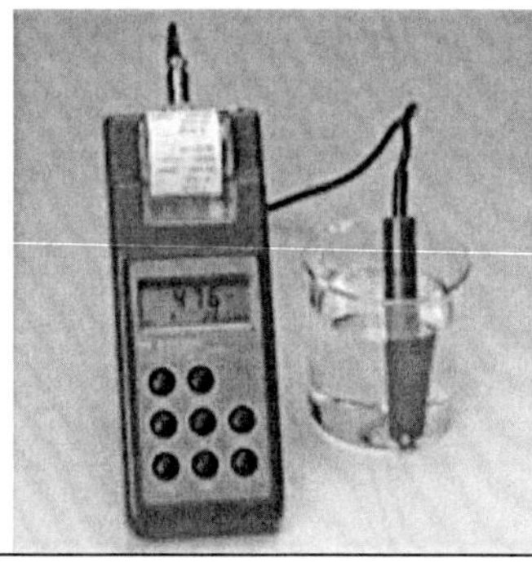
Oximeter	**Oximètre**	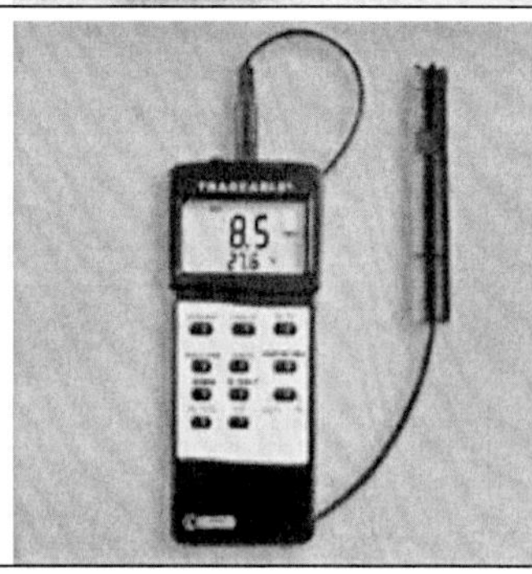

Flowmeter	**Débimètre**	
Hygrometer	**Hygromètre**	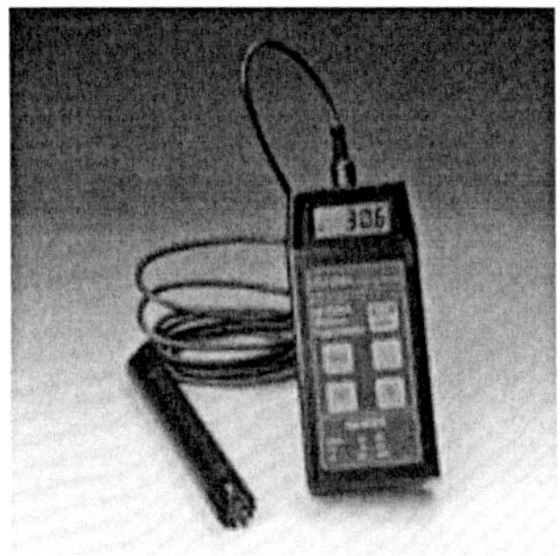
Lightmeter	**Luxmètre**	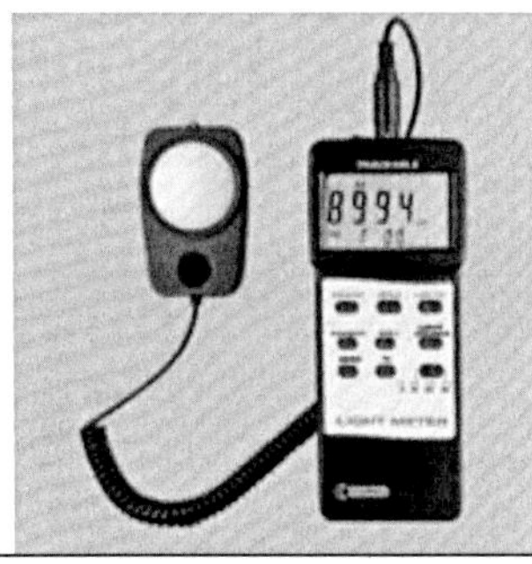
Multimeter	**Multimètre**	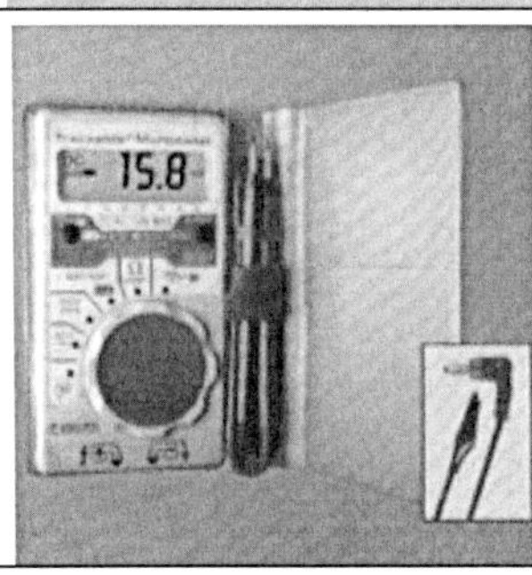

pH-meter	**pH-mètre**	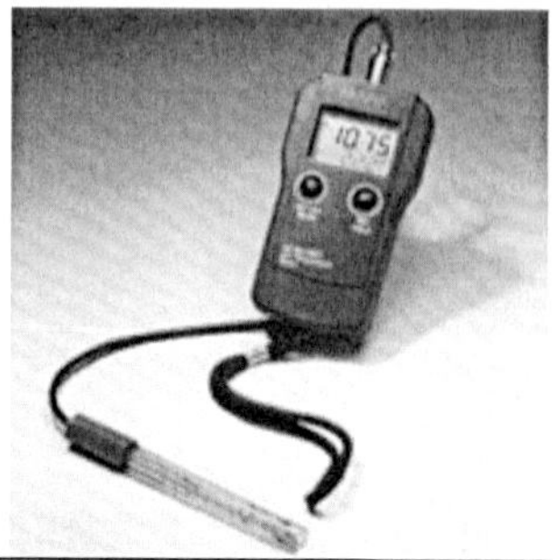
Soundmeter	**Sonomètre**	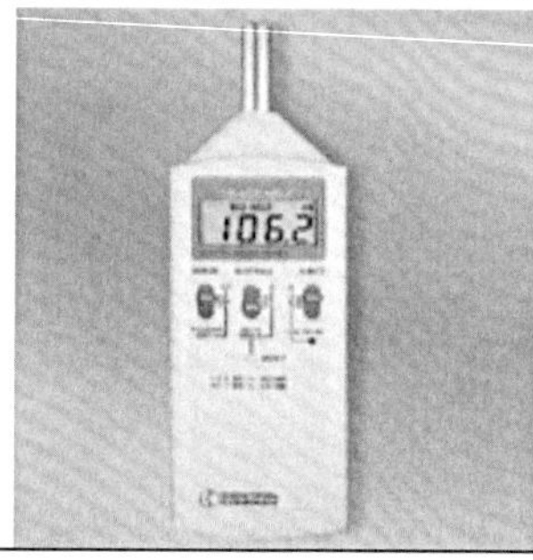
Refractometer	**Réfractomètre**	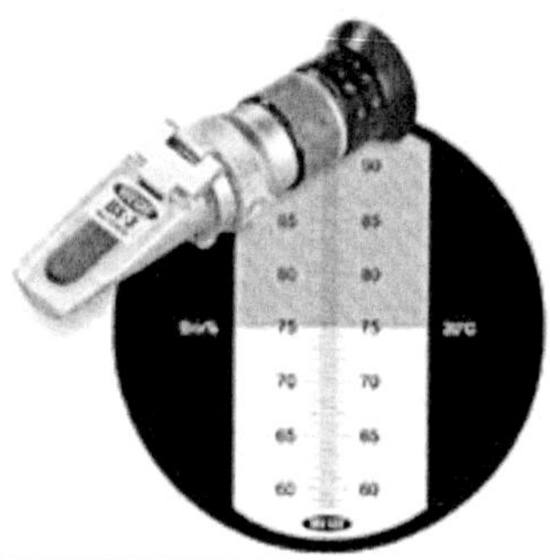
Newton's Spring Scales **Newtonmeter**	**Dynamomètre**	

Ammeter	**Ampèremètre**	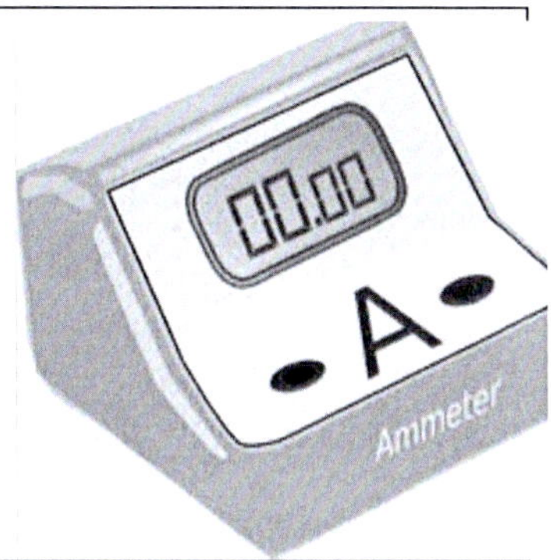
Voltmeter	**Voltmètre**	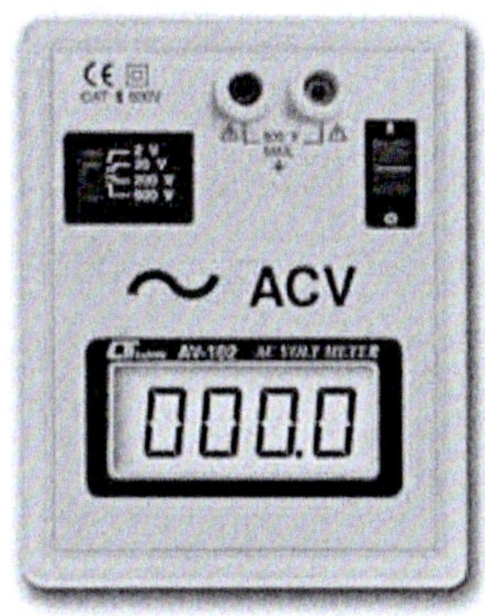

PHYSICAL QUANTITIES AND THEIR UNITS: BASIC AND DERIVED
GRANDEURS PHYSIQUES ET LEURS UNITÉ LÉGALES ET DÉRIVÉES

Common formulae – formules fondamentales

English	Français	Symbol Symbole	Unit Unité
Length	Longueur	l	m
Angle	Angle	θ	Rad, °
Distance	Distance	d	m
Distance travelled	Distance parcourue	d	m
Displacement	Déplacement	s,x	m
Amplitude	Amplitude	x_0,y_0	m
Wavelength	Longueur d'onde	λ	m
Area	Surface	A	m^2
Volume	Volume	V	m^3
Time	Temps	t	s
Frequency	Fréquence	f	Hz
Angular frequency or angular speed	Pulsation	ω	$rad.s^{-1}$
Speed	Vitesse	c	$m.s^{-2}$
Rate of change of speed	Taux de changement de vitesse		$m.s^{-2}$
Uniform, average, instantaneous velocities	Vitesse uniform, moyenne, instantannée	u,v	$m.s^{-1}$
Acceleration	Accélération	a	$m.s^{-2}$
Acceleration of free fall	Accélération de chute libre	g	$m.s^{-2}$
Gravitational field strength	Intensité de la pesanteur	g	$m.s^{-2}$
Mass	Masse	m	kg
Density	Masse volumique	ρ	$kg.m^{-3}$
Momentum	Quantité de mouvement	p,mv	$kg.m.s^{-1}$
Force	Force	F	N
Moment of force	Moment de force	M	N.m
Torque	Moment du couple	T	N.m
Pressure	Pression	p	Pa
Stress	Tenseur de contrainte	σ	Pa

Strain	**Déformation**	**ε**	**No unit**
Young's modulus	**Module d'élasticité ou de traction**	**E**	**Pa**
Gravitational constant	**Constante gravitationnelle**	**G**	**$N.kg^{-2}.m^2$**
Work done	**Travail**	**W**	**J**
Energy	**Energie**	**W,E**	**J**
Kinetic energy	**Energie cinétique**	**E_k**	**J**
Potential energy	**Energie potentielle**	**E_p**	**J**
Power	**Puissance**	**P**	**W**
Temperature	**Temperature**	**T**	**K**
Internal energy	**Energie interne**	**U**	**J**
Heating	**Chaleur ou transfert thermique**	**q**	**J**
Heat capacity	**Capacité thermique ou calorifique**	**C**	**$J.kg^{-1}$**
Specific heat capacity	**Capacité calorifique spécifique**	**c**	**$J.kg^{-1}.K^{-1}$**
Specific latent heat	**Chaleur spécifique latent**	**l**	**$J.kg^{-1}$**
Temperature gradient		**ΔT/Δx**	**$K.m^{-1}$**
Thermal conductivity	**Conductivité thermique**	**λ**	**$W.m^{-1}.K^{-1}$**
U value		**U**	**$W.m^{-2}.K^{-1}$**
Amount of substance	**Quantité de matière**	**n**	**mol**
Molar mass	**Masse molaire**	**M**	**$kg.mol^{-1}$**
Molar heat capacity	**Capacité molaire calorifique**	**C_m**	**$J.mol^{-1}$**
Molar gas constant	**Constant de gaz parfait**	**R**	**$J.mol^{-1}.K^{-1}$**
Avogadro constant	**Constant d'Avogadro**	**N_A**	**mol^{-1}**
Boltzmann constant	**Constant de Boltzmann**	**k**	**$J.k^{-1}$**
Current	**Courant électrique**	**I**	**A**
Charge	**Charge électrique**	**Q**	**C**
Electric field strength	**Intensité du champ électrique**	**E**	**$V.m^{-1}$**
Electric potential	**Potentiel électrique**	**V**	**V**
Permittivity of free space ou	**Permittivité du vide**	**$ε_0$**	**$F.m^{-1}$**

Relative permittivity	**Permittivité relative**	ε_r	**No unit**
Permeability of free space or vacuum permeability	**Perméabilité du vide ou constant magnétique**	μ_0	**$H.m^{-1}$**
Potential difference	**Différence de potentiel**	**V**	**V**
Electromotive force	**Force électromotrice**	**E**	**V**
Capacitance	**Capacité**	**C**	**F**
Resistance	**Résistance électrique**	**R**	**Ω**
Resistivity	**Résistivité**	ρ	**Ω.m**
Conductance	**Conductance**	**G**	**S**
Conductivity	**Conductivité**	σ	**$S.m^{-1}$**
Inductance	**Inductance**	**L**	**H**
Reactance	**Réactance**	**X**	**Ω**
Impedance	**Impédance**	**Z**	**Ω**
Time of constant	**Constant du temps**	τ	**s**
Magnetic field strength	**Intensité de champ magnétique**	**B**	**T**
Magnetic flux	**Flux magnétique**	ϕ	**Wb**
Magnetic flux linkages	**Flux magnétique totale (dans une bobine de N spires)**	**Nϕ**	**Wb turn**
Magnetic flux leakage	**Contrôle magnétique non destructif**		
Curie temperature	**Température de Curie**	T_c	**K**
Planck constant	**Constant de Planck**	**h**	**J.s**
Photon energy	**Energie de photon**	**hf**	**J**
Work function energy	**Energie minimum**	ϕ	**J**
Activity	**Activité (radioactive)**	**A**	**Bq**
Decay constant	**Décroissance exponentielle**	λ	**s^{-1}**
Half-life	**Demi-vie**	$T_{1/2}$	**s**
Mass excess	**Exces de masse**	**Δm**	**kg**
Binding energy	**Energie de liaison**	E_b	**J**
Mass number	**Nombre de masse**	**A**	
Atomic number,	**Numéro atomique,**	**Z**	

proton number	**nombre de proton**		
Neutron number	**Nombre de neutron**	**N**	

COMMON CIRCUIT SYMBOLS
SYMBOLES DES CIRCUITS ÉLECTRICITÉ

Component	Composant	Symbole
Lamp	Lampe	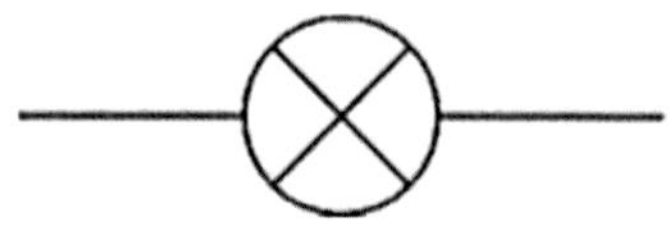
Dry cell	Pile	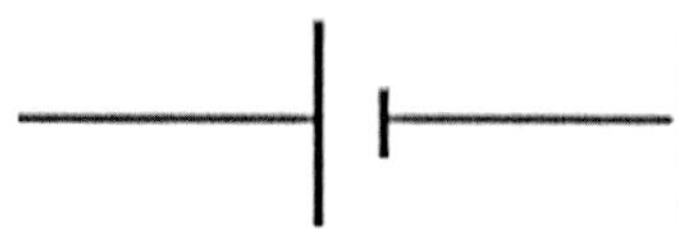
AC power supply	Source de tension alternative	
DC power supply	Source de tension continue	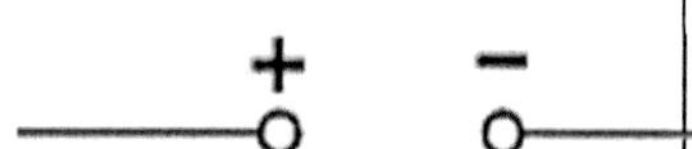
Diode	Diode	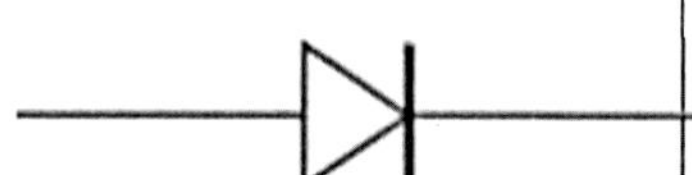
LED Light Emitting Diode	DEL Diode Electro Luminescente	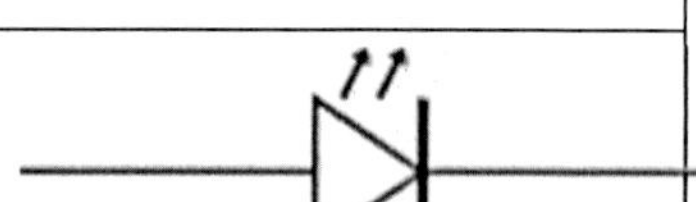
Tension generateur	Générateur de tension	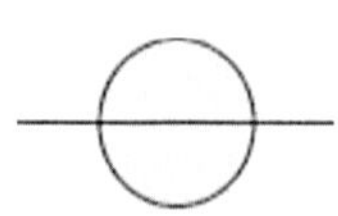
Resistor	Résistance	

Variable resistor	**Résistance variable**	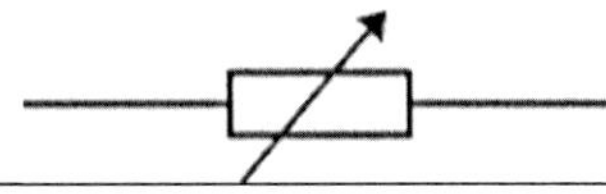
Capacitor	**Condensateur**	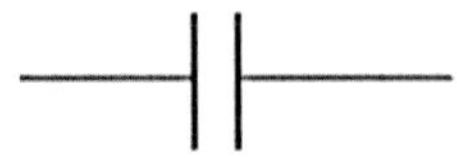
Inductor	**Bobine**	
Fuse	**Fusible**	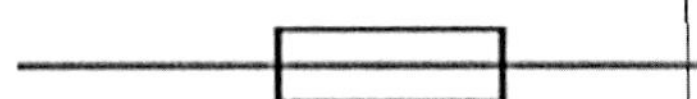
Transistor	**Transistor**	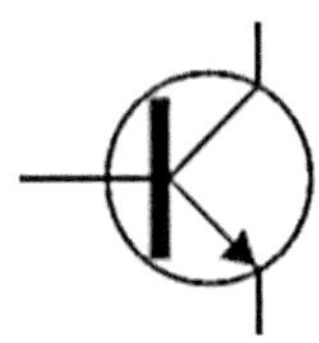
Motor	**Moteur**	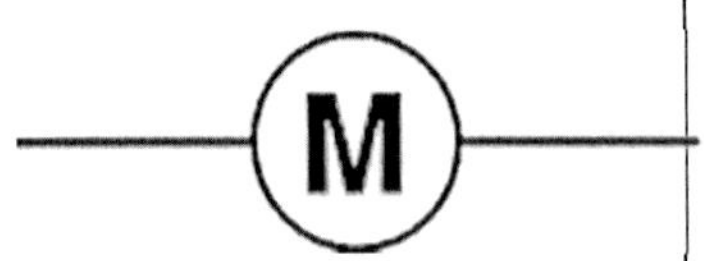
Switch	**Interrupteur**	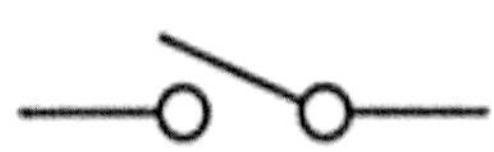
Ammeter	**Ampèremètre**	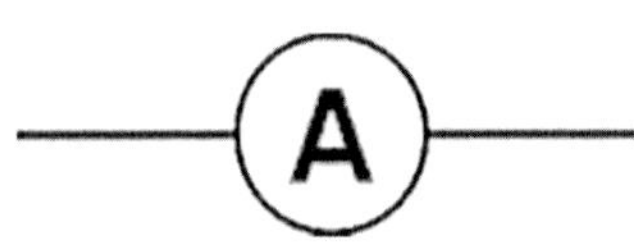

Voltmeter	**Voltmètre**	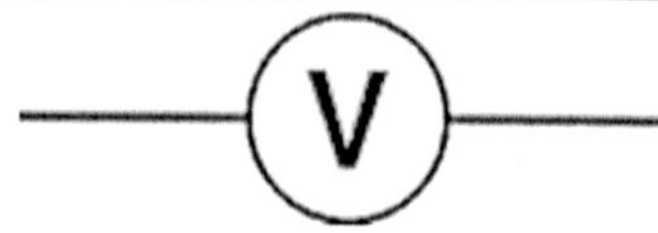
Ground connection	**Mise à la terre**	
Chassis ground	**Mise à la masse**	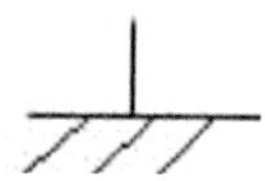
Transformer	**Transformateur**	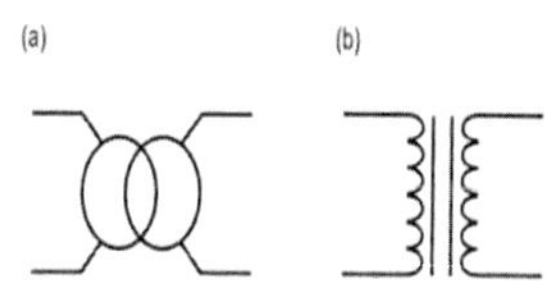
Joined wires	**Fils connectés**	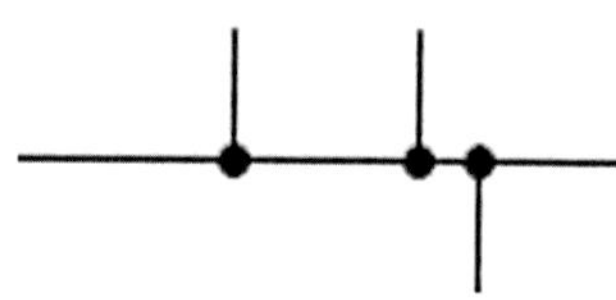
Wire crossing (not joined)	**Fils non connectés**	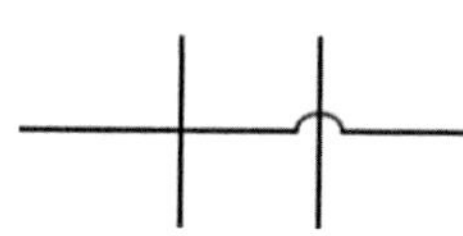
Oscilloscope	**Oscilloscope**	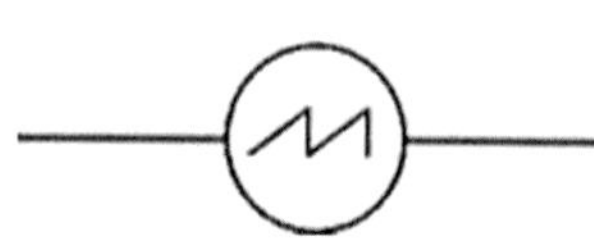

Ohmmeter	Ohmmètre	
Battery	Générateur	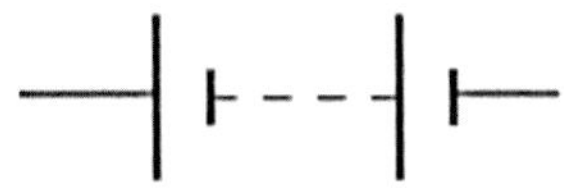
2-way switch	Inverseur	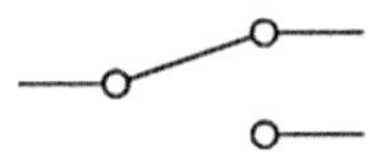

USEFUL FORMULAE AND EQUATIONS
EQUATIONS ET FORMULES

English	Français	
Pressure = force/area	Pression = force/surface	$p = F/A$
Speed = distance travelled/time taken	Vitesse = distance parcourue / temps correspondant	$v = d/t$
Acceleration = increase in velocity/time taken	Accélération = vitesse / temps correspondant	$a=\Delta v/\Delta t$
Momentum = mass x velocity	Quantité de mouvement = masse x vitesse	$p = m.v$
Resultant force = mass x acceleration	Force = masse x accélération	$F = m.a$
Weight = mass x gravitational field strength	Poids = masse x Intensité de la pesanteur	$W = m.g$
Work done = force x distance moved in the direction of the force	Travail =force x distance dans la direction de la force	$W = F.d.\cos \theta$
Power = work done/time taken	Puissance = travail effectué / temps correspondant	$P = \Delta E/\Delta t = \Delta W/\Delta t$
Kinetic energy = ½ masse x velocity²	Energie cinétique = ½ masse x vitesse²	$E_k = ½\ m.v^2$
Change in potential energy = mass x gravitational field strength x change in height	Energie potentielle = masse x intensité de la pesanteur x hauteur	$E_p = m.g.\Delta h$
Centripetal force = mass x speed²/ radius	Force centripète = masse x vitesse² / rayon	$F = m.v^2/r$
Moment of force = force x distance	Moment de force = force x déplacement	$M = F \times d$
Pressure x volume = number of moles x molar gas constant x absolute temperature	Pression x volume = nombre de mole x constant des gaz parfait x température	$p.V = n.R.T$

Wave speed = frequency x wavelength	**Vitesse d'onde (pulsation) = fréquence x longueur d'onde**	$c = f.\lambda$
Current = charge/time interval	**Courant électrique = charge électrique / temps correspondant**	$I = \Delta Q/\Delta t$
Potential difference = work done/charge	**Tension électrique = travail effectué / charge électrique**	$V = W/Q$
Electrical energy transfer = current x potential difference x time interval	**Transfert d'énergie électrique = courant x différence de potentiel x temps correspondant**	$\Delta W = I.V.\Delta t$
Electrical power = potential difference x current	**Puissance électrique = tension x courant électrique**	$P = V.I = R.I^2$
Resistance = (resistivity x length)/ cross-sectional area	**Résistance électrique = (résistivité d'un fil conducteur x longueur du fil)/ section**	$R = V/I = \rho.l/A$
Capacitance = charge stored/ potential difference	**Capacité d'un condensateur = charge stocké / tension électrique**	$C = Q/V$
Input voltage/output voltage = primary turns/secondary turns	**(Tension primaire/tension secondaire) = (nombre des spires primaire/nombre des spires secondaires)**	$V_p/V_s = N_p/N_s$

PHYSICAL CONSTANTS AND USEFUL DATA
CONSTANTES FONDAMENTALES

Acceleration of gravity at earth's surface	**Constant de gravité à la surface de la Terre**	g	9.81	$m.s^{-2}$
Avogadro's number	**Nombre d'Avogadro**	N_A	$6.02x10^{23}$	mol^{-1}
Boiling point at S.T.P.	**Point d'ebullition**		283.15	k
Boltzmann's constant	**Constante de Boltzmann**	k	$1.38x10^{-23}$	$J.K^{-1}$
Coulomb's law constant	**Constante de Coulomb**	$k=1/4\pi\varepsilon_0$	$9.0x10^9$	$N.m^2.C^{-2}$
Density of dry air at S.T.P.	**Densité de l'air dans les C.N.T.P.**		1.293	$kg.m^{-3}$
Density of water at S.T.P.	**Densité de l'eau dans les C.N.T.P.**		1000	$kg.m^{-3}$
Distance of Moon from Earth	**Distance Lune-Terre**		$3.844x10^8$	m
Distance of Sun from Earth	**Distance Soleil-Terre**		$1.496x10^{11}$	m
Electric permeability	**Perméabilité électrique**	ε_0	$8.85x10^{-12}$	$F.m^{-1}$
Electron mass	**Masse de l'électron**	m_e	$9.11x10^{-31}$	kg
Electron volt	**Electron-volt**	1 ev	$1.60x10^{-19}$	J
Escape speed at earth's surface	**Vitesse de la surface de la Terre**		11.2	$km.s^{-1}$
Fundamental charge	**Charge élémentaire**	e	$1.602x10^{-19}$	C
Gas constant	**Constant des gaz parfait**	R	8.31	$J.mol^{-1}.K^{-1}$
Gravitational constant	**Constante gravitationnelle**	G	$6.67x10^{-11}$	$N.m^2.kg^2$
Heat of fusion of water	**Température de fusion de l'eau**	L_f	33.5	kJ/kg
Heat of vaporization of water	**Température de vaporisation de l'eau**	L_v	2.257	MJ/kg
Ice point at S.T.P.	**Point de conjulation**		273.15	K
Mass of the earth	**Masse de la Terre**		$5.976x10^{24}$	kg
Mass of the Moon	**Masse de la Lune**		$7.36x10^{22}$	m
Mass of the Sun	**Masse du Soleil**		$1.99x10^{30}$	kg
Molar mass of air	**Masse molaire de l'air**		0.02898	$kg.mol^{-3}$

Molar volume at R.T.P.	**Volume molaire dans les C.L.T.P.**		**24.467×10^{-3}**	**m^3**
Molar volume of a gas at S.T.P.	**Volume molaire dans les C.N.T.P.**		**22.414×10^{-3}**	**m^3**
Neutron mass	**Masse du neutron**	**m_n**	**1.67×10^{-27}**	**kg**
Permeability of free space	**Perméabilité du vide**	μ_0	**$4\pi \times 10^{-7}$**	N/A^2
Permittivity of free space	**Permittivité du vide**	ε_0	**8.854187×10^{-12}**	**$C^2/N.m^2$**
Physical quantity	**Grandeur physique**	**Symbol Symbole**	**Value Valeur**	**Unit Unité**
Planck's constant	**Constante de Planck**	**h**	**6.63×10^{-34}**	**J.s**
Power radiated from Sun	**Puissance de la radiation solaire**		**3.85×10^{26}**	**W**
Proton mass	**Masse du proton**	**m_p**	**1.67×10^{-27}**	**kg**
R.T.P. Room conditions of temperature and pressure	**C.L.T.P. Condition du laboratoire de température et de pression**		**1.01325×10^5, 1atm 298.15 K, 0°C**	
Radius of Earth at equator	**Rayon de la Terre à l'équateur**		**6.378×10^6**	**m**
Radius of Earth at poles	**Rayon de la Terre aux pôles**		**6.357×10^6**	**m**
Radius of Moon	**Rayon de la Lune**		**1.739×10^6**	**m**
Radius of Sun	**Rayon du Soleil**		**6.96×10^8**	**m**
S.T.P. Standard conditions of temperature and pressure	**C.N.T.P. Conditions normales de température et de pression**		**1.01325×10^5, 1atm 273.15 K, 0°C**	
Speed of light in vacuum	**Célérité de la lumière dans le vide**	**c**	**2.99792458×10^8**	**$m.s^{-1}$**
Speed of sound in dry air at S.T.P	**Vitesse du son dans l'aire sec dans les C.N.T.P.**		**331**	**$m.s^{-1}$**
Standard atmosphere	**Pression atmosphérique standard**		**1.01325×10^5**	**Pa**
Standard pressure	**Pression standard**		**1.10^5**	**Pa**
Standard temperature	**Température standard**		**273.15 0°C**	**K**
Temperature of Sun's surface	**Température à la surface du Soleil**		**5770**	**K**
Unified mass unit	**Unité mass atomique**	**1u**	**1.660540×10^{-27}**	**kg**

ABBREVIATIONS FOR UNITS
ABRÉVIATIONS DES UNITÉS

A	**Ampere**	**lb**	**pound**
Å	**Angstrom**	**L**	**liter**
atm	**Atmosphere**	**m**	**meter**
Btu	**British thermal unit**	**MeV**	**mega-electron volts**
Bq	**Becquerel**	**Mm**	**megameter**
C	**Coulomb**	**mi**	**mile**
°C	**degree Celsius**	**min**	**minute**
cal	**calorie**	**mm**	**millimeter**
Ci	**Curie**	**ms**	**millisecond**
cm	**centimeter**	**N**	**Newton**
dyn	**Dyne**	**nm**	**nanometer**
eV	**Electron volt**	**pt**	**pint**
°F	**degree Fahrenheit**	**qt**	**quart**
fm	**femtometer**	**rev**	**revolution**
ft	**foot**	**R**	**Roentgen**
Gm	**Gigameter**	**Sv**	**Sievert**
G	**Gauss**	**s**	**second**
Gy	**Gray**	**T**	**Tesla**
g	**gram**	**u**	**unified mass unit**
H	**Henry**	**V**	**Volt**
h	**hour**	**W**	**Watt**
Hz	**Hertz**	**Wb**	**Weber**
in	**inch**	**y**	**year**
J	**Joule**	**yd**	**yard**
K	**Kelvin**	**µm**	**micrometer**
kg	**kilogram**	**µs**	**microsecond**
km	**kilometer**	**µC**	**microcoulomb**
keV	**kilo-electron volts**	**Ω**	**Ohm**

CONVERSION UNIT TABLE – PUISSANCES DE DIX ET CONVERSION D'UNITÉS

10^n	Symbol Symbole	Préfixe	Prefix
10^{24}	Y	yotta	yotta
10^{21}	Z	zetta	zetta
10^{18}	E	exa	exa
10^{15}	P	péta	peta
10^{12}	T	téra	tera
10^{9}	G	giga	giga
10^{6}	M	méga	mega
10^{3}	k	kilo	kilo
10^{2}	h	hecto	hecto
10^{1}	da	déca	deca
10^{0}			
10^{-1}	d	déci	deci
10^{-2}	c	centi	centi
10^{-3}	m	milli	milli
10^{-6}	μ	micro	micro
10^{-9}	n	nano	nano
10^{-12}	p	pico	pico
10^{-15}	f	femto	femto
10^{-18}	a	atto	atto
10^{-21}	z	zepto	zepto
10^{-24}	y	yocto	yocto

ORDER OF MAGNITUDE FREQUENCY AND WAVELENGTH
ORDRE DE GRANDEUR FRÉQUENCE ET LONGUEUR D'ONDE

Frequency Fréquence f(Hz)	Wavelength Longueur d'onde λ (m)	Domaine Field
10^6-10^4	10^2-10^4	Radio waves Ondes radio
10^7	10	TV waves Ondes TV
10^8	1	Talkywalky waves Ondes CB
10^{10}-10^9	10^{-2}-10^{-1}	Microwaves Micro-ondes
10^{13}-10^{11}	10^{-5}-10^{-3}	Infrared Infrarouge
10^{15}-10^{14}	10^{-7}-10^{-6}	Visible radiations Radiations visibles
10^{16}	10^{-8}	Ultraviolet radiation
10^{18}-10^{17}	10^{-10}-10^{-9}	X-Rays Rayons-X
10^{21}-10^{19}	10^{-13}-10^{-11}	Gamma radiation Radiation Gamma

SOME CONVERSION FACTORS
QUELQUES CONVERSIONS UTILES

1 m = 39.37 in = 3.281 ft = 1.094 yd

1 m = 10^{15} = 10^{10} Å = 10^{9} nm

1 km = 0.6215 mi

1 mi = 5280 ft 1.609 km

1 lightyear (année lumière) = 1 l.y = 9.46×10^{15} m≈10^{13}km

1 in = 2.540 cm

1 L = 10^{3} cm^{3} = 10^{-3} m^{3} = 1.057 qt

1 h = 3.6 ks

1 y = 365.24 d = 3.156×10^{7} s

1 km/h = 0.278 m/s = 0.6215 mi/h

1 ft/s = 0.3048 m/s = 0.6818 mi/h

1 rev = 2π rad = 360°

1 rad = 57.30°

1 rev/min = 0.1047 rad/s

1 slug = 14.59 kg

1 tonne = 10^{3} kg = 1 Mg

1 atm = 1013 hPa = 1.013 bar = 76.00 cm.Hg = 14.70 lb/in^{2}

1 N = 10^{5} dyn = 0.2248 lb

1 lb = 4.448 N

1 Pa.s = 10 poise

1 J = 9.869×10^{-3} L.atm

1 kW.h = 3.5 MJ

1 cal = 4.184 J

1 eV = 1.602×10^{-19} J

1 horsepower (cheval) = 746 W

1 kg = 2.205 lb

COMMON UNITS

Physical quantity Quantité physique	S.I. unit Unité S.I.	English units
Length (l) Longueur (l)	US : Meter (m) UK : Metre (m) FR : Mètre (m)	Inch (in or '') 1 in = 2.54.10-2 m = 2.54 cm Foot (ft or ') 1 ft = 12 in = 0.305 m Yard (yd) 1 yd = 3 ft = 0.914 m Statute (or land) Mile (mi) 1 mi = 1,609 m = 1.609 km
Area (A) Surface (A)	Square meter (m^2) Mètre carré (m^2)	Square inch (in^2) 1 $in^2 = 6.45.10^{-4}$ m^2 Square foot (ft^2) 1 ft^2 = 144 in^2
Volume (V) Volume (V)	Cubic meter (m^3) *[Remember : Liter (or litre) (L)* *1 L = 10^{-3} m^3 = 1 dm^3]* Mètre cube (m^3)	Cubic inch (in^3) 1 in^3 = 16.387 mL US Liquid ounce (liq oz) or fluid oz (floz) 1 floz = 29.574 mL US Gallon (gal) 1 gal = 3.795 mL UK fluid ounce (fl.oz) 1 floz = 28.413 mL UK (or Imperial) Gallon (UKgal) 1 UKgal = 4.546 mL
Velocity (v) Vitesse (v)	US : Meter per second ($m.s^{-1}$) UK : Metre per second ($m.s^{-1}$) Mètre par seconde ($m.s^{-1}$)	Mile per hour (mph) 1 mph = 0.447 m/s
	Radian per second ($rad.s^{-1}$)	

Angular velocity (ω) **Vitesse angulaire(ω)** **Rotational frequency (n)** **Fréquence de rotation (n)**	**Revolution per minute (rpm)** **or Round per minute** **1 rpm = $\frac{2\pi}{60}$ rad.s^{-1}**	
Mass (m) **Masse (m)**	**Kilogram (kg)** **Kilogramme (kg)**	**Pound mass (lbm)** **1 lbm = 0.454 kg**
Force (F) **Force (F)**	**Newton (N)**	**Pound (lb)** **1 lb = 4.448 N**
Torque (T) **Moment de couple (T)**	**Newton-meter (N.m)**	**Pound-foot (lb-ft)** **1 lb-ft = 1.356 N.m** **Pound-inch (lb-in)** **1 lb-in = 0.113 N.m**
Pressure (p) **Pression (p)**	**Pascal (Pa)** **1 Pa = 1 N.m^{-2}** **Bar (bar)** **1 bar = 10^5 Pa**	**Pound-force per square inch (lbf/in^2)** ***Also called :*** **Pound per square inch (psi)** **1 psi = 6.895.10^3 Pa**
Power (P) **Puissance (P)**	**Watt (W)**	**Horse-power (HP)** **1 HP = 745.7 W**

GREEK LETTERS IN PHYSICS
ALPHABET GREC EN SCIENCES PHYSIQUES

Upper case letter Majuscule	Lower case letter Minuscule	Pronounced Prononciation	Physics used Usage en physiques
Α	α	Alpha	Angle, coefficient …
Β	β	Bêta	Angle, coefficient …
Γ	γ	Gamma	Angle, coefficient …
Δ	δ	Delta	Δ: change in… Variation de…
Ε	ε	Epsilon	Small value - Petite valeur, Illuminance, permittivity – pérmittivité
Ζ	ζ	Zeta	
Η	η	Eta	Viscosity coefficient - Coefficient de viscosité
Θ	θ	Theta	Angle, temperature (°C)
Ι	ι	Iota	Moment of inertia – moment d'inertie
Κ	κ	Kappa	
Λ	λ	Lambda	Wavelength, ionique molar conductivity - Longueur d'onde, conductivité molaire ionique
Μ	μ	Mu	Micro symbol, volumic mass - Symbole du micro, masse volumique Permeability – pérmeabilité, viscosity - viscosité
Ν	ν	Nu	Light frequency - Fréquence de la lumière
Ξ	ξ	Xi	
Ο	ο	Omicron	
Π	π	Pi	Π: Arcimedes' principle- Poussée d'Archimède π: pi number-nombre pi
Ρ	ρ	Rho	Density - Masse volumique
Σ	σ	Sigma	Σ: summation-somme σ: molar conductivity-conductivité molaire
Τ	τ	Tau	Durée - Time
Υ	υ	Upsilon	Admittance
Φ	φ	Phi	Phase angle, magnetic flux – déphasage, flux magnétique

Χ	**χ**	**Chi**	**Reactance - réactance**
Ψ	**ψ**	**Psi**	**Electric flux – flux électrique**
Ω	**ω**	**Omega**	**Ω: ohms symbol – symbole des ohms** **ω: angular velocity, angular pulsation – vitesse angulaire, pulsation angulaire…**

VISIBLE SPECTRUM
SPECTRE VISIBLE

Colour	Wavelength range Longueur d'onde (nm)
Red	630-790
Orange	590-630
Yellow	560-590
Green	490-560
Blue	450-490
Violet	400-450

Outcomes over the Long-Term

Natural Law: loi naturelle
- **The same observation applies to many different systems. A law summarizes what happens.**
- **La même observation appliquée à des systèmes différents. Une loi resume ce qui se passe.**

Postulat: postulat
- **Principle that must be accepted as true without demonstration.**
- **Principe qui doit être admis comme vrai sans démonstration.**

Significant figures (sig figs): nombre significatif
- **Is the number of decimal in the result.**
- **C'est le nombre de chiffres dans un résultat.**

Theory (Model): théorème
- **A set of tested hypotheses that give an overall explanation of some natural phenomenon. A theory is an attempt to explain why it happens.**
- **Un ensemble d'hypothèses testé, qui donnent une explication générale de quelques phénomènes naturels.**

Uncertainty in measurement: incertitude dans les measures
- **A digit that must be estimated is called uncertain. A measurement always has some degree of uncertainty.**
- **Un nombre à estimer possède une incertitude. Chaque mesure a toujours un degré d'incertitude.**

THE SOLAR SYSTEM
LE SYSTÈME SOLAIRE

Planet planète	**Mercury**	**Venus**	**Earth**	**Mars**	**Jupiter**	**Saturn**	**Uranus**	**Neptune**
Mean distance from Sun Distance moyenne du Soleil (million km)	**57.91**	**108.21**	**149.60**	**227.94**	**778.34**	**1430**	**2869.6**	**4496.7**
Mass-masse (Earth masses par rapport à la Terre)	**0.054**	**0.815**	**1.000***	**0.107**	**317.89**	**95.14**	**14.52**	**17.46**
Sideral period période sedé-rale	**88d**	**224.7d**	**365.26d**	**687d**	**11.86y**	**29.46y**	**164.79y**	**164.79y**
Diameter diamètre	**4,878**	**12,104**	**12,756**	**6,794**	**142,800**	**120,000**	**51,000**	**49,500**
Satelleites satéllites	**0**	**0**	**1**	**2**	**16**	**18**	**15**	**2**
Atmosphere atmosphère	**H, He and Ne**	CO_2	**N, O**	CO_2	**H, and** CH_4	**H and He**	**H, He, and** CH_4	CH_4 **and H**
Axial rotation (equatorial) (km)	**58d16h**	**343d**	**23h56m 4s**	**24h37m 23s**	**9h50m 30s**	**10h14m**	**16-28h****	**18-20h****

d = days - jours
y = years - années
h = hours - heures
km = kilometers - kilomètres
***The mass of the Earth is** 5.976×10^{24} **kg – Masse de la Terre**
****Different latitudes rotate at different speeds**

ELECTROMAGNETIC SPECTRUM
SPECTRE ÉLECTROMAGNÉTIQUE

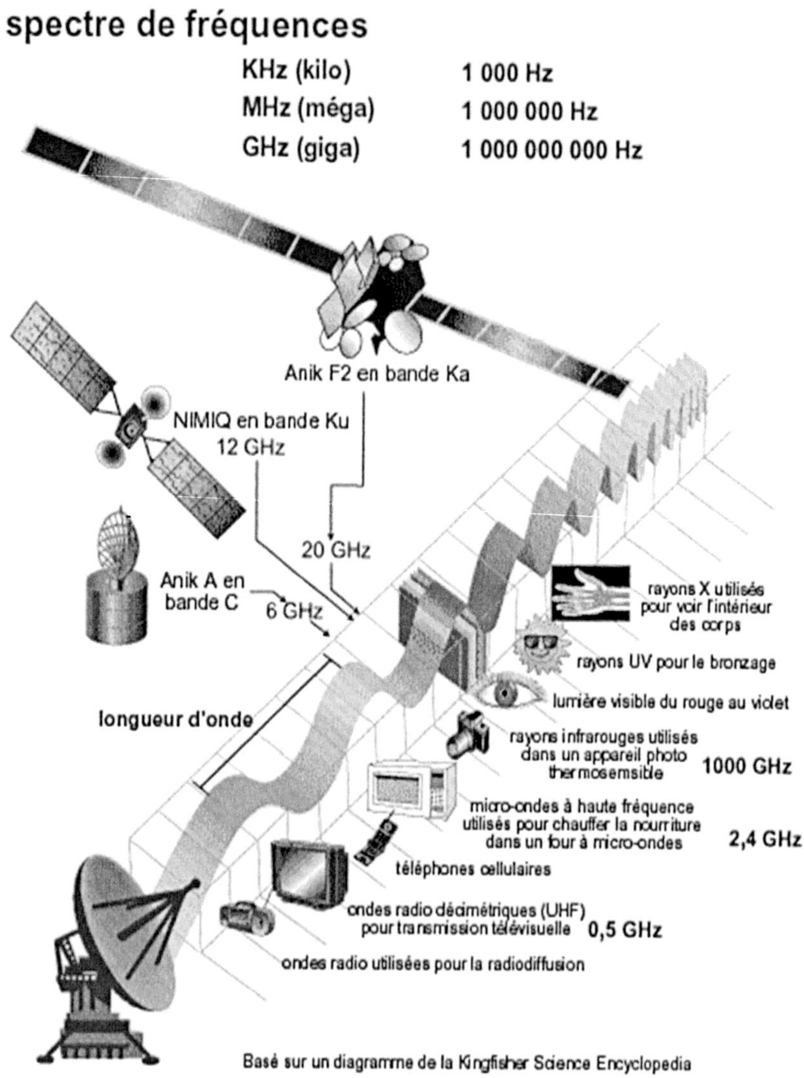

FLUID MECHANICS
MÉCANIQUE DES FLUIDES

Bernoulli equation: équation de Bernoulli

- **A statement of the conservation of energy in a form useful for solving problems involving fluids. For a non-viscous, incompressible fluid in steady flow, the sum of pressure, potential and kinetic energies per unit volume is constant at any point.**
- **Along a fluid flow streamline the Bernoulli Equation is written as:**

$$\frac{1}{2} \cdot \rho \cdot v^2 + \rho \cdot g \cdot z + p = \text{constante}$$

Where
p: pressure
ρ: density
g: gravity
v: flow speed
z: height
$\rho v^2/2$: is called dynamic pressure
ρgh: is called static pressure

- **C'est un énoncé de la conservation de l'énergie sous une forme utile pour résoudre des problèmes impliquant des fluides. Dans le cas d'un fluide non-visqueux, incompressible en flux continu, la somme des pressions, des énergies potentielles et cinétique par unité de volume est constante en tout point.**
- **Le long dc la ligne aérodynamique l'équation de Bernoulli s'écrit:**

$$\frac{1}{2} \cdot \rho \cdot v^2 + \rho \cdot g \cdot z + p = \text{constante}$$

Avec
p: la pression
ρ: la masse volumique
g: l'intensité de la pesanteur
v: la vitesse d'écoulement
z: la hauteur
$\rho v^2/2$: est la pression dynamique
ρgh: est la pression statique

Compressible fluids: fluides compressibles

- **A fluid is compressible if its volume changes significantly when it is pressurized. Gases are obviously compressible.**
- **Un fluide est compressible si son volume change de manière significative quand il est mis sous pression. Les gaz sont évidemment compressibles.**

Fluid: fluide

- **A body is called fluid if it may flows easily. Fluid must be deformable, that is to say, it has no shape of its own. A fluid is a continuous medium.**

The fluid state therefore includes mainly two physical states:

- Gaseous state
- Liquid state.

- On appelle fluide un corps susceptible de s'écouler facilement. Un fluide doit donc être déformable ; c'est-à-dire qu'il n'a pas de forme propre. Un fluide est un milieu continu.

  L'état fluide englobe donc principalement deux états physiques :
  - l'état gazeux
  - l'état liquide.

Fluid mechanics: mécanique des fluides

- The study of fluids - liquids and gases. Involves various properties of the fluid, such as velocity, pressure, density and temperature, as functions of space and time.
- L'étude des fluides - liquides et de gaz. Implique plusieurs propriétés du fluide, telles que la vitesse, la pression, la densité et la température, en tant que fonctions de l'espace et le temps.

Incompressible fluids: fluides incompressibles

- A fluid is incompressible if its volume does not change significantly when it is pressurized. Liquids are usually incompressible.
- Un fluide est incompressible si son volume ne change pas de manière significative lorsqu'il est mis sous pression. Les liquides sont généralement incompressibles.

Laminar and turbulent flow: flux laminaire et turbulent

- Experiments realized by Reynolds (1883) during the flow of a liquid in a straight cylindrical pipe which also comes in a net of colored liquid, showed the existence of two flow regimes: laminar and turbulent.

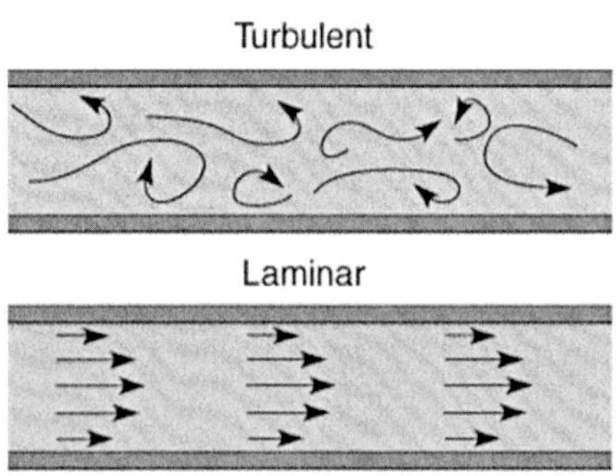

- Using various fluids (different viscosity), by varying the speed and the diameter of the pipe, Reynolds showed that the parameter determined whether the flow is laminar or turbulent is a dimensionless number called the Reynolds number Re.
- The experience shows that:

If $Re < 2000$ the scheme is LAMINAR

If $2000 < Re < 3000$ the scheme is intermediate

If $Re > 3000$ the scheme is TURBULENT

- Les expériences réalisées par ***Reynolds*** **(1883) lors de l'écoulement d'un liquide dans une conduite cylindrique rectiligne dans laquelle arrive également un filet de liquide coloré, ont montré l'existence de deux régimes d'écoulement: laminaire et turbulent.**
- **En utilisant des fluides divers (viscosité différente), en faisant varier le débit et le diamètre de la canalisation, Reynolds a montré que le paramètre qui permettait de déterminer si l'écoulement est laminaire ou turbulent est un nombre sans dimension appelé nombre de Reynolds Re.**
- **L'expérience montre que :**
  Si Re < 2000 le régime est LAMINAIRE
  Si 2000 < Re < 3000 le régime est intermédiaire
  Si Re > 3000 le régime est TURBULENT

Streamlines: lignes aérodynamiques (lignes de courant)
- **A streamline is a path traced out by a massless particle as it moves with the flow.**
- **Une ligne aérodynamique est une trajectoire tracée par une particule sans masse se déplaçant avec le courant.**

Torricelli's theorem (law): théorème (loi) de Torricelli
- **La loi énonce que le carré de la vitesse d'écoulement d'un fluide sous l'effet de la pesanteur est proportionnelle à la hauteur de fluide située au-dessus de l'ouverture par laquelle il s'échappe du cylindre qui le contient.**
- **The law states that the square of the flow velocity of a fluid under the effect of gravity is proportional to the height of the fluid located above the opening through which it escapes from the cylinder which contains it.**

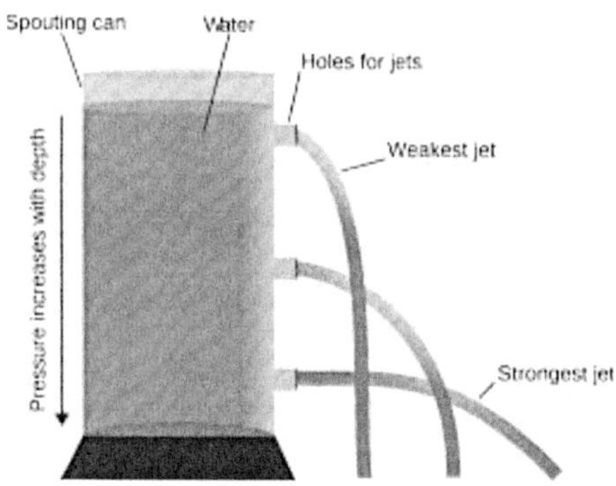

Venturi effect (Venturi meter): effet Venturi
- **If a liquid flows through a pipe, then as it is incompressible, the flow (volume passing through a surface per unit time) is constant. If the pipe widens, then speed decreases (since the flow rate is the product of the speed by the section, the two vary inversely).**

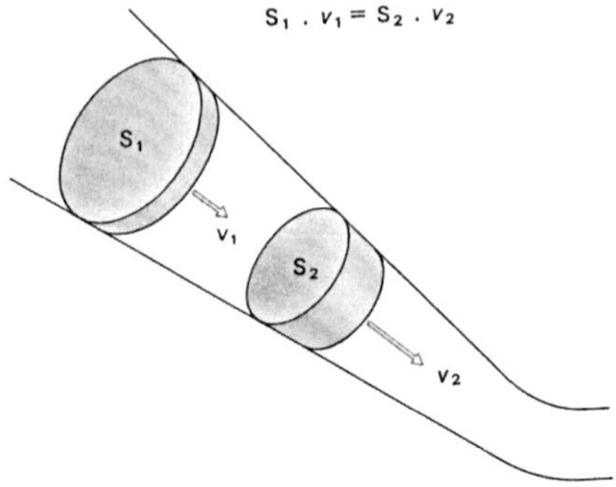

- Bernoulli's theorem then tells us that the pressure increases. Conversely, if the pipe narrows, the fluid accelerates and its pressure decreases. This experimental device describes the Venturi effect (Venturi meter).
- Si un liquide s'écoule dans une canalisation, alors comme il est incompressible, son débit (volume transitant à travers une surface par unité de temps) est constant. Si la canalisation s'élargit, alors la vitesse diminue (puisque le débit est le produit de la vitesse par la section, les deux varient à l'inverse).
- Le théorème de Bernoulli nous indique alors que la pression augmente. A l'inverse, si la canalisation se rétrécit, le fluide accélère et sa pression diminue. On qualifie ce dispositif expérimental de tube de Venturi.

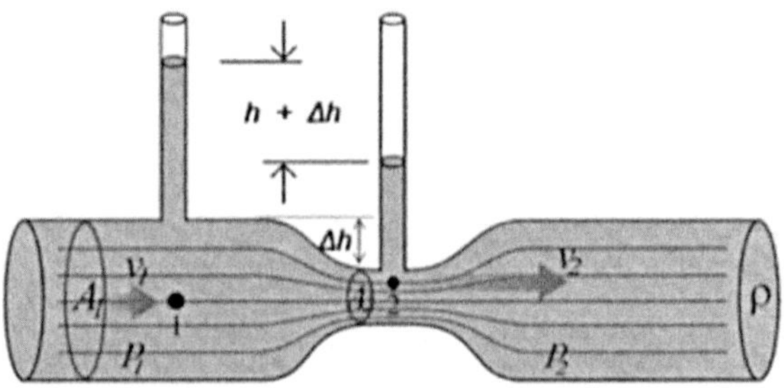

Viscosity: viscosité

- The viscosity of a liquid is a measure of its resistance to shear, and has an effect on its properties. There are two related measures of fluid viscosity - known as dynamic (or absolute) and kinematic viscosity.
  1- Dynamic (absolute) viscosity:
    - Absolute viscosity or the coefficient of absolute viscosity is a measure of the internal resistance.
  2- Kinematic viscosity:
    - Is the ratio of absolute or dynamic viscosity to density - a quantity in which no force is involved. Kinematic viscosity can be obtained by dividing the absolute viscosity of a fluid with its mass density
    - $\nu = \mu / \rho$

Where
v = kinematic viscosity
μ = absolute or dynamic viscosity
ρ = density

- **La viscosité d'un liquide est une mesure de sa résistance au cisaillement, et elle a un effet sur ses propriétés. Il y a deux mesures connexes de la viscosité du fluide - appelés viscosité dynamique (ou absolue) et viscosité cinématique.**

1- Viscosité dynamique (ou absolue) :

- **Viscosité absolue ou le coefficient de viscosité absolue est une mesure de la résistance interne.**

2- Viscosité cinématique :

- **C'est le rapport de la viscosité absolue ou dynamique à la masse volumique - une quantité dans laquelle aucune force n'est impliquée. La viscosité cinématique peut être obtenue en divisant la viscosité absolue d'un fluide avec la masse volumique.**
- $v = \mu / \rho$

  Avec
  v = viscosité cinématique
  μ = viscosité absolue ou dynamique
  ρ = densité

PART 2

CHEMISTRY – CHIMIE

Chemistry is the study
of the atomic building blocks of nature,
how they combine, and their combinations which form the solids, liquids, and gases
that make up most forms of matter.

La chimie est l'étude
de structure atomique de la nature,
comment elles se combinent, et de leurs combinaisons qui forment les solides, liquides, et gaz
qui composent la plupart des formes de la matière.

A

Absolute zero: zéro absolu

- **Is the temperature at which atoms and molecules are effectively motionless, 0 K or -273.15 °C.**
- **C'est la température à laquelle les atomes et les molécules sont immobiles, 0 K ou -273,15 °C.**

Absorbed dose: dose absorbée

Absorption of liquids and gases: absorption des liquides et des gaz

- **Happens when a fluid soaks into the pores of a material, like water soaks into a sponge.**
- **Lorsqu'un fluide est absorbé par une matière, c'est le cas de l'eau et une éponge.**

Absorption of radiation: absorption d'une radiation

- **Happens when a wavelength of a radiation is absorbed by a material, ozone absorbs harmful ultraviolet radiation.**
- **Lorsque les longueurs d'onde sont absorbées par une matière, l'ozone de la haute atmosphère absorbe les radiations ultraviolettes dangereuses.**

Absorption spectrum: spectre d'absorption

Accumulator: accumulateur

Accuracy of data: Exactitude des données

Acids: acides

- **According to Bronsted definition. An acid is a proton donator : $HA = H^+ + A^-$**
- **Substance which in solution gives a pH lowers than seven.**
- **Selon la définition de Bronsted. Un acide est un donneur de proton : $HA = H^+ + A^-$**
- **Une solution acide a un pH inférieur à 7.**

Acid anhydride: anhydride d'acide

- **R-CO-O-CO-R'**

- **Is an organic compound that has two acyl groups bound to the same oxygen atom.**
- **C'est un composé organique possédant deux groupes acyles attachés à un atome d'oxygène.**

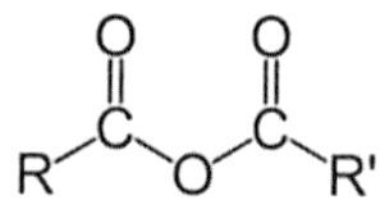

Acid-base equilibria: équilibre acido-basique

Acid-base indicators: indicateur acido-basique

Acid-base reactions: réaction acido-basique

Acid-base titration: titrage (dosage) acido-basique

Acid chlorides: acide chlorhydrique
- **Acid solution of hydrogen chloride in water.**
- **Solution acide de chlorure d'hydrogène.**

Acid-dissociation equilibrium constant or dissociation constant: constant d'équilibre ou constante d'acidité K
- $aA_{aq} + bB_{aq} = cC_{aq} + dD_{aq}$

$$K = \frac{[C]^{c}_{éq}[D]^{d}_{éq}}{[A]^{a}_{éq}[B]^{b}_{éq}}$$

Acid indicators: indicateurs colorés
- **Solutions used to find out whether a substance is an acid or an alkali (base).**
- **Indicators work by changing colour.**
- **BTB (Bromothymol blue) is a common indicator, it is yallow in acid solutions and bleu in alkaline solutions.**
- **Ce sont des solutions utilisées pour savoir si une solution est acide ou base.**
- **Les inducateurs fonctionnent en changeant de couleur.**

- **BBT (bleu de bromothymol) est l'indicateur le plus répondu. Il devient jaune en milieu acide et bleu en milieu basique.**

Acidic oxide: oxyde d'acide

Acid rain: pluie acide

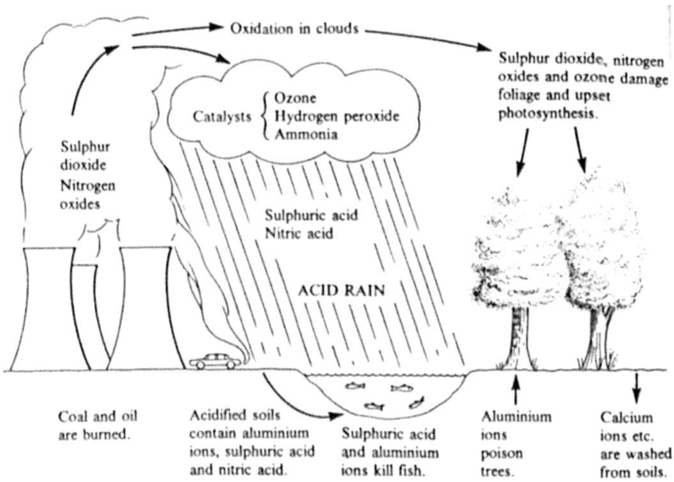

Acid salt: sel acide

Acid strength: force (concentration) d'un acide

Actinium: actinium

- **Is a radioactive chemical element.**
- **Discovered by Debierne (France) in 1899.**
- **Etymological origin: *aktis* (radius) from Greek.**
- **Its chemical symbol is Ac.**
- **Its atomic number is 89.**
- **Used in thermoelectric generators.**
- **C'est un élément de la classification périodique.**
- **Découvert par Debrierne (France) en 1899.**
- **Origine étymologique: *aktis* (rayon) du grec.**
- **Son symbole chimique est Ac.**
- **Son numéro atomique est 89.**
- **Utilisé dans les générateurs thermoélectriques.**

Activation energy: énergie d'activation

- **The minimum energy required to transform reactants into the activated complex.**
- **C'est l'énergie minimale nécessaire pour transformer des réactifs en complexe activé.**

Acyl chlorides: chlorure d'acyle

Addition-elimination reactions: réactions d'addition-élimination

Addition polymerization: réaction de polymérisation

Addition reaction: réaction d'addition

Aerosols: aérosols

Air: air

- **Gas principally composed of nitrogen and oxygen.**
- **Gaz composé essentiellement d'azote et d'oxygène.**

Air pollution: pollution de l'air

Alcohols: alcools

- $C_nH_{2n+1}OH$
- **They all possess the same functional group, a hydroxyl group attached to a saturated carbon atom.**
- **Ils possèdent tous le même groupe fonctionnel hydroxyde attaché à un atome de carbone saturé.**

Aldehydes: aldéhydes

- **Have a hydrogen atom attached to the carbonyl carbon atom.**
- **Les aldéhydes ont un atome d'hydrogène attaché au groupe carbonyle.**

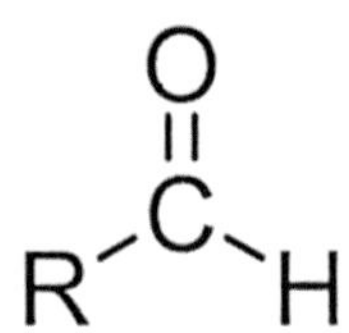

Alkali elements: éléments alcalins

- **Elements such as lithium, sodium and potassium in group one of the periodic table that share the same chemical properties.**
- **Les éléments tels que le lithium, sodium et le potassium dans le premier groupe de tableau périodique et qui partagent les mêmes propriétés chimiques.**

Alkaline earth metals: métaux alcalino-terreux

Alkanes: alcanes

- C_nH_{2n+2}
- **Are saturated hydrocarbons as they contain only single bonds between carbon atoms.**
- **Sont des hydrocarbures saturés ils contiennent une liaison simple entre les atomes de carbones.**

Alkenes: alcènes

- C_nH_{2n}
- **Are unsaturated hydrocarbons as they contain double bonds between carbon atoms.**
- **Sont des hydrocarbures insaturés ils contiennent une liaison double entre deux atomes de carbones.**

Alkyl group: groupe alkyle

- $-C_nH_{2n+1}$
- **Is a functional group, like an alkane, consists of single-bonded carbon and hydrogen atoms. Examples :**
- **Methyl group** $- CH_3$

$$R - CH_3$$

- **Ethyl group** $- CH_2 - CH_3$

$$R - CH_2 - CH_3$$

- **C'est un groupe fonctionnel, comme les alcanes, contient des liaisons simples des atomes de carbones et d'hydrogènes. Exemples : les groupes méthyle et éthyle.**

Alkynes: alcynes

- C_nH_{2n-2}

- **Are unsaturated hydrocarbons as they contain triple bonds between carbon atoms.**
- **Sont des hydrocarbures insaturés ils contiennent une liaison triple entre deux atomes de carbones.**

Alloys: alliages
- **An alloy is a metallic solid solution composed of two or more elements.**
- **Un alliage est une combinaison d'un métal composé d'au moins un élément chimique.**

Aluminium: aluminium
- **Is a metallic chemical element.**
- **Isolated by Orsted (Denmark) in 1825.**
- **Etymological origin: *alumen* in Latin.**
- **Its chemical symbol is Al.**
- **Its atomic number is 13.**
- **C'est un élément métallique de la classification périodique.**
- **Isolé par Orsted (Danemark) en 1825.**
- **Origine étymologique: *alumen* en latin.**
- **Son symbole chimique est Al.**
- **Son numéro atomique est 13.**

Americium: américium
- **Is a radioactive chemical element.**
- **Its chemical symbol is Am.**
- **Produced by Glenn T. Seaborg, Leon Morgan, Ralph James and Albert Ghiorso at the end of 1944.**
- **Etymological origin: *America* (continent).**
- **Its atomic number is 95.**
- **Used in most smoke detectors.**
- **C'est un élément radioactif de la classification périodique.**
- **Synthétisé par Glenn T. Seaborg, Leon Morgan, Ralph James et Albert Ghiorso vers la fin de l'année 1944.**
- **Origine étymologique: *america* (continent).**
- **Son numéro atomique est 95.**
- **Utilisé dans la plus part des détecteurs de fumé.**

Amides: amides
- **Is an organic compound that contains the functional group consisting of a carbonyl group linked to a nitrogen atom N.**

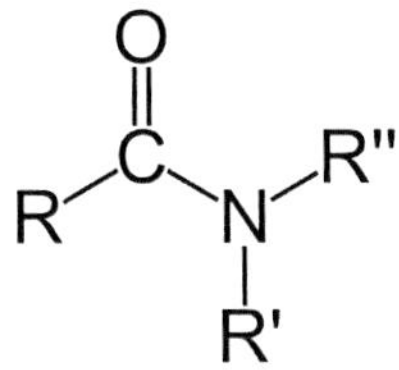

- **C’est un compose organique contenant un groupe fonctionnel carbonyle attaché à un atome d’azote N.**

Amines: amines

- **Are organic derivatives of ammonia. They are classified as primary, secondary or tertiary amines according to the number of alkyl or aryl groups attached to the nitrogen atom.**
- **Examples of the three categories of amines are shown below:**

	Complete Structural Formula	Condensed Structural Formula
Methylamine	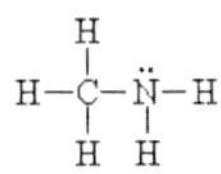	CH_3NH_2
Dimethylamine	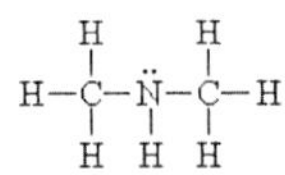	CH_3NHCH_3
Trimethylamine	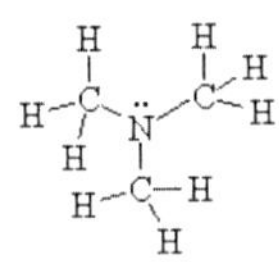	$CH_3-\underset{\underset{CH_3}{\vert}}{N}-CH_3$

- **Ce sont des dérivés organiques de l’ammonium. Ils sont classés en trois formes: primaire, secondaire et tertiaire selon les groupes d’alkyle ou aryle attachés à l’atome d’azote.**
- **Voir les exemples des formules développées et non développées dans le tableau ci-dessus.**

Amino group: groupe amine

Ammonia: ammoniac

- **Is a smelly colorless gas (NH_3), very soluble in water.**
- **C’est un gaz sans couleur d’une odeur caractéristique (NH_3), très soluble dans l’eau.**

Amount of substance: quantité de matière

Amphoteric oxide: oxyde amphotère
- **Is an oxide that can act either as an acid or a base.**
- **C'est un oxyde qui peut agir soit comme acide ou une base.**

Amount concentration: concentration molaire
- **Amount of a constituent (n) divided by the volume (V) of the mixture.**
- **C'est la quantité de matière d'un composé divisée par le volume total.**

Analgesics: analgésique
- **Is a painkiller, from Greek 'without pain'.**
- **C'est un antidouleur, vient du grec 'sans douleur'.**

Analytical chemistry: chimie analytique

Anhydrides: anhydrides

Anhydrous: anhydre
- **Not containing water.**
- **Ne contient pas de l'eau.**

Aniline: aniline
- **Is an aromatic organic compound, its moléculaire formula is $C_6H_5NH_2$.**
- **C'est un composé organique aromatique de formule chimique $C_6H_5NH_2$.**

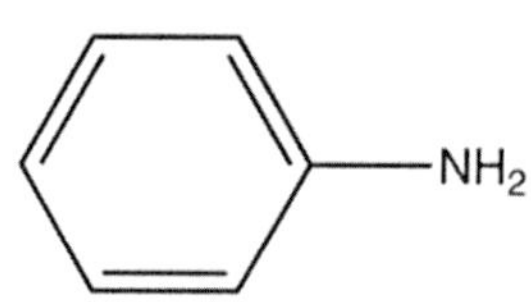

Anions: anions

Anode: anode

Antibiotics: antibiotiques

Antifreeze: antigel

Antimony: antimoine

- **Is a metallic chemical element.**
- **Its chemical symbol is Sb.**
- **Known by ancient Egyptian 3000 BC.**
- **Etymological origin: *athimar* (name of the metalloid) in Arab. Or *anti-monachos* (monk's killer) is explained by many early alchemists being monks, and antimony being poisonous.**
- **Its atomic number is 51.**
- **Most of it is melted down and added to lead to make bullets and batteries or alloyed with other metals.**
- **C'est un élément métallique de la classification périodique.**
- **Connu par les anciens égyptiens 3000 avant JC.**
- **Origine étymologique: *athimar* (nom de métalloïde) en arabe. Ou antimoines (tueur de moines) car les premiers alchimistes en occident étaient des moines et beaucoup ont été empoisonnés en manipulant l'antimoine.**
- **Son symbole chimique est Sb.**
- **Son numéro atomique est 51.**
- **Utilisé sous forme fondue et ajouté au plomb pour fabriquer des balles et des batteries ou en alliage avec d'autres métaux.**

Antiseptics: antiseptiques

Aqueous solution: solution aqueux

- **Describing a solution in water.**
- **Une solution dans l'eau.**

Arenes: arènes

- **Arenes is an aromatic hydrocarbon with alternating double and simple bonds between carbon atoms forming hydrocarbons rings.**

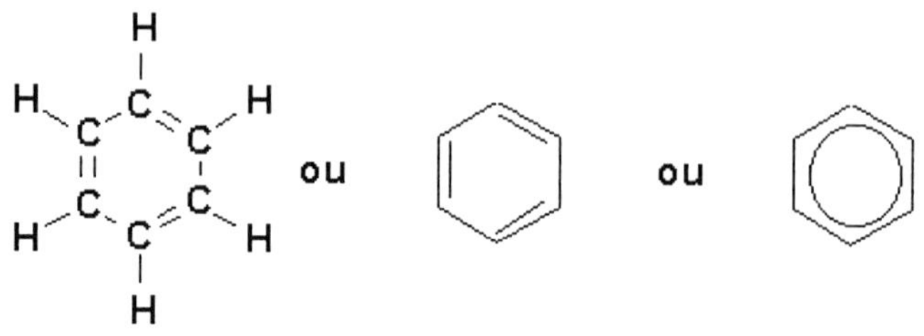

- **Les arènes sont des hydrocarbures aromatiques avec des liaisons doubles et des liaisons simples en alternance entre les atomes de carbones formant des cycles hydrocarbure.**

Argon: argon
- **Is a chemical element.**
- **Is a rare gas, colorless, odorless and tasteless.**
- **Discovered by Rayleigh (England) in 1894.**
- **Etymological origin: *argos* (inactive) in Greek.**
- **Its chemical symbol is Ar.**
- **Its atomic number is 18.**
- **Used as a shield gas to protect against oxidation.**
- **C'est un élément de la classification périodique.**
- **C'est un gaz rare, incolore, inodore et sans saveur.**
- **Découvert par Rayleigh (Angleterre) en 1894.**
- **Origine étymologique: *argos* (inactif) en grec.**
- **Son symbole chimique est Ar.**
- **Son numéro atomique est 18.**
- **Utilisé comme gaz bouclier anti oxidation.**

Aromatic hydrocarbons: hydrocarbons aromatique
- **Chemical compound responsible for the smell or for the taste of a substance.**
- **Composé chimique responsable d'une odeur ou un gout.**

Arsenic: arsenique
- **Is a chemical element.**
- **Discovered probably by Albert le Grand (Germany) in 1250. Systematically studied by Berzelius (Sweden) in the beginning of 19th century.**
- **Etymological origin: *arsên* (male) in Greek.**
- **Its chemical symbol is As.**
- **Its atomic number is 33.**

- **Combined with gallium it forms a semiconductor used in creating highspeed integrated circuits for supercomputers and cell phones.**
- **C'est un élément de la classification périodique.**
- **Découvert probablement par Albert le Grand (Allemagne) en 1250. Systématiquement étudiée par Berzelius (Suède) au début du 19ème siècle.**
- **Origine étymologique: *arsên* (mâle) en grec.**
- **Son symbole chimique est As.**
- **Son numéro atomique est 33.**
- **Combiné avec le gallium, ils forment des semi-conducteurs utilisés dans les circuits intégrés ultra rapide dans les super-ordinateurs et les téléphones portables.**

Aryl group: groupe aryle

- **Is a functional group or substituent derived from an aromatic ring. Examples :**
- **Phenyl C_6H_5**

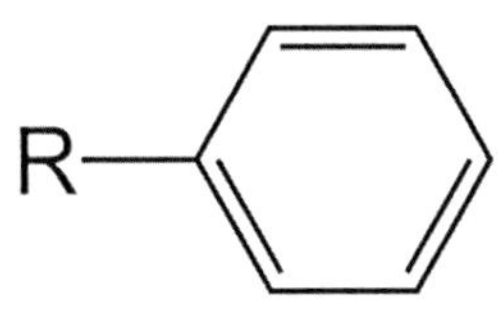

- **Benzyl C_6H_5-CH_2-**

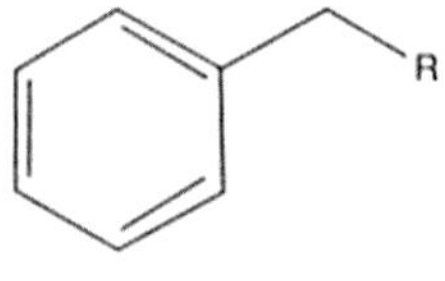

- **C'est un groupe fonctionnel ou substituant qui dérive d'un noyau aromatique. Exemples: phényle et benzyle.**

Ascorbic acid (vitamin C): acide ascorbique (vitamine C)

Aspirin: aspirine

- **Known as acetylsalicylic acid, is a salicylate drug, often used as an analgesic to relieve minor aches and pains, as an antipyretic to reduce fever, and as an anti-inflammatory medication. Aspirin was first isolated by Felix Hoffmann, a chemist with the German company Bayer in 1897.**
- **Connu sous le nom d'acide acétylsalicylique, c'est un médicament de salicylate, souvent utilisé comme un analgésique pour soulager les douleurs mineures, comme antipyrétique pour réduire la fièvre, et comme un médicament anti-inflammatoire. L'aspirine a été isolée par Felix Hoffmann, chimiste de la société allemande Bayer en 1897.**

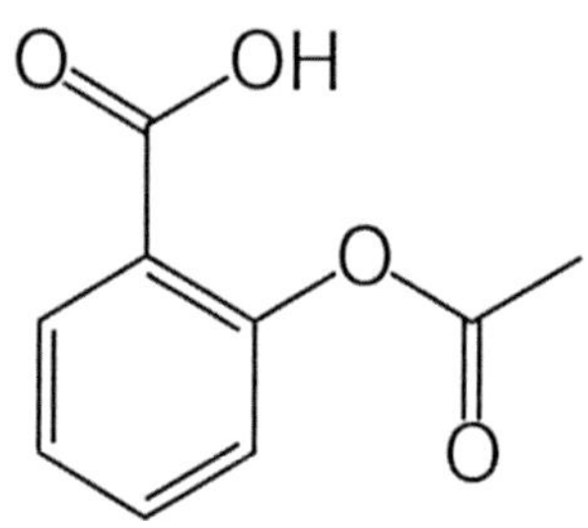

Astatine: astate

- **Is a chemical element.**
- **Synthesized by Coson, Mackenzie and Sergé (USA) in 1940.**
- **Etymological origin: *astatos* (unstable) in Greek.**
- **Its chemical symbol is At.**
- **Its atomique number is 85.**
- **C'est un élément de la classification périodique.**
- **Synthétisé par Corson, Mackenzie and Sergé (USA) en 1940.**
- **Origine étymologique: *astatos* (instable) en grec.**
- **Son symbole chimique est At.**
- **Son numéro atomique est 85.**

Asymmetric carbon: carbone asymétrique

- **An asymmetric carbon atom is a carbon atom that is attached to four different types of atoms or four different groups of atoms.**

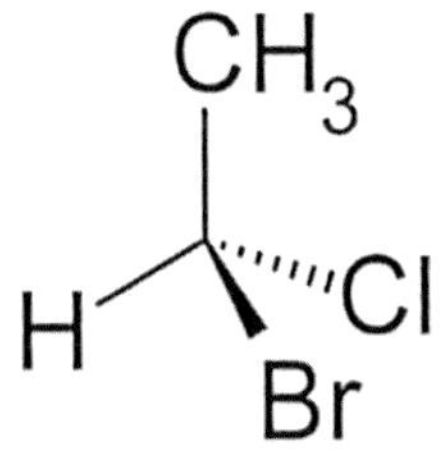

- Un atome de carbone asymétrique est un atome tétraédrique attaché à quatre atomes différents ou quatre groups d'atomes de substituant différents.

Atmosphere: atmosphère

Atmospheric pressure: pression atmosphérique

Atom: atome

- The smallest component of an element consisting of a positively-charged nucleus surrounded by a bound system of negatively-charged electrons. Since an atom is neutral, the number of positively-charged protons in the nucleus is equal to the number of electrons.
- La plus petite composante d'un élément constitué d'un noyau chargé positivement entouré d'un système d'électrons chargés négativement. Comme l'atome est neutre, le nombre de protons chargés positivement dans le noyau est égal au nombre d'électrons.

Atomic absorption spectroscopy: spectre d'absorption atomique

Atomic emission spectroscopy: spectre d'émission atomique

Atomic number: numéro atomique

- Is the number of protons found in the nucleus of an atom and therefore identical to the charge number of the nucleus. This number defines the chemical element.
- It is conventionally represented by the symbol Z.
- C'est le nombre de proton dans le noyau atomique et il est égal au nombre de charges électrique du noyau. Il définit l'élément chimique.
- Il est représenté par la lettre Z.

Atomic orbitals: trajectoire (orbite) atomique

Atomic radius: rayon atomique

Atomic spectrum: spectre atomique

Atomic theory: théorie atomique

Atomization: atomisation

Autocatalysis: autocatalyses

Autoionization: autoprotolyse

$$2H_2O = H_3O^+ + HO^-$$

Avogadro's constant (number): nombre d'Avogadro

- Is the number of elementary entities in a mole.
- C'est le nombre d'entités élémentaire dans une mole.
- $N_A = 6.02x10^{23}$ mol^{-1}

Avogadro's Law: loi d'Avogadro

- Is a gas law hypothesized that two given samples of an ideal gas, of the same volume and at the same temperature and pressure, contain the same number of molecules.
- P.V = n.R.T
- P is the pressure, in Pascal (Pa).
- V is the volume, in m^3.
- n is the amount of substance of the gas (in moles)
- R is the gas constant (8.314 $J \cdot K^{-1} mol^{-1}$)
- T is the absolute temperature en kelvin (K).
- Appelée aussi loi des gaz parfaits, spécifie que des volumes égaux de gaz parfaits différents, aux mêmes conditions de température et de pression, contiennent le même nombre de molécules.
- P.V = n.R.T
- P est la pression, s'exprime en Pascal (Pa).
- V est le volume, s'exprime en mètres cubes (m^3).
- n est la quantité de matière, s'exprime en moles (mol).

- **R est la constante de gaz, s'exprime en $J \cdot K^{-1} \cdot mol^{-1}$.**
- **T est la température, s'exprime en Kelvin.**

B

Back titration: dosage par retour

Bacteria: bactérie

- **Living things that have only one cell and are so small they can only be seen with a microscope. Measuring 0.2 µm.**
- **C'est un organisme vivant unicellulaire de l'ordre de 0,2 µm.**

Ball-and-stick model: modèle moléculaire eclaté

- **The ball-and-stick model represents the bonds that hold the atoms together by using balls and sticks. The atoms being the balls and the bonds that hold the atoms together being the sticks.**
- **Le modèle moléculaire représente les atomes et les liaisons qui les lient en utilisant des boules et des bâtons.**

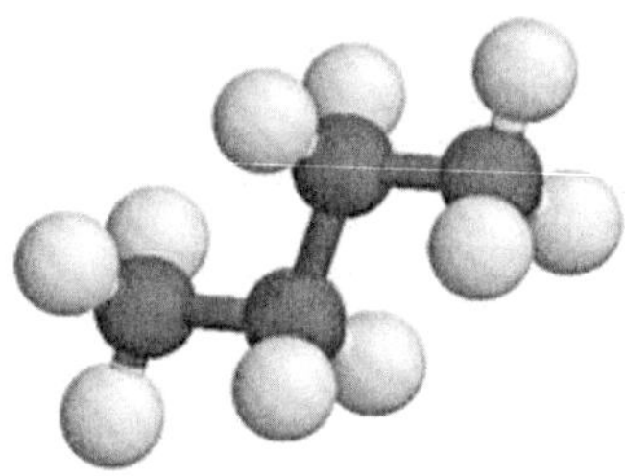

Bar: bar

- **Unit of pressure.**
- **Unité de pression.**

Barium: baryum

- **Is a chemical element.**
- **Discovered by Scheele (Sweden) in 1787.**
- **Etymological origin: *barus* (heavy) in Greek.**
- **Its chemical symbol is Ba.**
- **Its atomic number is 56.**
- **Barium in pure form is a metal, used as a ''getter'' in high-vacuum components such as vacuum tubes. Getters are used to remove residual gas, often to achieve a higher vacuum in sealed tubes.**
- **C'est un élément de la classification périodique.**
- **Découvert par Scheele (Suède) en 1787.**
- **Origine étymologique: *barus* (lourd) en grec.**

- **Son symbole chimique est Ba.**
- **Son numéro atomique est 56.**
- **A l'état pure le baryum est sous forme métallique, il est utilisé comme ''piège à gaz'' dans les composants fonctionnant à vide comme les tubes électroniques. Il évite l'apparition de gaz rémanents dans les tubes sellés.**

Base: base

- **According to the Bronsted definition a base is a proton acceptor : $A^- + H^+ = HA$**
- **Substance which in solution gives a pH higher than seven.**
- **Selon Bronsted une base est susceptible de capter un proton : $A^- + H^+ = HA$**
- **Solution de pH supérieure à 7.**

Battery: batterie

- **Is a device consisting of one or more electrochemical cells that convert stored chemical energy into electrical energy.**
- **C'est un dispositif constitué d'une ou plusieurs cellules électrochimiques qui convertissent l'énergie chimique stockée en énergie électrique.**

Beaker : bécher

- **A wide cylindrical glass vessel with a pouring lip, used as a laboratory container and mixing jar.**
- **Récipient cylindrique, utilisé dans les laboratoires.**

Benzene: benzene

- **C_6H_6**
- **Is the simplest member of the class of hydrocarbons called aromatic hydrocarbons or arenes.**
- **C'est la forme la plus simple des hydrocarbures aromatiques ou les arènes.**

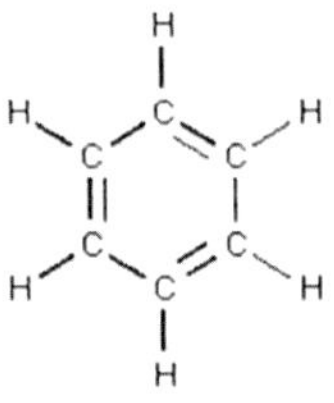

Berkelium: berkélium

- **Is a radioactive chemical element.**
- **Synthesized, isolated and identified in 1949 by Glenn T. Seaborg, Albert Ghiorso and Stanley G. Thompson.**
- **Etymological origin: University of California at *Berkeley* (city in USA).**
- **Its chemical symbol is Bk.**
- **Its atomic number is 97.**
- **It has no applications for the moment.**
- **C'est un élément radioactif de la classification périodique.**
- **Synthétisé, isolé et identifié en 1949 par Glenn T. Seaborg, Albert Ghiorso et Stanley G. Thompson.**
- **Origine étymologique: Université de Californie en *Berkeley* (cité en USA).**
- **Son symbole est Bk.**
- **Son numéro atomique est 97.**
- **Pas d'application pour le moment.**

Beryllium: béryllium
- **Is a metallic chemical element.**
- **Discovered by Vauquelin (France) in 1798.**
- **Etymological origin: takes its name from ore (mineral).**
- **Its chemical symbol is Be.**
- **Its atomic number is 4.**
- **Used as an alloy in the lightweight parts for missiles and spacecraft.**
- **C'est un élément métallique de la classification périodique.**
- **Découvert par Vauquelin (France) en 1798.**
- **Origine étymologique: tire son nom du minerai.**
- **Son symbole chimique est Be.**
- **Son numéro atomique est 4.**
- **Utilisé comme alliage dans les pièces légères dans les missiles et les vaisseaux spéciaux.**

Boron: bore
- **Is a chemical element.**
- **Discovered by Davy (England), Gay-Lussac and Thénard (France) in 1808.**
- **Etymological origin: *borax* from Persian.**
- **Its chemical symbol is B.**
- **Its atomic number is 5.**
- **While extremely hard, boron is too brittle in pure form to have any practical applications.**
- **C'est un élément de la classification périodique.**

- **Découvert par Davy (Angleterre), Gay-Lussac et Thénard (France) en 1808.**
- **Origine étymologique: *borax* du persan.**
- **Son symbole chimique est B.**
- **Son numéro atomique est 5.**
- **Bien qu'il soit extrêmement dur, le bore est trop fragile à l'état pur pour avoir des applications pratiques.**

Bunsen burner: bec Bunsen
- **Use to provide heat for chemical reaction**
- **Produit de la chaleur pour les réactions chimiques.**

Blast furnace: haut fournaux
- **Is a steel tower approximately 60 m high, lined with heat resistant bricks. Used to extract iron from its ores hematite and magnetite**
- **C'est un tour d'acier de 60 m de hauteur approximativement, renforcée par des briques résistants. Utilisé pour extraire le fer des minerais.**

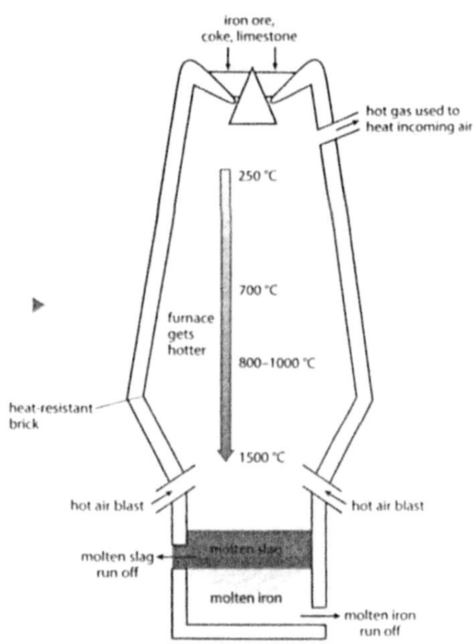

Biochemistry: biochimie
- **Is the research in the field of health.**
- **C'est la recherche dans le domaine de la santé.**

Bismuth: bismuth

- **Is a chemical element.**
- **Known since the 15th century. Studied by Geoffroy le Jeune (France) in 1753.**
- **Etymological origin: *Wismuth* from German.**
- **Its chemical symbol is Bi.**
- **Its atomic number is 83.**
- **Frequently used as fuse wire, an alloy of bismuth and tin (40% to 60%) having a low melting point.**
- **C'est un élément de la classification périodique.**
- **Connu depuis le 15ème siècle. Etudié par Geoffroy le Jeune (France) en 1753.**
- **Origine étymologique: *Wismuth* de l'allemand.**
- **Son symbole chimique est Bi.**
- **Son numéro atomique est 83.**
- **Utilisé fréquemment comme fil fusible, un alliage de bismuth et d'étain (40 % à 60 %), qui possède un point de fusion très bas.**

Boiling hot: bouillant

Boiling point: point (température) d'ébullition

- **The highest temperature attainable by a body to evaporate in gaseous form.**
- **La température la plus élevée que peut atteindre un corps avant de s'évaporer, sous forme gazeuse.**

Bond: liaison

- **Single, double, triple bond.**
- **Liaison simple, double et triple.**

Brine: saumure

- **Very salty water.**
- **Eau très salé.**

Bromine: brome

- **Is a chemical element.**
- **Bromine is a halogen. It is a volatile liquid dark red, irritating odor.**
- **Discovered by Balard (France) in 1826.**
- **Etymological origin: *bromôs* (stink) from Greek.**
- **Its chemical symbol is Br.**
- **Its atomic number is 35.**

- **Commonly used in lamps halogenated, fire extinguishers and colorants in cosmetics.**
- **C'est un élément de la classification périodique.**
- **Le brome un halogène. C'est un liquide volatil rouge sombre, d'odeur irritante.**
- **Découvert par Balard (France) en 1826.**
- **Origine étymologique: *bromôs* (puanteur) du grec.**
- **Son symbole chimique est Br.**
- **Son numéro atomique est 35.**
- **Couramment utilisé dans les lampes halogènes, les extincteurs et les colorants en cosmétique.**

Bronsted acid: acide de Bronsted
- **A molecular entity capable of donating a hydron (proton) to a base, (i.e. a 'hydron donor') or the corresponding chemical species.**
- **Une entité moléculaire capable de donner un ion H^+ (proton) à une base ou une autre espèce chimique.**

Buffer solution: solution tampon
- **A buffer solution is a solution where pH does not vary much when you add a small amount of acid, base or if we dilute it in moderation. A buffer solution is used to maintain a constant pH.**
- **Une solution tampon est une solution dont le pH varie peu lorsqu'on y ajoute une petite quantité d'acide, de base ou lorsqu'on la dilue de façon modérée. Une solution tampon est utilisée pour maintenir le pH d'une solution constante.**

Build up: assembler

C

Cadmium: cadmium

- **Is a metallic chemical element.**
- **Identified by Stromeyer (Germany) in 1817.**
- **Etymological origin: *Kadmeia* (Kadmos city) from Greek.**
- **Its chemical symbol is Cd.**
- **Its atomic number is 48.**
- **The hint of yellow is a bit of cadmium oxide, a favorite pigement of the impressionist painters.**
- **C'est un élément métallique de la classification périodique.**
- **Identifié par Stromeyer (Allemagne) en 1817.**
- **Origine étymologique: *Kadmeia* (cité de Kadmos) en grec.**
- **Son symbole chimique est Cd.**
- **Son numéro atomique est 48.**
- **La touche de jaune, c'est de l'oxyde de cadmium, un pigment de prédilection des peintres impressionnistes.**

Cesium: césium

- **Is a chemical element.**
- **Discovered by Robert Bunsen (Germany) and Gustav Kirchhoff (Prussia) in 1861.**
- **Etymological origin: *caesius* (bleu marin) from Latin.**
- **Its chemical symbol is Cs.**
- **Its atomic number is 55.**
- **Used in the atomic clock. Pure cesium is a silver-gold coloured metal that melts just above room temperature. It is uncommon only because it combines so easily with other common elements.**
- **C'est un élément de la classification périodique.**
- **Découvert par Robert Bunsen (Allemagne) et Gustav Kirchhoff (Prusse) en 1861.**
- **Origine étymologique: *caesius* (marine blue) du latin.**
- **Son symbole chimique est Cs.**
- **Son numéro atomique est 55.**
- **Utilisé dans l'horloge atomique. Le césium pur est un métal de couleur argent-or qui fond juste au-dessus de la température ambiante. Il n'est pas commun parce qu'elle s'associe si facilement avec d'autres éléments communs.**

Cesium atomic clock: horloge atomique au cesium

- **Cesium atomic clocks are used since 1950, which are the world's best timekeepers.**
- **Les horloges atomiques au césium sont utilisées depuis 1950, ce sont les meilleurs gardiens mondiaux du temps.**

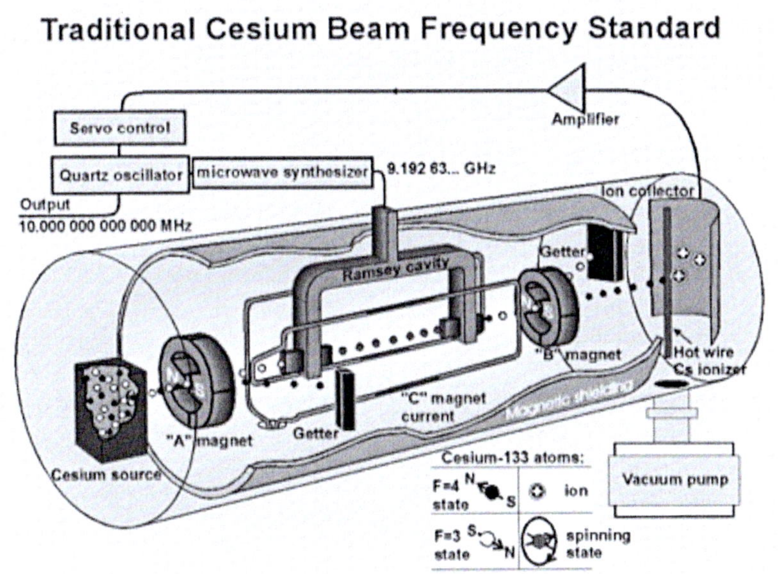

Calcium: calcium
- **Is a metallic chemical element.**
- **Isolated by Davy (England) in 1808.**
- **Etymological origin: *calx* (lime) from Latin.**
- **Its chemical symbol is Ca.**
- **Its atomic number is 20.**
- **Pure metallic calcium has few applications.**
- **C'est un élément métallique de la classification périodique.**
- **Isolé par Davy (Angleterre) en 1808.**
- **Origine étymologique: *cals* (chaux) du latin.**
- **Son symbole chimique est Ca.**
- **Son numéro atomique est 20.**
- **Le calcium à l'état pur a très peu d'utilisations.**

Calcium carbonate: carbonate de calcium

- White crystalline salt occurring in limestone, chalk, marble, calcite, coral, and pearl: used in the production of lime. Formula: $CaCO_3$.
- Sel cristallin blanc, on le trouve dans le calcaire, craie, marbre, calcite, corail et perle : utilisé dans la production de l'eau de chaux. Sa formule chimique: $CaCO_3$.

Californium: californium
- Is a radioactive chemical element.
- Fabricated by Thomson, Street, Ghioro and Seaborg in1950.
- Etymological origin: *California* (state in USA).
- Its chemical symbol is Cf.
- Its atomic number is 98.
- Used as convenient portable neutron source for detection of precious metals and in oil well logging.
- C'est un élément radioactif de la classification périodique.
- Origine étymologique: *California* (état aux USA).
- Son symbole chimique est Cf.
- Son numéro atomique est 98.
- Utilisé dans les détecteurs portables à source de neutrons pour la détection des métaux précieux et des puits de pétrole.

Calometer: calorimètre
- Is a device used for calorimetry, the science of measuring the heat of chemical reactions or physical changes as well as heat capacity.
- C'est un dispositif destiné à mesurer les échanges de chaleur d'une réaction chimique ou physique.

Carbon: carbone
- Is a chemical element.
- Known since the antiquity.
- Etymological origin: *carbo* (coal) from Latin.
- Its chemical symbol is C.
- Its atomic number is 6.
- Graphites and diamonds are pure carbon.
- C'est un élément de la classification périodique.
- Connu depuis l'antiquité.
- Origine étymologique: *carbo* (charbon) du latin.
- Son symbole chimique est C.
- Son numéro atomique est 6.
- Les graphites et les diamants sont de carbone pur.

Carbon dioxide: dioxyde de carbone

- **Gas produced during all processes of combustion. Chemical expression: CO2. It is responsible for the greenhouse effect.**
- **Gaz produit lors de combustion. Sa formule chimique est CO_2. Il est responsable de l'effet de Serre.**

Carbon monoxide: monoxyde de carbone

- **Gas produced during incomplete combustions. Scentless, uncolored, very toxic gas.**
- **Gaz produit lors des combustions incomplètes. Il est sans odeur, incolore et très toxique.**

Carbon nanotubes: tube nanocarbone

- **Are allotropes of carbon with a cylindrical nanostructure. These carbon molecules have new properties, making them potentially useful in many applications in nanotechnology, electronics, optics, and other fields of science materials.**
- **Ce sont des tubes en forme allotropique de carbone. Ils sont utilisé dans le demain de nanotechnologie, en électronique, en optique et dans d'autres domaine de matériels scientifiques.**

Carboxylic acid: acide carboxylique

- **RCOOH**

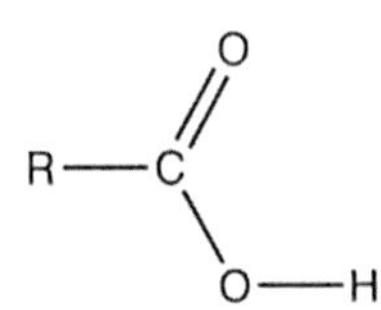

- **Is an organic compound that has one acyl group. The functional group for a carboxylic acid is a carbonyl group (-COOH), this group has one oxygen double bonded to the carbon atom and the OH group then bonded to the carbon atom.**
- **Example :**

Complete Structural Formula / Condensed Structural Formula

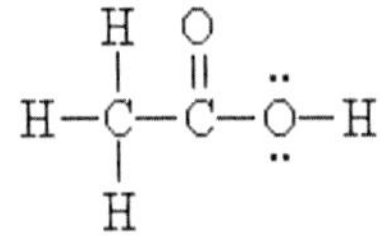

CH_3COOH

- **C'est un composé organique possédant un groupe acyle. Le groupe fonctionnel de l'acide carboxylique est (-COOH), l'atome de car-**

bone possède une liaison double avec un atome d'oxygène et une liaison simple avec OH.
- Voir l'exemple de l'acide acétique ci-dessus.

Cast: coulée

Cast iron: fonte

Catalyst: catalyseur
- A substance that speeds up a reaction without being consumed.
- Une substance qui accélère une réaction sans être consommée.
- When the catalyst and the reactants are all gaseous or in solution (in water or another solvent) it is called homogeneous catalysis. The catalyst and the reagents are in the same phase.
- In homogeneous catalysis, the catalyst efficiency is greater as its concentration in solution is high.
- When the catalyst is solid and the reactants are gaseous or aqueous solution, it is called heterogeneous catalysis.

  In heterogeneous catalysis, the surface of the solid catalyst in contact with the reactants plays an important role in the reaction.
- Enzymes are biological molecules that act as catalysts. These are proteins, that is to say molecules consisting of the sequence of several hundred amino acids.

  When a reaction is catalyzed by an enzyme is called enzymatic catalysis. During an enzymatically catalyzed reaction, the reactants are dissolved in the same liquid phase as the enzyme. Enzyme catalysis is a special case of homogeneous catalysis.
- Lorsque le catalyseur et les réactifs sont tous gazeux ou tous en solution (dans l'eau ou dans un autre solvant), on parle de catalyse homogène. Le catalyseur et les réactifs sont donc dans la même phase.
- En catalyse homogène, l'efficacité d'un catalyseur est d'autant plus grande que sa concentration en solution est élevée.
- Lorsque le catalyseur est solide et que les réactifs sont gazeux ou en solution aqueuse, on parle de catalyse hétérogène. En catalyse hétérogène, la surface du catalyseur solide en contact avec les réactifs joue un rôle primordial dans la réaction.
- Les enzymes sont des molécules biologiques agissant comme des catalyseurs. Ce sont des protéines, c'est-à-dire des molécules constituées par l'enchaînement de plusieurs centaines d'acides aminés.
- Lorsqu'une réaction est catalysée par une enzyme, on parle de catalyse enzymatique. Au cours d'une réaction de catalyse enzymatique,

les réactifs sont en solution dans la même phase liquide que l'enzyme. La catalyse enzymatique est donc un cas particulier de la catalyse homogène.

Celsius: célsius

- **A scale on a thermometer where the interval between the boiling point and the freezing point of water is divided into 100 degrees. Freezing point is represented by 0 degrees and boiling point is represented by 100 degrees. The same scale is also utilized in Centigrade.**
- **Unit of temperature.**
- **Symbol °C.**
- **C'est une échelle thermométrique ou l'intervalle entre le point d'ébullition et le point de congélation est divisé par cent. Le point de congélation est représenté par 0 et le point d'ébullition est représenté par 100. La même échelle est utilisée pour le Centigrade.**
- **Unité de la température.**

Centrifuging: centrifugation

- **The process of separating different particles in suspension in a liquid by a movement of very quick rotation.**
- **C'est le processus de séparation de diffèrent particules en suspension dans un liquide par un mouvement rotatif très rapide.**

Cerium: cérium

- **Is a radioactive chemical element.**
- **Discovered by Klaproth (Germany) and Berzelius (Sweden) in 1803.**
- **Etymological origin: *Ceres* (asteroid).**
- **Its chemical symbol is Ce.**
- **Its atomic number is 58.**
- **Used in lighter flints because it catches fire easily when struck.**
- **C'est un élément radioactif de la classification périodique.**
- **Découvert par Klaproth (Allemagne) et Berzelius (Suède) en 1803.**
- **Origine étymologique: *Cérès* (asteroïde).**
- **Son symbole chimique est Ce.**
- **Son numéro atomique est 58.**
- **Utilisé dans les pierres à briquet parce qu'il s'enflamme facilement lorsqu'il est frappé.**

Change of state: changement d'état

- **Change from one state (solid, liquid or gas) to another state.**
- **Changement d'un état solide, liquide ou gazeux en un autre.**

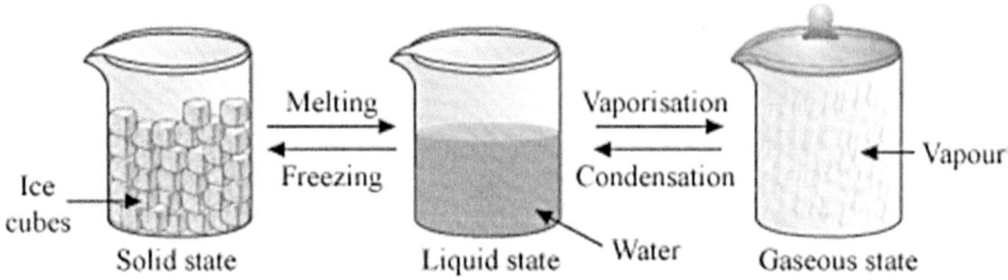

Chemical compound: composé chimique

- A chemical compound is a pure chemical substance consisting of two or more different chemical elements.
- C'est une substance chimique pure, composée d'atomes de deux ou plus d'éléments chimiques différents.

Chemical equilibrium: équilibre chimique

- When the rate of the forward reaction equals the rate of the reverse reaction and the concentration of products and reactants remains unchanged.
- Quand la réaction se fait dans les deux sens de façon identique et les concentrations des produits et les réactifs restent inchangés.

Chemical reaction rate: vitesse de réaction chimique

Chemistry: chimie

- Is the science of matter and the changes it undergoes.
- C'est la science de la matière et sa transformation.

Chemical energy: énergie chimique

- During a chemical reaction, energy appears: in the form of warmth, or light. There can be movement or an explosion.
- Lors des réactions chimiques, une énergie apparait sous forme de chaleur ou de lumière. Un mouvement peut avoir lieu ou une explosion.

Chemical species: espèces chimiques

Chemical symbol: symbole chimique

- Letter or group of letters representing a chemical element.

- **Une lettre ou un groupe de lettres qui représentent un élément chimique.**

Chemical dye: chimie de teinture

Chemical product: produit chimique

Chirality: chiralité

- **A chiral molecule is one that is not superimposable on its mirror image (our hands are chiral).**
- **The chiral molecules are called Enantiomers.**
- **Une molécule est chirale si elle non superposable à son image dans miroir (nos mains sont chirales).**
- **Les molécules chirales sont des Enantiomères.**

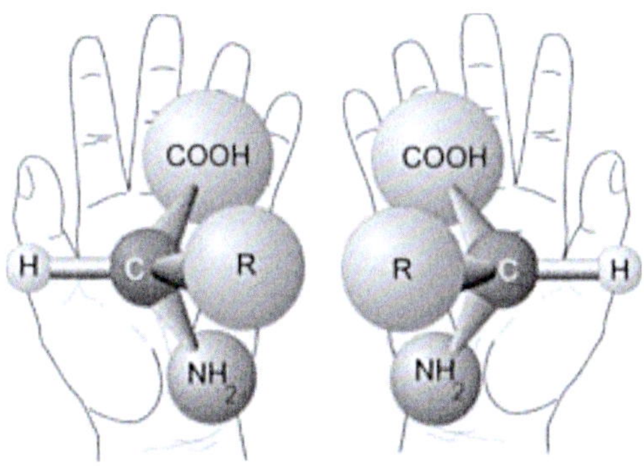

Chlorine: chlore

- **Is a chemical element.**
- **Known since ancient time.**
- **Etymological origin: *khlôros* (pale green) from Greek.**
- **Its chemical symbol is Cl.**
- **Its atomic number is 17.**
- **It is mainly used tu purifie drinking water and swimming pool. Combined with sodium, chlorine makes common table salt.**
- **C'est un élément de la classification périodique.**
- **Connu depuis l'antiquité.**
- **Origine étymologique: *khlôros* (vert pale) du grec.**
- **Son symbole chimique est Cl.**
- **Son numéro atomique est 17.**

- Utilisé essentiellement pour purifier l'eau potable et l'eau des piscines. Combiné avec le sodium, il devient le sel de cuisine.

Chlorofluorocarbon (CFC): chlorofluorocarbure (CFC)
- Is an organic compound that contains carbon, chlorine, and fluorine, produced as a volatile derivative of methane and ethane.
- Ce sont des gaz composés dérivés des alcanes, où tous les atomes d'hydrogène ont été substitués par des atomes de chlore et de fluor. Ce sont des produits dérivés de méthane et d'éthane.

Chromatography (thin layer chromatography TLC): chromatographie (chromatographie sur couche mince CCM)
- Technology of separation of chemical components in solution in a homogeneous mixture, which uses the difference in the rates of migration of components carried by a solvent called the eluent on a support.
- Technique physique de séparation et d'identification d'espèces chimique dans une solution appelée éluant.
- The component can be identified by calculating R_F.
- R_F = Distance travelled by the component / Distance travelled by the solvent front.
- Les espèces chimiques peuvent être identifiées en calculant le rapport frontal R_F.
- R_F = Distance parcourue par l'espèce chimique / Distance parcourue par le front de solvant.

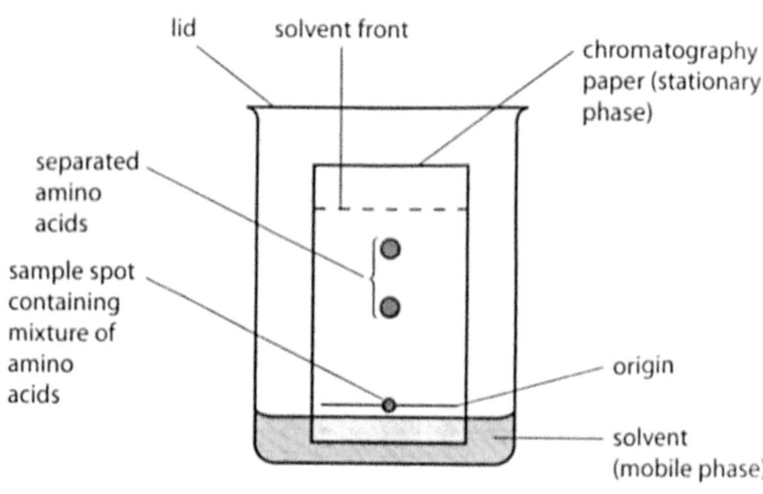

Chromium: chrome

- **Is a chemical element.**
- **Discovered by Vauquelin (France) in 1797.**
- **Etymological origin: *krôma* (color) from Greek.**
- **Its chemical symbol is Cr.**
- **Its atomic number is 24.**
- **Many things are chrome-plated. This process is called electrowinning.**
- **C'est un élément de la classification périodique.**
- **Découvert par vauquelin (France) en 1797.**
- **Origine étymologique : *krôma* (couleur) du grec.**
- **Son symbole chimique est Cr.**
- **Son numéro atomique est 24.**
- **Beaucoup de choses sont chromés. Ce processus est appelé extraction électrolytique.**

Cloud: nuage

- **A visible body of very fine water droplets or ice particles suspended in the atmosphere at altitudes ranging up to several kilometers above sea level.**
- **Un corps visible constitué de fine goulettes d'eau ou de particules de glaces suspendues dans l'atmosphère à des altitudes de plusieurs kilomètres au-dessus de niveau de la mer.**

Cobalt: cobalt

- **Is a metallic chemical element.**
- **Isolated by Brandt (Sweden) in 1735.**
- **Etymological origin: *kobold* (evil genius) from German.**
- **Its chemical symbol is Co.**
- **Its atomic number is 27.**
- **Used in pigments, notably cobalt blue, and in high-strength, high temperature steel alloys.**
- **C'est un élément métallique de la classification périodique.**
- **Isolé par Brandt (Suède) en 1735.**
- **Origine étymologique: *kobold* (mauvais génie) de l'Allemand.**
- **Son symbole chimique est Co.**
- **Son numéro atomique est 27.**
- **Utilisé dans les pigments, spécialement le cobalt bleu, et il est utilisé dans le domaine de haute résistance notamment les alliages des aciers à hautes température.**

Coulometry: coulométrie

- Is the technique in analytical chemistry that determines the amount of matter transformed during an electrolysis reaction by measuring the amount of electricity consumed or produced.
- C'est une technique utilisée en chimie analytique qui détermine la quantité de matière transformée lors d'une réaction d'électrolyse en mesurant la quantité d'électricité consommée ou produite.

Colourant: colorant

- A dye or similar reagent.
- C'est une teinture ou un réactif semblable.

Color indicator: indicateur coloré

- Large organic molecules with low acid-base properties and the color depend on the pH of the solution in which it is present.
- Grosse molécule organique ayant des propriétés acide-base faibles et dont la couleur dépend du pH de la solution dans laquelle elle se trouve.

Combustion: combustion

- A chemical process in which two compounds react together to produce heat and light.
- Une réaction chimique entre deux composants produisant chaleur et lumière.

Comet: comète

- Frozen masses of gas and dust which have a definite orbit through the solar system.
- Une masse congelée de gaz et de poussière qui a une orbite définie dans le système solaire.

Component: composant

Compact: compact

- Closely and firmly united or packed together.
- Étroitement et fermement uni ou empaqueté ensemble.

Compound: composé (chimique)

Compressible: compressible

- **A substance for which the volume can be reduced without changing the quantity.**
- **Une substance pour laquelle le volume peut être réduit sans changer la quantité.**

Compression: compression

- **The volume decreases as the pressure increases at constant temperature.**
- **Le volume décroit quand la pression augmente à température constante.**

Concrete: béton

- **Is a mixture of cement, sand and stones.**
- **C'est un mélange de ciment, du sable et des pierres.**

Condensation: condensation

- **Change of state from gas to solid.**
- **Changement d'état du gaz en solide.**

Concentrated sulphuric acid: acide sulfurique concentré

Concentration: concentration

- **Molar concentration C_n: is the amount of a constituent 'n' (mole) divided by the volume of the mixture 'V' (liter).**
- **$C_n = n/V$ ($mol.L^{-1}$).**
- **Concentration molaire C_n: est la quantité de matière 'n' (mole) divisée par le volume de la solution 'V' (litre).**
- **$C_n = n/V$ ($mol.L^{-1}$).**
- **Mass concentration C_m: is the amount of a constituent 'm' (grams) divided by the volume of the mixture 'V' (liter).**
- **$C_m = m/V$ ($g.L^{-1}$).**
- **Concentration massique C_m: est la masse d'une matière 'm' (gramme) divisée par le volume de la solution 'V' (litre).**
- **$C_m = m/V$ ($g.L^{-1}$).**

Condenser: réfrigérant

- **A piece of laboratory glassware used to cool hot vapors or liquids.**

- **Un instrument de verrerie du laboratoire utilisé pour refroidir les vapeurs ou les liquides.**

Condensed structural formula: formule semi-développée

- **Condensed structural formula.**
- **Formule semi-développée.**
- **Full structural formula.**
- **Formule développée.**

Conformational isomerism: stéréo-isomère de confirmation

- **A conformational molecule is a form of stereoisomerism in which the isomers can be interconverted by rotation around a single bond. It can takes infinity of rotational positions.**

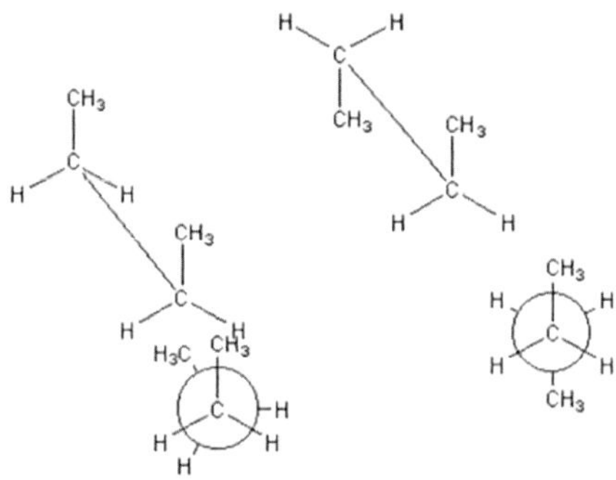

- **It is important to understand that the transition from one conformation to another happened without breaking the single bonds.**
- **On appelle conformations d'une molécule, les différentes structures spatiales qu'elle peut prendre par suite de rotations autour de ses liaisons simples : il en existe une infinité de rotation possible.**
- **Il est fondamental de comprendre que le passage d'une conformation à une autre se fait sans rupture des liaisons simples.**

Conservation of atoms: conservation des atoms

- **During a chemical reaction, the reacting atoms are conserved when the products are formed.**
- **Pendant une réaction chimique, les atomes réagissant sont conservés quand les produits sont formés.**

Contamination: contamination

Continuous Fractional Distillation of Petroleum: distillation frac-

tionnée continue du pétrole

- **The oil industry uses fractional distillation. Crude petroleum oil is vaporized and fed into a massive fractionating column, which may be 30 to 60 m high and 3 to 6 m in diameter. Different fractions, such as gasoline and kerosene, are drawn off continuously from the column at different levels.**
- **L'industrie pétrolière utilise une distillation fractionnée. Le pétrole brut est vaporisé et introduit dans une colonne de fractionnement massif, qui peut aller de 30 à 60 m de haut et de 3 à 6 m de diamètre. Différents produits fractionnés, comme l'essence et le kérosène, sont soutirés en continu de la colonne à des niveaux différents**

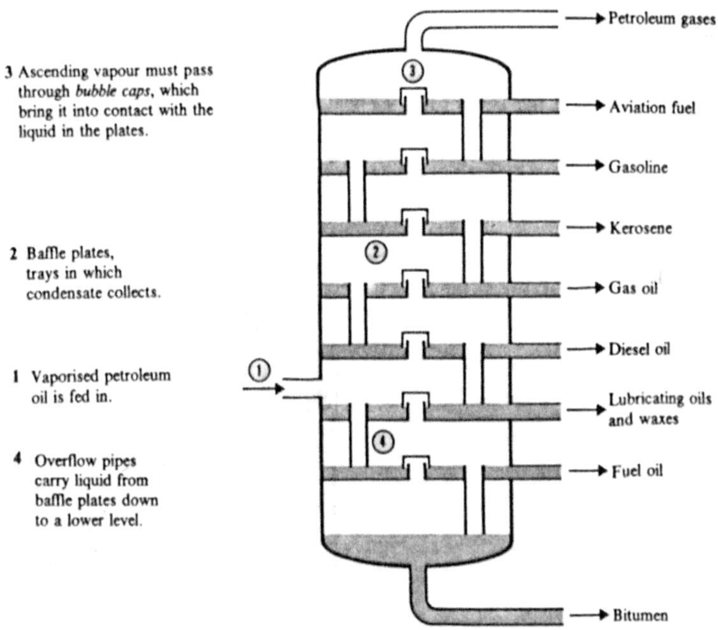

Copper: cuivre

- **Is a metallic chemical element.**
- **Probably discovered 6000 before JC.**
- **Etymological origin: *cypres* (Cyprus Island).**
- **Its chemical symbol is Cu.**
- **Its atomic number is 29.**
- **Used in the industry of wiring, heat sinks and coins.**
- **C'est un élément métallique de la classification périodique.**
- **Probablement découvert 6000 ans avant JC.**
- **Origine étymologique: *cypres* (Isle de Chypre).**

- **Son symbole chimique est Cu.**
- **So numéro atomique est 29.**
- **Utilisé dans l'industrie du câblage, les dissipateurs de chaleur et les pièces de monnaies.**

Corona: couronne
- **The very hot outermost layer of a star's atmosphere. Our Sun's corona can only be seen during a total solar eclipse.**
- **C'est une couche très chaude qui entoure une étoile. La couronne solaire peut être visible lors d'une éclipse totale de soleil.**

Corrosion: corrosion
- **Reaction between metal and the gas in air, the metal is oxidized to form an oxide layer on surface.**
- **Réaction entre un métal et un gaz dans l'air, le métal est oxydé pour former une couche de rouille à sa surface.**

Corrosive: corrosive
- **Responsible for corrosion.**
- **Agent responsable de la corrosion.**

Cosmological: cosmologique
- **Having to do with the study of the history, structure, and changes in the universe.**
- **C'est l'étude du changement dans l'univers de point de vue historique et structurelle.**

Coulometer: coulomètre
- **Is a cell in which measurements can be made of the quantity of electricity passed and the masses of substances liberated at or dissolved from the electrodes.**
- **C'est une cellule dans laquelle des mesures peuvent être faites de la quantité d'électricité transmise et les masses des substances libérées ou dissous à partir des électrodes.**

Covalent bond: liaison covalente
- **Is a form of chemical bonding that is characterized by the sharing of pairs of electrons between atoms, and other covalent bonds.**
- **C'est une liaison chimique dans laquelle chacun des atomes liés met en commun un électron d'une de ses couches externes afin de former un doublet d'électrons liant les deux atomes.**

Critical point: point critique

- Critical temperature and pressure (for water, T_c=374°C and Pc=218 atm).
- Température et pression critique (pour l'eau T_c=374°C et Pc=218 atm).

Critical pressure: pression critique

- Pressure required liquefying at the critical temperature.
- Pression atteint pour liquéfier à la température critique.

Critical temperature: température critique

- Temperature above which the vapor cannot be liquefied.
- Température au-dessus de laquelle le vapeur ne peut pas être liquéfié.

Curium: curium

- Is a radioactive chemical element.
- Fabricated by Seaborg, James and Ghiorso (USA) in 1944.
- Etymological origin: *Curie* (Pierre and Marie Curie).
- Its chemical symbol is Cm.
- Its atomic number is 96.
- Used in scientific specialized research institutions.
- C'est un élément radioactif de la classification périodique.
- Fabriqué par Seaborg, James et Ghiorso (USA) en 1944.
- Origine étymologique : *Curie* (Pierre et Marie Curie).
- Son symbole chimique est Cm.
- Son numéro atomique est 96.
- Utilisé dans les institutions spécialisées de recherches scientifiques.

Cyclohexane: cyclohexane

- Cyclohexane is a saturated cyclic hydrocarbon of the family cycloalkanes of molecular formula C_6H_{12}. Cyclohexane is used as a polar solvent in the chemical industry, but also as a reagent for the industrial production of nylon.
- Le cyclohexane est un hydrocarbure cyclique saturé de la famille des cyclo alcanes de formule brute C_6H_{12}. Le cyclohexane est utilisé comme solvant apolaire dans l'industrie chimique, mais aussi comme réactif pour la production industrielle du nylon.
- The structural formula of cyclohexane :

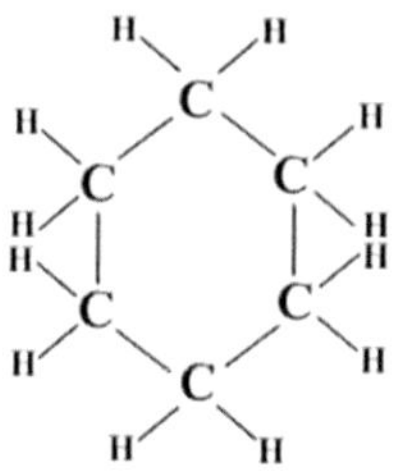

- **La formule développée de cyclohexane.**

Crystallizer: cristallisoir

- **Is a cylindrical container used for crystallization.**
- **C'est un récipient de forme cylindrique, dans lequel on effectue des cristallisations.**

D

Daniel cell (dry cell): pile Daniel

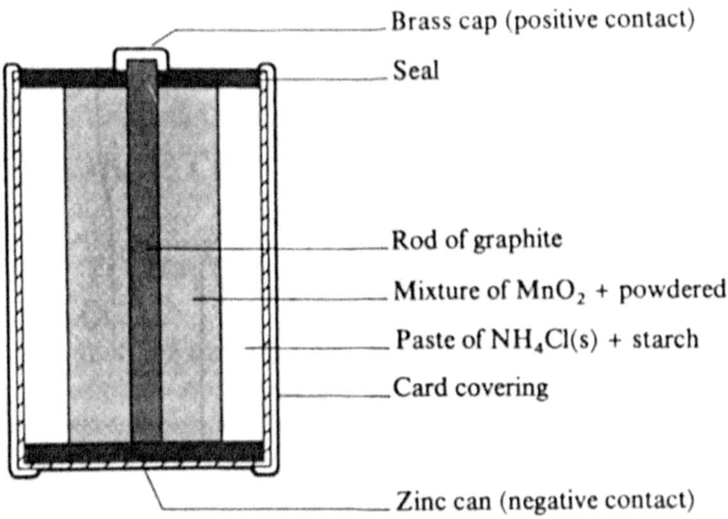

Dark matter: matière noire

- **Around 90 per cent of the Universe could be made from a mysterious type of matter known as dark matter. Scientists do not yet know what dark matte ris made from, but it could contain new types of particles that have not yet been discovered.dark matter cannot be seen or detected directly, but scientists beleive it is there because of the effect it seems to be because of the effect it seems to be having on matter that we can see.**
- **Environ 90 pour cent de l'Univers pourrait être fait à partir d'un type mystérieux de la matière appelée la matière noire. Les scientifiques ne savent pas encore à partir de quoi cette sombre matière est fabriquée mais il pourrait contenir de nouveaux types de particules qui n'ont pas encore été découvert. La matière noire ne peut pas être vu ou détecté directement, mais les scientifiques pensent qu'elle est là en raison de l'effet qu'elle semble avoir sur la matière que nous pouvons voir.**

Dew: rosée
- **Droplets of water deposited on grass in the morning due to the condensation of atmospheric moisture.**
- **Gouttes d'eau déposées sur l'herbe le matin par condensation de l'humidité atmosphérique.**

DNA (deoxyribonucleic acid): ADN acide désoxyribonucléique
- **Is a nucleic acid that contains the genetic instructions used in the development and functioning of all known living organisms.**
- **C'est une molécule, présente dans toutes les cellules vivantes, qui renferment l'ensemble des informations nécessaires au développement et au fonctionnement d'un organisme.**

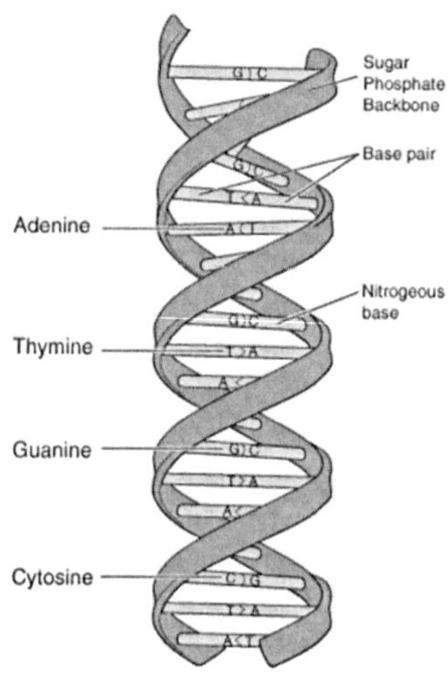

Drugs: drogues
- **A chemical that effects how the body works.**
- **Un produit chimique affectant le comportement du corps.**

Droplets: gouttes
- **Small quantity of a liquid in a round form.**
- **Petite quantité d'eau en forme arrondi.**

Diffusion: diffusion
- **The process of one substance spreading through another.**
- **Le processus de propagation d'une substance par une autre.**

Dilute (to): diluer

Dispersed: dispersé

- **Distributed throughout the whole of the volume.**
- **Dispersé partout dans un volume donné.**

Disinfectant: désinfectant

Dissolving: dissolution

- **The action of obtaining a homogeneous solution by stirring a solid, a liquid or a gas in a solvent.**
- **C'est l'action nécessaire pour obtenir une solution homogène en dissolvant un solide, un liquide ou un gaz dans un solvant.**

Dissolve: dissoudre

- **The substance (solute) added to a solvent becomes evenly dispersed.**
- **Une substance ajoutée à un solvant.**

Distillate: distillat

- **The liquid obtained by distillation.**
- **Un liquide obtenu par distillation.**

Distillation: distillation

- **The process of separating a mixture of liquids by heating, the vapor of the liquid with the lowest boiling point comes off first and is condensed back to a liquid in a condenser.**
- **C'est le processus de séparation des liquides dans une solution par chauffage, le premier liquide obtenu est celui qui possède la température d'ébullition la plus basse, qu'on refroidit grâce un réfrigérant.**

Divided: divisé

- **To become separated into components or parts.**
- **Séparer des composants.**

Distilled water: eau distillée

- **Water which has had salts removed by distillation. It is done by distillation or ion exchange.**
- **Eau sans sels minéraux, éliminé par distillation ou par échange ionique.**

Drinkable: potable

- **It can be drunk without any damage to health.**
- **Peut-être bu sans danger pour la santé.**

Dubnium: dubnium

- **Is a radioactive chemical element.**
- **Discovered by Russian scientists in 1968.**
- **Etymological origin: *Dubna* (city in Russia).**
- **Its chemical symbol is Db.**
- **Its atomic number is 105.**
- **C'est un élément radioactif de la classification périodique.**
- **Son symbole chimique est Db.**
- **Découvert par une équipe de scientifiques Russe en 1968.**
- **Origine étymologique: *Dubna* (ville Russe).**
- **Son numéro atomique est 105.**

Dyes: colorants, teintures

- **Is a colored substance that has an affinity to the substrate to which it is being applied.**
- **C'est l'action utilisée par le teinturier pour faire absorber un colorant par le support et qui se mélange à sa couleur initiale.**

Dysprosium: dysprosium

- **Is a radioactive chemical element.**
- **Its chemical symbol is Dy.**
- **Discovered by Lecoq de Boisbaudran (France) in 1886.**
- **Etymological origin: *dusprositos* (difficult to achieve) from Greek.**
- **Its atomic number is 66.**
- **Used in the coating of hard disk drives.**
- **C'est un élément radioactif de la classification périodique.**
- **Son symbole chimique est Dy.**
- **Découvert par Lecoq de Boisbaudran (France) en 1886.**
- **Origine étymologique: *dusprositos* (difficile à atteindre) du grec.**
- **Son numéro atomique est 66.**
- **Utilisé dans le revêtement des disques durs.**

E

Electrolysis: életrolyse
- **In an electrolysis cell, the positive electrode is called the cathode and the negative electrode is called the anode.**
- **L'électrode positive est appelée cathode et l'électrode négative est appelée anode.**

Electrolyte: électrolyte
- **A substance whose aqueous solution conducts an electric current.**
- **Une substance dans l'état aqueux conduit un courant électrique.**

Electronic shell: couche électronique
- **An electron shell is an orbit followed by electrons around an atom's nucleus. The closest shell to the nucleus is called the "K shell", followed by the "L shell", then the "M shell", and so on further and further from the nucleus. The shell letters K, L, M, are alphabetical.**
- **Un atome est composé d'un noyau entouré de couches électroniques qui contiennent chacune un nombre donné d'électrons qui gravitent autour du noyau. Les couches électroniques sont symbolisées par des lettres, successivement, en partant de la plus proche du noyau K, L, M, etc..... par ordre alphabétique.**

Electrophoresis: électrophorèse
- **C'est une technique qui permet la séparation des acides α-aminés, des protèines ou des fragments d'ADN.**
- **Is a technique that allows the separation of α-amino acids, proteins or DNA fragments.**

Effervescence: effervescence
- **The formation of gaseous bubbles in a liquid by chemical reaction.**
- **Formation des bulles de gaz dans un liquide par réaction chimique.**

Einsteinium: einsteinium
- **Is a radioactive chemical element.**
- **Its chemical symbol is Es.**
- **Synthesized by an American team such as Seaborg and Thomson in 1951.**
- **Etymological origin: *Einstein* (Albert Einstein).**
- **Its atomic number is 99.**
- **No known applications for the moment.**

- C'est un élément radioactif de la classification périodique.
- Son symbole chimique est Es.
- Synthétisé par une équipe américaine dont Seaborg et Thomson en 1950.
- Origine étymologique: *Einstein* (Albert Einstein).
- Son numéro atomique est 99.
- Pas d'application connue pour le moment.

Electrochemical cell: cellule électrochimique
- Is a cell in which a chemical reaction results in the production of an electric current.
- C'est une cellule dans laquelle une réaction produit un courant électrique.

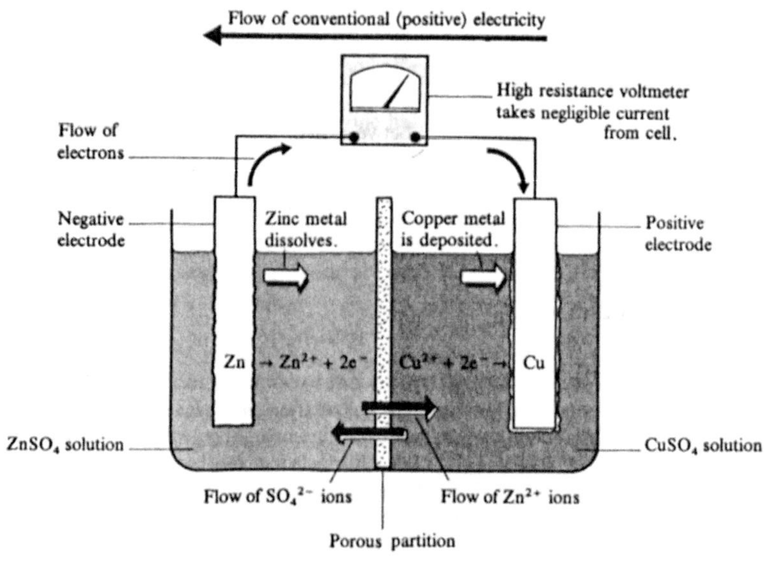

Electrode: électrode
- A piece of metal or graphite placed in an electrolyte via which current enters or leaves.
- Pièce métallique ou de graphites placés dans un électrolyte par laquelle un courant électrique passe.

Electron: électron
- Basic particle of negative load which orbits around the nucleus of the atom.

- **Particule basique de charge négative qui gravite autour du noyau atomique.**

Eluent: éluant

- **Liquid used during a chromatography, in which the bottom of the support is submerged.**
- **Solvant utilisé pour effectuer la chromatographie, dans lequel le bas du support est submergé.**

Erbium: erbium

- **Is a radioactive chemical element.**
- **Its chemical symbol is Er.**
- **Discovered by Mosander (Sweden) in 1842, isolated by Urbain (France) in 1905.**
- **Etymologic origin: *Ytterby* (Sweden city).**
- **Its atomic number is 68.**
- **Used to improve the information carrying capability in the fiber optic cables.**
- **C'est un élément radioactif de la classification périodique.**
- **Découvert par Mosander (Suède) en 1842, isolé par Urbain (France) en 1905.**
- **Origine étymologique: *Ytterby* (cité Suédoise).**
- **Son symbole chimique est Er.**
- **Son numéro atomique est 68.**
- **Utilisé pour améliorer la transmission des informations dans les cables de fibre optique.**

Esterification: esterification

- **Is a chemical reaction in which an ester – COO – is obtained by condensation of a carboxylic acid –COOH and an alcohol – OH.**
- **C'est une réaction chimique dans laquelle un ester – COO – est obtenu par condensation d'un groupe acide carboxylique – COOH et d'un groupe alcool – OH.**

$$R\text{-}COOH + R'\text{-}OH = R\text{-}COO\text{-}R' + H_20$$

Empirical formula: formule brute

- **In chemistry it is the simplest whole number ratio of the atoms it contains. For example, the empirical formula of the alkane C_2H_6 is CH_3.**
- **En chimie, la formule brute correspond au rapport de nombre entier le plus simple des atomes qu'il contient. Example, la formule brute de l'alcane C_2H_6 est le CH_3.**

Emulsion: émulsion

- Formed when fine droplets of one liquid are in suspension in another liquid. The two liquids are not miscible.
- Se forme lorsque des gouttes d'un liquide se forment en suspension dans un autre liquide.

Enantiomer: énantiomère

- One of two stereoisomers that are mirror images of each other and non-superimposable. Organic compounds that contain a chiral carbon usually have two non-superimposable structures. Example:

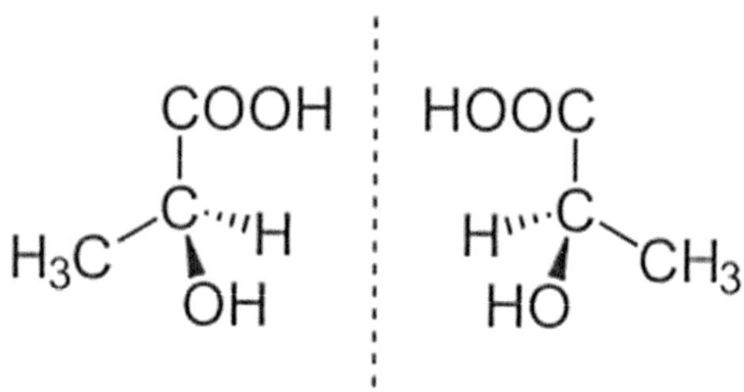

- Two stereoisomers non enantiomers are called diastereoisomers.
- Equal amounts of an enantiomers (chiral molecule) mixture are called racemic mixture.
- Deux stéréo-isomères de configuration, non superposables, et images l'un de l'autre dans un miroir plan, sont appelés énantiomères.
- Deux stéréo-isomères non énantiomères sont appelés diastéréoisomères.
- Un mélange équimolaire de deux énantiomères est dit racémique.

Endothermic reactions: réaction endothermique

- Processes in which energy is absorbed as it proceeds and surroundings become colder.
- Lorsqu'une réaction chimique absorbe de la chaleur pour se réaliser.

Energy transfer: transfert d'énergie

Enthalpy change: variation d'enthalpie

- The enthalpy change, ΔH, that accompanies a reaction is the amount of heat liberated or absorbed as a reaction proceeds at a given temperature, T, at constant pressure P.
- The SI units of enthalpy, H, are joules, J. Usually we work with molar quantities and then of H and ΔH are $Jmol^{-1}$ or $kJmol^{-1}$.
- $\Delta H = \Delta U + PV$
- La variation d'enthalpie, ΔH, qui accompagne une réaction est la quantité de chaleur libérée ou absorbée en tant que produit de réaction à une température donnée, T et à pression constante P.
- L'unité de l'enthalpie H dans le SI est exprimé en joule J. Souvent les calculs sont réalisés en quantités de matière donc H et ΔH sont exprimés en $J.mol^{-1}$ ou $kJ.mol^{-1}$.

Enthalpy of combustion: enthalpie de combustion

Enthalpy of formation: enthalpie de formation

Entropy: entropie

- Is the amount of heat in or out a body, or a system, divided by the temperature at which the transfer takes place. Entropy is the measure of the disorder of a system; the higher the entropy, the greater the disorder.
- C'est la quantité de chaleur dans ou hors d'un corps ou d'un système, divisée par la température à laquelle a lieu le transfert. L'entropie est la mesure du désordre d'un système, plus l'entropie est élevé, plus le désordre est élevé.

Enzyme (catalyst): catalyse enzymatique

- A large molecule (usually a protein) that catalyzes biological reactions.
- Une molécule (protéine) qui catalyse des réactions biologiques.
- The enzyme acts as catalysts.
- Lorsque le catalyseur est une enzyme.

Equivalent dose: dose équivalente

Ether: éther

- The functional group for ethers is –O– where the oxygen is bonded on both sides to a carbon atom.

- Example : dimethyl ether

Complete Structural Formula

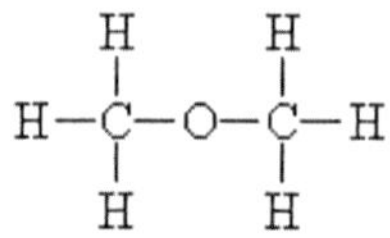

Condensed Structural Formula

CH_3OCH_3

- Le groupe fonctionnel des éthers est l'oxygène –O– attaché à deux atomes de carbone.
- Voir l'exemple ci-dessus.

Europium: europium
- Is a radioactive chemical element.
- Its chemical symbol is Eu.
- Discovered by Demarcay (France) in 1901.
- Etymologic origin: *Europe* (continent).
- Its atomic number is 63.
- Used in phosphors for cathode ray TV screens and in compact fluorescent bulbs.
- C'est un élément radioactif de la classification périodique.
- Découvert par Demarcay (France) en 1901.
- Origine étymologique: *Europe* (continent).
- Son symbole chimique est Eu.
- Son numéro atomique est 63.
- Utilisé dans les luminophores pour écrans cathodiques et des ampoules fluorescentes compactes.

Exothermic reaction: réaction exothermique
- Chemical reaction gives out heat and surroundings become warmer.
- Lorsqu'une réaction chimique dégage de la chaleur.

Eyepiece: oculaire
- Is a type of lens that is attached to a variety of optical devices such as telescopes and microscopes.
- C'est un système optique complémentaire de l'objectif. Il est utilisé dans les instruments tels que les microscopes ou les télescopes pour agrandir l'image.

F

Fat: corps grass, triester.

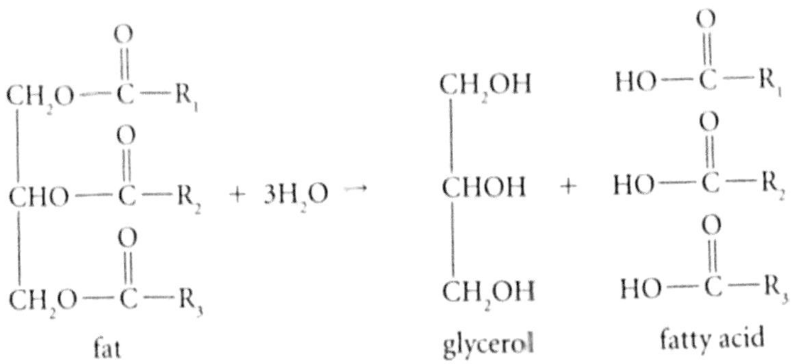

Fatty acid: acide gras

Fermium: fermium

- **Is a radioactive chemical element.**
- **Discovered by Albert Ghiorso in 1952.**
- **Etymological origin: *Fermi* (Enrico Fermi) Italian scientists.**
- **Its chemical symbol is Fm.**
- **Its atomic number is 100.**
- **No known applications.**
- **C'est un élément radioactif de la classification périodique.**
- **Son symbole chimique est Fm.**
- **Découvert par Albert Ghiorso en 1952.**
- **Origine étymologique: *Fermi* (Enrico Fermi) scientifique italien.**
- **Son numéro atomique est 100.**
- **Pas d'applications connues.**

Flammable: inflammable

Fluorine: fluor

- **Is a chemical element.**
- **Its chemical symbol is F.**

- **Identified by Scheele (Sweden) in 1771 and isolated by Moissan (France) in 1886.**
- **Etymologic origin: *fluor* (flowing) from Latin.**
- **Its atomic number is 9.**
- **C'est un élément de la classification périodique.**
- **Son symbole chimique est F.**
- **Identifié par Scheele (Suède) en 1771 et isolé par Moissan (France) en 1886.**
- **Origine étymologique: *fluor* (écoulement) du latin.**
- **Son numéro atomique est 9.**

Filtrate: filtrat
- **Product resulting from filtering.**
- **Produit obtenu par filtration.**

Filtration: filtration
- **Separation of the solid particles in suspension in a heterogeneous mixture often with the aid of filter paper.**
- **Séparation des particules solide dans une solution hétérogène, souvent grâce à un filtre.**

Floculation: floculation
- **Gathering in form of small flakes, of very fine solid particles in suspension in water.**
- **C'est une agrégation de matières en suspension formant des flocs dans l'eau.**

Flow measurement: débitmètre
- **Is a device used for measuring the flow of liquids.**
- **C'est un appareil qui sert à mesurer le débit des liquides.**

Fractional distillation: distillation fractionnée
- **Is a process used to separate the components of a mixture of liquids by means of the difference in their boiling temperatures.**
- **C'est un processus de séparation des composants dans un mélange grâce à leurs différentes températures d'ébullition.**

Francium: francium
- **Is a chemical radioactive element.**

- **Its chemical symbol is Fr.**
- **Discovered by Marguerite Perey (France) in 1939.**
- **Etymological origin: *France* (country).**
- **Its atomic number is 87.**
- **Uranium and thorium minerals produce francium in vanishingly small quantities.**
- **C'est un élément radioactif de la classification périodique.**
- **Son symbole chimique est Fr.**
- **Découvert par Marguerite Perey (France) en 1939.**
- **Origine étymologique: *france* (pays).**
- **Son numéro atomique est 87.**
- **L'uranium et le thorium produisent le francium en infinitésimale petites quantités.**

Frost (hard rime): givre (gelée blanche)
- **Ice deposited on objects, acquired by solidification of a mist.**
- **Glaces déposés sur les objets obtenus par solidification de brume.**

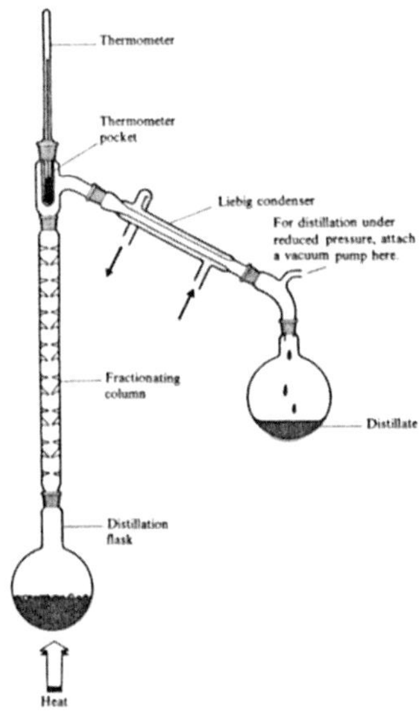

Free surface: surface libre
- **A boundary between two homogeneous fluids.**
- **Frontière entre deux liquides homogènes.**

Fog: brouillard

- Is a collection of water droplets or ice crystals suspended in the air.
- C'est un amas de fines gouttelettes ou de fins cristaux de glace suspendue dans l'air.

Fuel: combustible, carburant
- Substance which undergoes combustion.
- Substance qui peut bruler.

Fuel cell: pile à combustible

Functional group identeties: groupes fonctionnels
- Are sub molecular structural motifs, characterized by specific elemental composition and connectivity that confer reactivity upon the molecule that contains them.
- Common functional groups :

Chemical class	Group	Formula	Suffix
Amines	primary Amine	R−NH_2	-amine
	secondary Amine	R−N(−H)−R'	-amine
	tertiary Amine	R−N(−R')−R	-amine
Imines	primary Imine	R−C(=NH)−R'	-imine
	secondary Imine	R−C(−H)=N−R'	-imine
Amide	Amide	R−C(=O)N(−H)−R'	
Carboxylic acid	Carboxyl	R−C(=O)OH	-oic acid
Alcohol	Hydroxyl	R−OH	-ol
Carbonyl	Aldehyde	R−C(=O)H	-al
	Ketone	R−C(=O)−R'	-one

Ester	**Ester**	**R−C(=O)O−R'**	**-oate**
Ether	**Ether**	**R−O−R'**	
Alkanes	**Methyl**	**R−CH_3**	**-ane**
Alkenes	**Alkene**	**R−CH=CH−R'**	**-ene**
Alkynes	**Alkyne**	**R−CC−R'**	**-yne**
Phenyl	**Phenyl**	**R−C_6H_5**	**-yle**

- **Les groupes fonctionnels sont les motifs submoléculaires, caractérisés par la composition élémentaires spécifiques, qui confèrent la réactivité des molécules qui les contiennent.**
- **Les groupes fonctionnels les plus répondus sont dans le tableau ci-dessus.**

Fume hood: hotte
- **Is a type of local ventilation device that is designed to limit exposure to hazardous or noxious fumes, vapors or dusts.**
- **C'est un dispositif qui permet l'extraction des vapeurs toxiques des produits utilisés lors de manipulations.**

Fusion: fusion
- **Transition from solid state to liquid state**
- **Changement d'état solide en état liquide.**

G

Gadolinium: gadolinium

- **Is a radioactive chemical element.**
- **Its chemical symbol is Gd.**
- **Detected by Jean-Charles Galissard de Marigna in 1880 and isolated Paul-Émile Lecoq de Boisbaudran (France) in 1886.**
- **Etymological origin: *Gadolin* (Johan Gadolin) Finnish chemist and geologist.**
- **Its atomic number is 64.**
- **Used in patient RMI scan injections to improve the contrast.**
- **C'est un élément radioactif de la classification périodique.**
- **Son symbole chimique est Gd.**
- **Découvert Jean Charles Galissard de Marigna en 1880 et isolé par Paul-Émile Lecoq de Boisbaudran (France) en 1886.**
- **Origine étymologique: *Gadolin* (Johan Gadolin) chimiste et géologiste finlandais.**
- **Son numéro atomique est 64.**
- **Utilisé dans les injections des patients subissant de scan RMN pour améliorer le contraste.**

Gallium: gallium

- **Is a metallic chemical element.**
- **Its chemical symbol is Ga.**
- **Provided by Mendeleïev in 1871.**
- **Discovered by Lecoq de Boisbaudran (France) in 1875.**
- **Etymological origin: *gallus* (coq) inventor's name.**
- **Its atomic number is 31.**
- **Alloys of gallium, indium and tin are replacing mercury in thermometers.**
- **C'est un élément métallique de la classification périodique.**
- **Son symbole chimique est Ga.**
- **Prévu par Mendeleïev en 1871.**
- **Découvert par Lecoq de Boisbaudran (France) en 1875.**
- **Origine étymologique: *gallus* (coq) d'après le nom de son inventeur.**
- **Son numéro atomique est 31.**
- **Utilisé en alliage avec l'indium et de l'étain pour remplacer le mercure dans les thermomètres.**

Galvanic cell: Pile galvanique

- Galvanic cell (also called voltaic cell) uses chemical reaction to produce electrical energy (flow of electrons).
- Pile galvanique (également appelé cellule voltaïque) utilise une réaction chimique pour produire de l'énergie électrique (flux d'électrons).

Gas: gaz
- Compressible and expansible formless material.
- Matériaux compressible et expansible.

Germanium: germanium
- Is a metallic chemical element.
- Its chemical symbol is Ge.
- Provided by Mendeleïev in 1871.
- Discovered by Winkler (Germany) in 1886.
- Etymological origin: *Germania* (Germany).
- Its atomic number is 32.
- Used in light emitting diodes and semiconductors.
- C'est un élément métallique de la classification périodique.
- Son symbole chimique est Ge.
- Prédi par Mendeleïev en 1871.
- Découvert par Winkler (Allemagne) en 1886.
- Origine étymologique: *Germania* (Germany).
- Son numéro atomique est 32.
- Utilisé dans diodes électroluminescentes et les semi-conducteurs.

Glass fibre: fibre de glass
- A composite material.
- Matériaux composite.

GLP: GPL
- Gas of liquefied oil. Fuel used for car motors. It is a mixture of propane and butane.
- Gaz utilisé comme combustible pour les voitures. C'est un mélange de propane et butane.

Gloves: gants
- Used in chemistry laboratory for hand's protection.
- Utilisé pendant les séances de travaux pratiques pour protéger les mains.

Gold: or

- **Is a metallic chemical element.**
- **Known since ancient time.**
- **Etymological origin: *aurum* (shining dawn) from Latin.**
- **Its chemical symbol is Au.**
- **Its atomic number is 79.**
- **Used in jewelry and computer's microprocessors.**
- **C'est un élément métallique de la classification périodique.**
- **Connu depuis le temps ancien.**
- **Origine étymologique: aurum (aurore brillant) du latin.**
- **Son symbole est Au.**
- **Son numéro atomique est 79.**
- **Utilisé en bijouterie et dans les microprocesseurs des ordinateurs.**

Graph: graphe
- **Graphic presentation of the variations of a measurable greatness.**
- **Représentation graphique des variables des grandeurs mesurées.**

Group of materials: famille ou groupe de matériaux

H

Hafnium: hafnium

- **Is a metallic chemical element.**
- **Its chemical symbol is Hf.**
- **Identified by Hevesy de Heves (Sweden) and Coster (Hollande) in 1923.**
- **Etymological origin: *kobenhavn* (Copenhagen), capital of Denmark.**
- **Its atomic number is 72.**
- **C'est un élément métallique de la classification périodique.**
- **Identifié par Hevesy de Heves (Suède) et Coster (Pays Bas) en 1923.**
- **Origine étymologique : *kobenhavn* (Copenhagen), capital de Danemark.**
- **Son symbole chimique est Hf.**
- **Son numéro atomique est 72.**

Hassium: hassium

- **Is a radioactive chemical element.**
- **Its chemical symbol is Hs.**
- **Synthesized by Peter Armbruster and Gottfried Munzenberg (Germany) in 1984.**
- **Etymological origin: *Hessen* (state in Germany).**
- **Its atomic number is 108.**
- **No applications.**
- **C'est un élément métallique de la classification périodique.**
- **Synthétisé par Peter Armbruster et Gottfried Munzenberg (Allemagne) en 1984.**
- **Origine étymologique: *Hessen* (état en Allemagne).**
- **Son symbole chimique est Hs.**
- **Son numéro atomique est 108.**
- **Pas d'applications.**

Harmful: nocif

Hazard: danger, risque, péril

Heat: chauffer

Helium: helium

- Is a chemical element.
- Its chemical symbol is He.
- Discovered by Jansen (France) in 1868 and isolated by Ramsay (England) in 1895.
- Etymological origin: *hêlios* (sun) from Greek.
- Very light, colorless, not inflammable gas, glows pale peach when an electric current runs through it.
- Its atomic number is 2.
- C'est un élément de la classification périodique.
- Découvert par Jansen (France) en 1868 et isolé par Ramsay (Angleterre) en 1895.
- Origine étymologique : *hêlios* (soleil) du grec.
- Gaz non inflammable très léger.
- Son numéro atomique est 2.
- C'est un gaz très légèr, sans couleur, inflammable il a une lueur pâle pêche lorsqu'il est traversé par un courant électrique.

Heterogeneous: hétérogène
- A blend of several constituents which can be differentiated by the naked eye.
- Solution de plusieurs composants distingués à l'œil nu.

Heterogeneous catalyst: catalyse hétérogène
- Present in a different phase than reacting molecules.
- C'est un catalyse dans un état physique diffèrent que les réactifs.

Holmium: holmium
- Is a radioactive chemical element.
- Its chemical symbol is Ho.
- Discovered by Clève in 1879.
- Etymologic origin: *Stockholm* (Sweden city).
- Its atomic number is 67.
- Used in pole pieces of the medical imaging magnets.
- C'est un élément radioactif de la classification périodique.
- Découvert par Clève en 1879.
- Origine étymologique : *Stockholm* (cité Suédoise).
- Son symbole chimique est Ho.
- Son numéro atomique est 167.
- Utilisé dans les aimants d'imageries médicales.

Homogeneous catalyst: catalyse homogène
- Present in the same phase as the reacting molecules.

- **C'est une catalyse dans un état physique identique que les réactifs.**

Horizontal: horizontale
- **Perpendicular direction in the vertical direction given by a thread with lead.**
- **Droite perpendiculaire.**

Hydrate: hydrate
- **A salt that contains water of crystallization. (It is hydrated). The salt becomes an anhydrate if the water is removed.**
- **Sel qui contient de l'eau de cristallisation. Le sel devient anhydre si l'eau est retirée.**

Hydrocarbons: hydrocarbures
- **Hydrocarbons comprise the simplest series of organic compounds. These compounds are composed of carbon and hydrogen atoms in single, double, and triple bonds. Depending on the type of central bond present, the hydrocarbon can be classified as an alkane (single bond), alkene (double bond), or alkyne (triple bond). A diene contains two double bonds.**
- **Les hydrocarbures sont les composés organiques les plus simples. Ils sont constitués des atomes de carbones et d'hydrogènes liés par des liaisons simple, double ou triple. Selon les liaisons présentes, l'hydrocarbure est classé comme an alcane (liaison simple), alcène (liaison double) ou alcyne (liaison triple). Si la molécule contient deux liaisons double, elle est appelée diène.**

Hydrogen: hydrogène
- **Is a chemical element.**
- **Its chemical symbol is H.**
- **Isolated by Cavendish (England) in 1766.**
- **Etymological origin: *udôr* and *genos* (water) from Greek.**
- **Its atomic number is 1.**
- **Very light, inflammable, uncolored and scentless gas, 75% of the visible universe is hydrogen.**
- **C'est un élément de la classification périodique.**
- **Isolé par Cavendish (Angleterre) en 1766.**
- **Origine étymologique : *udôr* and *genos* (eau) du grec.**
- **Son symbole chimique est H.**
- **Son numéro atomique est 1.**
- **Gaz inflammable, incolore, sans odeur et très léger, 75% de l'univers visible est formé d'hydrogène.**

Hydrolysis: hydrolyse
- **Is the splitting of a compound by reaction with water.**
- **C'est la separation d'un compose par reaction avec de l'eau.**

Hydrous: hydraté
- **Substance that contains water.**
- **Substance qui contient de l'eau.**

Hydrophilic: hydrophile ou lipophobe
- **Attracted to the water (polar head), part of an emulsifier molecules.**
- **Attiré par l'eau, une partie d'une espèce amphiphile.**

Hydrophobic: hydrophobe ou lipophile
- **Attracted to oil (non-polar tail), part of an emulsifier molecule.**
- **Attiré par les huiles, possède une propriété détergente.**

I

Ideal gas equation, universal gas equation: equation du gaz parfait
- **The equation of state for an ideal gas.**
- **pV=nRT**

For a gas containing n moles of molecules, at a pressure p in a volume V,

Where T is the absolute temperature and R is the Molar Gas Constant, R=8.31 $JK^{-1}mol^{-1}$.
- **C'est l'équation d'état d'un gaz parfait.**
- **pV=nRT**

Pour un gaz qui contient n moles de molecules à une pression p dans un volume V,

Ou T est la temperature absolue et R est la constant molaire du gaz, R=8.31 $JK^{-1}mol^{-1}$.

Incandescence: incandescence
- **State of a chemical component which issues light when strongly heated.**
- **Etat d'un composant chimique qui émet de la lumière lorsqu'il est fortement chauffé.**

Industrial Fractionating Column: colonne industriel de distillation

(see Continuous Fractional Distillation of Petroleum)

Iron: fer
- **Is a metallic chemical element.**
- **Its chemical symbol is Fe.**
- **Known since 3000 years ago.**
- **Etymological origin: *ferrum* (iron) from Latin.**
- **Its atomic number is 26.**
- **Used in alloys and manufacturing tools.**
- **C'est un élément métallique de la classification périodique.**
- **Connu depuis 3000 ans.**
- **Origine étymologique : *ferrum* (fer) du latin.**
- **Son symbole chimique est Fe.**
- **Son numéro atomique est 26.**
- **Utilisé dans les alliages et la fabrication des outils.**

Iridium: iridium

- **Is a chemical element.**
- **Its chemical symbol is Ir.**
- **Discovered by Tennant (England) in 1803.**
- **Etymological origin: *iris* (rainbow) from Latin.**
- **Its atomic number is 77.**
- **Used in high-temperature situations, such as spark plug electrodes.**
- **C'est un élément de la classification périodique.**
- **Son symbole chimique est Ir.**
- **Découvert par Tennant (Angleterre) en1803.**
- **Origine étymologique : *iris* (arc en ciel) du latin.**
- **Son numéro atomique est 77.**
- **Utilisé dans des situations à haute température, tels que les électrodes des bougies d'allumage.**

Isomer: isomère

- **Isomers are compounds with different physical and chemical properties but the same molecular formula. In organic chemistry, there are many cases of isomerism. For example, the formula C_4H_{10} represents both butane and 2-methylpropane.**

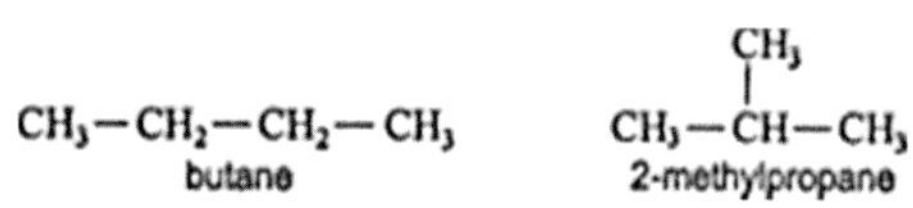

- **Structural isomers: same chemical formula but atoms are bonded in different orders. Example of structural isomers is given by propanol, it has the same chemical formula C_3H_8O but atoms are bonded in different orders:**

Propan-1-ol or propanol	Propan-2-ol
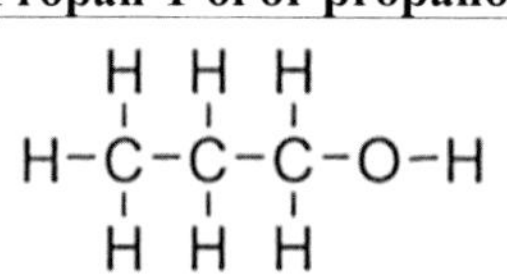	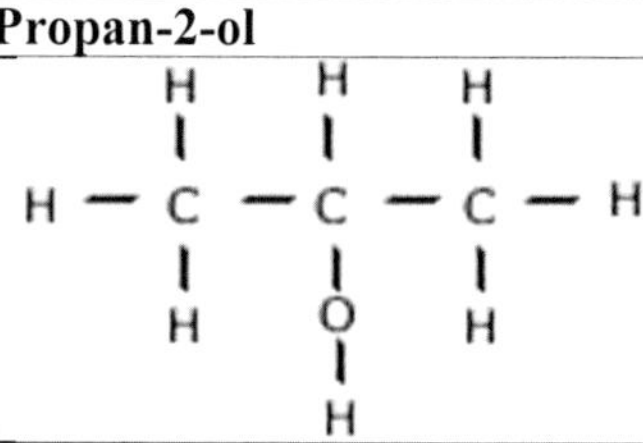

- **Stereoisomers have identical molecular formulas and arrangements of atoms. They differ from each other only in the spatial orientation of groups in the molecule. The simplest forms of stereoisomers are *cis* and *trans* isomers, both of which are created by the restricted ro-**

tation about a double bond or ring system. Butene, C_4H_8, exists in both *cis* and *trans* forms.

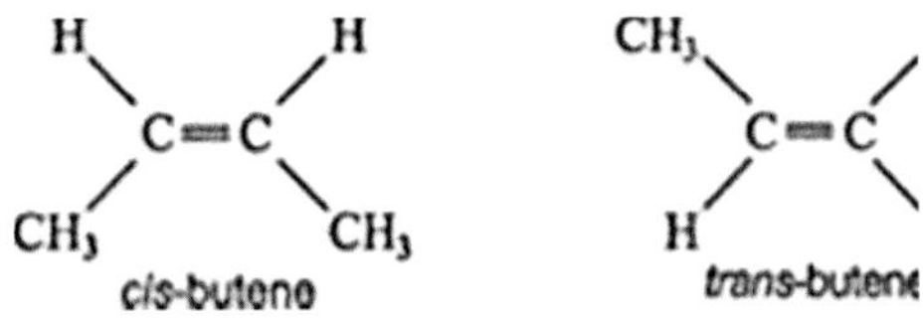

- **Diastereoisomers Z/E or geometric isomers: two or more stereoisomers of a compound that have different configurations and are not mirror images of each other and non-superimposable. Example:**

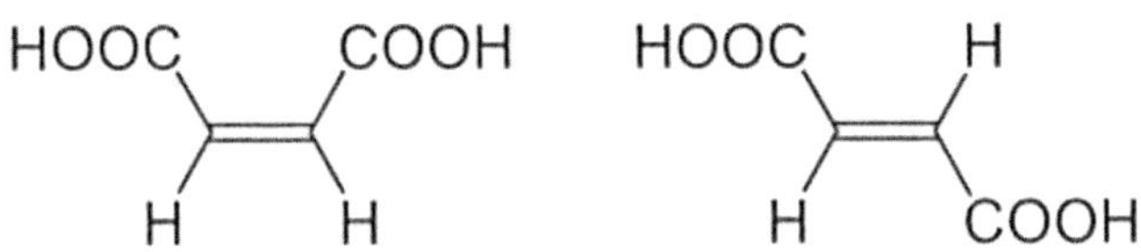

- **Asymmetric carbon atom or optical isomers: different arrangement of four different groups around central atom of carbon. Example:**

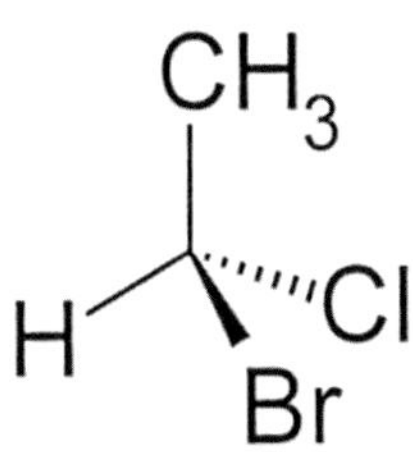

- **Deux molécules différentes ou plus de même formule brute mais de structure moléculaire différente.**
- **Isomères de structure: même formule brute mais les liaisons des atomes sont différentes. Exemple le propanol de formule brute C_3H_8O, il peut avoir deux représentations spatiales différentes, voir le tableau ci-dessus.**
- **Diasteréréoisomerie Z/E: deux molécules de même formule semi-développée, non superposable et qui ne sont pas images l'une de l'autre dans un miroir. Exemple:**

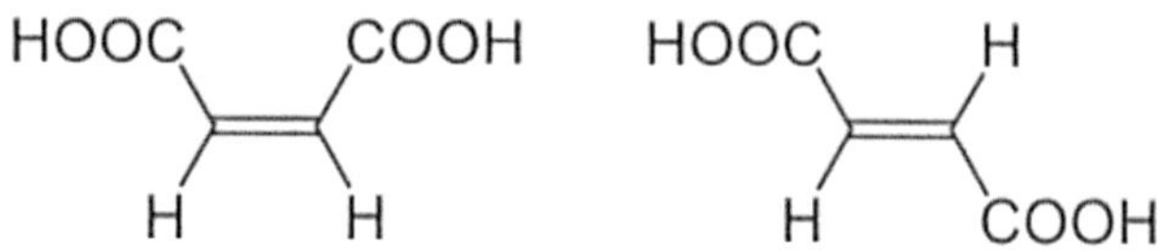

- **Carbone asymétrique: c'est un atome de carbone qui possède quatre substituants de nature différente. Exemple:**

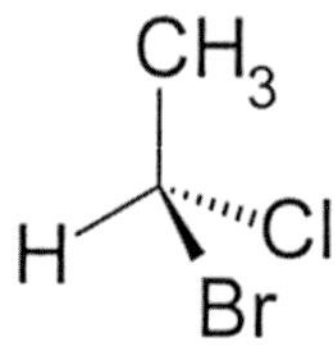

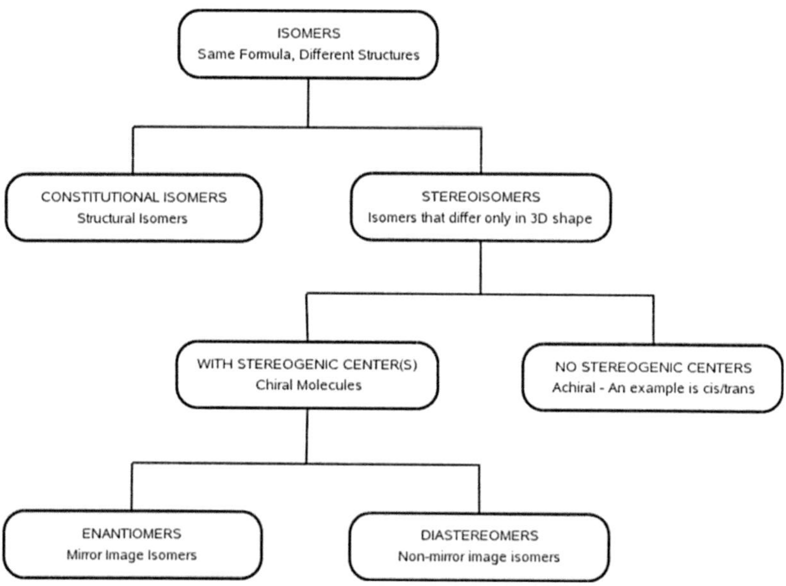

Isotope: isotope

- **Chemical elements can exist as two or more isotopes that have different numbers of neutrons in the nucleus, but they have the same number of protons.**
- **Les éléments chimiques peuvent exister sous forme de deux ou plusieurs isotopes qui ont un nombre différent de neutrons dans le noyau, mais ils ont le même nombre de protons.**

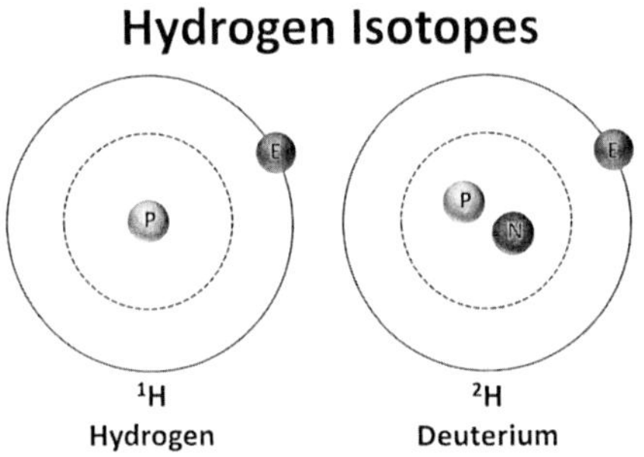

Insoluble: insoluble
- Means does not dissolve in a given solvent.
- Qu'on ne peut pas dissoudre dans solvant.

Iodine: iode
- Is a chemical element.
- Its chemical symbol is I.
- Discovered by Courtois (France) in 1811.
- Etymological origin: *iôdes* (purple) from Greek.
- Its atomic number is 53.
- Used as disinfectants.
- C'est un élément de la classification périodique.
- Son symbole chimique est I.
- Découvert par Courtois (France) en 1811.
- Origine étymologique : *iôdes* (violet) du grec.
- Son numéro atomique est 53.
- Utilisés comme désinfectants.

Ion: ion
- Holder of load in a solution, resulting from an atom or a group of atoms having lost or gained one or several electrons. Negatively charged ions are known as anions and positively charged ions are called cations.
- C'est un atome ou groupe d'atome ayant perdu ou gagné un ou plusieurs électrons. Les ions chargés négativement sont appelés anions et les chargés positivement sont appelés cations.

Ionizing radiation: rayonnement ionisant

Immiscible: non miscible

- **Incapable of being mixed or blended together. Immiscible liquids that are shaken together eventually separate into layers. Oil and water are immiscible.**
- **Incapable de se mélanger ou se combiner ensemble. Exemple l'eau et l'huile.**

Inidium: inidium

- **Is a chemical element.**
- **Its chemical symbol is In.**
- **Discovered by Reich and Richter (Germany) in 1863.**
- **Etymologic origin: *indigo* (blue color).**
- **Its atomic number is 49.**
- **Used in low-melting-point alloys that replace mercury in thermometers, and in flat screen televisions.**
- **C'est un élément de la classification périodique.**
- **Découvert par Reich et Richter (Allemagne) en 1863.**
- **Origine étymologique : *indigo* (couleur bleu).**
- **Son symbole chimique est In.**
- **Son numéro atomique est 49.**
- **Utilisé dans des alliages à bas point de fusion qui remplacent le mercure dans les thermomètres et il est utilisé dans les téléviseurs à écran plat.**

IUPAC: UICPA

- **International Union of Pure and Applied Chemistry.**
- **Union International de la Chimie Pure et Appliquée.**

K

Ketone: cétone

- **A ketone has the carbonyl group bonded through its carbon atom to two other carbon atoms**

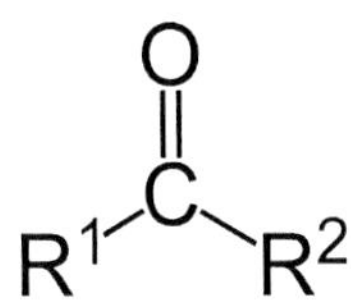

- **Example : acetone**

Complete Structural Formula

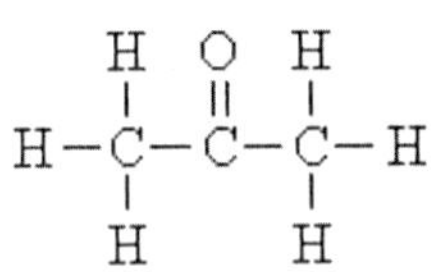

Condensed Structural Formula

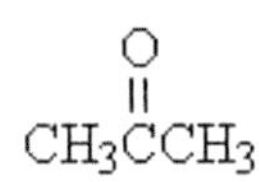

- **Une cétone possède un groupe carbonyle attaché à deux groups alkyls ou aryles.**
- **Exemple : acétone**

Krypton: krypton

- **Is a chemical element.**
- **Its chemical symbol is Kr.**
- **Isolated by Lord Rayleigh and Ramsey (England) in 1894.**
- **Etymologic origin: *kruptos* (hidden) from Greek.**
- **Its atomic number is 36.**
- **Inert gas, glows pale mauve color when excited with a high voltage electric current.**
- **C'est un élément de la classification périodique.**
- **Son symbole chimique est Kr.**
- **Isolé par Lord Rayleigh et Ramsey (Angleterre) en 1894.**
- **Origine étymologique: *kruptos* (caché) du grec.**
- **Son numéro atomique est 36.**
- **Gaz inerte, brille pâle couleur mauve lorsqu'il est excité par un courant électrique à haute tension.**

L

Lanthanum: lanthane

- Is a chemical element.
- Its chemical symbol is La.
- Isolated in 1839 by Carl Gastaf Masander (France). In 1923, lanthanum has been prepared in a pure metallic state.
- Etymologic origin: *lanthanien* (hidden) from Greek.
- Its atomic number is 57.
- Used in electron microscopy and in movie lighting to illuminate vast areas.
- C'est un élément de la classification périodique.
- Son symbole chimique est La.
- Isolé en 1839 par Carl Gustaf Mosander. En 1923, on a préparé pour la première fois du lanthane métallique pur.
- Origine étymologique: *lanthanien* (caché) du grec.
- Son numéro atomique est 57.
- Utilisé en microscopie électronique et de l'éclairage de cinéma pour éclairer de vastes zones.

Latent heat: chaleur latent

- ΔQ is the heat exchanged with the surroundings during a change of state without a change in temperature: freezing, melting, boiling. It is denoted L.
- ΔQ (J) = m (g) x L (J/g)
- C'est la chaleur ΔQ échangée avec le milieu extérieur lors d'un changement d'état sans changement de température: solidification, fusion, ébullition. Elle est notée L.

Lawrencium: lawrencium

- Is a radioactive chemical element.
- Its chemical symbol is Lr.
- Fabricated by Ghiorso, Sikkeland, Larsh and Latmer (USA) en 1961.
- Etymologic origin: Lawrence (Ernest Lawrence) inventeur du synchroton.
- Its atomic number is 103.
- No applications.
- C'est un élément radioactif de la classification périodique.
- Fabriqué par Ghiorso, Sikkeland, Larsh et Latmer (USA) en 1961.

- **Origine étymologique: Lawrence (Ernest Lawrence) inventor of synchroton.**
- **Son symbole chimique est Lr.**
- **Son numéro atomique est 103.**
- **Pas d'applications.**

Lead: plomb
- **Is a metallic chemical element.**
- **Its chemical symbol is Pb.**
- **Known since ancient times.**
- **Etymological origin: *plumbum* (Latin).**
- **Its atomic number is 82.**
- **Used in pipes for hundreds of years.**
- **C'est un élément métallique de la classification périodique.**
- **Connu depuis l'antiquité.**
- **Origine étymologique: *plumbum* (Latin).**
- **Son symbole chimique est Pb.**
- **Son numéro atomique est 82.**
- **Utilisé dans les tuyauteries pour des centaines d'années.**

Lead acid battery: accumulateur au plomb
- **Is used for heavy power applications as it can deliver a high current for short periods of time, which is needed to start an internal combustion engine.**
- **C'est une batterie utilisée pour délivrer un courant puissant pendant une courte durée pour démarrer un moteur à combustion.**

Limewater: eau de chaux
- **Calcium hydroxide ($Ca(OH)_2$ or slaked lime) : white solid which dissolves slightly in water to form limewater. This is weakly alkaline and is used to test for carbon dioxide.**
- **Hydroxyde de calcium $Ca(OH)_2$, solide blanc qu'on dessous dans l'eau distillée pour. Utilisée pour tester le dioxyde de carbone.**

Limestone: calcaire
- **Is a sedimentary rock composed largely of different crystal forms of calcium carbonate $CaCO_3$ and magnesium carbonate $MgCO_3$.**
- **Les calcaires sont des roches sédimentaires facilement solubles dans l'eau composées majoritairement de carbonate de calcium $CaCO_3$ mais aussi de carbonate de magnésium $MgCO_3$.**

Line formula: formule topologique

- A two-dimensional representation of molecular entities in which atoms are shown joined by lines representing single or multiple bonds, without any indication or implication concerning the spatial direction of bond.
- C'est une représentation bidimensionnelle d'une formule chimique ou figure les liaisons entre les atomes.

Lithium: lithium
- Is a chemical element.
- Its chemical symbol is Li.
- Discovered by Arfvedson (Sweden) in 1817 and isolated later by Bunsen (Germany).
- Etymological origin: *lithos* (stone) from Greek.
- Its atomic number is 3.
- Light element, reacts easily with water.
- C'est un élément de la classification périodique.
- Découvert par Arfvedson (Suède) en 1817 et isolé plus tard par Bunsen (Allemagne).
- Origine étymologique: *lithos* (pierre) du grec.
- Son symbole chimique est Li.
- Son numéro atomique est 3.
- Élément très léger et il réagit facilement avec l'eau.

Litmus paper: papier pH
- The litmus paper is a special paper that is soaked in a universal indicator. When you dip a piece of litmus paper in a solution, it takes the tone corresponding to the pH of the medium.
- Le papier pH est un papier spécial qui est imbibé d'un indicateur universel. Lorsque l'on trempe un morceau de papier pH dans une solution, il prend la tonalité correspondant au pH du milieu.

Liquide: liquide
- State of the material not having a clear form, and the volume of which is invariable.
- Etat de la matière qui n'a pas de forme ou de volume déterminés.

Liquid oxygen: oxygène liquide

Limpid: limpide
- Which is perfectly transparent.
- Solution parfaitement transparente.

Liquefaction: liquéfaction
- **Passage from the gaseous state to the liquid state.**
- **Passage de l’état gazeux à l’état liquide.**

LPG: GPL
- **Liquified propane gas.**
- **Gaz propane liquéfié.**

Lutetium: lutécium
- **Is a radioactive chemical element.**
- **Its chemical symbol is Lu.**
- **Discovered by Urbain (France) in 1907.**
- **Etymologic origin: *Lutèce* (ancient name of Paris).**
- **Its atomic number is 71.**
- **No applications.**
- **C’est un élément radioactif de la classification périodique.**
- **Son symbole chimique est Lu.**
- **Découvert par Urbain (France) en 1907.**
- **Origine étymologique: *Lutèce* (nom ancien de la ville de Paris).**
- **Son numéro atomique est 71.**
- **Pas d’applications.**

M

Magnesium: magnésium
- **Is a metallic chemical element.**
- **Its chemical symbol is Mg.**
- **Isolated by Bussy (France) in 1828;**
- **Etymological origin: *Magnesia* (ancient Greek city).**
- **Its atomic number is 12.**
- **Used in lightweight race car components and fire starters.**
- **C'est un élément métallique de la classification périodique.**
- **Son symbole chimique est Mg.**
- **Isolé par Bussy (France) en 1828.**
- **Origine étymologique: *Magnésie* (ancienne ville grecque).**
- **Son numéro atomique est 12.**
- **Utilisé dans les composants légers de voiture de course et les démarreurs.**

Manganese: manganèse
- **Is a metallic chemical element.**
- **Its chemical symbol is Mn.**
- **Discovered by Scheele (Sweden) and isolated by Gahn (Sweden) in 1774.**
- **Etymological origin: called manganese to avoid confusion with magnesium.**
- **Its atomic number is 25.**
- **C'est un élément métallique de la classification périodique.**
- **Découvert par Scheele (Suède) et isolé par Gahn (Suède) en 1774.**
- **Origine étymologique: appelé manganèse pour éviter la confusion avec le magnésium.**
- **Son symbole chimique est Mn.**
- **Son numéro atomique est 25.**

Mass: masse
- **Quantity of material measuring scales.**
- **Mesure d'une quantité de matière.**

Mass concentration: concentration massique
- **Is the mass of solute dissolved in one liter of solution**
- $C_m = m/V$

  C_m: **mass concentration** ($g.L^{-1}$)

  m: mass of the component (g)

V: total volume of the solution (L)

- **C'est la masse d'un soluté dissous dans un litre de solution**
- **$C_m = m/V$**

C_m: concentration massique ($g.L^{-1}$)

m: masse du constituant (g)

V: volume total de la solution (L)

Mass density or density: masse volumique

- **Is the mass of a material per unit volume.**
- **$\rho = m/V$**

ρ: masse density or density ($kg.m^{-3}$)

m: mass of the material (kg)

V: volume of the material (m^3)

- **C'est la masse d'un matériau par unité de volume.**
- **$\rho = m/V$**

ρ: masse volumique ($kg.m^{-3}$)

m: masse du matériau (kg)

V: volume du matériau (m^3)

Mass number (nucleon number) A: nombre de nucleon A

- **Is the number of protons plus the number of neutrons in the nucleus of an atom.**
- **C'est le nombre des protons et le nombre des neutrons dans le noyau d'un atome.**

Mechanical stress: contrainte mécanique

Meitnerium: meitnerium

- **Is a radioactive chemical element.**
- **Its chemical symbol is Mt.**
- **Fabricated by scientific team in Germany in 1982.**
- **Etymological origin: *Meitner* (Lise Meitner) Austrian physicist.**
- **Its atomic number is 109.**
- **No used applications.**
- **C'est un élément radioactif de la classification périodique.**
- **Fabriqué par une équipe scientifique allemande en 1982.**
- **Origine étymologique: *Meitner* (Lise Meitner) physicienne Autrichienne.**
- **Son symbole chimique est Mt.**

- Son numéro atomique est 109.
- Pas d'applications.

Mendelevium: mendélévium

- Is a radioactive chemical element.
- Its chemical symbol is Md.
- Fabricated by Ghiorso, Harvey, Choppin, Thomson and Seaborg (USA) in 1955.
- Etymological origin: *Mendeleïev* (Dimitri Mendeleïev).
- Its atomic number is 101.
- No used applications.
- C'est un élément radioactif de la classification périodique.
- Son symbole chimique est Md.
- Fabriqué par Ghiorso, Harvey, Choppin, Thomson et Seaborg (USA) en 1955.
- Origine étymologique : *Mendeleïev* (Dimitri Mendeleïev).
- Son numéro atomique est 101.
- Pas d'applications.

Meniscus: ménisque

- Is the curve in the upper surface of a liquid close to the surface of the container, caused by surface tension.
- C'est la courbure de la face supérieure d'un liquide dans un récipient à cause de l'attraction exercée par celui-ci.

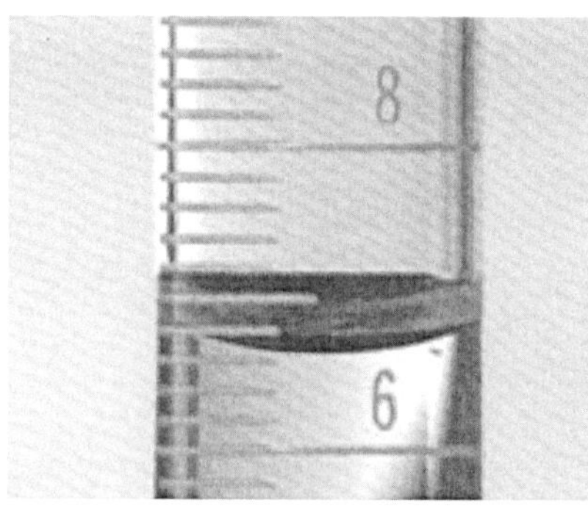

Mercury: mercure

- Is a metallic chemical element.
- Its chemical symbol is Hg.
- Known since ancient antiquity.
- Etymologic origin: *Mercurius* (Gods messenger) from Latin.

- Its atomic number is 80.
- Metal element liquid at room temperature.
- C'est un élément métallique de la classification périodique.
- Son symbole chimique est Hg.
- Connu depuis l'antiquité.
- Origine étymologique: *Mercurius* (messager des dieux) du latin.
- Son numéro atomique est 80.
- Le seul métal liquide à temperature ambiante.

Metallic material: matériau métallique

Mild: douce

Mineral material: matériau minéral

Mixture: mélange
- Solution containing several substances.
- Une solution contenant plusieurs substances.

Miscible: miscible
- Two liquids are miscible when they form a homogeneous mixture.
- Deux liquides sont miscibles lorsqu'ils forment un mélange homogène.

Mobile phase (elution): phase mobile
- Is a term used in analytical and organic chemistry to describe the emergence of chemicals from the column of a chromatograph.
- C'est un procédé permettant de mettre en solution (dite éluée) un composé adsorbé à l'aide d'un solvant nommé l'éluant.

Molar heat of Condensation: chaleur molaire de condensation
- The energy that must be removed in order to convert one mole of gas to liquid at its condensation point.
- C'est l'énergie dégagée pour transformer une mole de gaz en liquide à la température de condensation.

Molar Heat of Fusion: chaleur molaire de fusion
- The energy that must be absorbed in order to convert one mole of solid to liquid at its melting point.

- C'est l'énergie absorbée pour transformer une mole de solide en liquide à la température de fusion.

Molar heat of Solidification: chaleur molaire de solidification
- The energy that must be removed in order to convert one mole of liquid to solid at its freezing point.
- C'est l'énergie dégagée pour transformer une mole de liquide en solide à la température de congélation.

Molar Heat of Vaporization: chaleur molaire de vaporisation
- The energy that must be absorbed in order to convert one mole of liquid to gas at its boiling point.
- C'est l'énergie absorbée pour transformer une mole de liquide en gaz à la température d'ébullition.

Molar mass M: masse molaire M
- Is the mass in grams of one mole of molecule or atom that contains 6.022×10^{23} particles and has units of $g.mol^{-1}$.
- C'est la masse en grammes d'une mole de molécule ou d'un atome qui contient $6,022 \times 10^{23}$ particules et s'exprime en $g.mol^{-1}$.

Molarity: concentration molaire
- Molarity is the number of moles of solute dissolved in one liter of solution
- $C = n/V$

  C: molarity ($mol.L^{-1}$)

  n: quantity of material (mol.)

  V: total volume of the solution (L)
- C'est la quantité de matière d'un soluté dissous dans un litre de solution
- $C = n/V$

  C: concentration molaire ($mol.L^{-1}$)

  n: quantité de matière (mol.)

  V: volume total de la solution (L)

Mole: mole
- A mole (symbol: mol) is the amount of substance of a system which contains as many elementary entities as there are 6.02×10^{23} atoms, ions, molecules, electrons or other particles in 12 grams of carbon-12.

- La mole (symbole: mol) est la quantité de matière d'un système contenant autant d'entités élémentaires $6{,}02x10^{23}$ atomes, ions, molécules, électrons dans 12 g de carbone 12.

Molecule: molécule
- Grouping of atoms linked between them.
- Gouge d'atome lies entre eux.

Molecular formula: formule moléculaire
- The molecular formula of a compound is the actual number of atoms of each type present in a molecule. For example, the molecular formula of ethane is C_2H_6. The molecular formula is a multiple of the empirical formula.
- La formule moléculaire d'un composé est le nombre exact de chaque type d'atoms qui le composent. Example, la formule moléculaire de l'éthane est C_2H_6. La formule moléculaire est un multiple de la formule brute.

Molecular spectroscopy: spectroscopie moléculaire
- Is a device used to identify molecules in a compound.
- C'est un dispositif capable d'identifier les molécules dans un compose chimique.

Molybdenium: molybdène
- Is a metallic chemical element.
- Its chemical symbol is Mo.
- Discovered by Scheele (Sweden) in 1778 and isolated by Moissan (France) in 1895.
- Etymologic origin: *molubdos* (plumb) from Greek.
- Its atomic number is 42.
- Used in high temperature applications.
- C'est un élément métallique de la classification périodique.
- Son symbole chimique est Mo.
- Découvert par Scheele (Suède) en 1778 et isolé par Moissan (France) en 1895.
- Son numéro atomique est 42.
- Utilisé dans le domaine de haute température.

N

Nanotechnology: nanotéchnologie
- **Is the research and technology development in the 1-100 nm range.**
- **C'est la technologie à l'échelle de 1-100 nm.**

Natural compound: matériau naturel

Neodymium: néodyme
- **Is a radioactive chemical element.**
- **Its chemical symbol is Nd.**
- **Discovered by Carl Auer von Welsbach (Austria) in 1885.**
- **Etymological origin: *nêos* and *dîdymos* (new and twin) from Greek.**
- **Its atomic number is 60.**
- **Used in headphones and disk drives.**
- **C'est un élément radioactif de la classification périodique.**
- **Son symbole chimique est Nd.**
- **Découvert par Carl Auer von Welsbach (Autriche) en 1885.**
- **Origine étymologique: *nêos* et *dîdymos* (nouveau et jumeau) du grec.**
- **Son numéro atomique est 60.**
- **Utilisé dans les écouteurs et les lecteurs de disques.**

Neon: néon
- **Is a chemical element.**
- **Its chemical symbol is Ne.**
- **Isolated by Ramsey (England) in 1898.**
- **Etymological origin: *neos* (new) from Greek.**
- **Its atomic number is 10.**
- **Inert gaz, glows bright neon-red when excited by an electric current.**
- **C'est un élément de la classification périodique.**
- **Son symbole chimique est Ne.**
- **Isolé par Ramsey (Angleterre) en 1898.**
- **Origine étymologique: *neos* (nouveau) du grec.**
- **Son numéro atomique est 10.**
- **Gaz inerte, brille de couleur néon-rouge lorsqu'il est excité par un courant électrique.**

Neptunium: neptunium
- **Is a radioactive chemical element.**

- Its chemical symbol is Np.
- Fabricated by Edwin McMillan and Philip Abelson (USA) in 1940.
- Etymological origin: *Neptune* (planet)
- Its atomic number is 93.
- Used in nuclear research.
- C'est un élément radioactif de la classification périodique.
- Son symbole chimique est Np.
- Fabriqué par Edwin McMillan et Philip Abelson (USA) en 1940.
- Origine étymologique: *Neptune* (planète).
- Son numéro atomique est 93.
- Utilisé dans la recherche nucléaire.

Newman projection: projection de Newman

- A Newman projection, visualizes chemical conformations of a carbon-carbon chemical bond from front to back, with the front carbon represented by a dot and the back carbon as a circle.
- La représentation de Newman visualise les différentes conformations vues dans l'axe carbone-carbone, le carbone vu de face est représenté par un point et le carbone de derrière est représenté par un cercle.

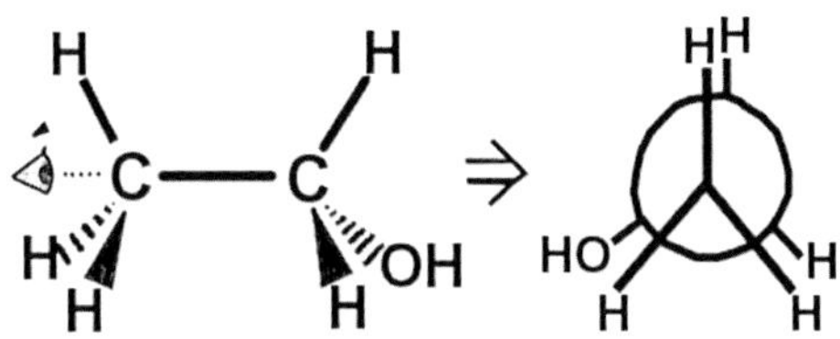

Nickel: nickel

- Is a metallic chemical element.
- Its chemical symbol is Ni.
- Isolated by Cronstedt (Sweden) in 1751.
- Etymological origin: *koppar nickel* (copper-nickel) in Sweden.
- Its atomic number is 28.
- Used in electroplating baths.
- C'est un élément métallique de la classification périodique.
- Son symbole chimique est Ni.
- Isolé par Cronstedt (Suède) en 1751.
- Origine étymologique: *koppar nickel* (cuivre-nickel) en suédois.
- Son numéro atomique est 28.
- Utilisé dans les bains de galvanisation.

Niobium: niobium

- **Is a metallic chemical element.**
- **Its chemical symbol is Nb.**
- **Discovered by Hatchett (USA) in 1801.**
- **Etymological origin: *Niobe* (daughter of Tantalus) from Greek mythology.**
- **Its atomic number is 41.**
- **Used in earrings and tongue studs.**
- **C'est un élément métallique de la classification périodique.**
- **Son symbole chimique est Nb.**
- **Découvert par Hatchett (USA) en 1801.**
- **Origine étymologique: *Niobe* (fille de Tantale) de la mythologie grec.**
- **Son numéro atomique est 41.**
- **Utilisé dans les boucles d'oreilles et les percing des langues.**

Nitrogen: azote

- **Is a chemical element.**
- **Its chemical symbol is N.**
- **Discovered by Rutherford (Scotland) in 1772.**
- **Etymologic origin: *a-zôê* (lifeless) from Greek.**
- **Its atomic number is 7.**
- **Colorless gas makes up 78% of the atmosphere.**
- **C'est un élément de la classification périodique.**
- **Découvert par Rutherford (Ecosse) en 1772.**
- **Origine étymologique: *a-zôê* (sans vie) du grec.**
- **Son symbole chimique est N.**
- **Son numéro atomique est 7.**
- **Gaz incolore qui constitue 78% de l'atmosphère.**

Nobelium: nobélium

- **Is a radioactive chemical element.**
- **Its chemical symbol is No.**
- **Fabricated by Hhiorso, Sikkeland, Walton and Seaborg (USA) in 1958.**
- **Etymologic origin: *Nobel* (Alfred Nobel).**
- **Its atomic number is 102.**
- **No applications.**
- **C'est un élément radioactif de la classification périodique.**
- **Son symbole chimique est No.**
- **Fabriqué par Ghiorso, Sikkeland, Walton et Seaborg (USA) en 1958.**
- **Origine étymologique: *Nobel* (Alfred Nobel).**

- **Son numéro atomique est 102.**
- **Pas d'applications.**

Nonstick: antiadhésif

Nonstick coating: revêtement antiadhésif

Nuclear waste: déchets radioactives
- **Radioactive wastes are wastes that contain radioactive material.**
- **C'est une matière radioactive pour laquelle aucun usage n'est prévu.**

Nucleus: noyau (pour un atome)

O

Octane number: indice d'octane

- **The octane number indicates the resistance of a motor fuel to knock. Octane numbers are based on a scale on which 2,2,4-trimethylpentane (isooctane) is 100 (minimal knock) and heptanes is 0 (maximum knock).**
- **L'indice d'octane est un chiffre permettant de déterminer la valeur antidétonant d'une essence. Les indices d'octane sont basées sur une échelle sur laquelle 2,2,4-triméthylpentane (isooctane) est de 100 (anti détonation minimale) et heptanes est 0 (anti détonation maximale).**

Octet rule: règle d'octet

- **The octet rule is a chemical rule of thumb that states that atoms of $Z>4$ atomic number tend to combine in such a way that they each have eight electrons in their valence shells, giving them the same electronic configuration as a noble gas.**
- **La règle de l'octet est une règle chimique simple qui énonce que les atomes avec un numéro atomique $Z>4$ tendent à se combiner de façon à avoir huit électrons dans leur couche de valence, ce qui leur donne la même structure électronique qu'un gaz noble.**

Osmosis: osmose

- **Is the movement of water from dilute to a concentrated solution through a semi-permeable membrane.**
- **C'est le mouvement des molécules d'eau traversent une membrane semi-perméable qui sépare deux liquides dont les concentrations en produits dissous sont différentes.**

Osmium: osmium

- **Is a metallic chemical element.**
- **Its chemical symbol is Os.**
- **Discovered by Tennant (England) in 1802.**
- **Etymological origin: *some* (smell) from Greek.**
- **Its atomic number is 76.**
- **Used in alloys and in fountain pen tips.**
- **C'est un élément métallique de la classification périodique.**
- **Son symbole chimique est Os.**
- **Découvert par Tenant (Angleterre) en 1802.**
- **Origine étymologique: *osé* (odeur) du grec.**

- **Son numéro atomique est 76.**
- **Utilisé dans les alliages et dans la fontaine de pointe de stylos.**

Organic compound: composé organique

Organic material: matériau organique

Origin: ligne de dépôt (CCM)
- **Line of deposit of chemical species on chromatography paper.**
- **Ligne de dépôt des espèces chimiques sur papier de chromatographie.**

Opaque: opaque
- **Does not allow any light to pass through.**
- **Ne permet à la lumière de passer.**

Overswing: suroscillation

Overtemperature: surchauffe

Overtone: harmonique (son)

Overweight: surcharge, surpoids

Oxidation: oxydation
- **Oxidation occurs when there is an increase in oxidation number of an element.**
- **Une oxydation survient lorsque le nombre d'oxydation d'un élément chimique augmente.**

Oxidation inhibitor: antioxydant

Oxidize: oxyder
- **Is a chemical process where oxygen react with another chemical element.**
- **C'est un processus chimique ou l'oxygène réagit avec un autre élément chimique.**

Oxidizer: oxydant, comburant

Oxidizing agent: oxydant

Oxygen: oxygène

- **Is a chemical element.**
- **Its chemical symbol is O.**
- **Discovered by Priestley (England) in 1774.**
- **Etymological origin: *oxus* and *genos* (generates acid) from Greek.**
- **Its atomic number is 8.**
- **Colorless gas at room temperature and makes up 20% of the atmosphere.**
- **C'est un élément de la classification périodique.**
- **Son symbole chimique est O.**
- **Découvert par Priestley (Angleterre) en 1774.**
- **Origine étymologique: *oxus* et *genos* (engendre l'acide) du grec.**
- **Son numéro atomique est 8.**
- **Gaz incolore à température ambiante et représente 20% de l'atmosphère.**

Oxygen bottle: bouteille d'oxygène

Oxygen mask: masque d'oxygène, inhalateur d'oxygène

Ozone: ozone

- **Is a trioxygen O_3.**
- **C'est un trioxygène O_3.**

Ozone layer: couche d'ozone

Ozonosphere: ozonosphère

P

Palladium: palladium

- **Is a metallic chemical element.**
- **Its chemical symbol is Pd.**
- **Discovered by Wollaston (England) in 1803.**
- **Etymological origin: *Pallas* (asteroid) Greek God of wisdom.**
- **Its atomic number is 46.**
- **Used in jewelery, in the spark plugs of the aircraft, in the production of surgical instruments and in the connections.**
- **C'est un élément métallique de la classification périodique.**
- **Son symbole chimique est Pd.**
- **Découvert par Wollaston (Angleterre) en 1803.**
- **Origine étymologique: *Pallas* (astéroïde) déesse grecque de la sagesse.**
- **Son numéro atomique est 46.**
- **Utilisé en bijouterie, dans les bougies d'allumage des avions, dans la production d'instruments chirurgicaux et dans la connectique.**

Paper of chromatography: papier de chromatographie

Pattern: motif

Parts per millions (ppm): unité de mesure de pollution (0.04 % = 400ppm)

Period (row): période (rangée)

Periodic table (Mendeleïev table of elements):tableau périodique des éléments (tableau de Mendeleïev)

- **The arrangement of the elements according to their atomic number into rows (period) and columns (groups) that displays their reccuring chemical properties.**
- **La disposition des éléments en fonction de leur numéro atomique en lignes (périodes) et en colonnes (groupes) qui affiche les propriétés chimiques récurrentes.**

pH: pH

- **The quantity pH is defined in terms of the activity of hydronium ions in solution.**

- **pH = - log [H_3O^+]**
- **[H_3O^+] = 10^{-pH}**
- **La quantité pH est définie par l'activité des ions hydronium dans une solution.**

pH scale: échèlle pH

- **pH (power of hydrogen).**
- **On this scale, a solution with a pH of 1 is strongly acidic, and a solution with a pH of 14 is strongly alkaline.**
- **Neutral solutions, which are neither acidic nor alkaline, have a pH of 7.**
- **pH (puissance d'hydrogène).**
- **Dans cette échelle, une solution de pH égal à 1 est un acide fort, et une solution de pH égal à 14 est une base forte.**
- **Une solution est neutre, ni acide ni base, son pH est égal à 7.**

Phase: phase

- **Is a homogeneous part of a system which is physically distinct from other parts of the system.**
- **C'est une partie homogène d'un système qui est physiquement distinct des autres parties du système.**

Phenols: phénols

- **Phenols belong to a class of chemical compounds consisting of a hydroxyl functional group (-OH) attached to an aromatic hydrocarbon group. The simplest of the class is phenol (C_6H_5OH).**
- **Phenol is a white crystalline solid, with a chemical formula of C_6H_5OH.**

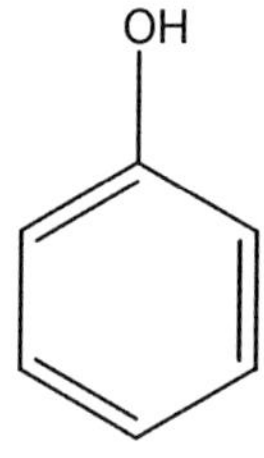

- **Phénols appartient à une classe de produit chimique d'un groupe fonctionnel hydroxyle (-OH) attaché à un groupe d'hydrocarbure aromatique. Le plus simple de la classe est phénol.**
- **C'est un crystal solide blanc dont la formule brute est C_6H_5OH.**

Phosphorus: phosphore

- **Is a chemical element.**
- **Its chemical symbol is P.**
- **Isolated by Brandt (England) in 1669.**
- **Etymological origin: *phôsphoros* (which carries light) from Greek.**
- **Its atomic number is 15.**
- **Used in matches.**
- **C'est un élément de la classification périodique.**
- **Son symbole chimique est P.**
- **Isolé par Brandt (Angleterre) en 1669.**
- **Origine étymologique: *phôsphoros* (qui porte la lumière) du grec.**
- **Son numéro atomique est 15.**
- **Utilisé dans les allumettes.**

Platinum: platine

- **Is a metallic chemical element.**
- **Its chemical symbol is Pt.**
- **Known by pre-Columbian civilization.**
- **Etymological origin: *platina* (small silver) from Spanish.**
- **Its atomic number is 78.**
- **Used in labware and in coins.**
- **C'est un élément métallique de la classification périodique.**
- **Son symbole chimique est Pt.**
- **Connu par la civilisation précolombienne.**
- **Origine étymologique: *platina* (petit argent) de l'espagnol.**
- **Son numéro atomique est 78.**
- **Utilisé dans les appareils de laboratoire et de pièces de monnaie.**

Plutonium: plutonium

- **Is a radioactive chemical element.**
- **Its chemical symbol is Pu.**
- **Fabricated by Seaborg, McMallin, Kennedy and Wahl (USA) in 1940.**
- **Etymological origin: *Pluton* (God of Hell) from Greek mythology.**
- **Its atomic number is 94.**
- **Used for military purposes to make nuclear bomb.**
- **C'est un élément radioactif de la classification périodique.**
- **Son symbole chimique est Pu.**
- **Fabriqué par Seaborg, McMallin, Kennedy et Wahl (USA) en 1940.**
- **Origine étymologique: *Pluton* (dieu des Enfers) de la mythologie grecque.**
- **Son numéro atomique est 94.**
- **Utilisé à des fins militaires pour fabriquer des bombes nucléaires.**

Processing: processus.

Protection shield: écran de protection

Photosynthesis: photosynthèse.

- **A metabolic process involving plants and some types of bacteria in which light energy absorbed by chlorophyll and other photosynthetic pigments results in the reduction of CO_2 followed by the formation of organic compounds. In plants the overall process involves the conversion of CO_2 and H_2O to carbohydrates and the release of O_2.**

Pollution: pollution.

- **Pollution happens when a harmful substance is released into the environment in such large quantities that it causes damage to people, wildlife and habitats.**
- **La pollution a lieu quand une substance nocive est libérée dans l'environnement en quantités tellement importantes qu'elle provoque des dommages aux personnes, la faune et des habitats.**

Polonium: polonium

- **Is a radioactive chemical element.**
- **Its chemical symbol is Po.**
- **Discovered by Pierre and Marie Curie (France) in 1898.**
- **Etymological origin: *Pologne* (country).**
- **Its atomic number is 84.**
- **Used to develop lightweight thermoelectric generators used for example in the spatial domain as a power source for satellites and planetary exploration robots.**
- **C'est un élément radioactif de la classification périodique.**
- **Son symbole chimique est Po.**
- **Découvert par Pierre et Marie Curie (France) en 1898.**
- **Origine étymologique: *Pologne* (pays).**
- **Son numéro atomique est 84.**
- **Utilisée pour développer des générateurs thermo-électriques légers utilisés par exemple dans le domaine spatial comme source d'énergie pour les satellites et de robots d'exploration planétaires.**

Polymer: polymère

- **Many molecules of monomer add together to form one large molecule of polymer.**

- **Addition des plusieurs monomères forment une large molécule appelée polymère.**

Potassium: potassium

- **Is a metallic chemical element.**
- **Its chemical symbol is K.**
- **Isolated by Davy (England) in 1807.**
- **Etymological origin: *qali* (jar) from Arabic.**
- **Its atomic number is 19.**
- **Used as a reagent in many reactions of fine chemicals and pharmaceuticals.**
- **C'est un élément métallique de la classification périodique.**
- **Son symbole chimique est K.**
- **Isolé par Davy (Angleterre) en 1807.**
- **Origine étymologique: *qali* (pot) de l'arabe.**
- **Son numéro atomique est 19.**
- **Utilisé comme réactif dans de nombreuses réactions de chimie fine et de pharmacie.**

Pyrolysis: pyrolyse

- **Splitting by heat, used in petroleum industry.**
- **Fractionnement par la chaleur, utilisée dans l'industrie pétrolière.**

Polymerization: polymérisation

- **Polymerization by addition**
- **Polymerization by condensation**
- **Polymérisation par addition**
- **Polymérisation par condensation**

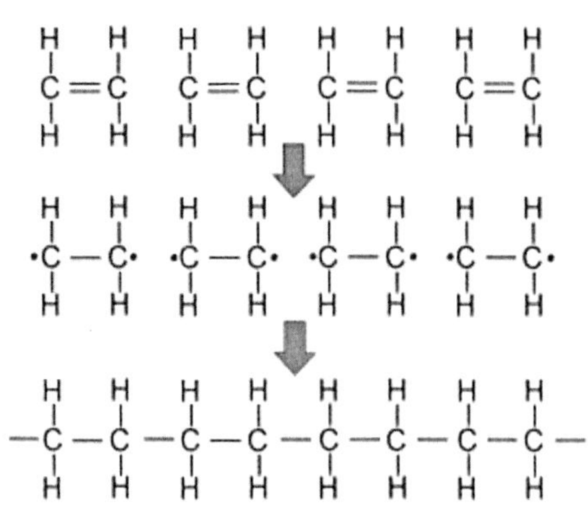

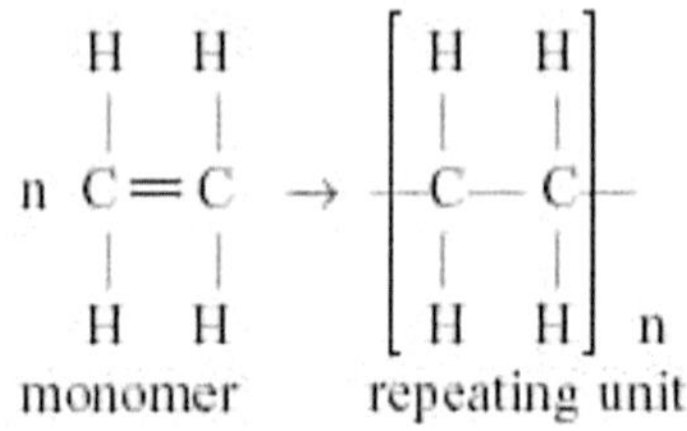

Polypropene	Propene	$-(CH_2-CH(CH_3))_n-$	Manufacture of ropes, toys, pipes, fibres, etc.
Polystyrene	Styrene	$-(CH_2-CH(C_6H_5))_n-$	As insulator, wrapping material, manufacture of toys, radio and television cabinets.
Polyvinyl chloride (PVC)	Vinyl chloride	$-(CH_2-CH(Cl))_n-$	Manufacture of rain coats, hand bags, vinyl flooring, water pipes.
Urea-formaldehyle Resin	(a) Urea (b) Formaldehyde	$-(NH-CO-NH-CH_2)_n-$	For making unbreak-able cups and laminated sheets.
Glyptal	(a) Ethylene glycol (b) Phthalic acid	$-(OCH_2-CH_2OOC-C_6H_4-CO)_n-$	Manufacture of paints and lacquers.
Bakelite	(a) Phenol (b) Formaldehyde	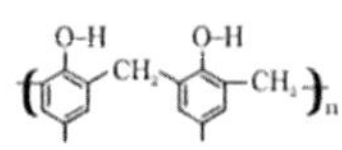	For making combs, electrical switches, handles of utensils and computer discs.

Polymerization degree: degré de polymérisation

Powder: poudre

Praseodyme: praséodyme

- **Is a radioactive chemical element.**
- **Its chemical symbol is Pr.**
- **Discovered by von Welsbach in 1885.**
- **Etymological origin: *praso* and *didymos* (leek and twin) from Greek.**
- **Its atomic number is 59.**
- **Used in glasses allowing glassblowers to see clearly.**
- **C'est un élément radioactif de la classification périodique.**
- **Son symbole chimique est Pr.**
- **Découvert par von Welsbach en 1885.**
- **Origine étymologique: *praso* and *didymos* (le poireau et jumeau) du grec.**
- **Son numéro atomique est 59.**

- **Utilisé dans les lunettes permettant aux souffleurs de verres de voir clairement.**

Promethium: prométhium
- **Is a radioactive chemical element.**
- **Its chemical symbol is Pm.**
- **Fabricated by Marinsky, Glendenin and Coryell (USA) in 1947.**
- **Etymological origin: *Prometheus* (the predictor) from the Greek mythology.**
- **Its atomic number is 61.**
- **Glows in the dark with a blue or green light.**
- **C'est un élément radioactif de la classification périodique.**
- **Son symbole chimique est Pm.**
- **Fabriqué par Marinsky, Glendenin et Coryell (USA) en 1947.**
- **Origine étymologique: *Prométhée* (le prévoyant) de la mythologie grecque.**
- **Son numéro atomique est 61.**
- **Luminescent dans le noir avec une lueur bleue ou verte.**

Protactinium: protactinium
- **Is a radioactive chemical element.**
- **Its chemical symbol is Pa.**
- **Discovered by Fajans and Göhring in 1913 and isolated by Grosse in 1934.**
- ***Etymological* origin: *protos* (first) from Greek.**
- **Its atomic number is 91.**
- **C'est un élément radioactif de la classification périodique.**
- **Son symbole chimique est Pa.**
- **No applications.**
- **Découvert par Fajans et Göhring en 1913 et isolé par Grosse en 1934.**
- **Origine étymologique: *protos* (premier) du grec.**
- **Son numéro atomique est 91.**
- **Pas d'applications.**

Precipitation: précipitation

Precipitate: précipité
- **A solid separated from a solution.**
- **Un solide séparé d'une solution.**

Polluted: pollué

- **Made unclean or impure; contaminated.**
- **Rendre impropre ou impur; contaminé.**

Pulse oximetry: oxymètre

- **Is a medical device that monitors the oxygen saturation.**
- **C’est un appareil qui mesure de la concentration en oxygène.**

Q

Quantum mechanics: mécanique quantique

- **Mathematical method of treating particles on the basis of quantum theory, which assumes that energy (of small particles) is not infinitely divisible.**
- **Méthode mathématique de l'étude des particules basée sur la théorie quantique qui stipule que l'énergie de petites particules n'est pas indéfiniment divisible.**

Quantum Number: nombre quantique

- **Numbers that describe the energies of electrons in atoms; derived from quantum mechanical treatment.**
- **Désigne les niveaux d'énergie des électrons dans l'atome. L'appellation vient de la mécanique quantique.**

R

Racimic mixture: mélange racémique

- **An equal amount of two enantiomers (chiral molecules) mixture is called racemic mixture.**
- **Un mélange équimolaire de deux énantiomères est dit racémique.**

Radium: radium

- **Is a radioactive chemical element.**
- **Its chemical symbol is Ra.**
- **Discovered by Pierre and Marie Curie (France) in 1898.**
- **Etymological origin: *radius* (radius) from Latin.**
- **Its atomic number is 88.**
- **Widely used at the beginning of the last century until its ban in civilian use since 1937 because of its high radioactivity.**
- **C'est un élément radioactif de la classification périodique.**
- **Son symbole chimique est Ra.**
- **Découvert par Pierre et Marie Curie (France) en 1898.**
- **Origine étymologique: *radius* (rayon) du latin.**
- **Son numéro atomique est 88.**
- **Très utilisé au début du siècle dernier jusque son interdiction dans l'utilisation civile depuis 1937 en raison de sa haute radioactivité.**

Radon: radon

- **Is a radioactive chemical gas element.**
- **Its chemical symbol is Rn.**
- **Discovered by Owens (England) in 1899 and isolated by Ramsey and Grey (USA) in 1908.**
- **Etymological origin: *radium* the element from which the radon it issued.**
- **Its atomic number is 86.**
- **Used in medicine including radiation kill cancer cells and is used as a tracer of continental air masses to study the atmospheric circulation in climatology.**
- **C'est un élément radioactif gazeux de la classification périodique.**
- **Son symbole chimique est Rn.**
- **Découvert par Owens (Angleterre) en 1899 et isolé par Ramsey et Grey (USA) en 1908.**
- **Origine étymologique: *radium*, l'élément dont il est issu.**
- **Son numéro atomique est 86.**

- **Utilisé en médecine dont les radiations tuent les cellules cancéreuses et on l'utilise comme traceur des masses d'air continentales pour étudier la circulation atmosphérique en climatologie.**

Rare earth elements: terre rares

React: réagit

Reaction time: durée d'une transformation
- **The period of time that elapse between the start of the reaction and the attainment of a given extent of a reaction.**
- **La durée nécessaire pour que l'avancement x atteigne une valeur déterminée par l'expérimentateur.**

Reagent: réactif

Rechargeable battery: pile rechargeable

Recycling: recyclage

Redox reaction: réaction redox
- **Is a chemical reaction in which changes in the oxidation numbers occur.**
- **C'est réaction chimique dans laquelle il y a changement de nombre d'oxydation.**

Reduction: réduction
- **Reduction occurs when there is a decrease in oxidation number of an element**
- **Une réduction survient lorsqu'il y a une diminution de nombre d'oxydation**

Reducing agent: réducteur

Regulator: détendeur

Reflux condense: chauffage à reflux

- **When a liquid mixture is heated, certain chemical compounds vaporize and become gaseous in a vertical column where they are cooled down by circulation of water and liquefy falling back into the liquid mixture again.**
- **Lorsqu'on chauffe un mélange liquide, certains composés chimiques se vaporise et deviennent gazeux dans une colonne verticale où ils sont refroidis par circulation d'eau et se liquéfient dans un mélange liquide à nouveau.**

Release: dégage

Residue: résidu
- **Matter remaining after completion of a chemical or physical process, such as evaporation, combustion, distillation or filtration.**
- **Reste de matières après avoir accompli une réaction chimique ou une procédure physique tels que : évaporation, combustion, distillation ou filtration.**

Retardation factor: rapport frontal (R_F)
- **Is the ratio of the distance travelled by the center of the spot to the distance simultaneously travelled by the mobile phase.**
- **C'est le rapport de la distance parcourue par la tache sur la distance parcourue par la phase mobile.**

Retention factor (R_f): rapport frontal (R_f)
- **Is the distance moved by component above the base line divided by the distance moved by the solvent front**
- **C'est la distance parcourue par l'espèce chimique divisé par le front de solvant**

Rhenium: rhénium
- **Is a metallic chemical element.**
- **Its chemical symbol is Re.**
- **Discovered by Noddack, Tacke and Berg (Germany) in 1925.**
- **Etymological origin: *Rhenus* (the Rhin) from Latin.**
- **Its atomic number is 75.**
- **Used for the production of superalloys for turbines, mainly aircraft.**
- **C'est un élément métallique de la classification périodique.**
- **Son symbole chimique est Re.**
- **Découvert par Noddack, Tacke et Berg (Allemagne) en 1925.**
- **Origine étymologique: *Rhenus* (le Rhin) du latin.**

- Son numéro atomique est 75.
- Utilisé pour la fabrication de superalliages pour les turbines, principalement aéronautiques.

Rhodium: rhodium
- Is a metallic chemical element.
- Its chemical symbol is Rh.
- Discovered by Wollaston (England) in 1803.
- Etymological origin: *rhodon* (pink) from Greek.
- Its atomic number is 45.
- C'est un élément métallique de la classification périodique.
- Son symbole chimique est Rh.
- Découvert par Wollaston (Angleterre) en 1803.
- Origine étymologique: *rhodon* (rose) du grec.
- Son numéro atomique est 45.

Rubidium: rubidium
- Is a metallic chemical element.
- Its chemical symbol is Rb.
- Discovered by Bunsen and Kirchhoff (Germany) in 1861.
- Etymological origin: *rubidus* (red) from Latin.
- Its atomic number is 37.
- Used in solar cells, in safety glasses in the fireworks (purple) and is used as a getter (gas sensor) in cathode ray tubes.
- C'est un élément métallique de la classification périodique.
- Son symbole chimique est Rb.
- Découvert par Bunsen et Kirchhoff (Allemagne) en 1861.
- Origine étymologique: *rubidus* (rouge) du latin.
- Son numéro atomique est 37.
- Utilisé dans Cellules photovoltaïques, dans les verres de sécurité, dans les feux d'artifice (couleur violette) et il est utilisé comme getter (capteur de gaz) dans les tubes cathodiques.

Rust: rouille
- Is a chemical reaction. Rusting occurs when air and water reach oxidisable metals
- C'est une réaction chimique. La rouille a lieu quand l'air et l'eau atteignent les métaux oxydables comme le fer, un oxyde métallique est ainsi formé

Ruthenium: ruthénium
- Is a metallic chemical element.

- **Its chemical symbol is Ru.**
- **Discovered by Claus (Russia) in 1844.**
- **Etymological origin: *Ruthenia* (Russia).**
- **Its atomic number is 44.**
- **Used in jewelry.**
- **C'est un élément métallique de la classification périodique.**
- **Son symbole chimique est Ru.**
- **Découvert par Claus (Russie) en 1844.**
- **Origine étymologique: *Ruthenia* (Russie).**
- **Sa masse atomique est 44.**
- **Utilisé en bijouterie.**

Rutherfordium: rutherfodium

- **Is a radioactive chemical element.**
- **Its chemical symbol is Rf.**
- **Discovered by Russian scientific team in 1964.**
- **Etymological origin: *Rutherford* (scientist).**
- **Its atomic number is 104.**
- **C'est un élément radioactif de la classification périodique.**
- **Son symbole chimique est Rf.**
- **Découvert par une équipe scientifique russe en 1964.**
- **Origine étymologique: *Rutherford* (scientifique).**
- **Son numéro atomique est 104.**

S

Safety goggles: lunettes de protection

- **Used in chemistry laboratory to protect our eyes during manipulation of chemical compounds.**
- **Utilisées en laboratoire pour protéger les yeux pendant les travaux pratiques.**

Saline: salin

- **Containing salt**
- **Contient du sel**

Saline solution: solution saline

- **A solution in which it is not possible to dissolve more solute.**
- **Une solution dans laquelle on ne peut plus de soluté.**

Saturated: saturé

- **A solution that contains the maximum amount of solute that the solvent can dissolve at a given temperature.**
- **Une solution qui contient un maximum de soluté que le solvant peut dissoudre à une température donnée.**

Salt bridge: pont salin

- **The salt bridge is necessary to complete the circuit and maintain charge neutrality in an electrochemical cell.**
- **Le pont salin est nécessaire pour maintenir l'électro neutralité d'une pile électrochimique.**

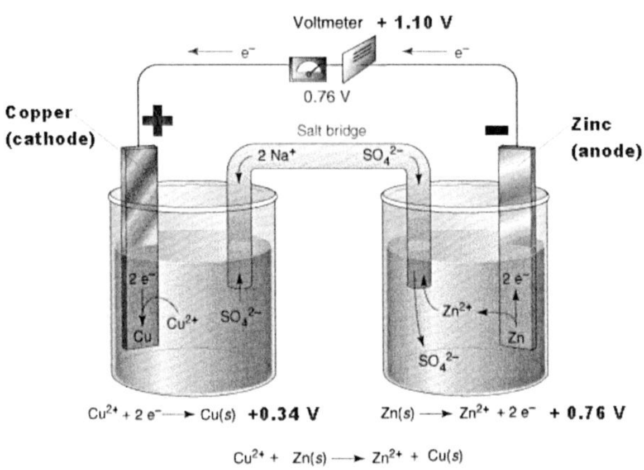

Samarium: samarium

- **Is a radioactive chemical element.**
- **Its chemical symbol is Sm.**
- **Discovered by Paul-Emile Lecoq de Boisbaudran (France) in 1879.**
- **Etymological origin: *samarskite* (mineral).**
- **Its atomic number is 62.**
- **As used with cobalt alloy they have the strength of the known higher demagnetization. It is found in microphones electric guitars as in the control rods of nuclear reactors.**
- **C'est un élément métallique de la classification périodique.**
- **Son symbole chimique est Sm.**
- **Découvert par Paul-Emile Lecoq de Boisbaudran (France) en 1879.**
- **Origine étymologique: *samarskite* (minerai).**
- **Son numéro atomique est 62.**
- **Utilisé en alliage avec le cobalt ils possèdent la résistance de démagnétisation la plus élevée connue. On le retrouve dans les microphones de guitares électriques comme dans les barres de contrôle de certains réacteurs nucléaires.**

Sampling: échantillonnage

Scandium: scandium

- **Is a metallic chemical element.**
- **Its chemical symbol is Sc.**
- **Discovered by Nilson (Norway) in 1879 and isolated by Fischer, Grieneisen and Brunger (Germany) in 1937.**
- **Etymological origin: *Scandinavia* (country).**
- **Its atomic number is 21.**
- **The main application of scandium by weight is in aluminium-scandium alloys for aerospace industry components. Some items of sports equipment, which rely on high performance materials, have been made with scandium-aluminium alloys, including baseball bats and bicycle frames and components.**
- **C'est un élément métallique de la classification périodique.**
- **Son symbole chimique est Sc.**
- **Découvert par Nilson (Norvège) en 1879 et isolé par Fischer, Grieneisen et Brunger (Allemagne) en 1937.**
- **Origine étymologique: *Scandinavie* (pays).**
- **Son numéro atomique est 21.**
- **L'application principale de scandium est en alliages d'aluminium-scandium pour les composants de l'industrie aérospatiale. Certains éléments de l'équipement sportif, qui s'appuient sur des matériaux de haute performance, ont été réalisés avec des alliages de scan-**

dium-aluminium, y compris des battes de baseball, les cadres de bicyclettes et des composants.

Seaborgium: seaborgium
- Is a radioactive chemical element.
- Its chemical symbol is Sg.
- Discovered by Russian scientific team and American scientific team in 1974.
- Etymological origin: *Seaborg* (Glenn Theodore Seaborg) American scientist.
- Its atomic number is 106.
- C'est un élément radioactif de la classification périodique.
- Son symbole chimique est Sg.
- Découvert par deux équipes scientifiques russe et américaine en 1974.
- Origine étymologique: *Seaborg* (Glenn Theodore Seaborg) scientifique Américan.
- Son numéro atomique est 106.

Selenium: sélénium
- Is a metallic chemical element.
- Its chemical symbol is Se.
- Discovered by Berzelius (Sweden) in 1817.
- Etymological origin: *selênê* (moon) from Greek.
- Its atomic number is 34.
- Used in light-sensing applications: light meters, photocopiers and automatic light switches.
- C'est un élément métallique de la classification périodique.
- Son symbole chimique est Se.
- Découvert par Berzelius (Suède) en 1817.
- Origine étymologique: *selênê* (lune) du grec.
- Son numéro atomique est 34.
- Utilisé dans des applications de détection de lumière: luxmètres, les photocopieurs et les interrupteurs automatiques.

Set fire: mettre à feu

Shell: couche
- Electronic shell
- Couche électronique

Shelf life: date limite de consommation

- **Is the length of time that food, drink, medicine, chemicals, and many other perishable items are given before they are considered unsuitable for sale, use, or consumption.**
- **La date limite de consommation, ou date de péremption, est une date figurant sur les denrées alimentaires microbiologiquement périssables susceptibles, après une courte période, de présenter un danger immédiat pour la santé humaine.**

Silicon: silicium

- **Is a metallic chemical element.**
- **Its chemical symbol is Si.**
- **Identified by Lavoisier (France) in 1787 and isolated by Berzelius (Sweden) in 1824.**
- **Etymological origin: *silex* (stone) from Latin.**
- **Its atomic number is 14.**
- **Used in computeur chips.**
- **C'est un élément métallique de la classification périodique.**
- **Son symbole chimique est Si.**
- **Identifié par Lavoisier (France) en 1787 et isolé par Berzelius (Suède) en 1824.**
- **Origine étymologique: *silex* (pierre) du latin.**
- **Son numéro atomique est 14.**
- **Utilisé dans les puces informatiques.**

Silver: argent

- **Is a metallic chemical element.**
- **Its chemical symbol is Ag.**
- **Known since antiquity.**
- **Etymological origin: *argentum* (silver money) from Latin.**
- **Its atomic number is 47.**
- **Used in jewelry.**
- **C'est un élément métallique de la classification périodique.**
- **Son symbole chimique est Ag.**
- **Connu depuis l'antiquité.**
- **Origine étymologique: *argentum* (monnaie en argent) du latin.**
- **Son numéro atomique est 47.**
- **Utilisé en bijoutrie.**

Single element molecule: corps simple

- **Is a chemical formula containing only one chemical element. Example: H_2, O_2.**

- **C'est une forme chimique ne comportant qu'un élément chimique. Exemple: H_2, O_2.**

Skeletal formula: formule moléculaire topologique

- **Is a simplified way of representing molecules such as butanol. The carbon atoms in this type of diagram are implied to be located at the vertices (corners) and termini of line segments rather than being indicated with the atomic symbol C. Hydrogen atoms attached to carbon atoms are not indicated: each carbon atom is understood to be associated with enough hydrogen atoms to give the carbon atom four bonds.**
- **C'est une façon simple de représenter les molécules complexes, exemple le butanol. Les sommets représentent les atomes de carbones, les atomes d'hydrogènes liés au carbone ne sont pas indiqués. Les groupes fonctionnels sont représentés.**

Sodium: sodium

- **Is a metallic chemical element.**
- **Its chemical symbol is Na.**
- **Predicted by Lavoisier (France) and isolated by Davy (England) in 1807.**
- **Etymological origin: *natron* (sodium carbonate) from Arabic.**
- **Its atomic number is 11.**
- **Explode in contact with water.**
- **Used in the manufacture of esters as well as that of other organic compounds, used in particular in the pharmaceutical, cosmetics and pesticides industries.**
- **C'est un élément métallique de la classification périodique.**
- **Son symbole chimique est Na.**
- **Prévu par Lavoisier (France) et isolé par Davy (Angleterre) en 1807.**
- **Origine étymologique: *natron* (carbonate de sodium) de l'arabe.**
- **Son numéro atomique est 11.**
- **Explose en contact avec l'eau.**
- **Utilisé dans la fabrication des esters ainsi que dans celle d'autres composés organiques, utilisés en particulier dans l'industrie pharmaceutique, les cosmétiques et les pesticides.**

Solvent front: front de solvant (CCM)
- **Is the mobile phase.**
- **C'est la phase mobile.**

Spot: tache

Stationary phase: phase stationnaire

Starch: amidon

Stereochemistry: stéréochimie
- **Stereochemistry is the study of the three-dimensional structure of molecules. The *cis* and *trans* isomers are forms of stereoisomers, differing structurally only in the location of the atoms of the molecule in three-dimensional space. Such stereoisomers can have different physical and chemical properties. For example, the *cis* and *trans* isomers of butenedioic acid show vast differences in their physical and chemical properties.**

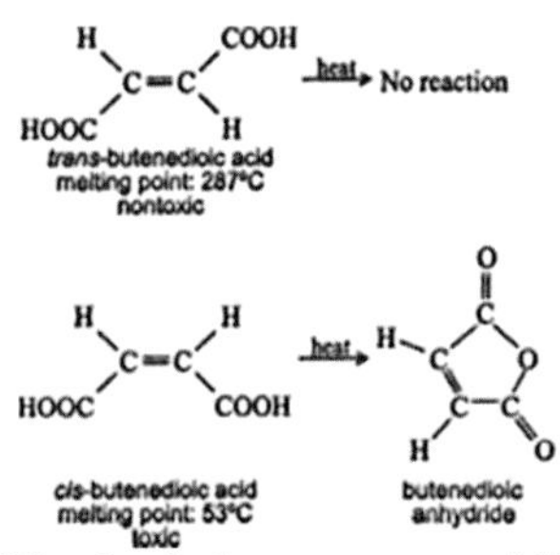

- **La stéréochimie est l'étude de la structure tridimensionnelle des molécules. Les isomères cis et trans sont des formes de stéréo-isomères, différant seulement dans la structure de l'emplacement des atomes de la molécule dans l'espace tridimensionnel. Ces stéréo-isomères peuvent avoir des propriétés physiques et chimiques différentes. Par exemple, les isomères cis et trans de l'acide butènedioïque montrent de grandes différences dans leurs propriétés physiques et chimiques.**

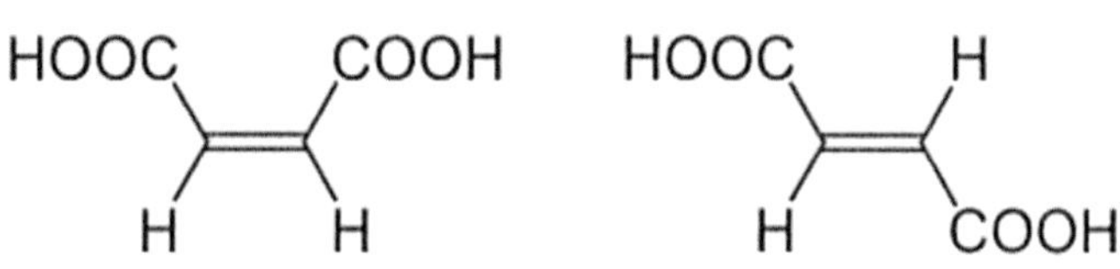

- **Stereochemistry is of particular interest to biochemists because the reactivity and toxicity of molecules change with their stereochemistry. Most body reactions are stereospecific, meaning that receptor sites on cells accept only molecules with specific spatial arrangements of their atoms. Other configurations of the same chemical either will not react or may be toxic to the living being. There are other types of stereoisomers in addition to the *cis* and *trans* arrangements of atoms**
- **La stéréochimie a un intérêt particulier pour les biochimistes car la réactivité et la toxicité des molécules changent avec leur stéréochimie. La plupart des réactions du corps sont stéréospécifique, ce qui signifie que les sites récepteurs des cellules n'acceptent que des molécules d'un arrangement partiel spécifique de leurs atomes. D'autres configurations de la même substance chimique peut ne pas réagir ou peut être toxique pour l'être vivant. Il existe d'autres types de stéréo-isomères, outre les arrangements cis et trans de atomes.**

Strontium: strontium
- **Is a chemical element.**
- **Its chemical symbol is Sr.**
- **Discovered by Klaproth (Germany) and Hope (Scotland) in 1792. Isolated by Davy (England) in 1808.**
- **Etymological origin: *Strontian* (Scottish city).**
- **Its atomic number is 38.**
- **Used in fireworks and distress flares.**
- **C'est un élément de la classification périodique.**
- **Son symbole chimique est Sr.**
- **Découvert par Klaproth (Allemagne) et Hope (Ecosse) en 1792. Isolé par Davy (Angleterre) en 1808.**
- **Origine étymologique: *Strontian* (ville Ecossaise).**
- **Son numéro atomique est 38.**
- **Utilisé dans les feux d'artifice et les fusées de détresse.**

Smog: brouillard de pollution
- **Mixture of smoke and fog.**
- **brouillard mêlé de fumée.**

Smoke: fumé
- **Mixture of fine solid particles in suspension in a gas.**
- **Mélange des fines particules solide suspendues dans un gaz.**

Soda: soude

- **Sodium hydroxide NaOH is a base solution.**
- **Hydroxyde de sodium NaOH c'est une base.**

Soda water: eau gazeuse

- **Water containing carbon dioxide.**
- **Eau chargée de dioxyde de carbone.**

Solid: solide

- **A state of matter. A substance having a definite shape and volume; one that is neither liquid nor gaseous.**
- **Etat de matière. Une substance qui a un aspect et un volume; ce qui est pas le cas des liquides ou les gaz.**

Solidification: solidification

- **The process of becoming hard or solid by cooling or drying or crystallization. Transition from liquid state to solid state**
- **C'est le processus de devenir dur ou solide par refroidissement ou séchage ou par cristallisation. C'est le passage de l'état liquide à l'état solide.**

Solute: solute

- **A substance that is dissolved in another substance (a solvent), forming a solution.**
- **Une substance dissoute dans une autre substance (un solvant) qui forme une solution.**

Solution: solution

- **The dissolution of a solute into a solvent forms a solution.**
- **C'est la dissolution d'un soluté dans un solvant formant une solution.**

Solvent: solvent

- **A substance, usually a liquid, in which another substance is dissolved, forming a solution.**
- **C'est une substance, souvent liquide, dans laquelle une autre substance est dissoute formant une solution.**

Solvent front: front de solvant

Space-filling model: modèle compact

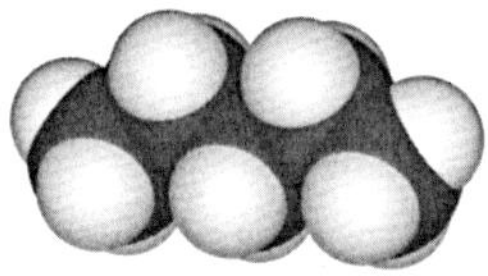

Specific heat: capacité thermique massique

- **Is the amount of energy to be provided by heat exchange to raise a kelvin temperature of a unit mass of a substance.**
- **Q (J) = m (g) x c (J/(g.K)) x ΔT (K)**
- **C'est la quantité d'énergie à apporter par échange thermique pour élever d'un kelvin la température de l'unité de masse d'une substance.**

Steam: vapeur

- **Gaseous state of water.**
- **Etat gazeux de l'eau.**

Standard Ambient Temperature and Pressure (SATP): Conditions du Laboratoire de Température et de Pression (CLTP)

- **In these conditions, temperature T = 298.15 K (25°C,) and absolute pressure 1 bar (1 atm).**
- **Dans ces conditions, la température T = 273.15 K (25°C, température ambiante) et la pression normale est de 1 bar (1 atm).**

Standard Temperature and Pressure (STP): Condition Normale de température et de Pression (CNTP)

- **In these conditions, temperature T = 273.15 K (0°C) and absolute pressure 1 bar (1 atm).**
- **Dans ces conditions, la température T = 273.15 K (0°C) et la pression normale est de 1 bar (1 atm).**

Structural formula: formule semi-développée

- **Is a graphical representation of the molecular structure.**
- **A full structural formula (graphique formula or displayed formula) shows every bond and atom.**

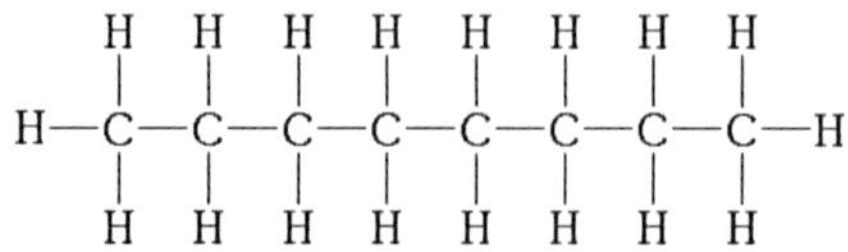

- **A condensed structural formula often omits bonds they can be assumed and groups atoms together.**

$$CH_3{-}CH_2{-}CH_2{-}CH_2{-}CH_2{-}CH_2{-}CH_2{-}CH_3$$

- **C'est une représentation graphique des molécules.**
- **La formule développée qui montre toutes les liaisons des atomes au sein de la molécule.**
- **La formule semi-développée est une simplification de la formule développée.**

Structure: structure

Stoichiometry: stœchiométrie
- **The term refers to the relationship between the amounts of substances that react together in a particular chemical reaction, and the amounts of products that are formed.**
- **C'est un terme qui correspond à la relation entre les quantités de matières des réactifs et la quantité de matière des produits formés.**

Sublimation: sublimation
- **Transition from the solid state to the gaseous state**
- **Passage de l'état solide à l'état gazeux.**

Substitution reaction: réaction de substitution
- **A reaction, elementary or stepwise, in which one atom or group in a molecular entity is replaced by another atom or group.**
- **C'est une réaction élémentaire dans laquelle un atome ou un groupe d'atome dans une entité moléculaire sont remplacés par un autre.**

Sulphur: soufre
- **Is a chemical element.**
- **Its chemical symbol is S.**
- **Known since antiquity.**

- **Etymological origin: *sulfur* (sulphur) from Latin.**
- **Its atomic number is 16.**
- **Used in the chemical industry as a precursor and is used in the vulcanization of rubber.**
- **C'est un élément de la classification périodique.**
- **Son symbole chimique est S.**
- **Connu depuis l'antiquité.**
- **Origine étymologique: *sulfur* (soufre) du latin.**
- **Son numéro atomique est 16.**
- **Utilisé dans l'industrie chimique comme precurseur et on l'utilise dans la vulcanisation du caoutchouc.**

Suspension: suspension
- **A dispersion of fine solid or liquid particles in a fluid. Particles in a suspension precipitate if the suspension is allowed to stand undisturbed.**
- **C'est une dispersion de fine solide ou liquide particules dans un fluide. Ces particules en suspension précipitent si la solution reste sans être perturbée.**

Super-freeze: surgeler

Synthesis: synthèse

Synthesize: synthétiser

Synthetic compound: matériau artificiel

T

Tantalum: tantale

- **Is a metallic chemical element.**
- **Its chemical symbol is Ta.**
- **Discovered by Anders Ekeberg (Sweden) in 1802.**
- **Etymological origin: *Tantalus* (father of Niobe) from Greek mythology.**
- **Its atomic number is 73.**
- **Used in the capacitors of high tech devices such as cell phones and laptop computeurs. We find it in medical implants like skull plates.**
- **C'est un élément métallique de la classification périodique.**
- **Son symbole chimique est Ta.**
- **Découvert par Anders Ekeberg (Suède) en 1802.**
- **Origine étymologique: *Tantalus* (père de Niobe) de la mythologie grecque.**
- **Son numéro atomique est 73.**
- **Utilisé dans les condensateurs des appareils de haute technologie tels que les téléphones cellulaires et ordinateurs portables. Nous le trouvons dans les implants médicaux tels que des plaques de crâne.**

Technetium: technétium

- **Is a radioactive chemical element.**
- **Its chemical symbol is Tc.**
- **Discovered by Carlo Perrier and Emilio Segrè (Italy) in 1937.**
- **Etymological origin: *teritos* (artificial) from Greek.**
- **Its atomic number is 43.**
- **Used in gamma rays imaging of skeletons.**
- **C'est un élément métallique de la classification périodique.**
- **Découvert par Carlo Perrier et Emilio Segrè (Italie) en 1937.**
- **Son symbole chimique est Tc.**
- **Origine étymologique: *teritos* (artificiel) du grec.**
- **Son numéro atomique est 43.**
- **Utilisé dans l'imagerie des squelettes par rayonnements gamma.**

Tellurium: tellure

- **Is a metallic chemical element.**
- **Its chemical symbol is Te.**
- **Discovered in Transylvania (today part of Romania) in 1782 by Franz-Joseph Müller von Reichenstein.**
- **Etymological origin: *tellus* (earth) from Latin.**
- **Its atomic number is 52.**

- Used in laser printers, detonators, some coclorants, semiconductors and in the vulcanization of rubber.
- C'est un élément métallique de la classification périodique.
- Découvert en Transsylvanie (actuellement la Romanie) en 1782 par Franz-Joseph Müller von Reichenstein.
- Son symbole chimique est Te.
- Origine étymologique: *tellus* (terre) du latin.
- Son numéro atomique est 52.
- Utilisé dans les imprimantes laser, les détonateurs, certains coclorants, les semi-conducteurs et dans la vulcanisation du caoutchouc.

Temperature: température
- Physical property that is measured with a thermometer. The unit often employed is the Degree Celsius (°C). The SI unit is the Kelvin (0 °C = 273.16 K).
- Propriété physique mesurable par un thermomètre. L'unité employée est souvent le °C. L'unité dans le SI est le Kelvin (0 °C = 273.16 K).

Temperatue dwell: palier de température
- Time during which a temperature does not change
- Palier de temps pendant lequel la température ne change pas

Terbium: terbium
- Is a radioactive chemical element.
- Its chemical symbol is Tb.
- Identified in 1843 by Carl Gustaf Mosander.
- Etymological origin: *Ytterby* (Sweden city).
- Its atomic number is 65.
- Used in X-ray screens in cathode ray tubes and as stabilizers in fuel cells.
- C'est un élément métallique de la classification périodique.
- Identifié en 1843 par Carl Gustaf Mosander.
- Son symbole est Tb.
- Origine étymologique: *Ytterby* (cité Suedoise).
- Son numéro atomique est 65.
- Utilisé dans les écrans à rayons X, dans les tubes cathodiques et comme stabilisateurs dans les piles à combustibles.

Thaw: dégel
- Is the period when the snow and ice melt.

- **C'est la période pendant laquelle la neige et la glace commence à fondre.**

Thallium: thallium

- **Is a metallic chemical element.**
- **Its chemical symbol is Tl.**
- **Discovered by William Crookes (England) and Claude-Auguste Lamy (France) independently in 1861**
- **Etymological origin: *thallus* (green twig) from Greek.**
- **Its atomic number is 81.**
- **Used in cardiac scintigraphy, infrared detectors and television cameras.**
- **C'est un élément métallique de la classification périodique.**
- **Découvert indépendamment par by William Crookes (England) et Claude-Auguste Lamy (France) en 186**
- **Son symbole chimique est Tl.**
- **Origine étymologique: *thallus* (brindille verte) du grec.**
- **Son numéro atomique est 81.**
- **Utilisé en scintigraphie cardiaque, détecteurs infrarouge et dans les caméras de télévision.**

Thorium: thorium

- **Is a radioactive chemical element.**
- **Its chemical symbol is Th.**
- **Discovered in 1828 by the Norwegian mineralogist Morten Thrane Esmark and identified by the Swedish chemist Jons Jakob Berzelius.**
- **Etymological origin: *Thor* (Norse god of thunder) from Greek mythology.**
- **Its atomic number is 90.**
- **Used in optical glasses of scientific instruments and electronics industry.**
- **C'est un élément radioactif de la classification périodique.**
- **Découvert en 1828 par le Norvégien minéralogiste Morten Thrane Esmark et identifié par le chimiste suédois Jons Jakob Berzelius.**
- **Son symbole chimique est Th.**
- **Origine étymologique: *Thor* (Dieu nordique de tonnerre) de la mythologie grecque.**
- **Son numéro atomique est 90.**
- **Utilisé dans les verres optiques des instruments scientifiques et dans l'industrie électronique.**

Thulium: thulium

- **Is a radioactive chemical element.**
- **Its chemical symbol is Tm.**
- **Discovered by Per Teodor Cleve (Sweden) in 1879.**
- **Etymological origin: *Thule* (region in the far North of Scandinavia).**
- **Its atomic number is 69.**
- **Used in portable X-ray equipment, in the pigments of cathode ray tubes and microwave generators in microwave devices.**
- **C'est un élément radioactif de la classification périodique.**
- **Son symbole est Tm.**
- **Découvert par Per Teodor Cleve (Suède) en 1879.**
- **Origine étymologique: *Thule* (région dans extrême Nord en Scandinavie).**
- **Son numéro atomique est 69.**
- **Utilisé dans les appareils radiographiques portables, dans les pigments des tubes cathodiques et dans les dispositifs générateurs hyperfréquences dans les micro-ondes.**

Thermal stress: contrainte thermique

Thermoplastic: thermoplastique

Thermometre: thermomètre

- **Device allowing temperature measurement.**
- **Instrument permettant de mesurer la température.**

Thermoset: thermodurcissable

Thin-layer chromatography (TLC): Chromatographie sur couche mince (CCM)

- **Is a physical method of separation and identification of chemical species.**
- **C'est une méthode physique de séparation et d'identification d'espèces chimiques.**

Tin: étain

- **Is a metallic chemical element.**
- **Its chemical symbol is Sn.**
- **Known since ancient time 3000 BC**
- **Etymological origin: *stagnum* (tin) in Latin.**
- **Its atomic number is 50.**

- **Used in coins, dishes and decorations in the form of alloy. Boat hulls are treated with a product containing tin that protect it from algae.**
- **C'est un élément métallique de la classification périodique.**
- **Son symbole chimique est Ti.**
- **Connu depuis l'antiquité 3000 avant JC.**
- **Origine étymologique: *stagnum* (étain) en latin.**
- **Son numéro atomique est 50.**
- **Utilisé dans les pièces de monnaies, dans les vaisselles et décorations sous forme d'alliage. On traite les coques des bateaux avec un produit contenant de l'étain qui les protègent des algues.**

Titanium: titane

- **Is a metallic chemical element.**
- **Its chemical symbol is Ti.**
- **Discovered in Cornwall (England) by William Gregor in 1791.**
- **Etymological origin: *Titans* (primordial deities) from Greek mythology.**
- **Its atomic number is 22.**
- **Used in jet engine because of its light weight and high strength.**
- **C'est un élément métallique de la classification périodique.**
- **Son symbole chimique est Ti.**
- **Découvert en Cornwall (Angleterre) par William Gregor en 1791.**
- **Origine étymologique: *Titans* (divinités primordiales) de la mythologie grecque.**
- **Son numéro atomique est 22.**
- **Utilisé dans le moteur de jet en raison de son poids léger et de sa haute résistance.**

Titration: dosage

- **Is an important laboratory technique used in chemical analysis. A solution containing an unknown quantity (unknown concentration) of a known substance is placed in a conical flask, and a solution of accurately known strength (called a standard solution) is then added from a burette. The addition of this solution continues until the end point of the titration is reached. This is signified by a colour change in an indicator (indicator well chosen), at this point the titration is stopped. The equivalence point of the titration occurs when the two solutions have reacted exactly (stoichiometric reaction).**
- **There are two methods of titration:**
  A- pH meter titration
  B- Color indicator titration

- **C'est une technique important de laboratoire utilisé dans l'analyse chimique. Une solution contenant une quantité inconnue (concentration inconnue) d'une substance connue est placé dans une fiole conique, et une solution de concentration connue avec précision (appelée solution standard) est ensuite ajoutée à partir d'une burette. L'addition de cette solution se poursuit jusqu'à ce que le point final du titrage est atteint. Ce qui est signifié par un changement de couleur d'un indicateur (indicateur bien choisi), à ce stade, le titrage est arrêté. Le point d'équivalence du titrage se produit lorsque les deux solutions ont réagi exactement (réaction stœchiométrique).**
- **Il y a deux méthodes de dosage:**
  A- Dosage pH métrique
  B- Dosage colorimétrique

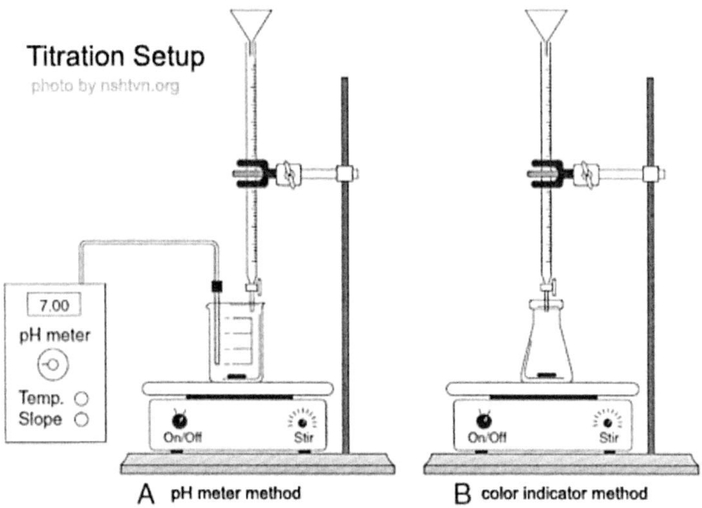

Transparent: transparent
- **A substance or object that allows all the light to pass through.**
- **Une substance ou un objet permettant à la lumière de passer à travers.**

Trigger (start off): déclencher (commencer)

Triple point: point triple (eutectique)
- **Describes the conditions under which three phases can coexist.**
- **Décrit les conditions dans lesquelles trios phases coexistent.**

Tungesten: tungstène

- **Is a metallic chemical element.**
- **Its chemical symbol is W.**
- **Discovered by Scheele and Torbern Torgman (Sweden) in 1781.**
- **Etymological origin: *tung sten* (heavy stone) in Swedish.**
- **Its atomic number is 74.**
- **Used as a filament in incandescent light bulbs.**
- **Découvert par Scheele et Torbern Torgman (Suède) en 1781.**
- **Origine étymologique: *tung sten* (pierre lourde) en suédois.**
- **Son numéro atomique est 74.**
- **Utilisé comme filament dans les ampoules à incandescence.**

U

Ultraviolet radiation: radiation ultraviolet

- **Is electromagnetic radiation with shorter wavelength than the violet end of the visible spectrum.**
- **C'est une radiation électromagnétique de longueur d'onde plus courte que le violet dans le spectre visible de la lumière.**

Ultraviolet spectroscopy: spectroscopie ultraviolet

- **Is used for studying colorless organic molecules with unsaturated functional groups such as C=C and C=O.**
- **Il est utilisé pour l'étude des molécules organiques incolores dont les groupes fonctionnels sont insaturés comme C=C et C=O.**

Universal indicator: indicateur coloré

- **Is a mixture of several acid-base indicators which changes color through of the spectrum from red to indigo as the pH rises from 0.1 to 14.0.**
- **C'est un mélange des couples acide-base dont les espèces conjuguées ont des teintes différentes allant de rouge au violet en fonction des valeurs de pH qui varie de 0,1 à 14,0.**

Uranium: uranium

- **Is a radioactive chemical element.**
- **Its chemical symbol is U.**
- **Discovered by Klaproth (Germany) in 1913 and isolated by Eugène-Melchiort Peligot (France) in 1841.**
- **Etymological origin: *Uranus* (sky) from Greek mythology.**
- **Its atomic number is 92.**
- **Used in piercing ammunition and nuclear power plants.**
- **C'est un élément radioactif de la classification périodique.**
- **Son symbole est U.**
- **Découvert par Klaproth (Allemagne) en 1913 et isolé par Eugène-Mélchior Peligot (France) en 1841.**
- **Origine étymologique: *Uranus* (ciel) de la mythologie grecque.**
- **Son numéro atomique est 92.**
- **Utilisé dans les munitions perforantes et dans les centrales nucléaires.**

Ununbium/Copernicium: ununbium/copernicium

- **Is a radioactive chemical element.**

- **Its symbol is Uub/Cn.**
- **Created by German scientific team in 1996.**
- **Etymological origin: *ununbium* (112 in Latin) and finally named Copernicium in honor to the astronomer Nicolas Copernicus.**
- **Its atomic number is 112.**
- **C'est un élément radioactif de la classification périodique.**
- **Son symbole est Uub/Cn.**
- **Créé par une équipe scientifique allemande en 1996.**
- **Origine étymologique: *ununbium* (112 en Latin) et finalement nommé Copernicium en hommage à l'astronome Nicolas Copernic.**
- **Son numéro atomique est 112.**

Ununhexium/Livermorium: ununhexium/livermorium
- **Is a radioactive chemical element.**
- **Its symbol is Uuh/Lv.**
- **Created by Yuri Oganessian (Russia) in 2000.**
- **Etymological origin: *ununhexium* (116 in Latin) and finally named Livermorium (Livermore city) in California.**
- **Its atomic number is 116.**
- **C'est un élément radioactif de la classification périodique.**
- **Son symbole est Uuh/Lv.**
- **Créé par Yuri Oganessian en 2000.**
- **Origine étymologique: *ununhexium* (116 en Latin) et finalement nommé Livermorium (cité de Livermore) en Californie.**
- **Son numéro atomique est 116.**

Ununnillium/Darmstadtium: ununnillium/darmstadtium
- **Is a radioactive chemical element.**
- **Its symbol is Uun/Ds.**
- **Created by German scientific team in 1994.**
- **Etymological origin: *Darmstadt* (German city).**
- **Its atomic number is 110.**
- **C'est un élément radioactif de la classification périodique.**
- **Son symbole est Uun/Ds.**
- **Créé par une équipe scientifique allemande en 1994.**
- **Origine étymologique: *Darmstadt* (cité allemande).**
- **Son numéro atomique est 110.**

Ununoctium: ununoctium
- **Is a radioactive chemical element.**
- **Its symbol is Uuo.**
- **Created by American and Russian scientific team in 2006.**

- **Etymological origin: *ununoctium* (118 in Latin).**
- **Its atomic number is 118.**
- **C'est un élément radioactif de la classification périodique.**
- **Son symbole est Uuo.**
- **Créé par une équipe scientifique américano-russe en 2006.**
- **Origine étymologique: *ununoctium* (118 en latin)**
- **Son numéro atomique est 118.**

Ununpentium: ununpentium

- **Is a radioactive chemical element.**
- **Its symbol is Uup.**
- **Created by Russian scientific team in 2004.**
- **Etymological origin: *Uup* (115 in Latin).**
- **Its atomic number is 115.**
- **C'est un élément radioactif de la classification périodique.**
- **Son symbole est Uup.**
- **Créé par une équipe scientifique russe en 2004.**
- **Origine étymologique: *Uup* (115 en latin).**
- **Son numéro atomique est 115.**

Ununquadium/Flerovium: ununquadium/Flérovium

- **Is a radioactive chemical element.**
- **Its symbol is Uuq/Fl.**
- **Created by Russian scientific team in 2011.**
- **Etymological origin: *Uuq* (114 in Latin).**
- **Its atomic number is 114.**
- **C'est un élément radioactif de la classification périodique.**
- **Son symbole est Uuq/Fl.**
- **Créé par une équipe scientifique russe en 2011.**
- **Origine étymologique: *Uuq* (114 en latin).**
- **Son numéro atomique est 114.**

Ununseptium: Ununseptium

- **Is a radioactive chemical element.**
- **Its symbol is Uus.**
- **Created by Russian scientific team in 2010.**
- **Etymological origin: *Uus* (117 in Latin).**
- **Its atomic number is 117.**
- **C'est un élément radioactif de la classification périodique.**
- **Son symbole est Uus/Fl.**
- **Créé par une équipe scientifique russe en 2010.**
- **Origine étymologique: *Uus* (117 en latin).**

- **Son numéro atomique est 117.**

Ununtrium: ununtrium
- **Is a chemical element.**
- **Its symbol is Uut.**
- **Created by Russian scientific team in 2004.**
- **Etymological origin: *Uut* (113 in Latin).**
- **Its atomic number is 113.**
- **C'est un élément de la classification périodique.**
- **Son symbole est Uut.**
- **Créé par une équipe scientifique russe en 2004.**
- **Origine étymologique: *Uut* (113 en latin).**
- **Son numéro atomique est 113.**

Unununium/Roentegenium: unununium/Roentegenium
- **Is a radioactive chemical element.**
- **Its symbol is Uuu/Rg.**
- **Created by German scientific team in 1994.**
- **Etymological origin: *Uuu* (111 in Latin) and finally named Roentegenium in honor to the German scientist Wilhem Röntegen.**
- **Its atomic number is 111.**
- **C'est un élément radioactif de la classification périodique.**
- **Son symbole est Uuu/Rg.**
- **Créé par une équipe scientifique allemande en 1994.**
- **Origine étymologique: *Uuu* (111 en latin) et finalement nommé Roentegenium en hommage au scientifique allemand Wilhem Röntegen.**
- **Son numéro atomique est 111.**

V

Vaporization: vaporisation
- **Transition from liquid state to gaseous state.**
- **Changement d'état d'un liquide en gaz.**

Vanadium: vanadium
- **Is a chemical element.**
- **Its chemical symbol is V.**
- **Discovered by Del Rio (Mexico) in 1801 and isolated by Roscoe in 1867.**
- **Etymological origin: *Vanadis* (Scandinavian goddess of beauty).**
- **Its atomic number is 23.**
- **Used with steel alloys.**
- **C'est un élément de la classification périodique.**
- **Son symbole chimique est V.**
- **Découvert par Del Rio (Mexique) en 1801 et isolé par Roscoe en 1867.**
- **Origine étymologique: *Vanadis* (déesse scandinave de la beauté).**
- **Son numéro atomique est 23.**
- **Utilisé dans les alliages avec l'acier.**

Van der Waals' bond: liaison de Van der Waals
- **Is a weak intermolecular bond.**
- **C'est une faible liaison intermoléculaire.**

Vn der Waals equation: équation Van der waals
- **An equation of state for a real gas.**
- $(p+a/V^2)(V-b)=NRT$

  For N moles of gas at an absolute temperature T and pressure p, in a volume V.

  Where R is the Universal Gas Constant and a and b are constants that represent the attractive Intermolecular Forces and the volume of molecules respectively.
- **C'est une équation d'état d'un gaz réel.**

  Pour N moles du gaz à une température absolue et à une pression p dans un volume V.

  Dont R est la constante universelle du gaz et a et b sont des constantes qui représentent les forces d'attraction intermoléculaires et le volume des molécules respectivement.

Vector quantity: quantité vectorielle

- **A mathematical or physical quantity which has both direction and magnitude.**
- **C'est une quantité mathématique ou physique qui a une direction et une norme.**

Velocity: vitesse

- **The SI unit is m/s.**
- **L'unité dans le SI est le m/s.**

Viscoelasticity: viscoélasticité

- **Is the liquid-like flow within a polymer or glass under the action of a long-term continued stress.**
- **C'est le flux semblable au liquide dans un polymère ou un verre sous l'action d'une contrainte continue à long terme.**

Viscosity: viscosité

- **It is the resistance to uniform flow and turbulence occurring in the mass of material.**
- **C'est la résistance à l'écoulement uniforme et sans turbulence se produisant dans la masse d'une matière.**

Voltaic cell: cellule voltaique

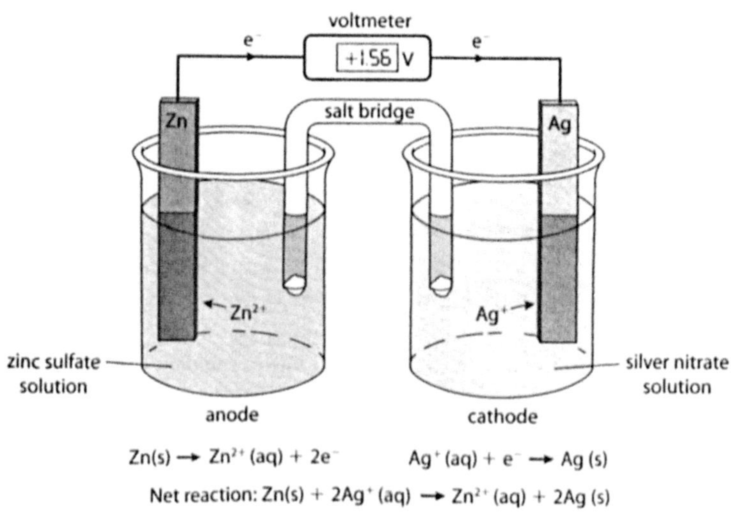

Volume: volume

- **The volume of an object is the space that this object occupies.**
- **C'est l'espace qu'un objet peut occuper.**

Vapour: vapeur

- **A substance that is in a gaseous state at a temperature below its boiling point.**
- **Une substance dans un état gazeuse à une température en dessous de point d'ébullition.**

W

Weak acids: acides faibles

- **Are only slightly ionizes when they dissolve in water. Only about one per cent of molecules reacts with water to form oxonium ions.**
- **Ils sont légèrement ionisés quand ils se dissolvent dans l'eau. Environ un pour cent des molécules réagit avec l'eau pour former des ions oxonium.**

Weak bases: bases faibles

- **Are only slightly ionizes when they dissolve in water. Only about one per cent of molecules react with water to form hydroxide ions.**
- **Ils sont légèrement ionisés quand ils se dissolvent dans l'eau. Environ un pour cent des molécules réagit avec l'eau pour former des ions hydroxyde.**

Weathering: désagrégation

- **Is a process which breaks down rocks physically and chemically.**
- **C'est un processus qui décompose les roches physiquement et chimiquement.**

Word equation: équation bilan en toutes lettres

- **An equation which describes a chemical change in words instead of symbols.**
- **C'est une équation bilan écrite en toutes lettres sans les symboles (formules brutes).**

X

X-rays: rayon X

- **Are electromagnetic radiations with very short wavelength in the region 1 nm ($1x10^{-9}$m).**
- **Ce sont des radiations électromagnétiques de longueurs d'ondes courtes, de l'ordre de 1 nm ($1x10^{-9}$m).**

Xenon: Xénon

- **Is a chemical element (noble gas) which makes up less than 0.1% of the atmosphere.**
- **Its chemical symbol is Xe.**
- **Isolated by Ramsey and Travers (England) in 1898.**
- **Etymological origin: *xenos* (stranger) from Greek.**
- **Its atomic number is 54.**
- **Excited by a high voltage, glows pale violet.**
- **C'est un gaz rare de la classification périodique formant moins de 0,1% de l'atmosphère.**
- **Son symbole chimique est Xe.**
- **Isolé par Ramsey et Travers (Angleterre) en 1898.**
- **Origine étymologique: *xenos* (étranger) du grec.**
- **Son numéro atomique est 54.**
- **Excité par une haute tension, il brille pâle violet.**

Y

Yield calculation: taux d'avancement

- **Is used to assess the efficiency of a chemical synthesis.**
- **Taux final d'une réaction chimique, se mesure en pourcentage.**

Ytterbium: yetterbium

- **A silvery metallic element.**
- **Its symbol is Yb.**
- **Discovered by Jean de Marignac in 1878.**
- **Etymological origin: *Ytterby* (Sweden city).**
- **Its atomic number is 70.**
- **Used in chemical industry.**
- **Elément métallique argenté de la classification périodique.**
- **Son symbole est Yb.**
- **Découvert en 1878 par Jean de Marignac.**
- **Origine étymologique: *Ytterby* (ville en Suède).**
- **Son numéro atomique est de 70.**
- **Utilisé dans l'industrie chimique.**

Yttrium: yttrium

- **Is a metallic chemical element.**
- **Its chemical symbol Y.**
- **Discovered by Johan Gadolin (Finland) in 1794 and isolated by Wöhler (Germany) in 1828.**
- **Etymological origin: *Ytterby* (Sweden village).**
- **Its atomic number 39.**
- **Used in lasers.**
- **C'est un élément métallique de la classification périodique.**
- **Son symbole chimique est Y.**
- **Découvert par Johan Gadolin (Finlande) en 1794 et isolé par Wöhler (Allemagne) en 1828.**
- **Origine étymologique: *Ytterby* (village suédois).**
- **Son numéro atomique est 39.**
- **Utilisé dans les lasers.**

Z

Zero order reaction: réaction d'ordre zéro

- **A reaction is zero order with respect to a reactant if the rate of reaction is unaffected by changes in the concentration of that reactant.**
- **Une réaction est dite d'ordre zéro par rapport à un réactif si le taux de la réaction n'est pas affecté par la variation de la concentration de ce réactif.**

Zinc: zinc

- **Is a metallic chemical element.**
- **Its chemical symbol is Zn.**
- **Known since antiquity. Isolated by Marggrat (Germany) in 1746.**
- **Etymological origin: *zangâr* (rust) from Persian or *alzanjâ* from Arabic.**
- **Its atomic number is 30.**
- **Used as sacrificial anodes to protect ship hulls, rails and steel tanks from rusting and oxidation.**
- **C'est un élément métallique de la classification périodique.**
- **Son symbole chimique est Zn.**
- **Connu depuis l'antiquité. Isolé par Marggrat (Allemagne) en 1746.**
- **Origine étymologique: *zangâr* (rouille) du persan ou *alzanjâ* de l'arabe.**
- **Son numéro atomique est 30.**
- **Utilisé comme anodes sacrificielles pour protéger la coque des navires, des rails et des réservoirs d'acier de la rouille et de l'oxydation.**

Zirconium: zirconium

- **Is a metallic chemical element.**
- **Its chemical symbol is Zr.**
- **Discovered by Klaproth (Germany) in 1789 and isolated by Berzelius (Sweden) in 1824.**
- **Etymological origin: *zarcoun* (precious stone) from Arabic.**
- **Its atomic number is 40.**
- **Used in body-piercing jewelry.**
- **C'est un élément métallique de la classification périodique.**
- **Son symbole chimique est Zr.**
- **Découvert par Klaproth (Allemagne) en 1789 et isolé par Berzelius (Suède) en 1824.**
- **Origine étymologique: *zarcoun* (pierre précieuse) de l'arabe.**

- **Son numéro atomique est 40.**
- **Utilisé dans les bijoux de piercing.**

Zwitterion: zwitterion

- **An ion that has a positive and a negative charge on the same group of atom.**
- **Ion possédant des charges négatives et positives dans le même groupe d'atome.**

Appendices

ELEMENTS WITH THEIR SYMBOLS IN ALPHABETICAL ORDER - LES ÉLÉMENTS CHIMIQUES ET LEURS SYMBOLES DANS L'ORDRE ALPHABÉTIQUE

Symbol-Symbole	English	Français	Etymology/ Etymologie	Discovered/ Découvert
Ac	Actinium	Actinium	Aktinos (Greek)	Andre Debierne 1899
Ag	Silver	Argent	Argyros (Greek)	Used since ancient times
Al	Aluminum	Aluminum	Alumen (latin)	Used since Antiquity
Am	Americium	Américium	Continent	Seaborg 1944
Ar	Argon	Argon	Argos (Greek)	Henry Cavendish 1785
As	Arsenic	Arsenic	Arsên (Greek)	used since Antiquity
At	Astatine	Astate	Astatos (Greek)	Dale Corson, Kenneth MacKenzie, and Emilio Segrè 1940
Au	Gold	Or	Aurum (Latin)	Used since Antiquity
B	Boron	Bore	Borax (Persiasn)	Used since Antiquity
Ba	Barium	Barium	Barus (Greek)	Humphrey Davy 1808
Be	Beryllium	Beryllium	Ore (minerai)	René Haüy 1798
Bh	Bohrium	Bohrium	Neils Bohr (scientists)	USSR in 1976
Bi	Bismuth	Bismuth	Wismuth (german)	Claude Geoffroy 1753
Bk	Berkelium	Berkélium	Berekely city (USA)	Stanley Thompson, Albert Ghiorso and Glenn Seaborg 1949
Br	Bromine	Brome	Bromôs (Greek)	Used since Antiquity
C	Carbon	Carbone	Carbo	Used since Antiquity

			(Latin)	
Ca	Calcium	Calcium	Cals (Latin)	Sir Humphry Davy in 1808
Cd	Cadmium	Cadmium	Kadmeia (Greek)	Fredrich Stromeyer 1817
Ce	Cerium	Cérium	Ceres (Greek)	Jöns J. Berzelius and Wilhelm von Hisinger 1808
Cf	Californium	Californium	Clifornia (USA)	Stanley Thompson, Kenneth Street, Albert Ghiorso and Glenn Seaborg 1950
Cl	Chlorine	Chlore	Khlôros (Greek)	Carl Wilhelm Scheele 1774
Co	Cobalt	Cobalt	Kobold (German)	Used since Antiquity
Cm	Curium	Curium	Marie Curie (scientists)	Glenn T. Seaborg, Ralph A.James, and Albert Ghiorso 1944
Cn	Copernicium	Copernicium	Johanos Copernic	Germany 1996
Cr	Chromium	Chrome	Krôma (Greek)	Nicolas-Louis Vanquelin 1780
Cs	Cesium	Césium	Caesius (Latin)	Robert Bunsen and Gustav Kirchhoff 1860
Cu	Copper	Cuivre	Cypres (Island)	used since Antiquity
Db	Dubnium	Dubnium	Dubna city (Russia)	Scientists 1967
Dy	Dysprosium	Dysprosium	Dusprositus (Greek)	Paul Émile Lecoq de Boisbaudran 1886
Er	Erbium	Erbium	Ytterby city (Sweden)	Carl Gustaf Mosande 1843
Es	Einsteinium	Einsteinium	Albert Einstein	Scientists 1952
Eu	Europium	Europium	Continent	Eugène-Antole Demarçay 1901
F	Fluorine	Flore	Fluor (Latin)	Georgius Agricola 1530
Fe	Iron	Fer	Ferrum (Latin)	Known since ancient times
Fm	Fermium	Fermium	Enrico fermi (scientists)	Teams of scientists 1952

Fr	Francium	Francium	France	Marguerite Perey in 1939
Ga	Gallium	Gallium	Gallus (Greek)	Paul E. Lecoq de Boisbaudran 1875
Gd	Gadolinium	Gadolinium	Johan Gadolin (scientists)	Jean Charles Galissard de Marigna 1880
Ge	Germanium	Germanium	Germany	Clemens A. Winkler 1886
H	Hydrogen	Hydrogene	Hydrogenes (Greek)	Theophrastus Paracelsus 1500
He	Helium	Hélium	Hélios (Latin)	Pierre Janssen 1886
Hf	Hafnium	Hafnium	Kobenhavn (Danemark)	Dirk Coster and Georg von Hevesey 1923
Hg	Mercury	Mercure	Mercury planet	Known since ancient times
Ho	Holmium	Holmium	Holmia (Latin)	Marc Delafontaine and Jacques-Louis Soret 1878
Hs	Hassium	Hassium	Hassia (Latin)	Peter Armbruster and Gottfried Münzenbes 1984
I	Iodine	Iode	Iôdes (Greek)	Bernard Courtois 1811
In	Indium	Indium	Indigo (Germany)	Ferdinand Reich and Hieronymous T. Richter 1863
Ir	Iridium	Iridium	Iris (Latin)	Smithson Tennant 1803
K	Potassium	Potassium	kali (Arab)	Sir Humphry Davy 1806
Kr	Krypton	Krypton	Kruptos (Greek)	William Ramsay and his assistant Morris Travers discovered krypton 1898
La	Lanthanum	Lanthane	Lanthanien (Greek)	Carl G. Mosander 1839
Li	Lithium	Lithium	Lithos (Greek)	Johan Arfvedson 1817
Lr	Lawrencium	Lawrencium	Ernest Lawrence (scientists)	Albert Ghiorso, Torbjørn Sikkeland, Almon Larsh and Robert Latimer 1961
Lu	Lutetium	Lutécium	Lutêce (Paris)	Carl Auer von Welsbach, Charles James, and Georges Urbain 1907
				Albert Ghiorso, Bernard

Md	**Mendelevium**	**Méndélevium**	**Dimitri Mende-leïev (scientists)**	**Harvey, Gregory Chop-pin, Stanley Thompson, and Glenn Seaborg 1955**
Mg	**Magnesium**	**Magnesium**	**Magnesia (Greek)**	**Joseph Black 1755**
Mn	**Manganese**	**Manganese**	**Magnesia (Greek city)**	**Known since ancient times**
Mo	**Molybdenum**	**Molybdene**	**Molubdos (Greek)**	**Extracted by Carl W. Scheele 1778, isolated by Peter J. Hjelm 1781**
Mt	**Meitnerium**	**Meitnerium**	**Lise Meitner (scientists)**	**Peter Armbruster and Gottfried Münzenber 1982**
N	**Nitrogen**	**Azote**	**a-zôê (Greek)**	**Daniel Rutherford, Carl Scheele 1772**
Na	**Sodium**	**Sodium**	**Natroun (Arab)**	**Sir Humphry Davy 1806**
Nb	**Niobium**	**Niobium**	**Niobe (Greek)**	**Charles Hatchett 1801**
Nd	**Neodymium**	**Néodyme**	**Nêos dîdymos (Greek)**	**Carl Auer von Welsbach 1885**
Ne	**Neon**	**Néon**	**Neos (Greek)**	**William Ramsay and Morris Travers 1898**
Ni	**Nickel**	**Nickel**	**Koppar nickel (Sweden)**	**Used since ancient times**
No	**Nobelium**	**Nobelium**	**Alfred Nobel (industrial)**	**Albert Ghiorso, Torbjørn Sikkeland, John Walton, and Glenn Seaborg 1958**
Np	**Neptunium**	**Neptunium**	**Neptune (Greek)**	**Edwin McMillan and Philip H. Abelson 1940**
O	**Oxygen**	**Oxygène**	**Oxus genos (Greek)**	**Joseph Priestley 1774**
Os	**Osmium**	**Osmium**	**Asmê (Greek)**	**Smithson Tennant 1803**
P	**Phosphorus**	**Phosphore**	**Phôsphoros (Greek)**	**Hennig Brand 1669**
Pa	**Protactinium**	**Protactinium**	**Protos (Greek)**	**Kasimir Fajans and Oswald Göhring 1913**
Pb	**Lead**	**Plomb**	**Plumbum (Latin)**	**Known since ancient times**

Pd	Palladium	Palladium	Pallas (Greek)	William.H. Wollaston 1803
Pm	Promethium	Promethium	Prometheus (Greek)	Isolated by Jacob. A. Marinsky, Lawrence E. Glendenin and Charles D. Coryell 1945
Po	Polonium	Polonium	Poland (Pologne)	Marie S. Curie 1898
Pr	Praseodymium	Praseodymium	Praso didymos (Greek)	Carl Auer von Welsbach 1885
Pt	Platinum	Platinum	Platina (Spain)	Used by Old South American peoples
Pu	Plutonium	Plutonium	Pluton (Greek)	Glenn Seaborg, Edwin McMillan, Joseph Kennedy, and Arthur Wahl 1940
Ra	Radium	Radium	Radius (Latin)	Pierre and Marie S. Curie 1898
Rb	Rubidium	Rubidium	Rubidus (Latin)	Robert Bunsen and Gustav Kirchhoff 1861
Re	Rhenium	Rhenium	Rhenus (Latin)	Walter Noddack, Ida Tacke, and Otto Berg first 1925
Rf	Rutherfordium	Rutherfordium	Ernest Rutherford (scientists)	Scientists 1964
Rg	Roentgenium	Roentgenium	Röntgen (scientists)	Scientists 1994
Rh	Rhodium	Rhodium	Rhodon (Greek)	William Hyde Wollaston 1803
Rn	Radon	Radon	Radium (from radium)	Fredrich E. Dorn 1900
Ru	Ruthenium	Ruthenium	Ruthenia (Russia)	Gottfried W. Osann 1827
S	Sulfur	Soufre	Sulfur (Latin)	Known since ancient times
Sb	Antimony	Antimoine	Althimar (Arab)	Egyptians 3000 BC
Sc	Scandium	Scandium	Scandinavia	Lars F. Nilson 1879
Se	Selenium	Selenium	Selênê	Arabs 1200
Sg	Seaborgium	Seaborgium	Glenn Seaborg	Scientists

Si	**Silicon**	**Silicium**	**Silex (stone)**	**Antoine Lavoisier 1789**
Sm	**Samarium**	**Samarium**	**Samarskite (ore)**	**Paul E. Lecoq de Boisbaudran 1875**
Sn	**Tin**	**Etain**	**Stagnum (Latin)**	**Known since ancient times**
Sr	**Strontium**	**Strontium**	**Strontian city (Scotland)**	**Adair Crawford 1790**
Ta	**Tantalum**	**Tantalum**	**Tantalus (Greek)**	**Anders G. Ekeberg in 1802**
Tb	**Terbium**	**Terbium**	**Ytterby (Sweden)**	**Carl Gustaf Mosander 1843**
Tc	**Technetium**	**Technetium**	**Teritos (Greek)**	**Carlo Perrier and Emilio Segrè 1937**
Te	**Tellurium**	**Tellurium**	**Tellus (Latin)**	**Baron Franz Muller von Reichenstein 1783**
Th	**Thorium**	**Thorium**	**Thor (Greek)**	**Jöns Jacob Berzelius 1828**
Ti	**Titanium**	**Titanium**	**Titans (Greek)**	**William Gregor 1791**
Tl	**Thallium**	**Thallium**	**Thallos (Greek)**	**William Crookes 1861**
Tm	**Thulium**	**Thulium**	**Thule (Latin)**	**Per Teodor Cleve 1879**
U	**Uranium**	**Uranium**	**Uranus (Greek)**	**Martin Heinrich Klaproth 1789**
Uub/Cn	**Ununbium/ Copernicium**	**Ununbium/ Copernicium**	**Nicolaus Copernicus (scientists)**	**Scientists 1996**
Uuh/Lv	**Ununhexium/ Livermorium**	**Ununhexium/ Livermorium**	**Lawrence Livermore (scientists)**	**Scientists 2000**
Uun/Ds	**Ununnillium/ Darmstadtium**	**Ununnillium/ Darmstadtium**	**Darmstadt (German city)**	**Scientists 1994**
Uuo	**Ununoctium**	**Ununoctium**	**118 (Latin)**	**Scientists 2002**
Uup	**Unupentium**	**Unupentium**	**115 (Latin)**	**Scientists 2003**
Uuq/Fl	**Ununquadium/ Flerovium**	**Ununquadium/ Flérovium**	**Georgy Flyorov (scientists)**	**Russian Scientists 1998**
Uus	**Ununseptium**	**Ununseptium**	**117 (Latin)**	**Scientists 2010**
Uut	**Ununtrium**	**Ununtrium**	**113 (Latin)**	**Scientists 2003**
Uuu/Rg	**Unununium/ Roentgenium**	**Unununium/ Roentgenium**	**Röntgen (scientists)**	**Scientists 1994**

V	**Vanadium**	**Vanadium**	**Vanadis (Scandinavian)**	**Andreas.M. del Rio 1801**
W	**Tungsten**	**Tungstene**	**Tung sten (Swedish)**	**Carl W. Scheele 1781**
Xe	**Xenon**	**Xénon**	**Xenos (Greek)**	**William Ramsay and Morris Travers. 1898**
Y	**Yttrium**	**Yttrium**	***Ytterby*** **(Stockholm archipelago)**	**Nicolas Louis Vauquelin 1798**
Yb	**Ytterbium**	**Ytterbium**	***Ytterby (Sweden)***	**Jean Charles Galissard de Marignac 1878**
Zn	**Zinc**	**Zinc**	**Alzanji (Arab)**	**Used since Antiquity**
Zr	**Zirconium**	**Zirconium**	**Zarcoun (Arab)**	**Martin Heinrich Klaproth in 1789**

LA VERRERIE DE LABORATOIRE
LABORATORY GLASSWARE

Magnetic stirrers	**Agitateur magnètique**	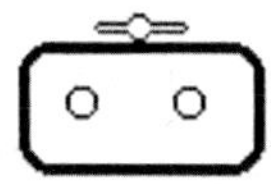
Beaker	**Bécher**	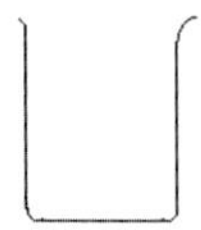
Bulb fillers	**Poire d'aspiration**	
Capsule	**Capsule**	
Liebig Condenser	**Réfrigérant**	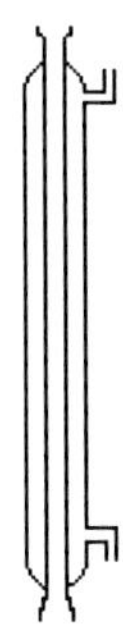
Crystallizer	**Cristallisoire**	

Erlenmeyer	**Erlenmeyer**	
Funnel	**Entonnoir**	
Graduated burette	**Burette graduée**	
Wash bottle	**Pissettes**	
Graduated cylinder	**Eprouvette graduée**	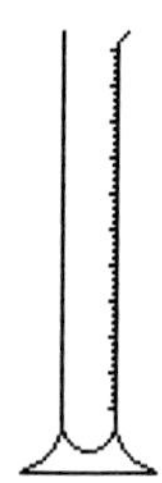

Graduated pipette	**Pipette graduée**	
Pasteur pipette	**Pipette Pasteur (micro-pipette)**	
Spatula	**Spatule**	
Pipette pumps	**Pro pipette ou pipeteur**	
Round-bottom flask	**Ballon**	

Separatory funnel	**Ampoule à décanter**	
Simple pipette	**Pipette simple**	
Watch glass	**Verre de montre**	
Test tube	**Tube à essai**	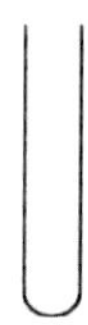
Vigreux column	**Colonne de Vigreux**	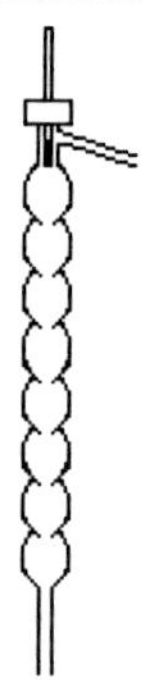

Volumetric flask	**Fiole jaugée**	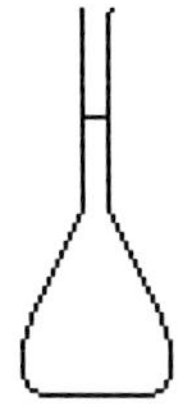
Volumetric pipette	**Pipette jaugée**	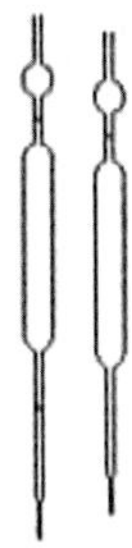
Stopper (U.S.) / bung	**Bouchon**	

THE FORMULAS OF SOME INORGANIC COMPOUNDS
FORMULES DE QUELQUES COMPOSÉS INORGANICS

Name	Nom	Other name	Nom usuel	Formula formule
Aluminium oxide	Oxyde d'aluminium			Al_2O_3
Ammonia	Ammoniac			NH_3
Ammonium chloride	Chlorure d'ammonium			NH_4Cl
Ammonium nitrate	Nitrate d'ammonium	NITRAM		NH_4NO_3
Calcium carbonate	Carbonate de calcium	Limestone, chalk	Calcaire, crée	$CaCO_3$
Calcium chloride	Chlorure de calcium			$CaCl_2$
Calcium hydroxide	Hydroxyde de calcium	Slaked lime	Eau de chaux	$Ca(OH)_2$
Calcium oxide	Monoxyde de calcium	Quicklime		CaO
Carbon monoxide	Monoxyde de carbone			CO
Carbon dioxide	Dioxyde de carbone			CO_2
Cobalt chloride	Dichlorure de cobalte			$CoCl_2$
Copper chloride	Dichlorure de cuivre			$CuCl_2$
Copper sulphate	Sulphate de cuivre			$CuSO_4$
Hydrochloric acide	Acide chlorhydrique			$HCl_{(aq)}$
Hydrogen fluoride	Fluorure d'hydrogène			HF
Hydrogen peroxide	Peroxyde d'hydrogène		Eau oxygénée	H_2O_2
Hydrogen sulphide	Sulfure d'hydrogène			H_2S
Iron(II) chloride	Chlorure de fer (II)			$FeCl_2$
Iron(III) chloride	Chlorure de fer (III)			$FeCl_3$
Magnesium carbonate	Carbonate de magnésium			$MgCO_3$
Magnesium chloride	Chlorure de magnésium			$MgCl_2$

Magnesium oxide	**Monoxide de magnésium**	**Magnesia**		**MgO**
Manganese dioxide	**Dioxyde de manganèse**			**MnO_2**
Nitric acid	**Acide nitrique**			**HNO_3**
Nitrogen moboxide	**Monoxyde d'azote**			**NO**
Nitrogen dioxide	**Dioxyde d'azote**			**NO_2**
Potassium chloride	**Chlorure de potassium**			**KCl**
Potassium hydroxide	**Hydroxyde de potassium**	**Caustic potash**		**KOH**
Potassium permanganate	**Permanganate de potassium**			**$KMnO_4$**
Potassium nitrate	**Nitrate de potassium**	**Salpetre**	**Salpètre**	**KNO_3**
Silicon dioxide	**Dioxyde de silicium**	**Silica**	**Silice**	**SiO_2**
Sodium carbonate	**Carbonate de sodium**	**Soda ash, washing soda**		**Na_2CO_3**
Sodium chloride	**Chlorure de sodium**	**Salt**	**Sel**	**NaCl**
Sodium hydrogencarbonate	**Hydrogénocarbonate de sodium**	**Sodium bicarbonate**		**$NaHCO_3$**
Sodium hydroxide	**Hydroxide de sodium**	**Caustic soda**	**Soude caustique**	**NaOH**
Sodium nitrate	**Nitrate de sodium**			**$NaNO_3$**
Sodium sulphate	**Sulphate de sodium**			**Na_2SO_4**
Sulphur dioxide	**Dioxyde de soufre**			**SO_2**
Sulphur trioxide	**Trioxyde de soufre**			**SO_3**
Sulphuric acid	**Acide sulphirique**			**H_2SO_4**
Zinc oxide	**Monoxide de zinc**			**ZnO**
Water	**Eau**			**H_2O**

PICTOGRAM - PICTOGRAMMES

Corrosion	**Corrosif**	
Compressed gases	**Gaz sous pression**	
Skin irritation	**Irritant**	
Exploding	**Explosif**	
Flame	**Inflammable**	

Acute hazards to the environment	**Dangereux pour l'environnement**	
Rondflam	**Comburant**	
Respiratory sensitization	**Cancérogène, mutgène et reprotoxique**	
Toxic	**Toxique**	

CHEMICAL TESTS
TESTES DE RECONAISSANCE

Various chemical tests can be done to find out a mystery substance.

Flame tests:

Potassium (K) burns with a lilac flame.
Sodium (Na) burns with a yellow/orange flame.
Calcium (Ca) burns with a brick-red flame.
Copper (Cu) burns with a blue-green flame.

Colored precipitate:

Ion name	Iron (II)	Iron (III)	Copper (II)	Chlorine	Zinc	Potassium	Calcium	Magnesium
Formula	e^{2+}	Fe^{3+}	Cu^{2+}	Cl^-	Zn^{2+}	K^+	Ca^{2+}	Mg^{2+}
Reactive	NaOH	NaOH	NaOH	$AgNO_3$	NaOH	Picrate de sodium	Oxalate d'ammonium	NaOH
Precipitation Colour	Green	Brick-red	Blue	White	White	Yellow	White	White

Common gases tests:

Chlorine bleaches damp litmus paper, turning it white.
Oxygen relights a glowing splint.
Carbon dioxide turns limewater cloudy.
Hydrogen makes a 'squeaky pop' with lighted splint.
Ammonia turns damp red litmus paper blue.

MAIN FUNCTIONAL GROUPS
PRINCIPAUX GROUPES FONCTIONNELS

Chemical class	Group	Formula	Structural Formula	Prefix	Suffix	Example
Alcohol	Hydroxyl	ROH	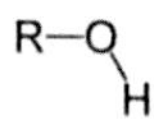	hydroxy-	-ol	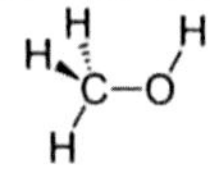 Methanol
Ketone	Carbonyl	RCOR'	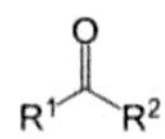	keto-, oxo-	-one	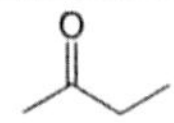 Methyl ethyl ketone *(Butanone)*
Aldehyde	Aldehyde	RCHO	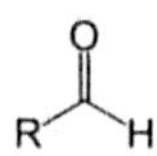	aldo-	-al	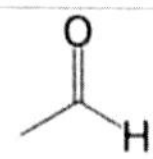 Acetaldehyde *(Ethanal)*
Carboxylic acid	Carboxyl	RCOOH	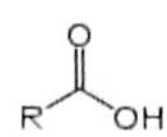	carboxy-	-oic acid	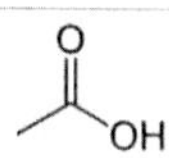 Acetic acid *(Ethanoic acid)*
Ether	Ether	ROR'	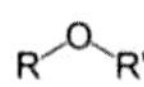	alkoxy-	alkyl alkyl **ether**	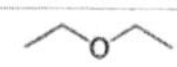 Diethyl ether *(Ethoxyethane)*
Ester	Ester	RCOOR'	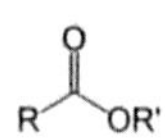		alkyl alkan**oate**	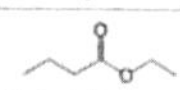 Ethyl butyrate *(Ethyl butanoate)*
Amide	Carboxamide	$RCONR_2$	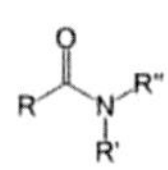	carboxamido	-amide	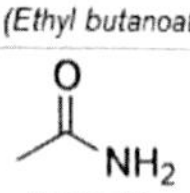 Acetamide *(Ethanamide)*
Amines	Primary amine	RNH_2	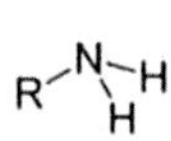	amino-	-amine	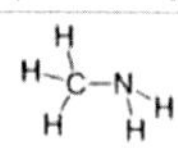 Methylamine *(Methanamine)*

THE PERIODIC TABLE OF ELEMENTS
TABLEAU PÉRIODIQUE DES ÉLEMENTS

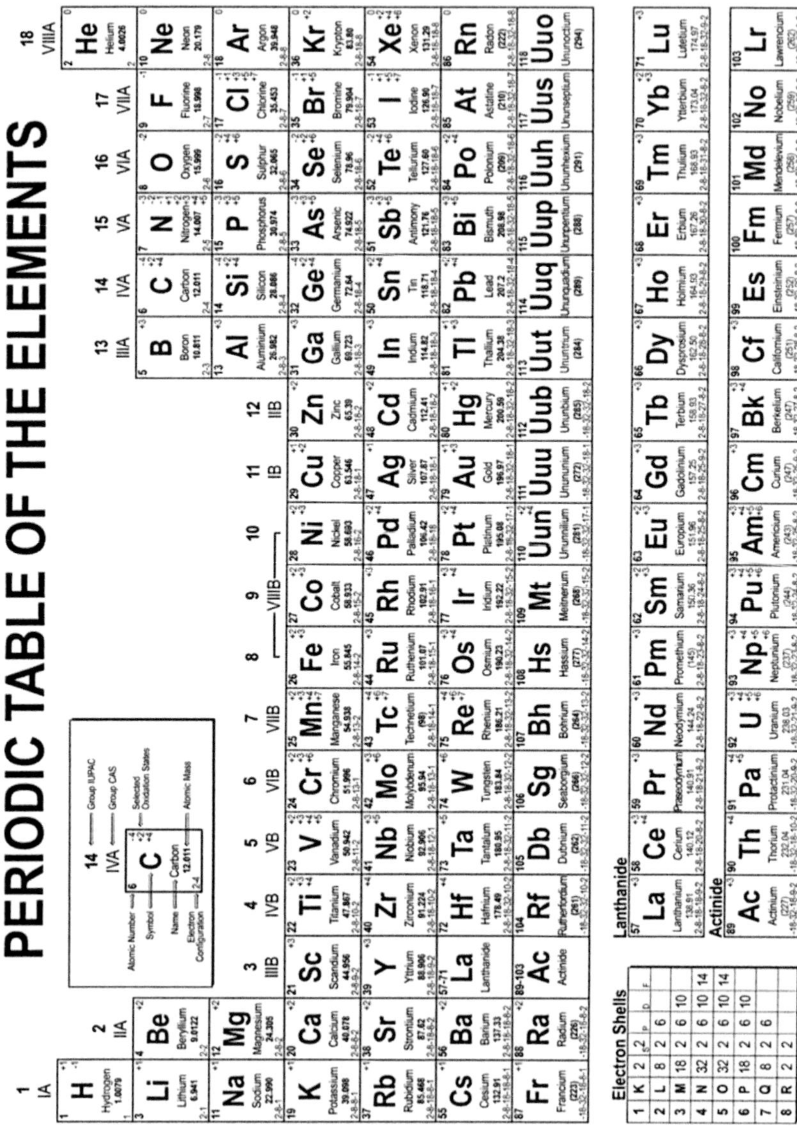

ISOMERS
ISOMÈRES

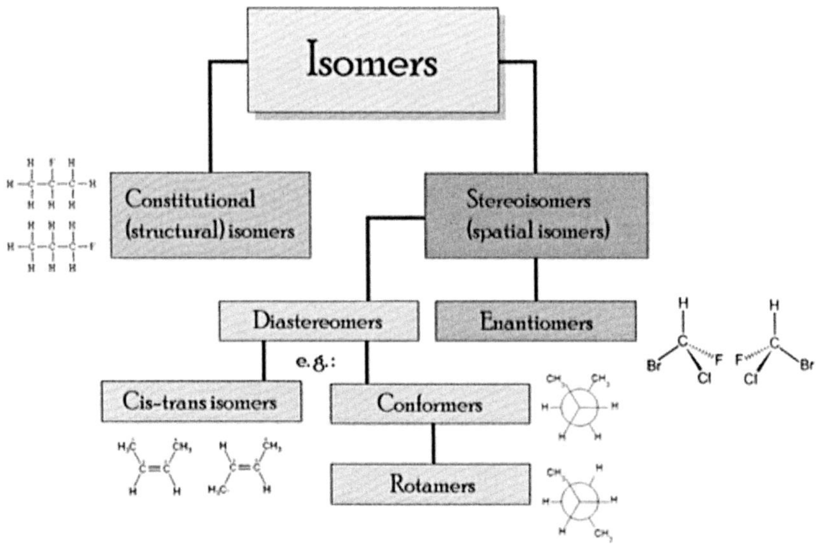

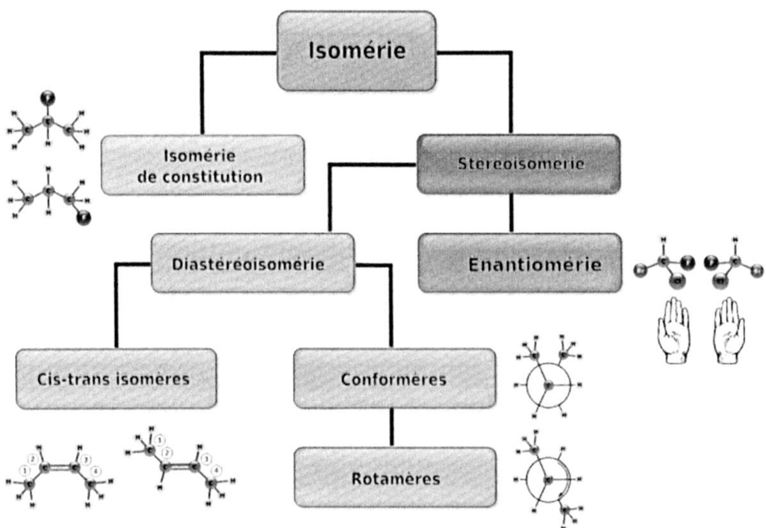

DIFFERENT FORMULAS APPLIED TO TWO COMPOUNDS
LES DIFFÉRENTES FORMULES APPLIQUÉES À DEUX COMPOSÉS CHIMIQUES

Compound / Composé	**Butane**	**Ethanoic acid / acide éthanoique**
Empirical formula / Formule brute	C_2H_5	CH_2O
Molecular formula / Formule moléculaire	C_4H_{10}	$C_2H_4O_2$
Full structural formula / Formule développée	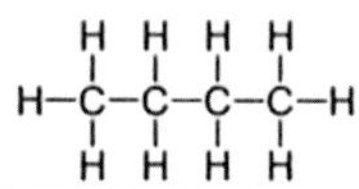	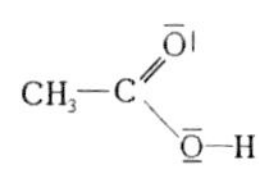
Condensed structural formula / Formule semi-développée	$CH_3-CH_2-CH_2-CH_3$	CH_3-COOH
Skeletal formula / Formule topoloqiue		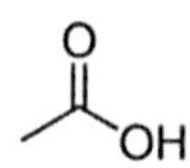
Ball-and-stick model / Modèle moléculaire eclaté	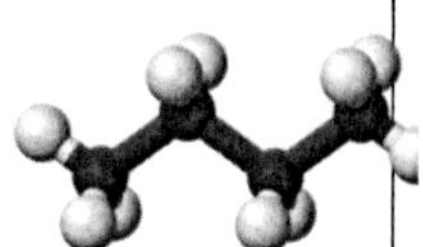	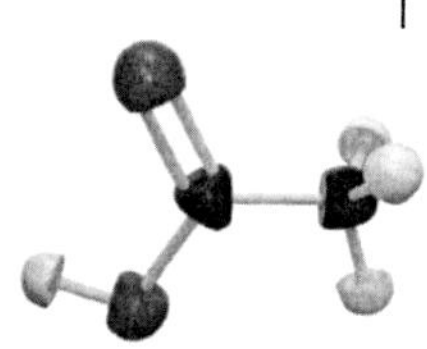
Space-filling model / Modèle compact	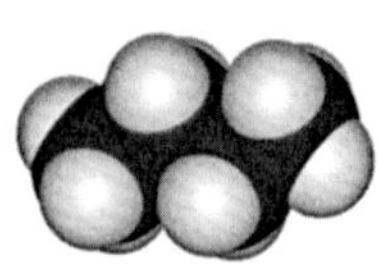	

PART 3

MATHEMATICS – MATHEMATIQUES

Mathematics is the language which explains how the Universe behaves.

Les mathématiques est un langage qui explique comment l'Univers se comporte.

A

Abacus: boulier.
Abelian group: groupe abélien.
Abscissa: abscisse.
Absolute value: valeur absolue.
Absolute: absolue.
Absorption laws: loi d'absorption.
Abstraction: abstraction.
Abundant numbers: nombre abondant.
Acceleration: accélération.
Accuracy: précision.
Acute angle: angle aigue (inférieur à 90°).

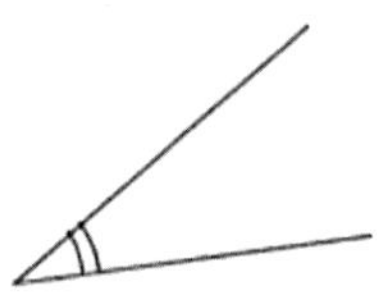

Addend: terme (est à l'addition ce que le facteur est à la multiplication).
Addition: addition.
Adjacent angles: angles adjacent.

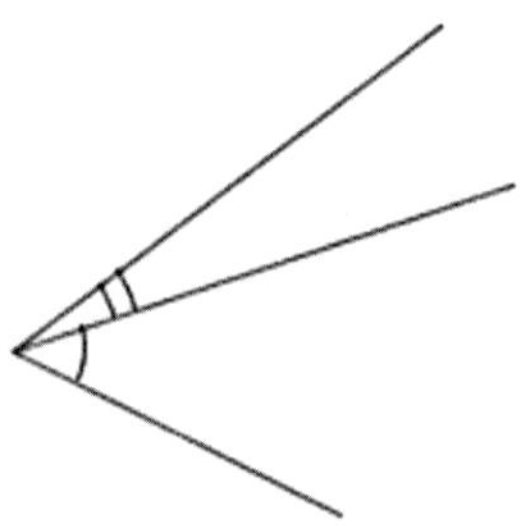

Adjugate matrix: comatrice.
Affine: affine (fonction).
Algebra: algèbre.

Algebraic functions: fonctions algébrique.
Algorithm: algorithme.
Alphabet: alphabet.
Alphanumeric: caractère alphanumérique.
Alternate exterior angles: angles alternes externes.

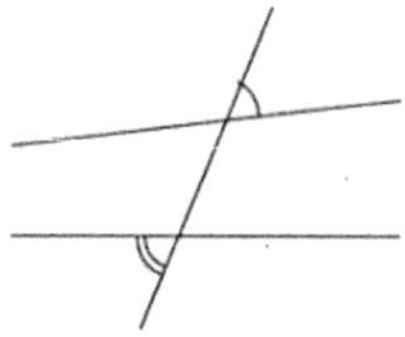

Alternate interior angles: angles alternes internes.

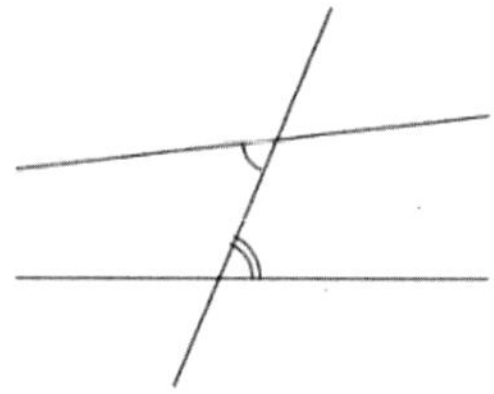

Altitude: hauteur (triangle).

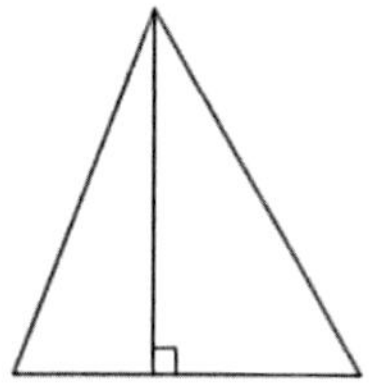

Altitude: hauteur.
Amicable numbers: nombre amiable.
Amplitude: amplitude.
Analog: analogique.
Analytic geometry: géométrie analytique.
Analysis: analyse.
Angle: angle.
Angle-hook: équerre.

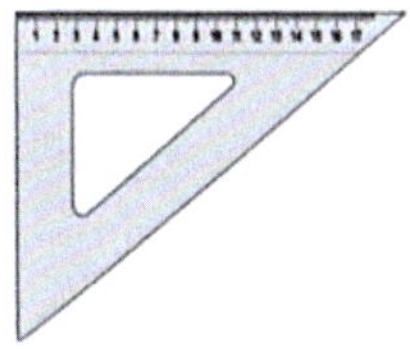

Angstrom: angstrom (unite), 10^{-15}.

Antecedent: antecedent.

Anticlockwise: dans le sens contraire du clockwise (U.K.).

Annulus: anneaux.

Apex apex (sommet le plus élevé)

- **The highest point of a solid or plane figure relative to a base plane or line**
- **Le point le plus haut d'une figure solide ou plane.**

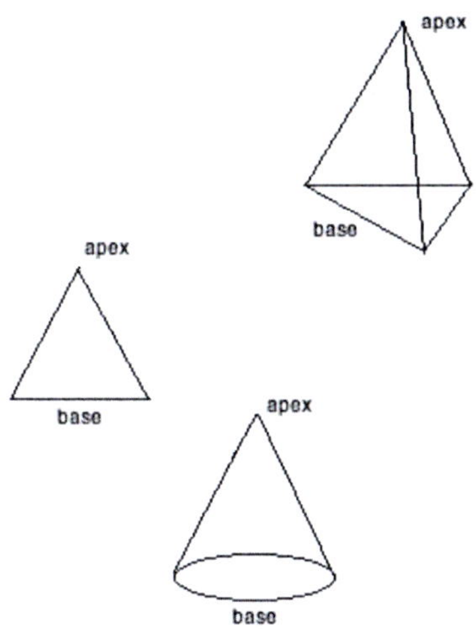

Apex, apices: sommet(s) (pour un volume).

Approximation: approximation.

Arabic numerals: chiffres Arabe.

Area: aire.

Arc: arc.

Arccot: arc cotangent.

Arcctg: arctangent.

Archimedes' constant: pi.
Arcos: arc cosinus.
Area: aire, surface.
Argument: argument.
Arithmetic: arithmétique.
Arms: côtés (d'un angle), côtés de l'angle droit (d'un triangle rectangle).

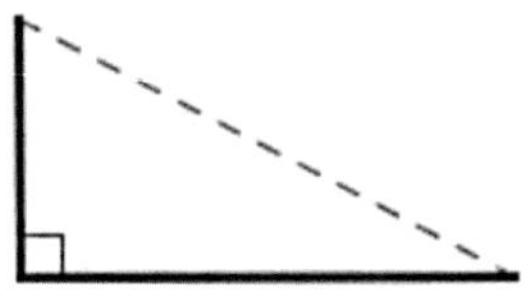

Associative laws: loi des associations.
Assume (to): supposer, prendre (une valeur).
Assumption: hypothèse.
Asymptote: asymptote.

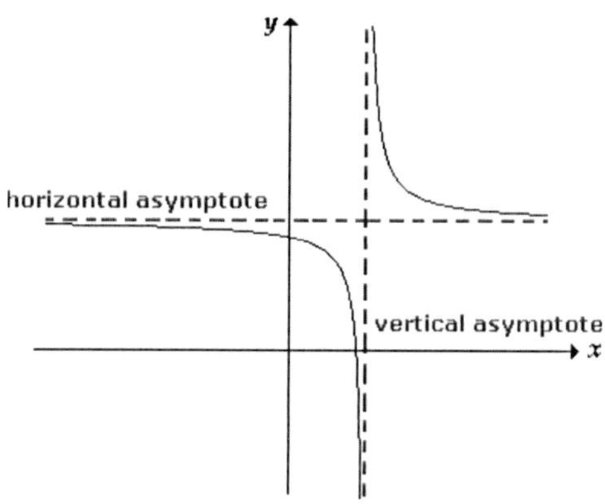

Auxiliary equation: équation caractéristique.
Average: moyenne.
Axiom: axiom.
Axis/axes: axes.

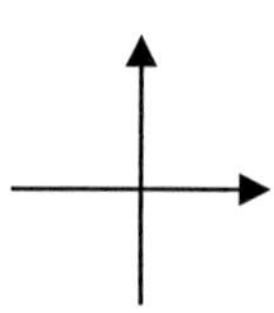

Azimuth: azimute.
Aztec numeration: numération Aztèque.

B

Babylonian sexagesimal system: système sexagésimal. Babylonien.
Bar: barre (verticale, cf. vinculum), bâton (diagramme).
Bar chart: diagramme à baton.

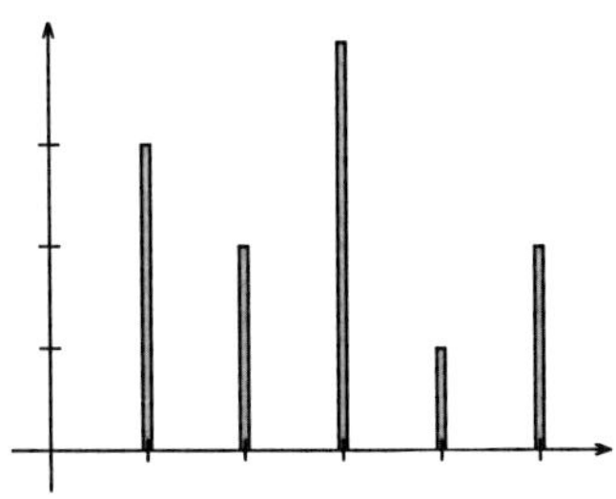

Barber paradox: Paradoxe du barbier.
Barycenter: barycentre.

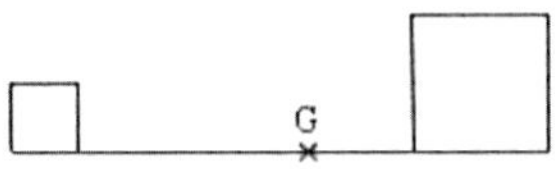

Base: base.
Bearings: palier.
Belong (to): appartenir.
Bernoulli equation: équation de Bernoulli.
Bijective: bijectif.
Billion: milliard, 10^9.
Binary numeration: numération binaire.
Binomial coefficient: coefficient binomial.
Biquadtratic equation: équation biquadratique.
Bisection method: Méthode de dichotomie.
Bisector: bissectrice (U.S.).

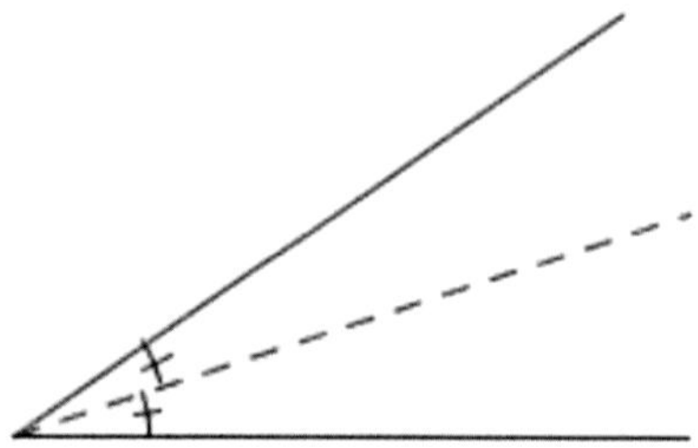

Bit: binary digit.
Block of elements: bloc d'éléments.
Body: corps, solide.
Boolean algebra: Algèbre de Boole (logique).
Borromean rings: Anneaux borroméens.
Borrow (to): retenir (= faire une retenue) (emprunter dans le civil).
Boundary value problem: conditions aux limites.
Bounded: borne.
Boxplot: diagramme en boîte (ou boîte à moustaches
Brace: accolade.
Bracket: (curly -) accolade; (round -) parenthèse; (square -) crochet.

C

Calculate: calculer.
Calculus: branch d'étude des fonctions.
Cancel (to): éliminer, simplifier par.
Cancellation: élimination, simplification.
Canonical: canonique.
Cardinal number: nombre cardinal.
Cardinality: cardinal.
Cartesian coordinates: coordonnées cartésien.

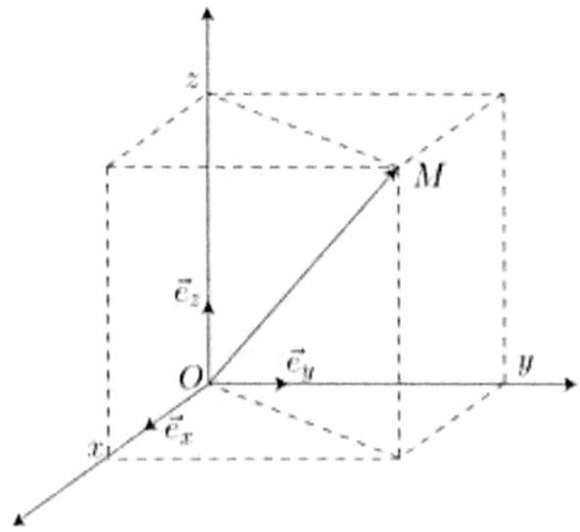

Centroid: centre de gravité.

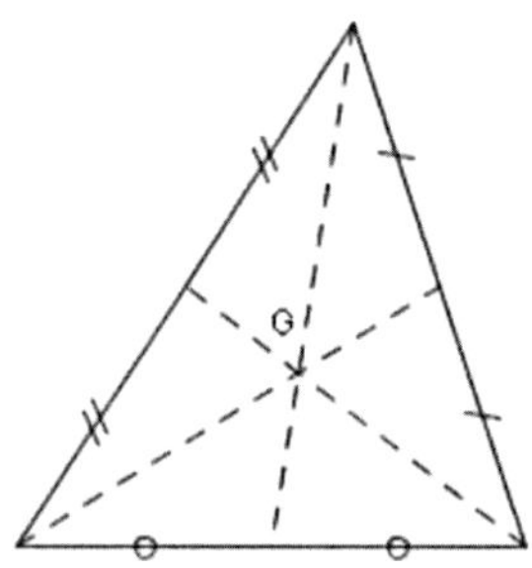

Check (to): vérifier (un calcul).
Cipher: chiffre, zéro.
Circum: concerne le cercle circonscrit(e) (circumcercle),
Circumcenter of a triangle: centre du cercle circonscrit à un triangle.

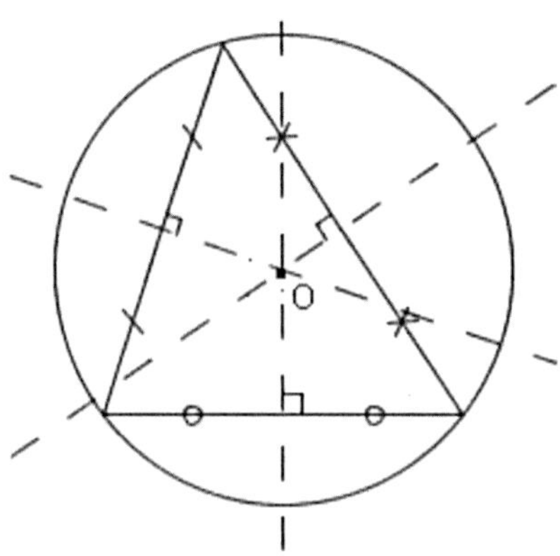

Clockwise: dans le sens des aiguilles d'une montre.
Coincident: confondu.
Collinear: alignés (points).

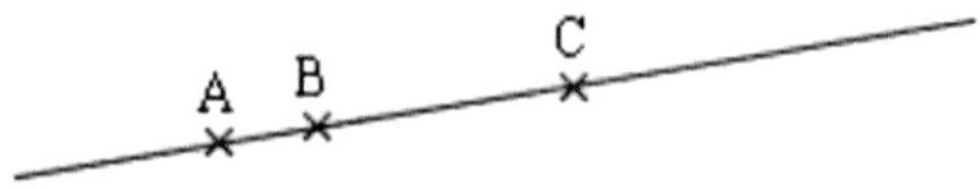

Combination: combinaison.
Comma: virgule.
Complex: complexe.
Compute (to): calculer.
Conjecture: conjecture.
Conjugate: conjugué.
Conjugation: conjugaison.
Continuos (fucntion): continue (fonction).
Convergent: concourantes.

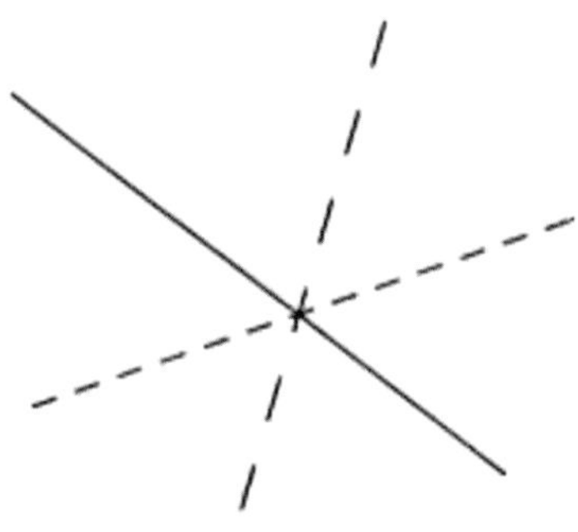

Coordinates: coordonnées.

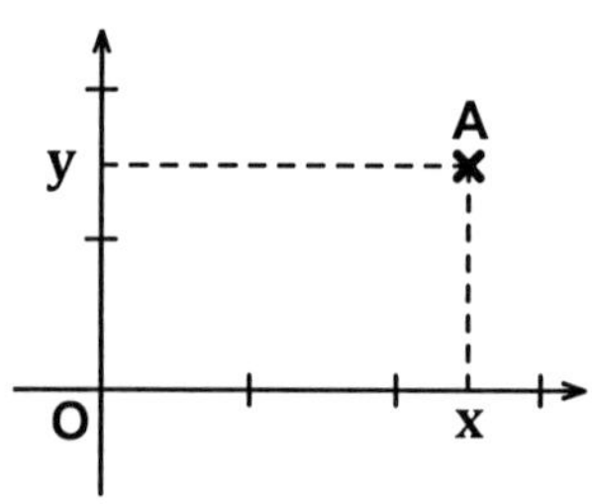

Coprime: premiers entre eux.
Correct: exact (calcul, décimales).
Corresponding angles: angles correspondants

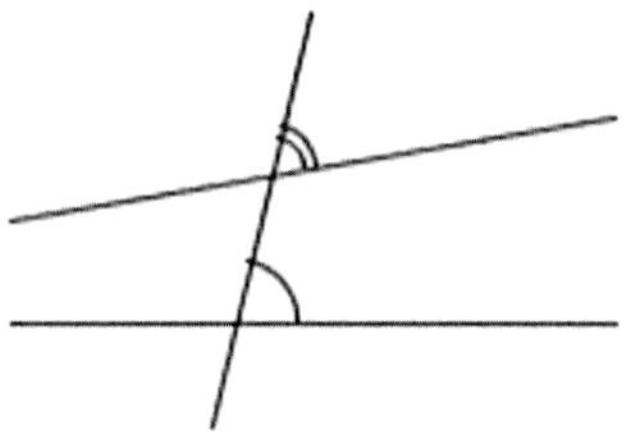

Cosine: cosinus.
Count: compter.
Counterclockwise: dans le sens contraire du des aiguilles d'une montre (U.S.).
Counterexample: contre-exemple.
Cross section: section droite.
Cross-sum: somme des chiffres (d'un entier).
Cube (to): élevé au cube.
Cube: cube.

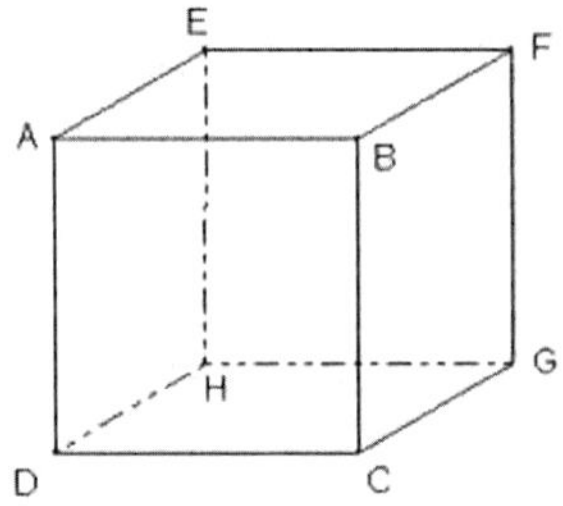

Cubed: au cube.
Cuboid: parallélépipède rectangle.

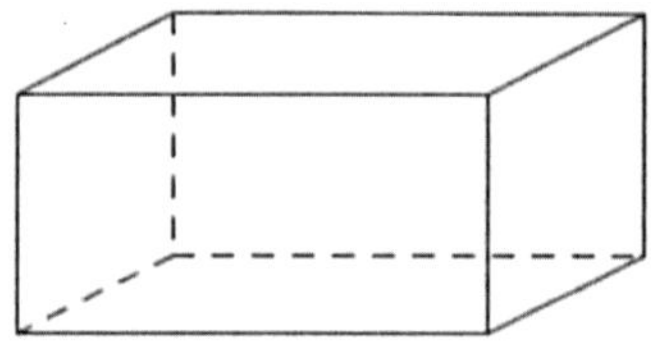

Curve: courbe.

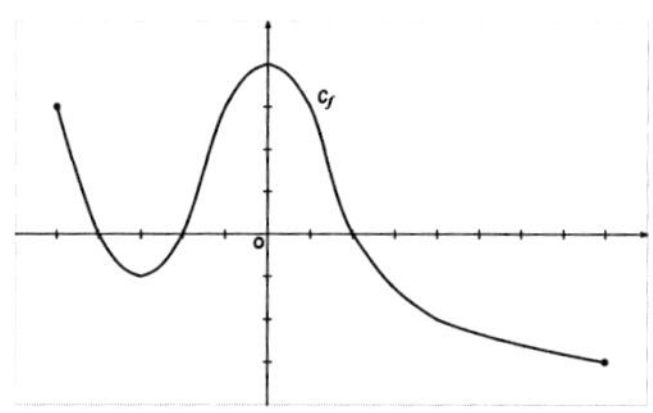

D

Dash: prime (′), tiret.
Data: données.
Decadic: décimal.
Decimal (place): décimale.
Digit: = décimale digit.
Deduce (to): déduire (raisonnement).
Deduct (to): déduire (calcul).
Definite: définie.
Degree: degré.
Denominator: dénominateur.
Denote (to): appeler, représenter, noter.
Derivative: dérivé.
Determinant: déterminant.
Diagram: diagramme.
Diameter: diamètre.

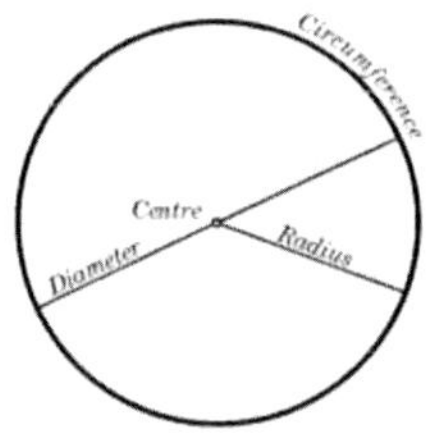

Diamond: losange.

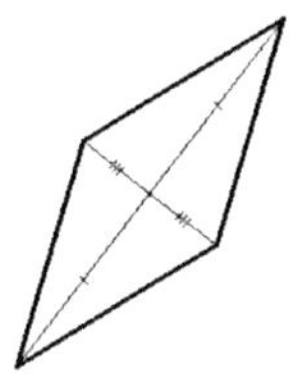

Die, dice: dé(s).

Difference quotient: taux d'accroissement.
Digit: chiffre.
Dimension: dimension.
Discrete: discret.
Disk: disque.
Distributed algorithms: algorithme réparti.
Distributivity: distributivité.
Divide: diviser.
Dividers (plur.): compas.

Division: division.
Divisor: diviseur.
Dot: point.
Dotted: pointillé.
Double dash: seconde (").

E

E.g.: par ex. (= exempli gratia).
Ede: arrête.
Edge: arête, côté.
Ellipse: ellipse.

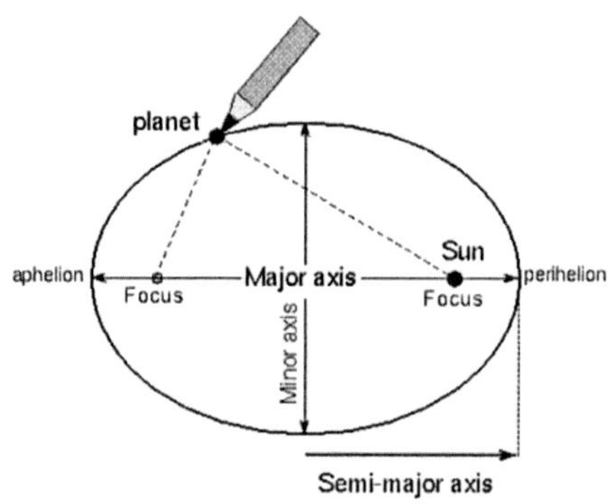

Enlargement: agrandissement.
Equilateral: équilatérale.

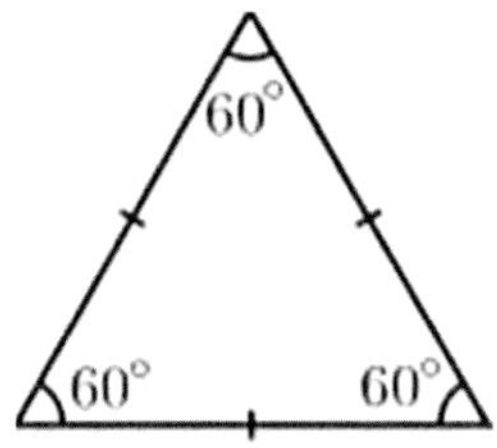

Equirectangular projection: Projection cylindrique équidistante.
Erect (to): construire (une perpendiculaire).

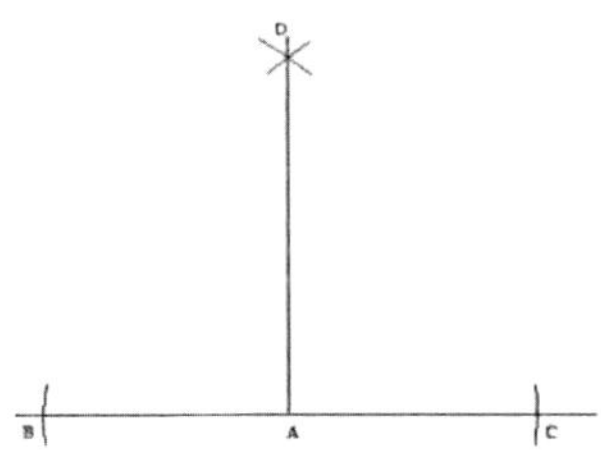

Euclidean algorithm: algorithme d'Euclide.
Euler line: droite d'Euler.
Even (number): pair (nombre)
Even: pair.
Ex: concerne un cercle ou une sphère exinscrit(e) (excercle),
Expacted value: espérance.
Expand (to): développer (un calcul), compléter (une base).
Expansion: développement.
Exponent: exposant.
Exponential: exponentiel.
Extrapolate: extrapoler

F

Factor (to): factoriser, décomposer.
Factor: facteur, diviseur.
Fewer: strictement moins de.
Fibonacci sequence: série de Fibonacci.

Figure(s): nombre, chiffres (statistiques).
Figures: je suis nul en calcul.
First quartile: premier quartile.
Fitting: ajustement (affine).
Floor (to): arrondir par défaut (contraire de "to ceil").
Floor: partie entière (sol dans le civil).
Flow charts: ordinogramme.

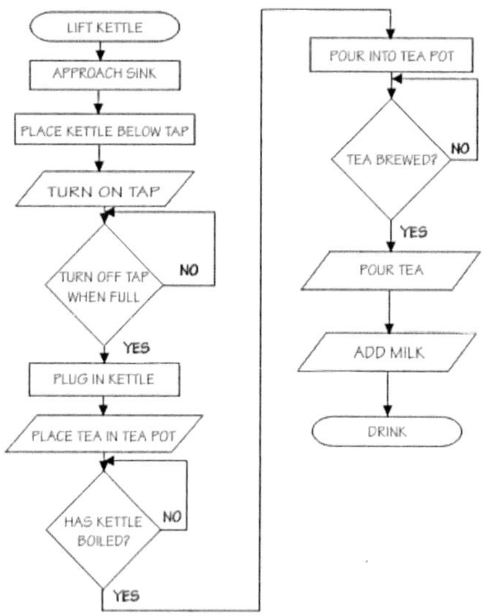

Focus: foyer.
Formula: formule.
Fraction: fraction.
Frame: repère.
Frieze: frise.
Frustrum: tronc (de cône).

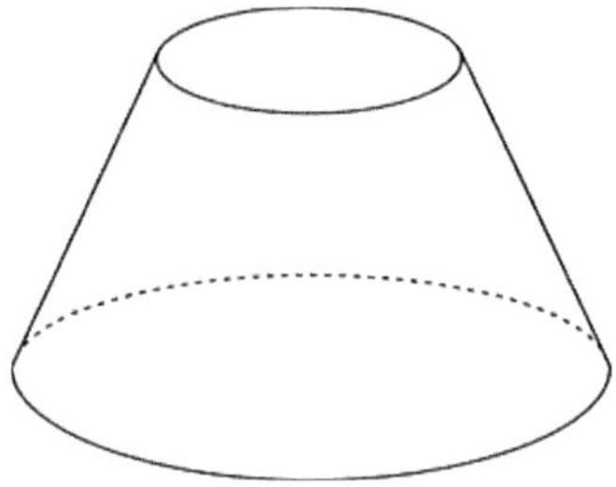

G

G.c.d. (greatest common divisor): p.g.c.d. plus grand commun diviseur.
Golden ratio: nombre d'or.
Golden rule: règle de trois.
Greater than (higher than): plus grand que, supérieur à.
Greatest lower bound: borne inférieure.

H

H.c.d. (highest common divisor): p.g.c.d. plus grand commun diviseur.
Heads or tails: pile ou face.
Height: hauteur.
Hence: donc.
Higher than (greater than): plus grand que, supérieur à.
Histograms: histogrammes.

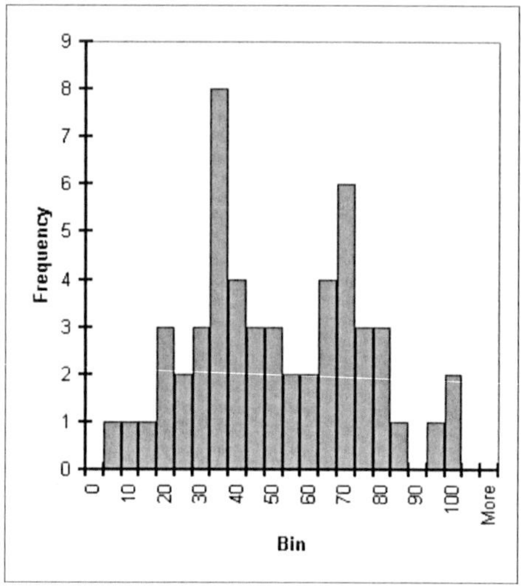

Hundred: cent.
Hundredth part of a number: centième partie d'un nombre.
Hyperbola: hyperbole.

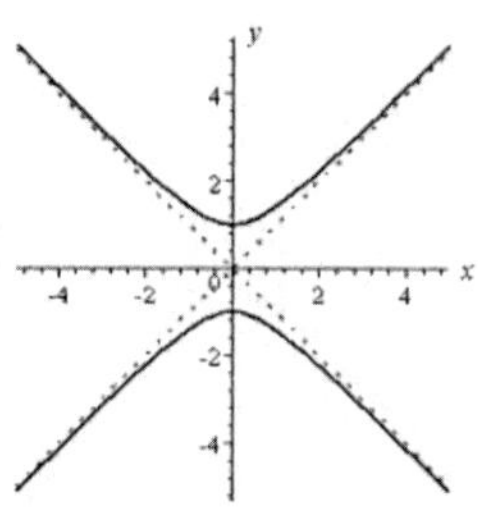

Hypotenuse: hypoténuse.

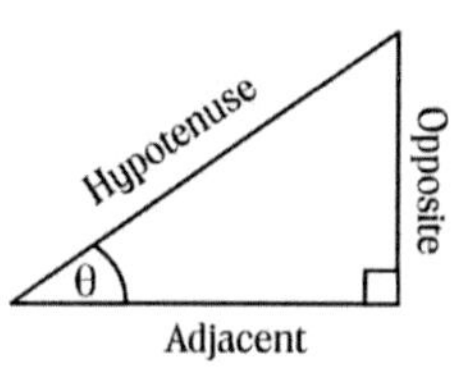

Hypothesis: hypothèse.

I

In: concerne le cercle ou la sphère inscrit(e) (incercle, insphere, incenter, inradius).
Inaccurate: inexact.
Incenter of a triangle: centre du cercle inscrit à un triangle.
Increment: accroissement.
Index: indice (base 100 par exemple)
Inequality: inégalité.
Infinite: infinité.
Inflection point: point d'inflexion.

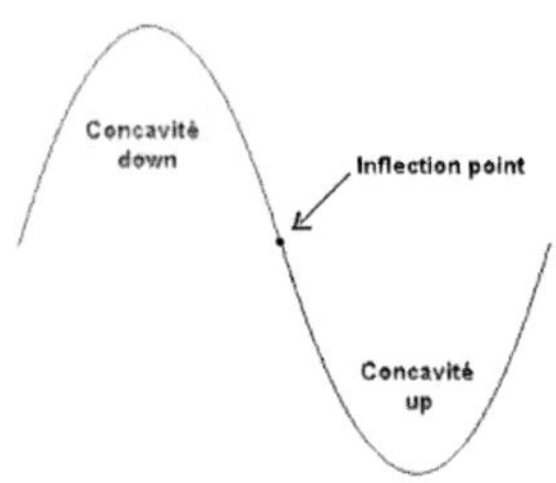

Integer (nom): entier (relatif) (entier naturel, natural number.
Integral (adj.): entier.
Intercept theorem: théorème de Thalès.

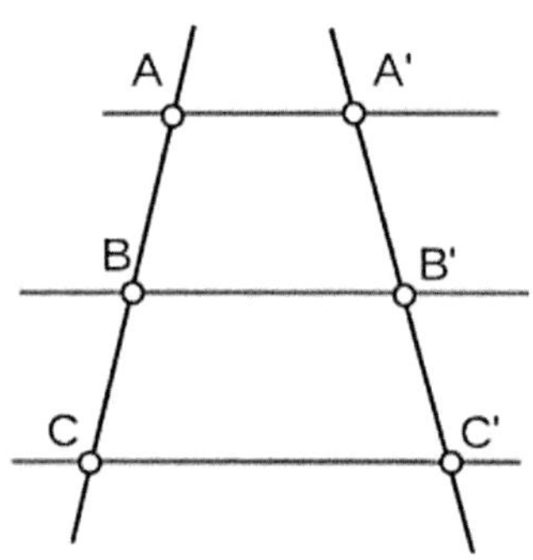

Intersection: intersection.
Interval: intervalle.

Into: facteur de (dans a(b+c)), divisé par (dans a : b).
Inversely as: inversement proportionnellement à.
Isoceles: isocèles.

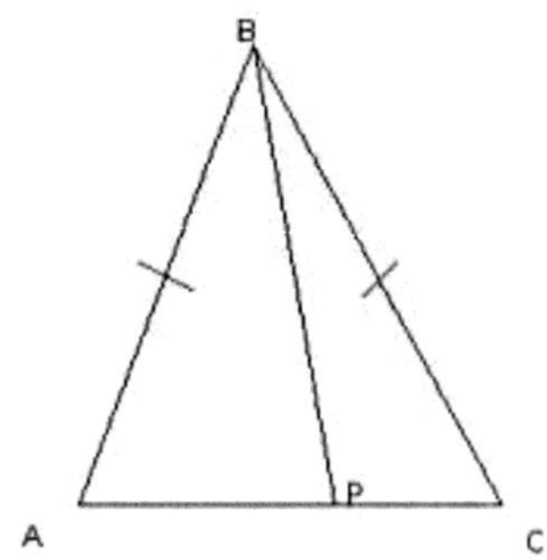

K

Kilogram: kilogramme.
Kilometer: kilomètre.
Knot (unit speed): noeud (unité).

L

L.c.m. (least common multiple): p.p.c.m.
Label: graduation (sur les axes).
Least (the): (le) plus petit, moindre, at least : au moins.
Least upper bound: borne supérieure.
Lecture: cours.
Left-hand(ed): vers la gauche (rotation), rétrograde (repère), ouvrante (parenthèse).
Leg: côté de l'angle droit (dans un triangle rectangle), branche (d'un compas) (jambe dans le civil).
Length: longueur.
Less than (lower than): plus petit que, inférieur à

Line: droite.

Line segment: segment droit.

Linear: linéaire.

M

Magic square: carrée magique.

Magnitude (vector): norme (vecteur).

Matrix: matrice.

$$\mathbf{A} = \begin{pmatrix} 9 & 13 & 6 \\ 1 & 11 & 7 \\ 3 & 9 & 2 \\ 6 & 0 & 7 \end{pmatrix}.$$

Mean: moyenne.

Mean value: valeur moyenne.

Median: médiane d'un triangle ou d'une série statistique.

Minus: moins.

Moreover: de plus.

Mutually independet events: événements indépendants.

N

Necessary condition: condition nécessaire.

Negative: strictement négatif.

Non-negative: positif ou nul.

Non-positive: négatif ou nul.

Nought: zéro.
Numeral: chiffre.
Numerator: numérateur.

O

Obtuse: obtus (angle supérieur à 90°).

Odd: impair.
Opposite: opposé.
Ordered pair: couple.
Ordinate: ordonnée.
Out of: sur (pour la lecture d'une note, 15/20 par ex.).

P

Parabola: parabole.

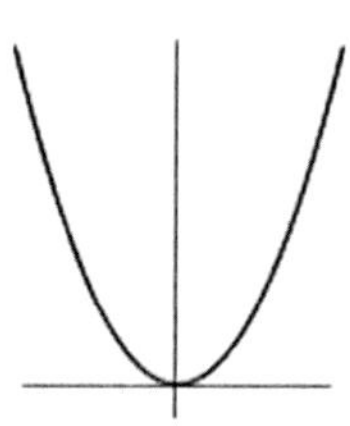

Parameter: paramètre.
Pattern: motif (d'un pavage), patron (d'un polyèdre).
Perform (to): effectuer (des simplifications par exemple).
Perigon: angle plat.
Perpendicular bisector: médiatrice

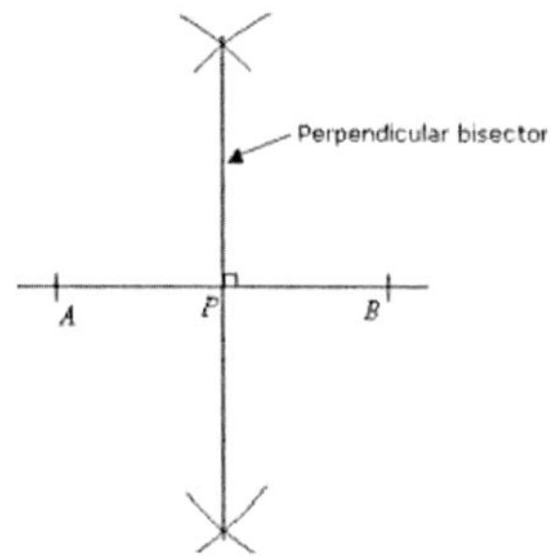

Pi (π): pie $\pi = 3.1415$

Pie chart: graphique circulaire (camembert).

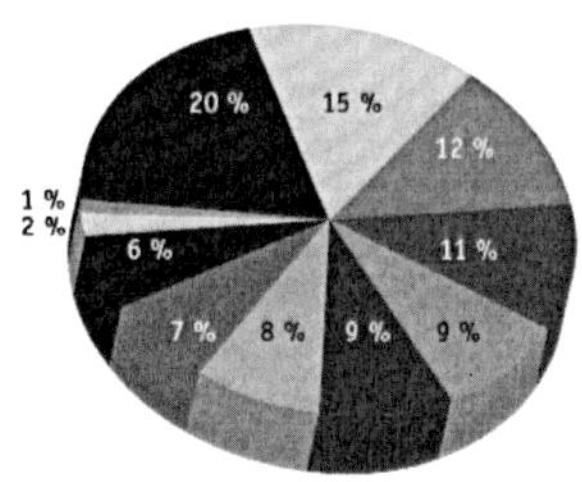

Piecewise continuous: continu par morceaux.

Plane: plan.

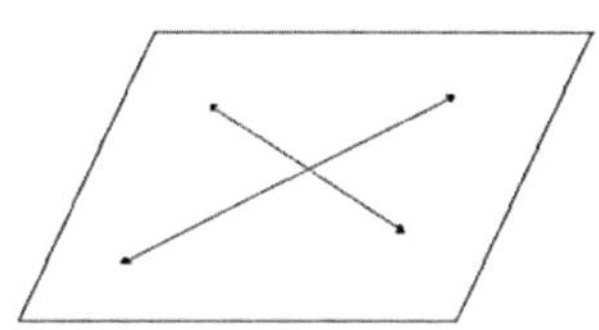

Plot (to): traçer (point par point).

Polar coordinates: coordonnées polaires.

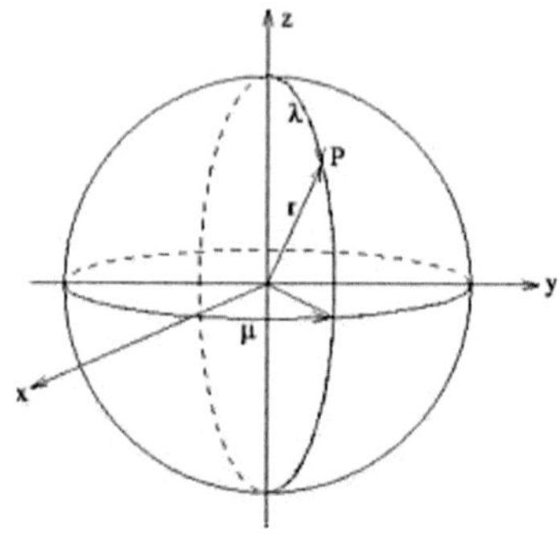

Polyhedron: polyédre.

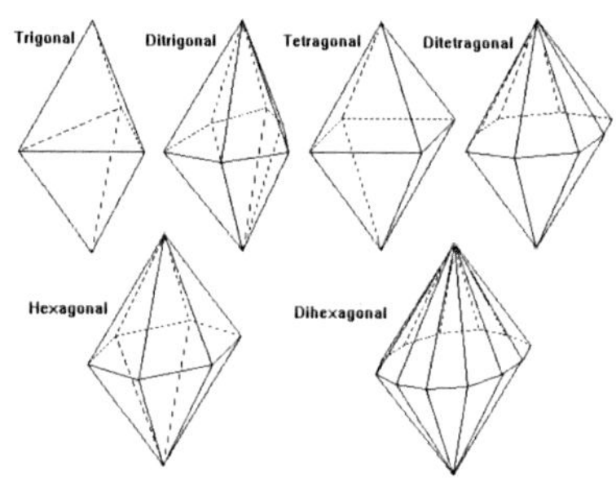

Positive: strictement positif.
Power: puissance.
Probability: probabilité
Product: produit.
Proof: prouver.
Protractor: rapporteur.

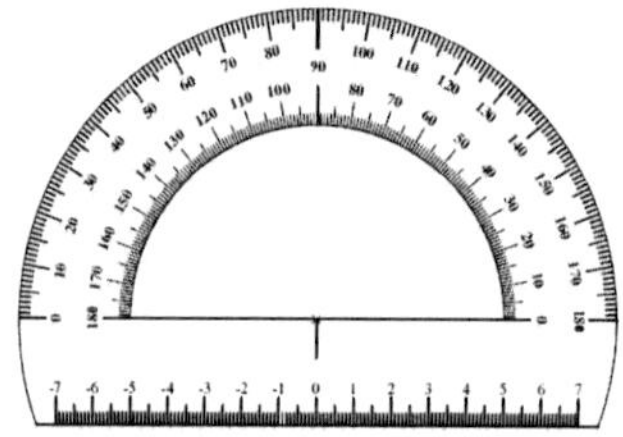

Provided: si, à condition que, vérifiant.

Pyramid: pyramide.

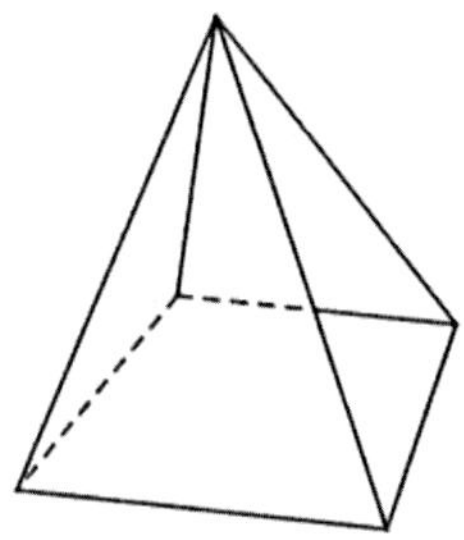

Pythagoras' constant: racine carée de deux.

Q

Q.e.d. (quod erat demonstrandum): c.q.f.d.
Quadrant: quartier d'un cercle.
Quadrilateral: quadrilatérale.

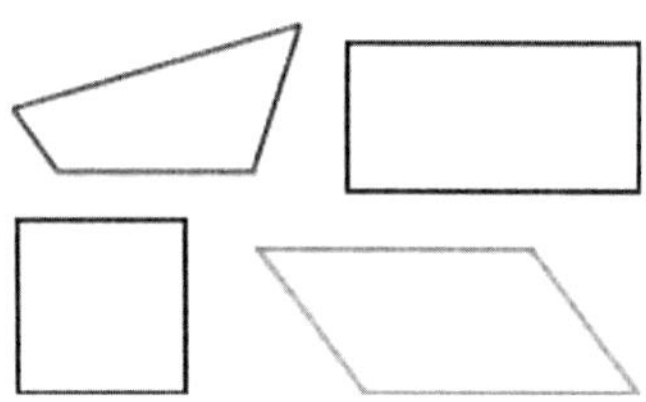

Quarter: un quart.

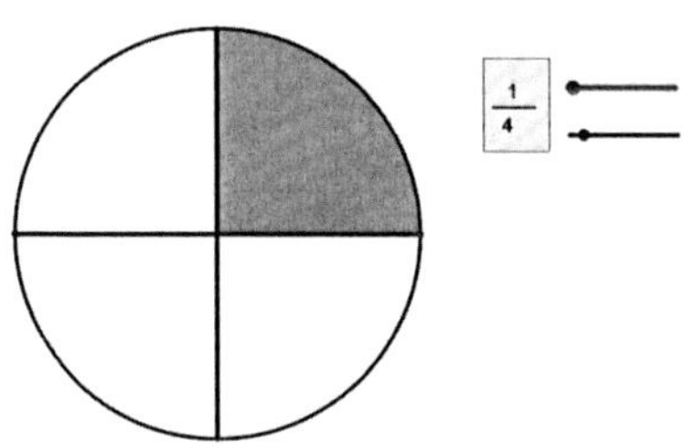

Quotient: quotient.

R

Radius: rayon (d'un cercle).

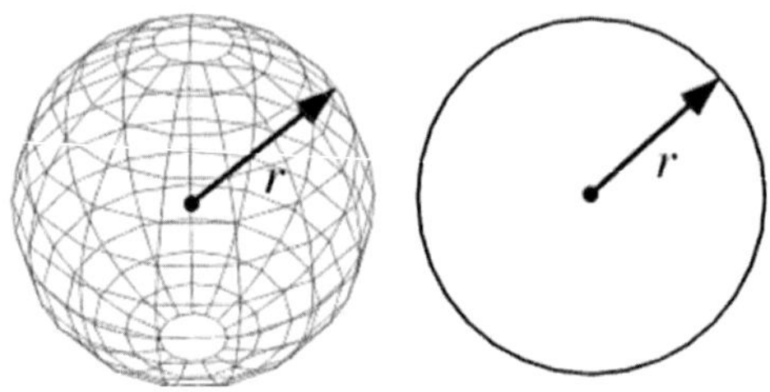

Radix, radices: base de numération.
Raise to the power n: élever à la puissance n.
Random: aléatoire.
Range: domaine, portée.
Rank: rang.
Ratio: quotient, rapport.
Ray: rayon, demi-droite.
Real numbers: nombres réels.
Reciprocal: inverse (d'un nombre).
Rectangle: rectangle.
Rectilinear: rectiligne.
Reflex: croisé (polygone), rentrant (angle).
Regular: régulier.
Relatively prime: premiers entre eux.
Remainder: reste (d'une division).
Resolve: résoudre.
Reversed (to be): changer de sens (pour une inégalité).
Revolve: rotation.
Rhomboid: rhomboïde.

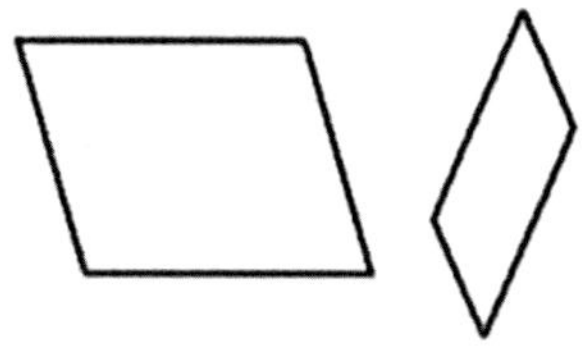

Rhombus: losange.
Right: droit (angle), rectangle (triangle).
Right angle: angle droit.
Right hand (ed): vers la droite (rotation), direct (repère), rermante (parenthèse).
Rise: différence des ordonnées (de deux points).
Roof: chapeau (^).
Root (square root): racine (racine carrée).
Rough: approximatif, approché, grossier.
Rounding off: arrondir.
Rule: règle, loi.
Ruler: règle (instrument).

Run : différence des abscisses (de 2 points).

S

Salient: saillant (angle), anguleux (point).
Sample: échantillon.
Sampling: échantillonage.
Scale: échelle.
Secant: sécante

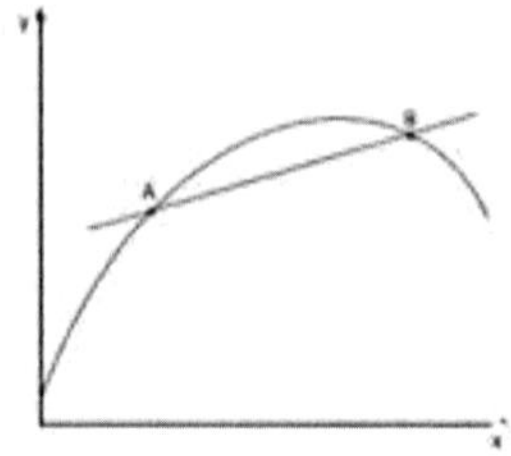

Section (cross): section (droite)
Seek (to): chercher.
Segment: segment
Sequence: suite.
Set: ensemble.
Settle (to): résoudre.
Shape: allure, profil, forme ("mettre sous la forme...")
Shift (to): faire passer (un terme d'un membre d'une équation dans un autre), décaler.
Shift: translation.
Side: côté (polygone), face (polyèdre).
Sieve: crible (d'Eratosthène).
Sign: signe
Significant digit: chiffre significatif.
Since: puisque.
Sine: sinus.
Solve: résoudre.
Sort (to): trier, ordonner.
Sphérical coordinates: coordonnées sphériques.
Squar mean root: racine carré de.
Square (to): élever au carré.
Squared: au carré.
Standard deviation: écart-type.
Statistics: statistique
Straightedge: équerre.

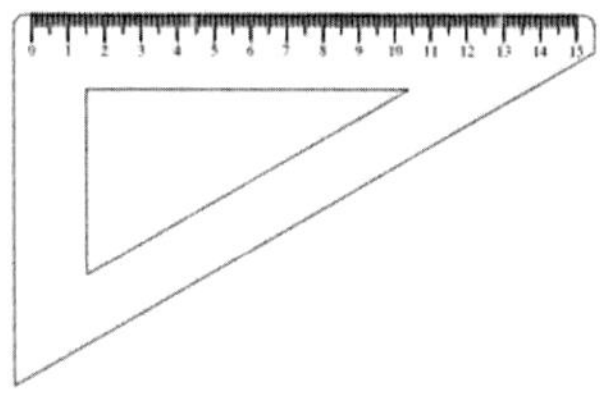

Stick diagram: diagramme à baton
Subscript: indice (écrire en indice).
Substraction: soustraction.
Sufficient condition: condition suffisante.
Sum: somme.
Superscript: exposant (écrire en exposant).
Supplementary: supplimentaire
Swap (to): échanger.
Symmetry transformation (of a figure): transformation laissant invariant(e) (une figure).

T

Tangent: tangent.
Term of (in): en fonction de.
Tesselation: pavage.
Test: critère.
Th.: ième.
Theorem: théorem.
Therefore: par conséquent.
Third quartile: troisième quartile
Though: bien que.
Thus: ainsi.
Tick mark: graduation.
Tiling: pavage (tile, tuile).
Time: fois.
Tip: extrémité.
Trajectory: trajectoire.

Trapezium: trapèze (U.K.), quadrilatère qui n'est pas un trapèze (U.S.).

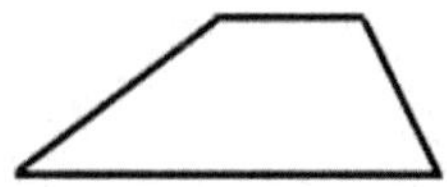

Trapezoid: quadrilatère qui n'est pas un trapèze (U.K.), trapèze (U.S.).

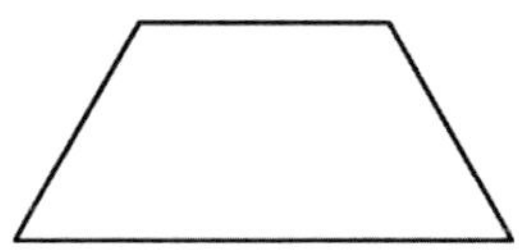

Treble (to): tripler.
Tree: arbre (de probabilités).
Triangle: triangle.
Trigonometry: trigonemétrie.
Triple dash: tierce (''').
Truncated: trunqué.
Turning point (inflection point): point d'inflexion.

U

Unequal: inégal.
Unity: unité.
Upon: sur (dans a/b).
Upper bound: limite spérieure.

V

Valid: exacte (décimale).
Value: valeur.
Vanish (to): s'annuler.
Variable: variable
Vector: vecteur.
Vertex, vertices: sommet(s) (en géométrie plane).
Vertical: verticale.
View from above: vue de dessus.
View from underneath: vue de dessous.
Vinculum: barre (au dessus d'une expression).
Volume: volume.

W

Well-defined: bien défini (pour une fonction).
Width: largeur.

X

X-axis: axe des abscisses.
X-coordinate: axe des abscisses.

Y

Yard: yard.
Yard axis: axe de lacet.
Yardage: métrage.
Y-coordinate: axe des ordonnées.

Z

Zero: zéro.
Zero adjustement: réglage à zéro.
Zero level: niveau zéro.
Zero meridian: méridien zéro.

Zero pitch: pas nul.

Zero offset: décalage de zéro.

Zero reset: remise à zéro.

Zeroed: centré.

Z – section: section en Z.

Appendices

MATHEMATICAL SYMBOLS IN COMMON USE

The most common mathematical symbols actually used in schools education programs, the dates and the names of mathematicians who discovered it.

= Is equal to	Recorde -1557 - England
< and > Is less or greater than	Thomas Harriot -1621- England
+ and - Plus and minus	Widmann - 1460 - Germany
+ and - Sign of number	Oughtred - 1631 - England
A x B Cross for multiplication	Oughtred - 1631 - England
A * B Star for multiplication	Johann Rahn - 1659 - Germany
A . B Point for multiplication	Leibniz - 1698 - Germany
AB A multiplied by B	Stifel - 1544
X^n X exposant n	René Descartes - France - (1596 – 1650)
÷ Division	Rahn - 1659 - Germany
: Division	Leibniz - 1698 - Germany
/ Division	De Morgan -England- (1806-1871)
¾ Fraction with horizontal line ex. 3 upon 4	Oresme -Franc- (1325-1382)
r.q. 5 Square root of 5	Bombelli -Italy- in 1572
$\sqrt{2}$ Square root of	Descartes – Holland- 1637
( ) Brackets	Tartaglia – (1506-1557)
[ ] Square brackets	Bombelli- Italy- (1526-1572)
{ } Braces	Viète – 1593- France
____ Underline	Choquet – France –born in 1915
, « comma » for decimal separation	Rodolphe Snellius- Pays bas – 1608
. « point » for decimal separation	Magini – Italy
π pi	Oughtred en 1647, imposé par Jones W. en 1706, ensuite définitivement par Euler (suisse) en 1748
Using « vowels » to design the un-	Vieta in 1600

known in the equations	
Using letters x, y and z to design the unknown in the equations	**Descartes – (1596- 1650)**
N Natural numbers	**Peano – Italy - (1858-1932) from the Italian *naturale***
Z Relative numbers	**Dedekind – Germany - (1831-1916) from German language *Zahl, zahlen***
D Decimal numbers	**French notation 1970**
Q Rational numbers	**Peano – Italy - (1858-1932) from the Italian *quotiente***
R Real numbers	**Dedekind – Germany - (1831-1916) from German language *real***
Sin, cos and tan	**Girard – (1595-1632)**
∫ Integral	**Leibniz – (1646-1716)**
∞ Infinity	**John Wallis -England- in 1655.** **This sign probably come from Greek alphabet ω « omega »**
i Complex	**Euler - Switzerland- 1777**
e Exponential base 10	**Euler in 1727**
e^x Exponential of x	**Euler in 1777**
F(x) Notation for functions	**Euler in 1734**
Σ Summation of (sigma)	**Euler in 1755**
Π Pi in capital letter	**Gauss –Germany-1855)**
∃ it exists …	**Giuseppe Peano (1858-1932). From German language *existieren.***
∀ Whatever or For every	**David Hilbert-Germany-1943**
∈ Belong to	**Peano in 1890. This sign probably come from Greek alphabet « epsilon ».**
Set of figures	**Georges Cantor –Germany**
Group	**Evariste Galois-France-1830**
Ring	**Dedekind – Germany-1871**
Fields	**Dedekind – Germany -1871**
f'(x) Derivative	**Lagrange-France-(1736-1813)**
n! Factoriel	**Kramp (1760-1826)**

C	**Complementary**	**Bourbaki – France - 1933**
$\|x\|$	**Modulus of x**	**Fréchet – France-(1878-1973)**

SYMBOLE MATHÉMATIQUES

Un aperçu général de quelques symboles utilisés actuellement dans les manuels scolaires et les dates de leurs apparitions ainsi que les noms de leurs inventeurs.

= Egale	Recorde -1557 - Angleterre
< et > Plus petit et plus grand	Thomas Harriot -1621- Angleterre
+ et - Addition et soustraction	Widmann - 1460 - Allemagne
+ et - Signe d'un nombre	Oughtred - 1631 - Angleterre
A x B Croix pour multiplication	Oughtred - 1631 - Angleterre
A * B Etoile pour la multiplication	Johann Rahn - 1659 - Allemagne
A . B Point pour la multiplication	Leibniz - 1698 - Allemagne
AB A multiplié par B	Stifel - 1544
X^n X exposant n	René Descartes - France - (1596 – 1650)
÷ Division	Rahn - 1659 - Allemagne
: Division	Leibniz - 1698 - Allemagne
/ Division	De Morgan – Angleterre – (1806-1871)
¾ Fraction avec trait horizontal	Oresme – France- (1325-1382)
r.q. 5 Racine carrée de 5	Bombelli -Italie- en 1572
$\sqrt{2}$ Racine carrée avec une barre supérieure	Descartes – Pays-Bas - 1637
( ) Parenthèses	Tartaglia – (1506-1557)
[ ] Crochets	Bombelli- Italie- (1526-1572)
{ } Accolades	Viète – 1593- France
____ Soulignement	Choquet – France –né en 1915
, « virgule » comme séparateur décimal	Rodolphe Snellius- Pays bas - 1608
. « point » comme séparateur décimal	Magini – Italie
π pi	Oughtred en 1647, imposé par Jones W. en 1706, ensuite définitivement par

	Euler (suisse) en 1748
Utilisation des "voyelles" pour désigner l'inconnue d'une équation	**Viète en 1600**
Utilisation des lettres x, y et z pour désigner l'inconnue d'une équation	**Descartes – (1596- 1650)**
N Ensemble des entiers naturels	**Giuseppe Peano – Italie - (1858-1932) de l'Italien *naturale***
Z Ensemble des entiers relatifs	**Dedekind – Allemagne- (1831-1916) de l'allemand *Zahl, zahlen***
D Ensemble des nombres décimaux	**Notation franco-française 1970**
Q Ensemble des nombres rationnels	**Giuseppe Peano – Italie - (1858-1932) de l'italien *quotiente***
R Ensemble des nombres réels	**Dedekind –Allemagne- (1831-1916) de l'allemand *real***
Sin, cos et tan	**Girard – (1595-1632)**
$\int$ **Intégrale (somme)**	**Leibniz – (1646-1716)**
∞ **Infini**	**John Wallis -Angleterre- en 1655. Le symbole vient probablement de l'alphabet grec ω « oméga »**
i Complexe	**Euler - Suisse- 1777**
e Base de l'exponentielle	**Euler en 1727**
e^x **Exponentiel de x**	**Euler en 1777**
F(x) Notation pour les fonctions	**Euler en 1734**
Σ Somme (sigma)	**Euler en 1755**
Π Pi majuscule; produit	**Gauss – Allemagne – (1777-1855)**
$\exists$ **il existe …**	**Giuseppe Peano (1858-1932). De l'allemand *existieren.***
$\forall$ Quel que soit	**David Hilbert- Allemagne- (1862-1943)**
$\in$ **Appartient à**	**Giuseppe Peano en 1890. Le symbole vient de la lettre grecque « epsilon ».**
Ensemble	**Georges Cantor –Allemagne- 1883**
Groupe	**Evariste Galois-France-1830**
Anneau	**Dedekind – Allemagne-1871**
Corps	**Dedekind – Allemagne-1871**

f'(x) Dérivée	**Lagrange-France-(1736-1813)**
n! Factorielle	**Kramp (1760-1826)**
C Complémentaire	**Bourbaki – France - 1933**
|x| Norme	**Fréchet – France-(1878-1973)**
→ Flèche surlignée pour désigner un vecteur	**Notation franco-française 20e siècle**

PART 4

SUSTAINABLE DEVELOPMENT AND RENEWABLE ENERGY

DEVELOPPEMENT DURABLE ET ENERGIE RENOUVELABLE

A

Assessment: évaluation, estimation

B

Blade: lame ou pale

Bioenergy: bioénergie
- **Is a renewable energy made available from materials derived from biological sources**
- **C'est une énergie renouvelable issue des matières dérivée de re-soupes biologiques**

Biofuels: biocarburant
- **Is a type of fuel which is in some way derived from biomass.**
- **Biocarburant est un carburant produit à partir de matériaux organiques non fossiles, provenant de la biomasse.**

Biomass: biomasse
- **Is a renewable energy source, is biological material from living, or recently living organisms**
- **C'est une source d'énergie renouvelable constituée l'ensemble des matières organiques d'origine végétale ou d'organisme vivant**

Bodywork: carrosserie

Brake: freins

Bulb: ampoule

C

Cardboard: carton
- **Heavy-duty paper**
- **Papier rigid**

Coastal area: zone costale

Coil of pipes: tubes en serpentin
- **It is a spiral tube used in the heating mantle and the distillation of perfumes**
- **C'est un tube en forme de spirale utilisé dans les chauffes ballon et dans la distillation des parfums**

Computer-aided design: conception assisté par ordinateur
- **Is the use of computer technology for the process of design and design-documentation**
- **C'est une technique de modélisation géométrique permettant de concevoir, de tester virtuellement à l'aide d'un ordinateur**

Containerboard: boite de carton

Consumer: consommateur

Corrugated fiberboard: (matériau) carton ondulé
- **Is a paper-based material consisting of a fluted corrugated sheet and one or two flat linerboards.**
- **Matériau de base pour fabriquer des cartons d'emballage.**

Crucible: creuset

- **Is a container used in modern laboratory processes, which can withstand temperatures high enough to melt its contents.**
- **C'est un récipient utilisé dans les laboratoires pour faire fondre des substances à haute température.**

D

Double glazing: double vitrage
- **Two layers of glass with an air gap reduce heat conduction and radiation.**
- **Vitres constitué de deux plaques de verres qui réduisent la perte de chaleur par conduction et par radiation.**

Disposable: jetable
- **Product only intended for single use**
- **Produit à usage unique**

Draft tubes: tubes traités
- **Is one of important part of a turbine, which is used to transform water into energy.**
- **C'est un tube utilisé dans une turbine pour conduire l'eau vers les pales qui produisent de l'énergie grace à leurs rotations.**

Drinking water: eau potable

E

Ecodesign: éco conception
- **Is an approach to design of a product with special consideration for the environmental impacts of the product during its whole life cycle.**
- **C'est un terme désignant la volonté de concevoir des produits respectant les principes de développement durable.**

Electrical impulses: des impulsions électriques

F

Fan: ventilateur

Flying kite: un cerf-volant

Freewheel: roue libre

G

Gear box: boîte de vitesses

- **A machine consists an assembly of parts including the speed-changing gears and refers simply to the gearbox that uses gears and gear trains to provide speed and torque conversions from a rotating power source to another device.**
- **C'est un dispositif mécanique permettant d'adapter la transmission d'un mouvement entre un arbre moteur et un arbre récepteur. Utilisée dans pour la transformation et la transmission de la puissance d'un moteur thermique aux roues motrices d'une voiture.**

Geothermal energy: énergie géothermique

- **Thermal energy generated and stored in the Earth.**
- **C'est l'énergie thermique produite et stockée par la Terre.**

Greenhouse (glasshouse): serre

- **Is a structure where plants are grown.**
- **C'est une structure destinée à la production agricole.**

Greenhouse effect: effet de Serre

- **Is a process by which thermal radiation from a planetary surface is absorbed by atmospheric greenhouse gases, and is re-radiated in all directions. As a result, the temperature there is higher than it would be if direct heating by solar radiation were the only warming mechanism.**
- **C'est un processus naturel qui, pour une absorption donnée d'énergie électromagnétique, provenant du Soleil confère au corps qui reçoit cette énergie une température de surface nettement supérieure à une situation.**

Greenhouse gas: gaz à effet de Serre

- **Is a gas in an atmosphere that absorbs and emits radiation within the thermal infrared range.**
- **Ce sont des composants gazeux qui absorbent et émettent le rayonnement infrarouge émis par la surface terrestre, contribuant à l'effet de serre.**

Grinding: moudre

- **Grinding the grain**
- **Moudre le grain**

H

Harness: exploiter

Has been shelved: a été mis en arrêt

Heat exchanger: échangeur de chaleur

Heliostat: héliostat

- **Is a device that includes a mirror, which turns so as to keep reflecting sunlight toward a predetermined target.**
- **Un héliostat est un dispositif permettant de suivre la course du Soleil, pour orienter toute la journée les rayons solaires vers une petite surface fixe, à l'aide de miroirs.**

Hydroelectricity: énergie hydroélectrique

- **Is the production of electrical power through the use of the gravitational force of falling or flowing water.**

- **C'est une énergie électrique obtenue par conversion de l'énergie hydraulique des différents flux d'eau.**

I

Ignite: s'enflammer

Impinging: empiéter

Impoundement facility: installation de retenu

Improve: améliorer

Incoming tide: marée montante

Ingoing tide: marée sortante

Iron ore: minerai de fer

K

Kilowatt-hours (kWh): kilowatt-heure
- **Is the amount of electrical energy used by a 1 kW appliance left on for 1 hour.**
- **C'est la quantité d'électricité consomée par 1 KW en 1 heure.**

L

Land lease: bail foncier

Large scale: grande échelle

Lightweight materials: matériaux légers

Loft insulation: laine de verre

- **Is a thick layer of 398tilizes398s wool laid reduce heat conduction and radiation.**
- **C'est couche épaisse de laine de verre qui réduit la perte de chaleur par conduction et par convection.**

M

Mill stone: pierre de moulin de forme cylindrique

Molten: fusion

N

National Electricity Grid: Réseaux d'Electricité National

Natural rubber: caoutchouc
- **Is an elastomer that was originally derived from latex, a milky colloid produced by rubber tree called Hevea brasiliensis.**
- **C'est un matériau élastomère obtenu par la transformation du latex naturellement sécrété par un arbre appelé Hévéa.**

Notch: encoche, entaille, brèche

Nozzle: bec

O

Off-grid: hors réseau

Off-shelf: hors plate-forme

Offshore: proche de littoral

Outgoing tide: marée descendante

Ozone: ozone

- **Is a triatomic molecule, consisting of three oxygen atoms. Ozone in the lower atmosphere is an air pollutant.**
- **trioxygène, est une molécule triatomique formée de trois atomes d'oxygène et donc de formule chimique O_3. La couche d'ozone est une concentration d'ozone qui filtre une partie des rayons ultraviolets émis par le Soleil, ultraviolets notamment responsables de cancers de la peau.**

P

Packaging: emballage

- **Technology of enclosing and protecting products.**
- **Technique destinée à contenir et protéger des marchandises.**

Passive house : maison ou habitat passive

- **Is a low-enegy house.**
- **C'est une maison à faible consommation énergétique.**

Pawl: cliquet, crochet, gâchette, arrêtoir

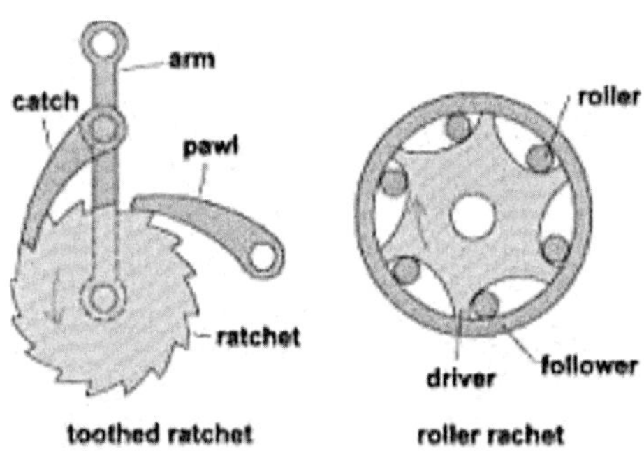

Penstock: conduite pour Controller l'écoulement

Photovoltaic system: Centrale solaire photovoltaïque

- **Is a system which uses one or more solar panels to convert sunlight into electricity.**
- **C'est un système permettant la production d'électricité constitué d'un ensemble de modules solaires photovoltaïques.**

Propellers: propulseur

Provide bulk power: fournir de l'électricité en vrac

Ponds: Etang

Pour: verser

Power: puissance
- **Is the rate of doing work, it's work done divided by time taken.**
- **C'est le travail éffectué divisé par le temps correspondant.**

Power station: centrale électrique
- **All power stations have a boiler of some sort, which makes steam, which drives a turbine, which drives a generator. The generator produces electricity (by induction) by rotating an electromagnet within coils of wire.**
- **Toutes les centrales électriques fonctionnent de la même façon, ils possèdent une Chaudière qui produit de la vapeur qui fait tourner une turbine liée à un générateur qui produit à son tour de l'électricité par induction magnétoélectrique.**

Purpose: objectif

R

Remote villages: villages reculés

Renewable resources : ressources renouvelables
- **Are parts of our natural environment and form our eco-system.**
- **Ce sont des resources naturelle de notre environement et forment notre eco-système.**

Renewable energy: énergie renouvelable
- **Is the energy which comes from natural resources which are renewable such as sunlight, wind, rain, tides, and geothermal heat. Renewable energy resources will never run out.**
- **Ce sont des formes d'énergies dont la consommation ne diminue pas la ressource à l'échelle humaine comme le rayonement solaire, le**

vent, la pluie, l'humidité et la chaleur géothermique. Les ressources d'énergie renouvelables ne s'épuiseront jamais.

Riverbed: chemin de rivière

Rotor: rotor
- **Rotational part of an electric motor.**
- **Partie rotative d'un motor électrique.**

Rushing: précipiter

S

Sail vessels: vaisseaux marines à voiles

Scroll: rouleau

Sealed: scellée

Shaft: arbre
- **A bar or rod that moves or turns to transmit motion in a machine.**
- **Une barre ou un cylindre en se tournant transmet un mouvement dans une machine.**

Shuts off: s'éteint

Sluice gates: écluses, vannes
- **Used to control water levels and flow rates in rivers and canals.**
- **Utilizes pour controller le flue d'eau dans les rivières et les canaux.**

Solar cells: panneaux photovoltaiques

- **Generate a lot of electric currents directly from sunlight.**
- **Produisent un courant électrique grace au soleil.**

Solar cooker (oven): four solaire (cuiseur solaire)

- **Is a device which concentrates sunlight for use as a heat source.**
- **C'est un système de chauffage ou de cuisson basé sur la capture des rayonnements lumineux émis par le Soleil.**

Solar furnace: four solaire

- **Is a large array of curved mirrors which are all focused onto one spot to produce very high temperature so water can be turned to steam to drive turbine.**
- **C'est un dispositive constitué des mirroirs qui focalise les rayonnements solaire vers un four qui chauffe de l'eau à haute température en la transformant en vapeur qui fait tourner une tubine.**

Solar panels: panneaux solaire

- **Contain water pipes under a black surface. Heat radiation from the Sun is absorbed by the black surface to heat the water in the pipes. The heat energy is used directly, rather than to create electricity.**
- **Ils contiennent des tubes sous une surface noire qui chauffe sous l'effet des rayonnements solaire absorbés. L'énergie absorbée est utilisée pour fabriquer de l'électricité.**

Solar power tower: tour solaire

- **Is a type of solar furnace using a tower to receive the focused sunlight.**
- **C'est un four monté sur une tour qui chauffe grace à l'énergie solaire.**

Solar power: centrale solaire

- **Is the conversion of sunlight into electricity.**
- **C'est la conversion des rayonnements solaire en énergie électrique.**

Sprang up: surgir

Sprocket: pignon, roué dentée

Spin vertically: tourner verticalement

Stator: stator d'un moteur
- **Fixed part of an electric motor**
- **Parie fixe d'un moteur électrique**

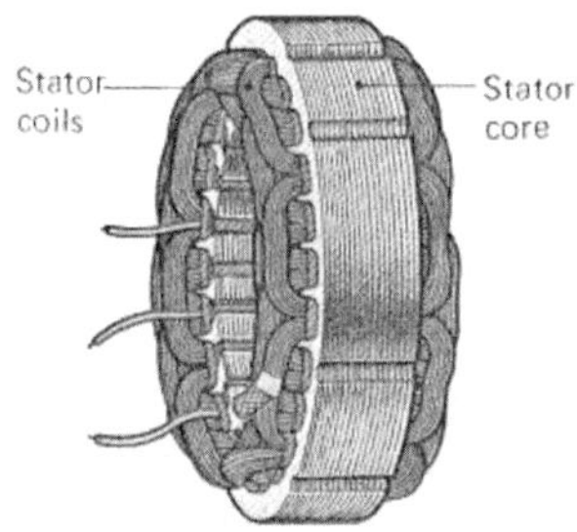

Steam engine: machine à vapeur
- **Is a heat engine that generates mechanical work using steam as its working fluid.**
- **C'est une machine qui porduit une énegie mécanique à partir de vapeur.**

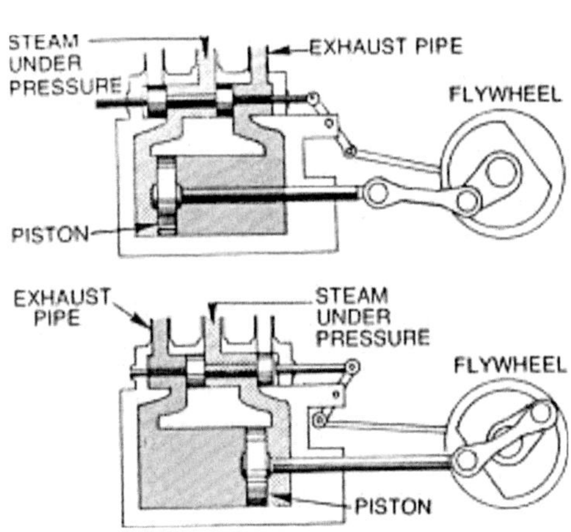

Steel lattice: treillis d'acier

Stir: remuer

Sustainable development (SD): développment durable (DD)
- **Is a pattern of resource use, which aims to meet human needs while preserving the environment so that these needs can be met not only in the present, but also for future generations.**
- **C'est la réponse aux besoins des générations du présent sans compromettre la capacité des générations futures à répondre aux leurs.**

Sunlight: rayonnement solaire
- **Is the total frequency spectrum of electromagnetic radiation given off by the Sun.**
- **C'est l'émission solaire totale de spectre de fréquences de radiation électromagnétique.**

Sun rise: lever de soleil

Sun set: coucher de soleil

T

Tailraces: canaux dérivés

Tank: réservoir, citerne

Task: tâche

Technical standard and resouces: norme et resources
- **Is an established norm or requirement about technical systems. It is usually a formal document that establishes uniform engineering or technical criteria, methods, processes and practices.**
- **C'est le fait d'établir respectivement des normes et standards industriels, c'est-à-dire un référentiel commun et documenté destiné à harmoniser l'activité d'un secteur.**

Tide: marée

Tidal barrages: barrages des marées

- **Are big dams built across river estuaries with turbines in them.**
- **Ce sont des barrages hydroélectriques construits dans lcs estuaires.**

Tidal power: énergie marémotrice
- **Is a form of hydropower that converts the energy of tides into useful forms of power.**
- **C'est une énergie issue des mouvements de l'eau créés par les marées.**

Thermal energy: énergie thermique
- **Is the portion of internal energy that is responsible for a system's temperature.**
- **C'est une part de l'énergie interne qui est responsible de l'échauffement d'un système.**

Turbine: turbine
- **A machine with blades that are turned by the movement of a liquid or gas such as air, steam or water.**
- **Une machine avec des pales qui tourne grace au mouvement d'un liquide, d'un gaz tel que l'air, vapeur ou de l'eau.**

Twilight: crépuscule

U

Unequal: inégale

W

Watermill: moulin à eau
- **Is a structure that uses a water wheel or turbine to drive a mechanical process.**
- **C'est une structure qui utilize une roué à eau ou une turbine pour produire une énergie mécanique.**

Water wheel: roué à eau
- **Is a machine for converting the energy of free-flowing or falling water into useful forms of power.**
- **C'est une machine qui permet de convertir l'énergie de la chute d'eau en une énergie utile.**

Wave power: énergie des vagues
- **Is the transport of energy by ocean surface waves, and the capture of that energy to do useful work.**
- **C'est une énergie marine utilisant la puissance du mouvement des vagues.**

Wells: puits

Wicket: guichet

Windmill: Moulin à vent
- **A windmill is a machine which converts the energy of wind into rotational energy by means of vanes called sails or blades.**
- **Le moulin à vent est un dispositif qui transforme l'énergie du vent en mouvement rotatif au moyen d'ailes ajustables.**

Wind flow patterns: modèles d'écoulement du vent

Wind turbine: éolienne
- **Une éolienne est un dispositif qui transforme l'énergie du vent en énergie électrique ou mécanique.**
- **A wind turbine is a device that converts energy from the wind into electrical ou mechanical energy.**

Wind power: énergie du vent
- **Wind power is the conversion of wind energy into a useful form of energy, such as using wind turbines to make electricity.**
- **C'est la conversion de l'énergie du vent en une énergie utile comme les éoliennes qui transforme l'énergie du vent en une énergie électrique.**

Y

Yaw: dispositive d'orientation, embarder, dévier la route
- **Used in wind turbines**
- **Utilisé dans les éoliennes**

Appendices

Strength of Materials - Résistance des matériaux

Allowable stress: contrainte admissible

Apparent elastic limit: limite élastique apparente
- **The stress at which the slope of the stress-strain curve in relation to the axis of constraints is 50% greater than the initial slope.**
- **La contrainte à laquelle la pente de la courbe contraintes-déformation par rapport à l'axe des contraintes est de 50 % supérieures à la pente initiale.**

Area-moment method: méthode de l'aire de moment

Beam: poutre
- **Part subject to bending.**
- **Pièce soumise à la flexion.**

Beam in flexure: poutre flèche

Bending: flexion

Bending moment: moment fléchissant

Bending strength: résistance à la flexion

Buckling: flambage
- **Bending sharp side of a column under axial load, a beam under transverse load, etc.., associated with the unstable equilibrium.**
- **Fléchissement brusque latéral d'une colonne sous charge axiale, d'une poutre sous charge transversal, etc., associé à l'équilibre instable.**

Cantilever beam: poutre en porte-à-faux, poutre console
- **Beam fixed at one end and free at the other.**
- **Poutre encastrée à une extrémité et libre à l'autre.**

Collapse: effondrement

Column: colonne
- **Part of a construction vertical compression.**
- **Pièce verticale d'une construction en compression.**

Combined bending and axial load: flexion compose

Compressive strength: résistance à la compression
- **Compressive maximum stress a material can build up.**
- **Contrainte de compression maximum qu'un matériau peut développer.**

Concrete: béton

Conjugate beam method: méthode de la poutre conjuguée

Continuous beam: poutre continue
- **Beam with more than two support points.**
- **Poutre ayant plus de deux points d'appui.**

Creep: fluage
- **Increased continuous deformation under a force constant or decreasing.**
- **Augmentation continuelle de déformation sous un effort constant ou décroissant.**

Dead load: charge permanente, poids mort

Deflection: flèche, déformation de flexion

Distributed load: charge répartie

Double integration method: méthode de la double intégration

Effective length: longueur équivalente

Elastic curve: courbe élastique

- **The curve taken by the axis of a beam or column when it bent by loads that does not seek beyond the elastic limit.**
- **La courbe prise par l'axe d'une poutre ou colonne normalement droite quand elle fléchie par des charges qui ne la sollicitent pas au-delà de la limite élastique.**

Elastic limit: limite élastique

- **The greatest stress that a material is capable of developing without a permanent deformation remains after total unloading.**
- **La plus grande contrainte qu'un matériau soit capable de développer sans qu'une déformation permanente subsiste après le déchargement total.**

Elongation: allongement

Failure: effondrement

Fixed beam: poutre encastré

Fixed-end moment: moment d'encastrement

Haunched beam: poutre à goussets

Hinge: articulation, rotule

Live load: charge vive

Member (structural): élément, membrure (de construction)

Modulus of elasticity: module d'élasticité

- **The report, below the proportional limit of a material, the stress to corresponding strain. Except, specification, the term can also be applied to compression than in tension.**
- **Le rapport, au-dessous de la limite de proportionnalité d'un matériau, de la contrainte à la déformation correspondante. Sauf, spécification, le terme peut aussi bien s'appliquer à la compression qu'à la traction.**

Overhanging beam : poutre avec porte-à-faux

- **Beam whose length exceeds one or both supports.**
- **Poutre dont la longueur dépasse l'un ou les deux appuis.**

Poisson's ratio: coefficient de Poisson

- **The ratio of lateral contraction per unit and per unit axial elongation of a bar stressed in axial tension in the elastic range.**
- **Le rapport entre la contraction latérale unitaire et l'allongement axial unitaire d'une barre sollicitée en traction axiale dans le domaine élastique.**

Pressure vessel: enveloppe sous pression

Prestressed concrete: béton précontraint

Proportional limit: limite de proportionnalité

- **The greatest stress a material can develop without deviating from Hooke's law.**
- **La plus grande contrainte qu'un matériau peut développer sans dévier de la loi de Hooke.**

Pure shear: cisaillement simple

Reinforced concrete: béton armé

Safety factor: coefficient de sécurité

Section modulus: module d'inertie

- **Moment of inertia divided by the distance between the neutral axis and extreme fiber of a beam.**
- **Moment d'inertie divisé par la distance entre l'axe neutre et la fibre extrême d'une poutre.**

Shear: cisaillement

Shear modulus of elasticity: module de rigidité

- **The report, below the proportional limit of a material, the stress to corresponding strain in shear. This value is usually obtained from a torsion test on a simple circular bar.**
- **Le rapport, au-dessous de la limite de proportionnalité d'un matériau, de la contrainte à la déformation correspondante, en cisaillement. Cette valeur s'obtient généralement d'un essai de torsion simple sur une barre circulaire.**

Simple beam: poutre simple

Slenderness ratio: élancement

- **In a column, the ratio between the length and the smallest radius of gyration.**
- **Dans une colonne, le rapport entre la longueur et le plus petit rayon de giration.**

Statically determinate structure: structure isostatique

Stiff: rigide

Stiffness: rigidité

Strain: déformation

- **Strain = extension/original length**
- **Déformation = extension/longueur originale**

Strain energy: énergie de déformation

Strain gage: jauge, extensomètre

Strength (ultimate): résistance maximum

Stress: contrainte

- **Tensile stress = tension/cross-sectional area.**
- **Unity in Pascal (Pa).**
- **Contrainte de traction = tension/aire de la section droite.**

- **Unité en Pascal (Pa).**

Tensile strength: résistance à la traction

Thermal stress: contrainte thermique

Torque: moment de torsion

Ultimate load: charge ultime
Uniform load: charge uniformément répartie

Vertical shear wind load: effort tranchant surcharge de vent

Weakness: faiblesse

Yield point: limite d'écoulement
- **Stress in a material, which occurs a significant increase of the deformation without increase of the load.**
- **Contrainte dans un matériau, à laquelle se produit un accroissement sensible de la déformation sans accroissement de la contrainte.**

Yield strength: limite conventionnelle d'élasticité
- **The stress at which a material shows a permanent deformation limit. The magnitude of the maximum deformation that one considers should not cause material damage.**
- **La contrainte à laquelle un matériau accuse une déformation permanente limite donnée. La grandeur de la déformation maximum que l'on estime ne pas devoir provoquer l'endommagement du matériau.**

Young modulus: module de Young
- **Is a measure of the stiffness of the material.**
- **Young modulus = stress/strain or $E = \sigma/\varepsilon$.**
- **C'est la mesure de la rigidité d'un matériau.**
- **Module de Young = contrainte/déformation ou $E = \sigma/\varepsilon$**

Inside Wind turbine – l'intérieur d'une éolienne

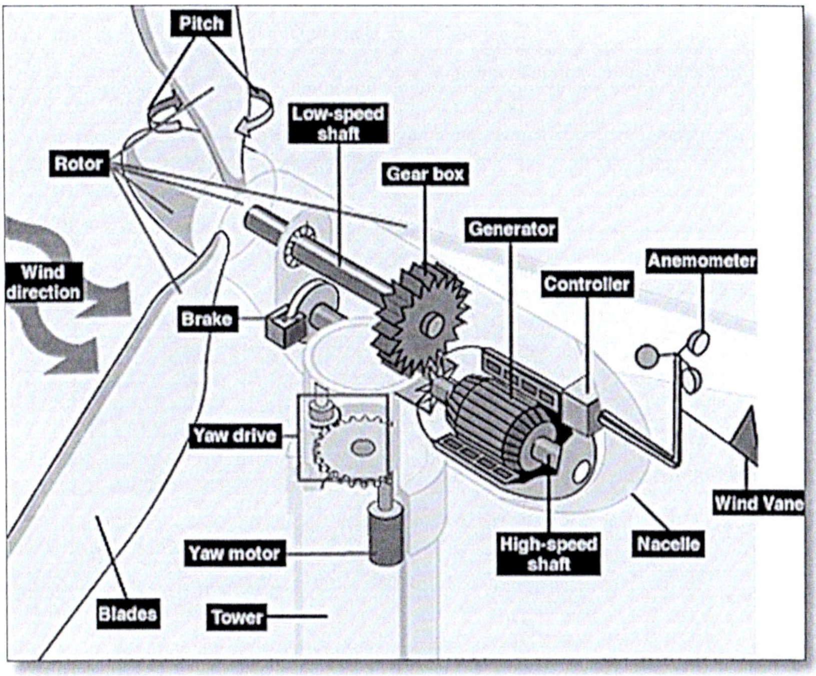

Anemometer: anemometer

- **Measures the wind speed and transmits wind speed data to the controller.**
- **Mesure la vitesse du vent et transmet les données de la vitesse du vent vers le contrôleur.**

Blades: pales

- **Most turbines have either two or three blades. Wind blowing over the blades causes the blades to "lift" and rotate.**
- **La plupart des éoliennes ont deux ou trois pales. Le vent qui souffle sur les pales entraîne les pales et les fais tourner.**

Brake: freins

- **A disc brake, which can be applied mechanically, electrically, or hydraulically to stop the rotor in emergencies.**
- **Frein à disque, qui peut être appliqué mécaniquement, électriquement ou hydrauliquement pour arrêter le rotor en cas d'urgence.**

Controller: contrôleur

- **The controller starts up the machine at wind speeds of about 8 to 16 miles per hour (mph) and shuts off the machine at about 55 mph. Turbines do not operate at wind speeds above about 55 mph because they might be damaged by the high winds.**
- **Le contrôleur démarre la machine à des vitesses de vent d'environ 8 à 16 miles par heure (mph) et éteint la machine à environ 55 mph. Les turbines ne fonctionnent pas à des vitesses de vent supérieures à environ 55 mph, car ils pourraient être endommagés par les vents violents.**

Gear box: boite de vitesse

- **Gears connect the low-speed shaft to the high-speed shaft and increase the rotational speeds from about 30 to 60 rotations per minute (rpm) to about 1000 to 1800 rpm, the rotational speed required by most generators to produce electricity. The gear box is a costly (and heavy) part of the wind turbine and engineers are exploring "direct-drive" generators that operate at lower rotational speeds and don't need gear boxes.**
- **L'engrenage relie l'arbre à basse vitesse à l'arbre à grande vitesse de rotation et augmente la vitesse d'environ 30 à 60 tours par minute à environ 1000 à 1800 tr/min, la vitesse de rotation requis par la plupart des générateurs pour produire de l'électricité. La boîte de vitesses est tès coûteuse et les ingénieurs sont en train d'explorer "un entraînement direct" des générateurs qui fonctionnen à des vitesses plus faibles de rotation sans avoir besoin de boîtes de vitesses.**

Generator: générateur

- **Usually an off-the-shelf induction generator that produces 50 Hertz AC electricity.**
- **Habituellement, un générateur à induction qui produit 50 Hertz de courant alternatif.**

High-speed shaft: arbre à grande vitesse (engrenage)

- **Drives the generator.**
- **Pilote le générateur.**

Low-speed shaft: arbre réductrice de vitesse (engrenage)
- **The rotor turns the low-speed shaft at about 30 to 60 rotations per minute.**
- **Le rotor tourne l'arbre à basse vitesse à environs 30 à 60 tours par minute.**

Nacelle: nacelle
- **The nacelle sits atop the tower and contains the gear box, low and high-speed shafts, generator, controller, and brake. Some nacelles are large enough for a helicopter to land on.**
- **La nacelle se trouve au sommet de la tour et contient la boîte de vitesses, arbres à faible et à grande vitesse, le générateur, le contrôleur et le frein. Certaines nacelles sont assez grandes pour qu'un hélicoptère puisse atterrir dessus.**

Pitch: tangage
- **Blades are turned, or pitched, out of the wind to control the rotor speed and keep the rotor from turning in winds that are too high or too low to produce electricity.**
- **Les pales sont tournées, ou pivotées, en fonction de l'intensité du vent pour contrôler la vitesse du rotor dans des vents qui sont trop élevés ou trop bas pour produire de l'électricité.**

Rotor: rotor
- **The blades and the hub together are called the rotor.**
- **Les pales et le moyeu sont appelés rotor.**

Tower: tour
- **Towers are made from tubular steel, concrete, or steel lattice. Because wind speed increases with height, taller towers enable turbines to capture more energy and generate more electricity.**
- **Les towers sont fabriqués de tube en acier, en beton ou en d'acier en treillis. Parce que la vitesse du vent augmente avec la hauteur, les tours les plus hauts permettent aux turbines de capturer plus d'énergie et produire plus d'électricité.**

Wind direction: direction du vent
- **This is an "upwind" turbine, so-called because it operates facing into the wind. Other turbines are designed to run "downwind," facing away from the wind.**

- **Il s'agit d'une turbine fonctionnant face au vent. D'autres éoliennes sont conçues pour fonctionner dans la direction opposée au vent.**

Wind vane: girouette
- **Measures wind direction and communicate with the yaw drive to orient the turbine properly with respect to the wind.**
- **Mesure et détecte la direction du vent et le communique au dispositif d'orientation qui à son tour l'oriente face au vent.**

Yaw drive: dispositif d'orientation
- **Upwind turbines face into the wind; the yaw drive is used to keep the rotor facing into the wind as the wind direction changes. Downwind turbines don't require a yaw drive; the wind blows the rotor downwind.**
- **Les turbines fonctionnant face au vent, ont besoin d'un dispositif d'orientation. Les autres turbines qui fonctionnent le dos tourné par rapport à la direction du vent ne nécessite pas l'utilisation d'un dispositif d'orientation. C'est le vent qui les oriente.**

Yaw motor: moteur de dispositive d'orientation
- **Powers the yaw drive.**
- **Le moteur faisant tourner le dispositive d'orientation.**

Glossary of Hydropower Terms – Glossaire des termes Hydroélectriques

The glossary of terms defines the components that make up hydro turbines and hydropower plants.

Le glossaire des termes qui définissent les éléments qui composent les turbines hydroélectriques et les centrales hydroélectriques.

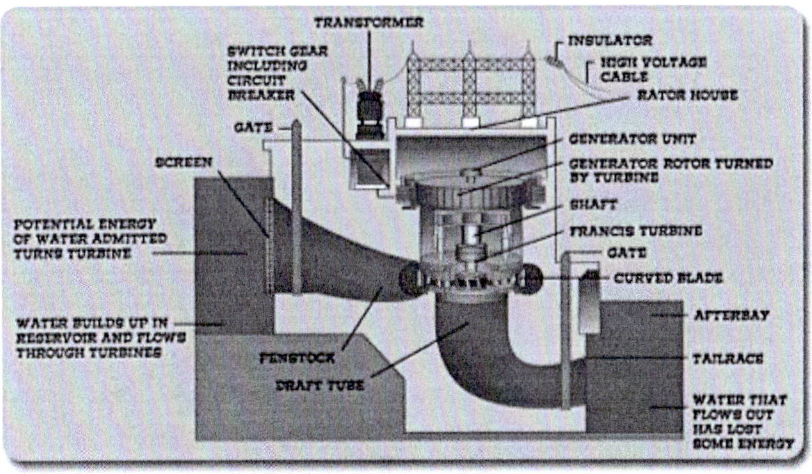

Alternating current (AC): courant altenatif

- **Electric current that reverses direction many times per second.**
- **Courant électrique qui inverse la direction plusieurs fois par seconde.**

Ancillary services: services auxiliaires

- **Operations provided by hydroelectric plants that ensure stable electricity delivery and optimize transmission system efficiency.**
- **Opérations fournies par les centrales hydroélectriques qui assurent la fourniture d'électricité stable et optimiser l'efficacité du système de transmission**

Cavitation: cavitation

- **Noise or vibration causing damage to the turbine blades as a results of bubbles that form in the water as it goes through the turbine which causes a loss in capacity, head loss, efficiency loss, and the**

cavity or bubble collapses when they pass into higher regions of pressure.
- **Du bruit ou des vibrations causant des dommages aux aubes de turbine comme un résultat de bulles qui se forment dans l'eau car il passe par la turbine qui entraîne une perte de capacité, perte de charge, perte d'efficacité, et les effondrements de cavités ou de bulles lors de leur passage à plus forte des régions de pression.**

Direct current (DC): courant continu (DC)
- **Electric current which flows in one direction.**
- **Courant électrique dans une seul direction.**

Draft tube: tube d'aspiration
- **A water conduit, which can be straight or curved depending upon the turbine installation that maintains a column of water from the turbine outlet and the downstream water level.**
- **Un conduit d'eau, qui peut être rectiligne ou courbe en fonction de l'installation de la turbine à maintenir une colonne d'eau de la sortie de la turbine et le niveau d'eau en aval.**

Efficiency: rendement
- **A percentage obtained by dividing the actual power or energy by the theoretical power or energy. It represents how well the hydropower plant converts the energy of the water into electrical energy.**
- **Un pourcentage obtenu en divisant la puissance effective ou de l'énergie par la puissance ou de l'énergie théorique. Il représente la façon dont la centrale hydroélectrique transforme l'énergie de l'eau en énergie électrique.**

Head: chevet
- **Vertical change in elevation, expressed in meters, between the head water level and the tail water level.**
- **Exprimée en mètres, entre le niveau supérieur de l'eau et le niveau inférieur de l'eau.**

Flow: flux
- **Volume of water, expressed as cubic meters per second, passing a point in a given amount of time.**
- **Volume d'eau, exprimé en mètre cube par seconde, passant un point donné par un temps donné.**

Headwater: cours supérieur
- **The water level above the powerhouse.**
- **Le niveau d'eau supérieure au central.**

Penstock: conduit force
- **A closed conduit or pipe for conducting water to the powerhouse.**
- **Conduit fermé ou un tuyau pour conduire l'eau jusqu'à la centrale.**

Runner: coolant
- **The rotating part of the turbine that converts the energy of falling water into mechanical energy.**
- **La partie tournante de la turbine qui convertit l'énergie des chutes d'eau en énergie mécanique.**

Scroll case: tube de defilement
- **A spiral-shaped steel intake guiding the flow into the wicket gates located just prior to the turbine.**
- **Une forme spirale d'acier qui guide l'écoulement dans les aubes directrices situées juste avant la turbine.**

Small hydro: central électrique de petite puissance
- **Projects that produce 30 MW or less.**
- **Central produisant 30 MW ou moins.**

Tailrace: canal de fuite
- **The channel that carries water away from a dam.**
- **Le canal qui ramène l'eau loins du barrage.**

Tail water: chute d'eau, eau d'aval
- **The water downstream of the powerhouse.**
- **L'eau en aval du central.**

Wicket gates: vannage, aubes directrices
- **Adjustable elements that control the flow of water to the turbine passage.**
- **Les elements réglables qui contrôlent l'écoulement d'eau vers le passage de turbine.**

Tools – Outillages

Awl: alêne.
Belt sander: ponceuse à bande.
Box cutter: cutteur.
Bucket: seau.
Dril bit: mèche à perçeuse.
Drill: perceuse.
Drilling: perçage.
Flexible-blades knives (mason's trowel): couteau à enduit.
Grindeur: meuleuse.
Hammer: marteau.
Holesaw: scie cloche.
Japanese chisel: ciseau à bois.
Jigsaw: scie sauteuse.
Machine plane: ponceuse électrique.
Nail: clou.
Pitchfork: fourche.
Plier: pince.
Sander: ponceuse.
Saw: scie.
Scaffolding : échaffaudage.
Screw gun: visseuse.
Screw: vise.
Screwdriver: tournevise.
Smoothing plane: ponceuse à bois.
Twist drills: mèche à perceuse.
Wire cutter: coupe cable (électricité).

PART 5

COMPUTEUR SCIENCE – INFORMATIQUE

A

Abnormal: anomalie
Abortion: arret prématuré
Acces key: clé d'accès
Account: compte internet
Acronym: sigle
Add-on: produit additionnel
Address resolved: adresse résolue
Administrator access: accès administrateur
Alias: nom d'emprunt
Align: se mettre en ligne
All rights reserved: tous droite réservés
Allow: authoriser
Append: ajout
Area: zone
Array: tableau
Assembler: assembleur
Asymmetric Digital Subscriber Line (ADSL): liaison numérique asymétrique
Attempt: essais
Away: absent

B

Back: page précédente
Backdoor: secret
Banner: bandeau publicitaire
Binary digit (ou number): Bit ou système binaire 0 et 1
Bit: bit 0 ou 1
Black hat: pirate informatique
Blacklink: lien entrant
Blogstream: source d'information altenative
Blow out: se planter
Bookmark: favoris

Boot disk: disque de démarrage

Box: boite

Break: coupure

Broaden: élargissez

Browse: naviguer

Browser: naviguer sur le Web

Bug: défaut

Bullets: puce

Button: interrupteur

Bypass: ignorer

Byte: byte, un mot constitué de 0 et de 1

C

Cache: cache mémoire (mémoire tampon)

Caching: stocker dans la mémoire

Cancel (to): éliminer, simplifier par.

Caption: titre d'un tableau

Card cage: fond de panier

Card reader: lecteur de carte

Card: carte

Carry: report

Cartridge: cartouche

Cash memory: cache mémoire

CD-ROM: disque compacte

Central processing unit (CPU): composant de l'ordinateur qui exécute les programmes informatiques.

Centronics: connexion parallèle

Character: caractère

Chat room: salon de bavardage

Chatter: bavarder

Check: cocher une case

Chip holders: détenteurs de puce

Chipset: jeu de composants

Close: fermer

Cipher: coder
Click rate: taux de clic
Command window: fenetre window
Compact disc CD: dique compacte
Completion: fin, terminé
Computer network: réseau informatique
Computer processors CPU: processeurs informatiques
Computer science: informatique
Computer: ordinateur
Computeur programs: programmes informatique
Computeur unit: unité centrale
Connect: se connecter
Consumption: consommation
Content provider: foirnisseur
Content: contenu
Cookie: fichier de témoins, programme mouchard
Cooleur: reroidisseur
Copy to: copier vers un fichier
Copyfile: copie de fichier
Cordless: sans fil
Core: coeur (connecteur)
Counter: compteur
Crack: percer
Cracker: perceur des programmes informatiques
Crasher: pirates informatiques qui détruisent pour le plaisir
Create table: création d'un tableau
Current time: heure actuelle
Cursor: index
Customizing: personnalisation

D

Damage: dégâts
Dash: prime (′), tiret.

Data (singulier): données.
Data processing: traitement de données
Data sheets: fiches de données
Date last modified: date de dernière modification d'un fichier
Debug: dépanner, corriger
Debugging: dépanner
Defender: défenseur
Define: définit une constante
Delete: supprimer
Delete: suprimer
Deletefile: supprimer des fichiers
Deriver class: sous-classe
Design: architecture
Desktop: ordinateur de bureau
Developer: développeur
Device: périphérique
Dialing modem: numérotation du modem
Digital wallet: porte monnaie électronique
DIN audio: connecteur audio
Directive: instruction
Directory: annuaire
Disabled: désactiveé
Disclaimer: dégagement de responsabilité
Disk: disc dur
Diskless: sans disc
Display: affichage
Docking station: station d'accueil
Done: fait, terminé
Door (access panel): panneau d'accès
Download: télécharger
Dual core: double cœur
Dummy: internaute novice
DVD: disque DVD

E

E-business: commerce électronique
E-cash: argent électronique
Echo: afficher
E-commerce: commerce électronique
Electrically-Erasable Programmable Read-Only Memory (EEPROM) : mémoire morte effaçable électriquement et programmable
Embedded : incorporé
Electronic components: composants électroniques
Electronic key : clé électronique
Empty : vide
Enable : disponible, activé
Encoding : cryptage
Encrypted : codé
Enter : entrer
Entry : saisie
Equal to : égal à
Erasable Programmable Read Only Memory (EPROM) : mémoire morte reprogrammable
Ethernet : architecture réseau
Euroconector : péritel

Examine: examiner
Example: exemple
Exit: sortir

F

Fake: faux, truqué
Fan: ventilateur

Favorite: favourie

Fax: télécopieur

Feature: fonctionnalité

Fee: taxe

Feeback: contactez-nous

Feeder line: cable d'alimentation

Fiber-optic cable: cable fibre optique

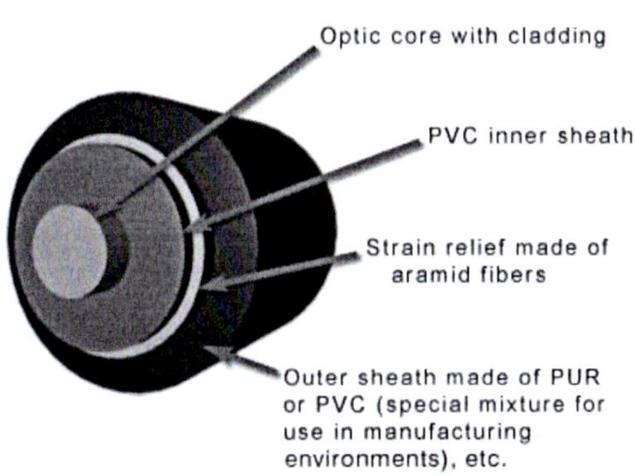

Field length: longueur de champ
File name: nom de fichier
Firewall: barrier de sécurité
First name: prénom
Fix: corriger
Flag: drapeau
Flat monitor: écran plat
Floating: flottante
Flooding: saturé
Floppy disk: disquette
Floppy: lecteur de disquette

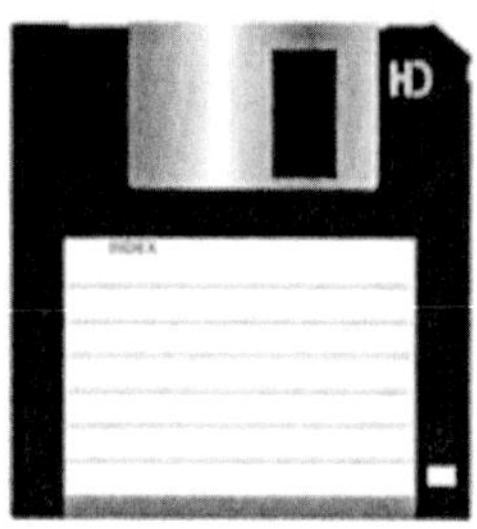

Flow chart: ordinogramme
Fopen: ouverture d'un fichier
Forbidden: interdit
Force: forcer
Form label: étiquette de formulaire
Format a web page: mettre en forme une page Web
Format: formatage
Forward hyperlink: transfère le lien hypertexte
Found: trouver
Free: libre
Frequency: fréquence
Friendly: Claire
Full path: chemin d'accès complet

G

Gathered: amassé
Glossy: glacé
Go to: aller à
Go top: aller au début
Google: moteur de recherché
Gosub: sous-routine
Graphic card: carte graphique

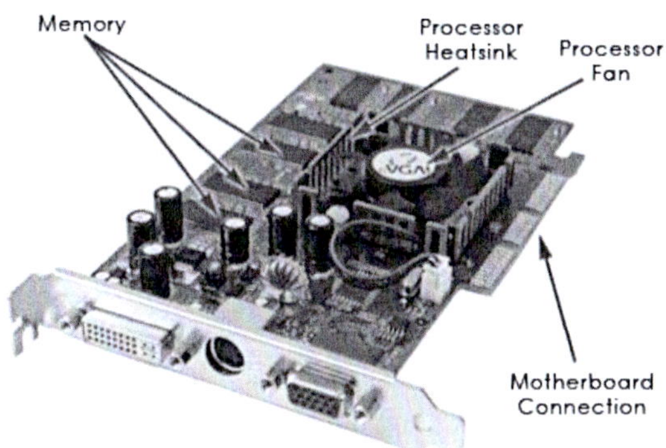

Grid: quadrillage
Groupbox: zone de groupe
Guarding: surveiller
Guestbook: livre d'or

H

Hack: pirater
Hacker: pirate du net
Handle: identificateur
Handling: gestion
Hard disc: disc dur

Hardware: matériel
Hash: hachage
Heading: en-tête
Helpprovider: founiseur
Highlight: éclairage
Home page: page d'accueil
Home: accueil
Host name: nom de l'hote ou l'hébergeur
Host: hôte
Hosting: hébergement

I

Id thread: numéro de thread
ID: numéro d'identification
Identifier: identificateur
Image map: image interactive
Image research: recherche d'image
In focus: au point
Include: inclure
Infoaddict: accro de l'internet

Inherit: héritage
Ink cartridge: cartouche d'encre
Integrated circuits, silicon chips or micrchips: circuits intégrés

Input: signal d'entrée
Internet account: compte internet
Internet relay chat: service de discussion internet
Interrupt: arrêter

J

Jack: prise
Jacket: couverture
Join: joindre
Jump: saut

K

Key: touche
Keyboard shortcut: touche de raccourci
Keyboard: clavier

Keypad: pavé numérique

Keyword: mot clé
Keylogger: clé d'enregistrement
Kill: stopper un processus
Knob: poussoir

L

Laptop: ordinateur portable

Last name: nom de famille
Launch: lancer
Lbx: etiquette
Leakage: perte
Leave: quitter
Less than: plus petit que
Let: permettre
Line fee: interligne
Lineage: enregistrement en ligne
Link: lien
Live cam: caméra internet
Local area network: réseau local

Locate: trouver
Logger: journal
Look online: recherche en ligne
Lurk: rôder
M

Malware: logiciel malveillant
Mapping: correspondence de type
Markup: balise, marqueur
Megahertz: mégahertz
Microcontroller circuits: circuits microcontrôleurs
Micropresessor: microprocesseur

Modem: modem

Modify structure: modifier la structure
Monitor: écran
Monthcalendar: calendrier mensuel
Mother board: carte mère

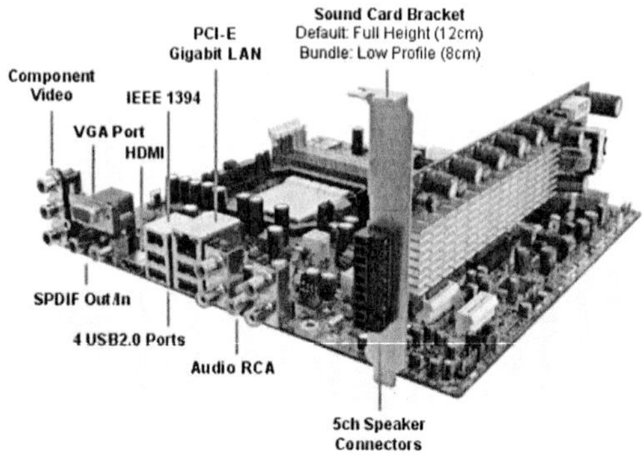

Mouse: souris

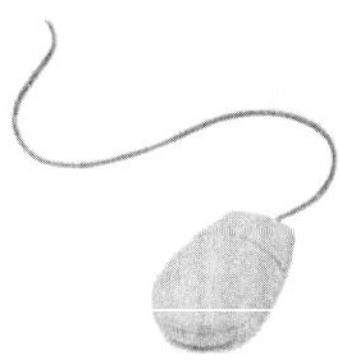

N

Native: mode natural
Nest: imbriquer
Network adapter card: carte réseau
Nickname: surnom
Node: nœud
Notch: encoche
Notebook: PC portable

Notify: notifier
Num lock: touché de verrouillage numérique

O

Office computer: ordinatuer de bureau

Offline browser: navigateur hors connexion
Offline: hors connexion
Oneseek: moteur de recheche
Online advertising: publicité en ligne
Online: en ligne
Order: commande
Outline process: analyse générale d'opération
Outline processor: organisateur d'idées
Outline: schèma
Overflow: dépassement de capacité
Overlay: superposition
Overload: surcharge
Override: remplacement, suppelanter
Overrun: débordement, dépassement

P

Pack: compacter, comprimer, paquet
Package: paquetage
Palmtop: ordinateur de poche

Panner: sous-fenêtrage
Parsed: données analysées
Pass-through: passé système
Paste: coller
Patch: raccordement
Pathway: chemin d'accès
Pattern: modèle
Peer to peer: égal à égal
Peripheral: péripherique
Phishing: hamçennage
Phreaker: pirate du réseau téléphonique
Pin out: brochage
Pins of integrated circuits: broches des circuits intégrés
Pit: trou
Pixel: pixel
Placeholder: emplacement
Playback: relecture, reproduction
Plotter: traceur
Plug: fiche
Plug-in: module d'extension
Pop-up: qui apparaît à l'écran
Port: point d'accès
Postmaster: administrateur de courrier électronique
Power cable: cable alimentation
Power supply: alimentation électrique
Power: puissance
Preclude: arrêter, empêcher
Print server: serveur d'impression
Printer: imprimante

Printhead: tête d'impression
Printing: impression en cours
Privacy: confidentialité
Processing: traitement
Processor: processeur
Programmable Read Only Memory (PROM): mémoire morte
Programming: programmer, programmation
Provider: fournisseur d'accès à internet
Publish: publier

Q

Quarantine: quarantaine
Queue: en file d'attente
Quoting: citation

R

Random: aléatoire, au hazard
Random-access memory (RAM): mémoire vive, mémoire système ou mémoire volatile.
Range: intervalle, gamme
Rank: rang, classer, grade
Rating: évaluation
Readdress: faire suivre
Readline: lecture d'une ligne
Read-only memory (ROM): mémoire non volatile
Ready: prêt
Reboot: redémarrer
Rebrush: faraîchir
Rebuild: régènérer, reconstruire
Related: page similaire
Remote control: télécommande
Remoting: accès à distance
Required: obligatoire

Reset: réintialiser
Resize: redimensionner
Resolution: résolution
Restart: redémarrer
Restore: restaurer
Rewriter: graveur
Ribbon: ruban
Right arrow: flèche droite
Router: routeur

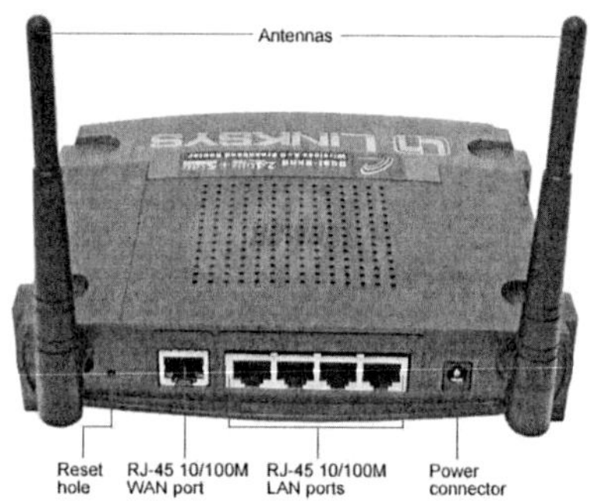

S
Safety: sûreté
Scanning: balayage
Screen shot: saisie d'écran
Screen: écran
Search engine: moteur de recherche
Select: choisi
Setting: réglage
Shared assembly: assemblage partagé
Shell: interréteur de commande
Shift: décalage
Shortcut: raccourci
Skip: sauter
Slider: curseur
Smart: intelligent
Smiley: souriard (binette)
Snippet: fragment

Solving: résoudre
Sound card: carte son

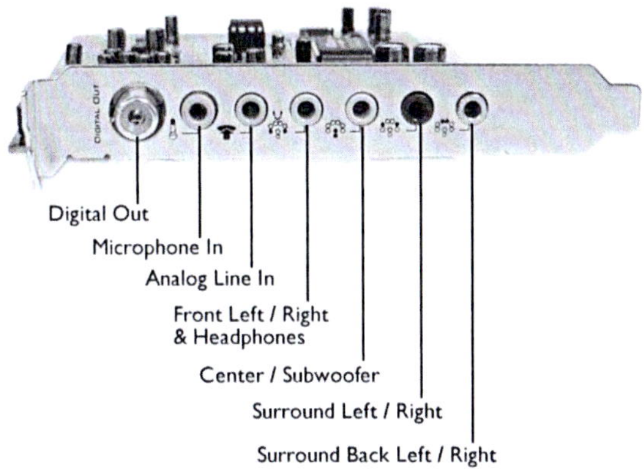

Space: laisser un intervalle
Spider: robot
Spin: tourner
Split: découper
Splitter: séparateur
Spyware: espion
Stack: empiler, tas, pile
Starter pack: kit de connexion
Stop: arrêt
Storage: capacité
Stream: flot
String: chaine de caractères
Subsystem: sous-système
Switch: commutateur
Scanner: scanneur, numériseur de document
Switch: interrupteur

T

Tab: onglet
Tag: renvoi

Temporary Internet File: répertoire des fichiers temporaire
Title: titre, intitulé
Toggle on and off: basculer en ou hors fonction
Toggle switch: interrupteur à bascule
Toggle: bouton bascule
Topping: au début
Torjan: cheval de Troie (virus)
Tracing: traçage
Track: trace
Trackbar: barre de suivi
Trails system: réseau de sentiers
Tray: intercalaire, tablette
Treat: traiter

U

Ultra Violet Programmable Read Only Memory (UVPROM):mémoire non volatile
Unavailable: non disponible
Underlying: sous-jacent
Uniqueness: caractère unique
Unmanaged: non géré
Unparsed: non analysé
Upload: télécharger
Uploading data: téléchargements des données
Use control: contrôle utilisateur
Use: utiliser

V

Valid: valider
Video card: carte vidéo

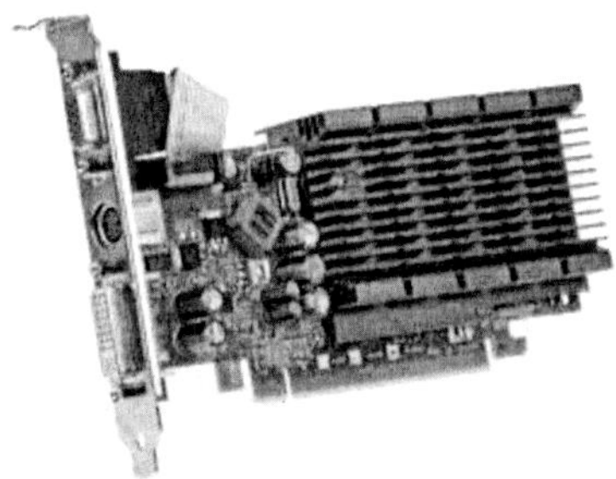

View state: état d'affichage
View: affichage
Virtual card: carte virtuelle
Virus: virus
Visual: visual

W

Wait: attente
Warm: ver (virus)
Web hosting: hébergement Web
Web Slide Show: diaporama Web
Webcast: Web diffusion
Webcam: camera web

Webmaster: administrateur Web
Website: siteweb
Webzine: magazine Web

While: tandis que
Widget: composant d’interface graphique
Window pane: sous fenetre
Wireless: sans fil
Workspace: espace de travail
Worldwide: mondial
Worm: virus-vers
Writeline: écrire une ligne
WRQ write request: requête d'écriture

Z

Zap: détruire
Zoom-in: zoom avant, agrandire

COMPUTER CONTENTS

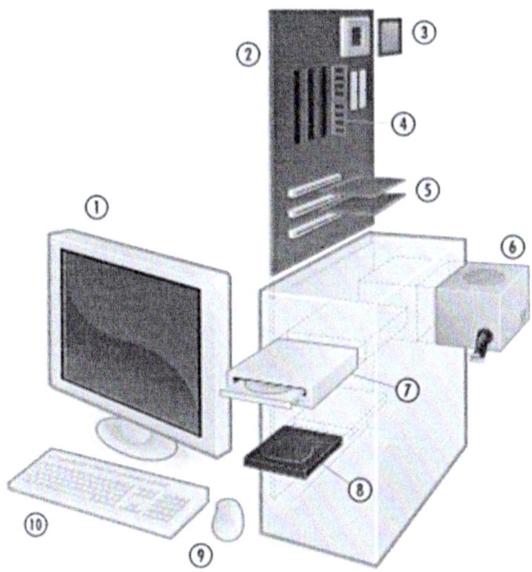

1- Screen: écran
2- Mother board: carte mère
3- Microprocessor: microprocesseu
4- Memory: mémoire
5- Chips: puce électronique
6- Power supplier: alimentation
7- CD/DVD reader: lecteur CD/DVD
8- Floppy: disquette
9- Mouse: souris
10- Keyboard: clavier

PART 6

GENERAL APPENDICES - GENERALITES

OUTCOMES OVER THE LONG-TERM

Theory (Model): théorème

- **A set of tested hypotheses that give an overall explanation of some natural phenomenon. A theory is an attempt to explain why it happens.**
- **Un ensemble d'hypothèses testé, qui donnent une explication générale de quelques phénomènes naturels.**

Natural Law: loi naturelle

- **The same observation applies to many different systems. A law summarizes what happens**
- **La même observation appliquée à des systèmes différents. Une loi resume ce qui se passe.**

Uncertainty in measurement: incertitude dans les measures

- **A digit that must be estimated is called uncertain. A measurement always has some degree of uncertainty.**
- **Un nombre à estimer possède une incertitude. Chaque mesure a toujours un degré d'incertitude.**

Significant figures (sig figs): nombre significatif

- **Is the number of decimal in the result.**
- **Ce le nombre de chiffres dans un résultat.**

EXAMINERS' TERMS
TERMES D'EXAMEN

Calculate: means that the answer will include a number.

Comment: means that you should interpret information given in the question.

Compare: means that you should say something definite about each of the things to be compared.

Deduce: implies that you will workout your answer with the help of information given in the question but using your understanding of the principles involved.

Define: requires a precise statement, make a definition clearer.

Describe: asks you to describe in words, and diagrams if helpful, the main points of a topic.

Determine: tells you to work out a quantity, formula or equation from the information given in the question.

Discuss: except you to give an argument reflecting on the key points in the topic of the question.

Explain: you have to write down some information and then give an explanation for your answer.

Estimate: probably means that you will have to calculate but that you can make simplifying assumptions to arrive at an order of magnitude answer to the question.

List: asks for a list of points, probably just one or two words each.

Name: you are quite likely to be asked to give the name of an organic structure.

Outline: tells you that the answer can be short with only the key points.

Predict: means that you cannot simply recall the answer. You must use information given in the question.

Sketch a graph: means that what you draw should be the right general shape in the right proportions. The axes should be labeled.

Sketch a diagram: means that a simple outline drawing will be acceptable to the examiners.

State or give: both ask for short and simple, factual statements.

Suggest: means that you need to apply your knowledge to answer the question in an unfamiliar situation.

Why: means 'explain' or 'give reasons'.

Write, or construct: means that you should describe a situation.

IRREGULAR VERBS
LES VERBS IRRÉGULIERS

Infinitiive	Past	Past participle	Français
abide	abode	abode	demeurer
arise	arose	arisen	s'élever, survenir
awake	awoke	awoken	(se) réveiller
be	was/were	been	être
bear	bore	borne	supporter
beat	beat	beaten	battre
become	became	become	devenir
begin	began	begun	commencer
bend	bent	bent	(se) courber
bet	bet	bet	parier
bid	bid	bid	offrir (un prix)
bind	bound	bound	lier, relier
bite	bit	bitten	mordre
bleed	bled	bled	saigner
blow	blew	blown	souffler
break	broke	broken	casser
breed	bred	bred	élever (du bétail)
bring	brought	brought	apporter
build	built	built	construire
burn	burnt	burnt	brûler
burst	burst	burst	éclater

buy	**bought**	**bought**	**acheter**
cast	**cast**	**cast**	**jeter, lancer**
catch	**caught**	**caught**	**attraper**
choose	**chose**	**chosen**	**choisir**
cling	**clung**	**clung**	**s'accrocher**
come	**came**	**come**	**venir**
cost	**cost**	**cost**	**coûter**
creep	**crept**	**crept**	**ramper**
cut	**cut**	**cut**	**couper**
deal	**dealt**	**dealt**	**distribuer**
dig	**dug**	**dug**	**creuser**
do	**did**	**done**	**faire**
draw	**drew**	**drawn**	**dessiner**
dream	**dreamt**	**dreamt**	**rêver**
drink	**drank**	**drunk**	**boire**
drive	**drove**	**driven**	**conduire**
dwell	**dwelt**	**dwelt**	**habiter**
eat	**ate**	**eaten**	**manger**
fall	**fell**	**fallen**	**tomber**
feed	**fed**	**fed**	**nourrir**
feel	**felt**	**felt**	**sentir, éprouver**
fight	**fought**	**fought**	**combattre**
find	**found**	**found**	**trouver**
flee	**fled**	**fled**	**s'enfuir**

fling	flung	flung	jeter violemment
fly	flew	flown	voler
forbid	forbade	forbidden	interdire
forget	forgot	forgotten	oublier
forgive	forgave	forgiven	pardonner
freeze	froze	frozen	geler
get	got	got	obtenir
give	gave	given	donner
go	went	gone	aller
grind	ground	ground	moudre
grow	grew	grown	grandir
hang	hung	hung	pendre, accrocher
have	had	had	avoir
hear	heard	heard	entendre
hide	hid	hidden	(se) cacher
hit	hit	hit	frapper
hold	held	held	tenir
hurt	hurt	hurt	blesser
keep	kept	kept	garder
kneel	knelt	knelt	s'agenouiller
know	knew	known	savoir, connaître
lay	laid	laid	poser à plat
lead	led	led	mener
lean	leant	leant	s'appuyer

leap	**leapt**	**leapt**	**sauter**
learn	**learnt**	**learnt**	**apprendre**
leave	**left**	**left**	**laisser, quitter**
lend	**lent**	**lent**	**prêter**
let	**let**	**let**	**permettre, louer**
lie	**lay**	**lain**	**être étendu**
light	**lit**	**lit**	**allumer**
lose	**lost**	**lost**	**perdre**
make	**made**	**made**	**faire, fabriquer**
mean	**meant**	**meant**	**signifier**
meet	**met**	**met**	**(se) rencontrer**
mow	**mowed**	**mown**	**tondre**
overcome	**overcame**	**overcome**	**surmonter, vaincre**
pay	**paid**	**paid**	**payer**
put	**put**	**put**	**mettre**
quit	**quit**	**quit**	**cesser (de)**
read	**read**	**read**	**lire**
rid	**rid**	**rid**	**débarrasser**
ride	**rode**	**ridden**	**chevaucher**
ring	**rang**	**rung**	**sonner**
rise	**rose**	**risen**	**s'élever, se lever**
run	**ran**	**run**	**courir**
saw	**sawed**	**sawn**	**scier**

say	said	said	dirc
see	saw	seen	voir
seek	sought	sought	chercher
sell	sold	sold	vendre
send	sent	sent	envoyer
set	set	set	fixer
sew	sewed	sewn	coudre
shake	shook	shaken	secouer
shear	sheared	shorn	tondre
shed	shed	shed	verser
shine	shone	shone	briller
shoe	shod	shod	ferrer, chausser
shoot	shot	shot	tirer
show	showed	shown	montrer
shrink	shrank	shrunk	rétrécir
shut	shut	shut	fermer
sing	sang	sung	chanter
sink	sank	sunk	couler
sit	sat	sat	être assis
sleep	slept	slept	dormir
slide	slid	slid	glisser
sling	slung	slung	lancer
slink	slunk	slunk	aller furtivement
slit	slit	slit	fendre, inciser

smell	smelt	smelt	sentir
sow	sowed	sown	semer
speak	spoke	spoken	parler
speed	sped	sped	aller à toute vitesse
spell	spelt	spelt	épeler
spend	spent	spent	dépenser
spill	spilt	spilt	renverser
spit	spat	spat	cracher
split	split	split	fendre
spoil	spoilt	spoilt	gâcher, gâter
spread	spread	spread	répandre
spring	sprang	sprung	jaillir, bondir
stand	stood	stood	être debout
steal	stole	stolen	voler, dérober
stick	stuck	stuck	coller
sting	stung	stung	piquer
stink	stank	stunk	puer
stride	strode	stridden	marcher à grands pas
strike	struck	struck	frapper
string	strung	strung	enfiler, tendre
strive	strove	striven	s'efforcer
swear	swore	sworn	jurer
sweep	swept	swept	balayer
swell	swelled	swollen	enfler

swim	swam	swum	nager
swing	swung	swung	se balancer
take	took	taken	prendre
teach	taught	taught	enseigner
tear	tore	torn	déchirer
tell	told	told	dire, raconter
think	thought	thought	penser
throw	threw	thrown	jeter
thrust	thrust	thrust	enfoncer
tread	trod	trodden	fouler aux pieds
undergo	underwent	undergone	subir
understand	understood	understood	comprendre
upset	upset	upset	bouleverser
wake	woke	woken	(se) réveiller
wear	wore	worn	porter
weave	wove	woven	tisser
weep	wept	wept	pleurer
win	won	won	gagner
wind	wound	wound	enrouler
withdraw	withdrew	withdrawn	(se) retirer
wring	wrung	wrung	tordre
write	wrote	written	écrire

ENGLISH EXPRESSIONS

Backward: vers l'arrière

Backup: sauvegarde

Carried out: réalisées

Cheer up: courage

Climb up: monter

Come up: venir

Drin up: boire

Fed up: ras-le-bol

Forwards: vers l'avant

Give a hand: donner un coup de main

Give up: abandonner

Grow up: grandir

Hands up: lever les mains

Look down: détecter

Look for: chercher

Look up: chercher

Make up: fabriquer

Open up: ouvrir

Run off: s'enfuir

Run out: s'épuiser

Run up: courir jusqu'à

Save up: économiser jusqu'à

Shorthand notation: notation abrégées

Sit up: s'asseoir

Speak up: parler

Stand up: debout

Sum up: résumer

Take off: décoller

Take up: prendre jusqu'à

Tear up: déchirer

Think up: pense jusqu'à

Throw up: jeter

Turn up: tournez jusqu'à

Upside down: à l'envers

Wake up: réveiller

Walk up: monter

Warm up: s'entrainer

PART 7

FRENCH - ENGLISH

PHYSIQUE - PHYSICS

A

Aberration: aberration
Absorbance: Absorbance
AC/DC: AC/DC
Accélération angulaire: angular acceleration
Accélération moyenne: average acceleration
Accélération: acceleration
Accommodation: accommodation
Accumulateur électrique: rechargeable battery
Acier: steel
Action et réaction: action and reaction
Activité: activity
AEPHT: COSTEP
Aérodynamiques: aerodynamics
Agitateur magnétique: Magnetic stirrers
Agrandissement: zooming
Aiguille aimantée: magnetized needle
Aimant en forme de fer à cheval: horseshoe magnet
Aimant permanent: hard magnets
Aimant temporaire: soft magnets
Aimant: magnet
Alimentation électrique: power supply
Alimentation sans interruption: uninterruptible power supply
Allumer, éteindre: switch on (off)
AM/FM: AM/FM
Amont: upstream
Amortissement du mouvement oscillatoire: damped harmonique motion
Amortissement: damping
Ampère: Ampere
Ampèremètre: ammeters
Amplificateur: amplifier
Amplitude: amplitude
Ampoule: bulb
Anémomètre: anemometer

Angle balayé: angle swept
Angstrom (ångström): Angstrom
Année lumière (a.l.): light year (l.y.)
Antenne: antenna
Apesanteur, gravité zéro: zero-gravity
Appareil radiographique: X-ray apparatus
Appareil: apparatus
Arc en ciel: rainbow
Aspirateur: vacuum cleaner
Astigmatisme: astigmatism
Astréroide: asteroid
Astronaute: astronaut
Astronome: astronomer
Astrophysique: astrophysics
Atmosphère (atm): atmosphere (atm)
Atome d'hydrogène: hydrogen atom
Aurore: aurora
Axe: axis

B
Bagues collectrices: slip rings
Balls: bullets
Bande de conduction: conduction band
Bande de valence: valence band
Bande passante: passband
Bar combustible (uranium): fuel rod
Bar: bar
Baromètre: barometre
Barycentre: barycentre
Basse tension: low voltage
Becquerel: Becquerel
Big Crunch: Big Crunch
Bilan d'énergie: energy balance
Bobine: coil
Boson de Higgs: Higgs boson

Bouée: buoy
Boulon d'articulation: yoke bolt
Boulon d'articulation: yoke bolt
Boussole: compass
Brancher, débrancher: plug in (out)
Bruit: disturbance

C

Câblage: wiring
Cable de liaison, rallonge: extention cord
Cadran solaire: sundial
Cadre en Z: Zee frame
Capacité (C): capacitance (C)
Capacité calorifique: heat capacity
Capacité thermique: heat capacity
Capteur solaire thermique: thermal solar sensor
Capteur: sensor
Carburant fissile: fossil fuels
CCD: CCD
Célérité: celerity
CELIAS: CELIAS
Cellule photovoltaïque: photovoltaic cell
Centimètre-Gramme-Seconde CGS: Centimeter-Gram-Second (CGS)
Centre de gravité: centre of gravity
Chaine d'énergie: energy chain
Chaleur: heat
Champ électrique: electric field
Champ gravitationnel: gravitational field strength
Champ magétique: magnetic field
Champ nul: zero field
Champ: field
Changement isothermique: isothermal changes
Charbon: coal
Charge à vide: zero load

Charge électrique: electric charge
Charge électronique: electronic charge
Charge élémentaire: elementary charge
Charge limite d'élasticité: yield load
Chargeur solaire: solar powered charger
Charnière: hinge
Chiffres significatif: significant figures
Chirurgie des yeux: eye surgery
Chromosphère: chromosphere
Chronomètre: stopwatch (chronometer)
Chute libre: free fall
Cible, objectif, but: target
Circuit électrique: electric circuit
Clepsydre: water clock (clypsydra)
Cloche sous vide: glass bell jar
Code postal: zip-code
Coefficient de transmission: transmission coefficient
Coeur solaire: solar core
Cohérence: coherence
Coil (solenoid): Spire (bobine)
Collision nonélastique: inelastic collision
Compacté: zipped
Compressibilité: compression
Condensateur: capacitor
Conducteurs: conductors
Conduction: conduction (see heat conduction)
Conductivité thermique: thermal conductivity
Conservation de l'énergie : conservation of energy
Constante d'Avogadro: Avogadro constant
Constante de Planck: Planck's constant
Constante de raideur: spring constant
Constante gravitationnelle: gravitational constant
Constellation: constellation
Contrainte à la rupture: yield stress
Convection: convection (see heat convection)

Convertisseur analogique numérique: digital analog converter
Convertisseur d'énergie: energy converter
Convertisseur électromagnétique: electromagnetic converter
Convertisseur: inverter dc-ac
Corona, couronne: corona
Coronagraphe: coronagraph
Corps noir: Black body
Cosmodétecteur: cosmodetector
Coulomb: Coulomb (C)
Couple (d'un moteur): torque
Couple de forces: couple of forces
Courant électrique: electric current
Courant et tension alternaif: alternating current and voltage
Courant: current
Court-circuit: short circuit
Cratère: crater
Crête: crest
Culasse: yoke piece
Cuvette: trough
Cycle d'énergie: energy cycle

D

Datation par carbone 14: radioactive-carbon dating
Datation par le carbon 14: radioactive-carbon dating
Débimètre: flowmeter
Débit massique: masse flowrate
Débit volumique: volumetric flowrate
Décibel: decibel
Décroissance alpha: alpha decay
Décroissance exponentielle: exponential decay
Décroissance gamma: gamma decay
Déformation et courbes (relativité générale): warps and curves (general relativity)
Degré d'arc: Arc Degree
Demi-vie: Half-life

Densité: density (relative density R_d)
Déplacement angulaire: angular displacement
Déplacement: displacement
Désintégration, décroissance radioactive: radioactive decay
Détecteur: detector
Détection et détermination de distance par ondes radio:
Détente (decompression): rarefaction
Diagramme de Feynman: Feynman diagrams
Diamagnétique: diamagnetic
Diffraction à travers un trou circulaire: Diffraction at a Small circular hole
Diffraction à travers une fente: diffraction at a single slit
Diffraction d'électron: electron diffraction
Diffraction: diffraction
Diode de Zener: Zener diode
Diode: diode
Disjoncteur: circuit breaker
Dispersion de la lumière: dispersion of light
Dispersion ou diffusion: scattering
Dispositif: device
Distance parcourue: distance travelled
Distance: distance
Domaine visible: visible range
Domaine visible: visible range
Dose absorbée: absorbed dose
Dose équivalente: equivalent dose
Dualité onde-particule: wave-particle duality
Ductilité: ductility
Dureté: hardness
Dynamomètre: spring scale (dynamometer)

E

Echange de particules: exchange particles
Echanges d'énergie: energy exchanges

Echantillanage: sampling
Echantillon: sample
Echèlle célsius de température: Celsius temperature scale
Echèlle centigrade de température: Centigrade temperature scale
Echographie (imagerie par ultrason): ultrasound imaging
Echographie: ultrasonography, ecography
Eclairement: illuminance
Ecoulement: flow
Ecran de plomb: lead screen
Ecran de protection: protection shield
Effet Doppler: Doppler Effect
Effet Hall: Hall Effect
Effet Joule: Joule's Effect
Effet photoélectrique: photoelectric Effect
Effet Tunnel: Tunnel Effect
Effet Venturi: Venturi effect (Venturi meter)
Effet Zeeman: Zeeman Effect
Ejection de la masse couronnale: coronal mass ejection
Elasticité: elasticity
Electrocardiogramme (ECG): electrocardiogram
Electrolyse: electrolysis
Electrolytes: electrolytes
Electron: electron
Electronique de puissance: Power electronics
Electron-volt: electron volt
Electrostatique: electrostatics
Embarder, pivoter: Yaw
Emission stimulée: stimulated emission (see optical pumping)
Endoscopie: endoscopy
Energie cinétique: kinetic energy
Energie de liaison: binding energy
Energie de rayonnement: radiation energy
Energie de tension élastique: elastic strain energy
Energie du vide: vacuum energy
Energie éolienne: wind power

Energie géothermique: geothermal energy
Energie interne: internal energy
Energie mécanique: mechanical energy
Energie noire: black energy
Energie perdue: wasted energy
Energie potentielle de pesanteur: potential energy of gravity
Energie potentielle élastique d'un ressort: potential energy of a spring
Energie potentielle: potential energy
Energie solaire: sun energy
Energie thermique: thermal energy
Energie zéro: zero-point energy
Energie: energy
Enthalpie: Enthalpy
Equation d'un mouvement circulaire: equation of rotational motion
Equation d'un mouvement linèaire: equation of straight line motion
Equation de Bernoulli: Bernoulli equation
Equation de Schrodinger: Schrodinger equation
Equation de transformateur: transformer equation
Equation des gaz parfaits: ideal gas equation
Equation générale des gaz: general gas equation
Equation photoélectrique d'Einstein: Einstein's photoelectric equation
Equation sous forme de mot: word equation
Equation: equation
Erreur alétoire: random error
Erreur systématique: systematic error
Erreur: error
Etalonnage: Calibration
Etat de repos: zero state
Etoile: star
Evaporation et refroidissement: evaporation and cooling
Examen radiographique: X-ray analysis
Excitation: excitation
Exigences: requirements

Exoplanète: extrasolar planet
Expériences: experiments
Extincteur: fire extinguisher

F
F.e.m. force éléctromagnétique induite: induced e.m.f. (electromagnetic force)
Farad: Farad
Fer doux: soft iron
Fer dur: hard iron
Fermeture éclair: zip fastener
Ferrites: ferrites
Ferromagnétisme: ferromagnetism
Feuille de zinc: zinc foil
Feuille: foil
Fibre optique: optical fibre
Fibres de verre: glass fibres
Fiche (électrique): plug
Fil conducteur: wire
Fil de terre: ground wire
Filament d'une lampe: filament lamp
Film antireflet: anti-reflective film
Filter passe-bas: low pass-filter
Filtre passe-bande: band pass filter
Filtre passe-haut: high pass-filter
Fissile: fissile
Fission nucléaire: nuclear fission
Fission: fission
Flexibilité: fexibility
Flotaison: flotation
Fluide: fluid
Fluides compressibles : compressible fluids
Fluides incompressibles : incompressible fluids
Flux couronnale: Coronal Streamer
Flux énergétique: energy flux

Flux laminaire et turbulent: laminar and turbulent flow
Flux lumineux: luminous flux
Flux magnétique: magnetic flux
Force centrifuge: Centrifugal force
Force de frottement: drag
Force de résistance aérodynamique: aerodynamic drag fprce
Force électromagnétique induite: induced electrmagnetic force
Force électromotrice f.é.m: Electromotive force, e.m.f
Force insaisissable: Elusive force
Force magnétique: magnetic force
Force: force
Formule de conjugaison: thin lens formula
Foudre: lightning
Fourche, cadran: yoke
Fractionnement: splitting up
Fracture, cassure: fracture
Fragile, fragilité: brittle (ness)
Franges de Young: Young's fringes
Fréquence angulaire: Angular frequency (angular speed)
Fréquence de coupure: cut-off frequency
Fréquence: frequency
Front d'onde: wavefront
Frottement: friction
Fusible: fuse
Fusion nucléaire: nuclear fusion
Fusion thermonucléaire: thermonuclear Fusion
Fusion: fusion (see thermonuclear fusion)

G

Galaxies: galaxies
Galvanisation au zinc: zinc plating
Gaz: gas
Générateur: generator
Giantes rouge: red giants
Glissement: slipping

Gluons (particule): gluons
Gradient: gradient (grad)
Grandissement: magnification
Graphe: graph
Graver: etch
Gravimètre: gravimeter
Gravitation: gravitation

H
Habitat: housing
Hadrons (particules): hadrons
Haute tension: high voltage
Hauteur d'un son: pitch of a sound
Henry (H): Henry (H)
Homogène: homogeneity
Horologe atomique: atomic clock
Horologe: wall clock
Hypothèse de De Broglie: De Broglie relation (see: wave particle duality)

I
Imagerie médicale: medical imaging
Imagerie par résonance magnétique (IRM): Magnetic resonance imaging (MRI)
Impesanteur: weightlessness
Impulsion: impulsion
Incident: incident (see reflaction)
Indicateur de vitesse: speedometer
Inductance: inductance (L)
Induction électromagnétique: electromagnetic induction
Infrarouge (IR): infra-red (IR)
Intensité de la pésanteur (g): strength of gravity (g)
Intensité du champ gravitationnel: gravitational field strength
Intensité sonore: sound intensity
Interactions élémentaire: fundamental interactions

Interférence destructive: destructive interference
Interférence: interference
Interrupteur: switch
Ionisation: ionisation
Isolant: insulators
Isolation: insulation
Isotope: isotope

J
Jauge de pression: jauge pressure
Joule: Joule

K
Kelvin: Kelvin
Kilogramme: kilogram
Kilowatt-heure: kilowatt-hour

L
La voie lactée: Milky way
Lampe à décharge à gaz: gas discharge lamp
Lampe à incandescence: incandescent light bulb (lamp)
Laser: Laser (Light Amplification by Stimulated Emission of Radiation)
Lentilles: lens
Liaison ionique: ionic bond
Ligne d'absorption (raie de Fraunhoffer): absorption Line
Lignes aérodynamiques (lignes de courant): Streamlines
Limite d'élasticité: Elastic limit
Limite de résistance: yield strength
Limite élastique: yield point
Loi d'Ohm: Ohm's law
Loi de Boyle-Mariotte: Boyles law
Loi de Charles: Charles law
Loi de Coulomb: Coulomb's law
Loi de Dalton de pression partielle: Dalton's law of partial pressure

Loi de décroissance exponentielle de radioactivité: Exponential law of radioactive decay
Loi de faraday: Faraday's law
Loi de Hooke: Hooke's law
Loi de Hubble: Hubble's law
Loi de Mariotte: Boyle's law
Loi de Wein: Wein's law
Lois de kepler: Kepler's laws
Lois de Kirchhoff: Kirchhoff's laws
Lois de Newton: Newton's laws
Lois de Soddy : Soddy's law
Longueur d'onde de De Broglie: De Broglie wavelength
Longueur d'onde électromagnètique: electromagnetic waves
Longueur d'onde: wavelength
Longueur: length
Loupe: magnifying glass (hand lens, magnefier)
Lumière blanche: white Light
Lumière ultraviolet: ultraviolet light
Lunettes: glasses

M
Machine à chaleur: heat engine
Machine: machine
Manomètre: manometer
Maser: Maser (Microwave Amplification by Stimulated Emission Radiation)
Matériaux composites: composite materials
Matériaux fissiles: fissile materials
Matière amorphe: amorphous solide
Matière fluide: fluid matter
Matière fluide: fluid matter
Matière noire: dark matter
Mécanique des fluides: fluid mechanics
Mécanique quantique: quantum mecanics
Mécanique quantique: Quantum mecanics

Médecine nucléaire: nuclear medicine
Micro-ondes (hyperfréquences): microwaves
Minute d'arc: arc Minute
Modulation: modulation
Module de cisaillement: shear modulus
Module de Young, module d'élasticité: Young's modulus
Moment d'inertie: momentum of inertia
Moment d'une force: momentum of force
Moteur à courant continu: direct current (DC) motor
Moteur asynchrone: asynchronous motor
Moteur électrique sans balais: brushless motor
Moteur électrique: electric motor
Moteur pas à pas: stepper motor
Moteur synchrone: synchronous motor
Moteur, engin: motor
Mouvement Brownien: Brownian motion
Mouvement circulaire: circular motion
Mouvement de translation rectiligne: rectilinear movement
Mouvement orbital: orbital motion
Mouvement: motion
Muons (voir cosmodétecteur): muons

N
Naine blanche: White Dwarf
Nebuleuse: Nebula
Neutrino: Neutrino
Niveau d'énergie: energy level
Niveau sonore: sound level
Niveau zéro: Zero level
Nœud: knot
Nombre atomique: Atomic number
Nombre de Mach: Mach number
Noyau: Nucleus
Numéro atomique: atomic number

O

Onde acoustique: acoustic wave
Onde électromagnétique: electromagnetic waves
Onde porteuse: carrier wave
Onde sonore: sound waves
Onde: wave
Ondemètre: wavemeter
Ondes à haute fréquence: higher frequency waves
Ondes longitudinales: longitudinal waves
Ondes radio et micro-ondes: radio waves and microwaves
Ondes sismiques: seismic waves
Ondes transversales: transverse waves
Onduleur: inverter dc-ac
Ouragan: hurricane
Outil: tool

P

Pale d'une éoliènne: blade
Palier: bearing
Panneaux solaire: solar panels
Particules fondamentales: fundamental particles
Pendule: pendulum
Pente: slope
Performance énergétique: energy efficiency
Période: period
Perméabilité relative: relative permeability
Perméabilité relative: relative permeability
Photon: photon
Pic: Spike
Pierre angulaire: stone corner
Pignon, roué dentée: sprocket
Pile: battery
Pivoter, embarder: yaw
Planète: planet
Plomb: lead

Poids: weight
Point de congélation: ice point
Point de fonctionnement: operating point
Point fixe: Fixed point
Polarization linéaire: linear polarisation
Pompage optique: optical pumping
Pompe à chaleur: heat pump
Pompe à vide: vacuum pump
Porte logique: logic gate
Potentiel électrique (tension): electric potential
Potentiel gravitationnel (champ radial): gravitational potential (radial fields)
Potentiel gravitationnel (champ uniform): Gravaitational potential (uniform fields)
Poulie: pulley
Poussée: thrust
Pouvoir calorifique: heating value
Pression absolue: absolute pressure
Pression atmosphèrique: atmospheric pressure
Pression différentielle: differential pressure
Pression relative: relative pressure
Pression: pressure
Principe d'Archimède: Archimedes' principle
Prise de courant (douille d'une ampoule): socket
Prise de terre: earth connection
Productivité: yield capacity
Puce électronique: microchip
Puissance électrique: electrical power
Puissance moyenne: average power
Puissance nucléaire: nuclear power
Puissance solaire: solar power
Pulsars: pulsars
Pulsation: impulse

Q

Quantité de mouvement: momentum
Quantité dérivée: derived quantity
Quantum: quantum
Quark: quark
Quasar: quasar

R
Raccord de graissage: Zerk fitting
Radar et sonar: radar and sonar
Radiation : radiation
Radiation alpha: alpha radiation
Radiation beta : beta radiation
Radiation d'ionisation: ionising radiation
Radiation gamma: gamma radiation
Radiations alpha: alpha rays
Radio Detection And Ranging (RADAR): Radar
Radio: radio
Radioactivité: radioactivity
Radioactivité: radioactivity
Radiogramme, radiographie: X-ray photogrph
Radioprotection: radio protection
Radiothérapie: radiotherapy
Raie d'absorption (raie de Fraunhoffer): absorption line
Rayon (faisceau): ray (beam)
Rayonnement cosmique: Cosmic Ray
Rayonnement de vision: Beam's eye view
Rayonnement ionisant: ionizing radiation
Rayonnement: radiation
Rayons d'électron: Electron beams
Rayon-X (imagerie): X-ray radiography
Rayon-X: X-rays
Réactance inductive: inductive reactance
Réaction en chaine: chain reaction
Réactions nucléaire: nuclear reactions
Récepteur: receiver

Réducteur de pression (détendeur): pressure reducing valve
Référence zéro: zero datum
Référentiel: frame of reference
Réflection: reflection
Réfraction: refraction
Réfrigérateur: refrigerators
Région active: active region
Région de transition: transition region
Réglage à zéro: zero adjustement
Règle de la main droite de Fleming: Fleming's right hand rule
Règle de la main gauche de Fleming: Fleming's left hand rule
Régler: adjust
Relativité: relativity
Remise à zéro: zero reset
Rendement: efficiency (machines)
Rendement: yield
Réqction de fission: fission reaction
Réseaux d'électricité: National grid
Réseaux électrique: high-volatage transmission
Réservoir: reservoir
Residue: residu
Résistance interne: internal resistance
Résistance: resistance
Résolution optique: optical resolution
Résonance Magnètique Nucliaire: Nuclear Magnetic Resonance
Ressort hélicoïdal: helical spring (coil spring)
Ressort: spring
Robot (automate): robot
Robuste: rugged
Rondelle: washer or hardeware
Rouge: red
Roulement à palier: bearing tube
Roulement: bearing

S

S’user: wear out
Sablier: hourglass
Sans interruption: uninterruptible power supply
Sans poids: weightless
Satellite: satellite
Scintigraphie: scan
SCUV: UVCS (Ultraviolet Coronagraph Spectrmeter)
Seconde d’arc: Arc Second
Section en Z: Z-section
Seismologie: seismology
Seismologiste: seismologist
Sémi-conducteur: semiconductor
Sensibilité: sensitivity
Séquence de mise à fe : sequence of firing
Seuil d’audibilité: audibility threshold
Seuil de coupure: Cutoff threshold
Signal analogique: analog signal
Signal numérique: digital signal
Signal: signal
S'imbriquer, chevauchement: overlap
Soleil: sun
Son audible: audible sound
Son: sound
SONAR: SONAR (SOund Navigation And Ranging)
Sonde à effet Hall pour mesurer le champ: Hall probe
Sonde spatiale: space probe
Sonomètre: sound level meter
Soulèvement: upthrust
Source d’énergie: energy sources
Sources d’énergie finies: finite energy sources
Spectre continue: continuous spectrum
Spectre d’un champ électrique: field lines (electric)
Spectre d’un champ magnétique: field lines (magnetic)
Spectre électromagnétique: electromagnetic spectrum
Spectre magnétique: magentic spectrum

Spectroscope: spectroscopy
Spetre d'émission: emission spectrum
Suivre: track
Supernova: supernovae
Surface d'émission: surface of emission
Surtension: overcurrent
Système de guidage, giration: yaw system
Système international SI: SI system (International System)
Système solaire: solar system

T

Taches solaires: coronal Hole
Technologie: technology
Télécommunication: telecommunication
Téléphone: telephone
Téléscope: telescope
Télévision: television
Température de Curie: Curie temperature
Température: temperature
Temps Atomique International (TAI): International Atomic Time (TAI)
Temps universel: Universal Time
Temps: time
Théorème (loi) de Torcelli: Torricelli's theorem (law)
Théorie de Big Bang: Big Bang theory
Théorie des cordes : string theory
Théorie quantique des champs: quantum field theory
Therapie par rayon X: X-ray therapy
Thermodynamique (lois): thermodynamics laws
Thermographie: thermography
Tornade: tornado
Tournant: turning point
TRACE: TRACE (Transition Region and Coronal Explore)
Traînée: drag
Transducteur ultrason: utrasound transducer

Transducteurs: transducers
Transfert d'énergie: energy transfer
Transfert de chaleur par conduction, convection ou par radiation: heat transfer
Transfert de chaleur par conduction: heat conduction
Transfert de chaleur par convection: heat convection
Transfert de chaleur par radiation: heat radiation
Transformateur: transformer
Travail d'extraction: work function
Travail: work
Traverse cruciforme, croisillon: X-member
Tremblement de terre: earthquake
Trou Noir: Black Hole
Trous (encoches): slots
Turbine: turbine

U
Ultrason: ultrasound
Unité Astronomique (U.A.): Astronomical Unit (A.U)
Unité de mass atomique: atomic masse unit
Unité dérivée: derived unity

V
Vagues: water waves
Vaisseau spatial: spacecraft
Vergence: vergence
Vide: vacuum
Vis d'Archimède: Archimedes' screw
Vis: screw
Viscossité: viscosity
Vitesee d'onde: wave speed
Vitesse angulaire: angular velocity
Vitesse d'échapement: escape speed
Vitesse d'écoulement: flow speed or velocity
Vitesse de la lumière: speed of light

Vitesse de synchronisme: synchronous speed
Vitesse limite: terminal speed
Vitesse moyenne des particules: drift speed
Vitesse uniform: steady speed
Vitesse: velocity
Voiture lunaire: Rover
Voltage: voltage
Voltmètre: voltmeter

W
Watt: watt
Wattemètre: wattemètre
Weber: weber

Z
Zénith: zenith
Zéro absolue: absolute zero
Zinc: zinc

CHIMIE - CHEMISTRY

A

Absorption d'une radiation: absorption of radiation

Absorption des liquides et des gaz: absorption of liquids and gases

Accumulateur au plomb: lead acid battery

Accumulateur: accumulator

Acide ascorbique (vitamin C): ascorbic acid (vitamin C)

Acide carboxylique: carboxylic acid

Acide catalysis: catalyse acide

Acide chlorhydrique: acid chlorides

Acide de Bronsted: Bronsted acid

Acide dissociation constants: constant de dissociation

Acide gras: fatty acid

Acide sulfurique concentré: concentrated sulphuric acid

Acides faibles: weak acids

Acides: acids

Actinium: actinium

Acyl chlorides

ADN acide désoxyribonucléique: DNA (deoxyribonucleic acid)

Aérosols: aerosols

Agrochimie: agrochemistry

Air: air

Alcanes: alkanes

Alcènes: alkenes

Alcools: alcohols

Alcynes: alkynes

Aldéhydes: aldehydes

Alliages: alloys

Aluminium: aluminium

Américium: americium

Amides: amides

Amidon: starch

Amines: amines

Amino acides: amino acids

Ammonic: ammonia

Amphétamines: amphetamines

Analgésiques: analgesic
Anhydre: anhydrous
Anhydride d'acide: acid anhydride
Anhydride: anhydride
Aniline: aniline
Anion: anion
Anode: anode
Anodisation: anodizing
Antiadhésif: nonstick
Antibiotiques: antibiotics
Antigel: antifreeze
Antimoine (Sb): antimony
Antioxidant: oxidation inhibiter
Antiseptiques: antiseptics
Arènes: arenes
Argent (Ag): silver
Argon (Ar): argon
Arsenique (As): arsenic
Aspirine: aspirine
Assembler: build up
Astate (At): astatine
Atmosphère: atmosphere
Atome: atom
Atomisation: atomization
Autocatalyse: autocatalysis
Autoprotolyse: autoionization
Azote (N): nitrogen

B
Bactérie: bacteria
Bar: bar
Baryum (Ba): barium
Base: base
Bases faibles: weak bases
Batterie: battery

Bec Bunsen: Bunsen burner
Bécher: beaker
Benzène: benzene
Berkélium (Bk): berkelium
Béryllium (Be): beryllium
Béton: concrete
Biochimie: biochemistry
Bismuth (Bi): bismuth
Bore (B): boron
Bouillant: boiling hot
Bouteille d'oxygène: oxygen bottle
Brome (Br): bromine
Brouillard de pollution: smog
Brouillard: fog
Buée: vapour

C

Cadmium (Cd): cadmium
Calcaire: Limestone
Calcium (Ca): calcium
Californium (Cf): californium
Calorimètre: calorimeter
Capacité thermique massique: specific heat
Carbonate de calcium: calcium carbonate
Carbone (C): carbon
Carbone assymétrique: stereoogenic center (chiral center)
Carbone: carbon
Catalyse enzymatique: enzyme (catalyst)
Catalyse hétérogène: heterogeneous catalyst
Catalyse homogène: homogeneous catalyst
Catalyse homogène: homogeneous catalyst
Catalyseur: catalyst
Cellule électrochimique: electrochemical cell
Cellule voltaique: voltaic cell
Célsius: celsius

Centrifugation: centrifuging
Cerium (Ce): cérium
Césium (Cs): cesium
Cétone: ketone
Chaleur latent: latent heat
Chaleur molaire de condensation: molar heat of condensation
Chaleur molaire de fusion: molar heat of fusion
Chaleur molaire de solidification: molar heat of solidification
Chaleur molaire de vaporisation: molar heat of vaporization
Changement d'état: change of state
Chauffage à reflux: reflux condense
Chauffer: heat
Chimie analytique: analytical chemistry
Chimie de teinture: chemical dye
Chimie: chemistry
Chiralité: chirality
Chlore (Cl): chlorine
Chlorofluorocarbure (CFC): chlorofluorocarbon (CFC)
Chlorure d'acyle: acyl chlorides
Chromatographie (chromatographie sur couche mince CCM): chromatography (thin layer chromatography TLC)
Chromatographie sur couche mince (CCM): thin-layer chromatography (TLC)
Chrome (Cr): chromium
CLTP: standard ambient temperature and pressure SATP
CNTP: standard temperature and pressure STP
Cobalt (Co): cobalt
Colonne industriel de distillation (see Continuous Fractional Distillation of Petroleum): Industrial Fractionating Column
Colorant: dyes
Colorants, teintures: dyes
Combustible: combustible (fuel)
Combustion: combustion
Comète: comet
Compact: compact

Composant: component
Composé chimique: chemical compound
Composé organique: organic compound
Compressible: compressible
Compression: compression
Concentration massique: mass concentration
Concentration molaire: amount (molarity)
Concentration: concentration
Condensation: condensation
Conservation des atoms: conservation of atoms
Contamination: contamination
Contrainte mécanique: mechanical stress
Contrainte thermique: thermal stress
Coronne: courona
Corps gras, triester: fat
Corps simple: single element molecule
Corrosion: corrosion
Corrosive: corrosive
Cosmologique: cosmologic
Couche d'ozone: ozone layer
Couche électronique: electronic shell
Couche: shell
Coulée: cast
Coulomètre: coulometer
Cristallisoir: crystallizer
Cuivre (Cu): Copper
Curium (Cm): curium
Cyclohexane: cyclohexane

D

Danger, risque, péril: hazard
Date limite de consomation: shelf life
Débimètre: flowmeter, flow measurement
Déchets radioactives: nuclear waste
Déclencher: trigger

Dégage: release
Dégel: thaw
Degree de polymerisation: polymerization degree
Désagrégation: weathering
Détendeur: regulator
Diastéréoisomères: diastereoisomers
Diffusion: diffusion
Diluer: dilute (to)
Dioxyde de carbone: carbon dioxide
Disinfectant: disinfectant
Dispersé: dispersed
Dissolution: dissolving
Dissoudre: dissolve
Distillat: distillate
Distillation fractionnée continue du pétrole: continuous fractional distillation of petroleum
Distillation fractionnée: fractional distillation
Distillation: distillation
Divisé: divided
Dosage: titration
Dose absorbée: dose absorbed
Dose équivalente: equivalent dose
Dosge par retour: back titration
Douce: mild
Drogues: drugs
Dubnium (Db): dubnium
Dysprosium (Dy): dysprosium

E

Eau de chaux: limewater
Eau distillée: distilled water
Eau gazeuse: soda water
Echantillonage: sampling
Ecran de protection: protection shield
Effervescence : effervescence

Einsteinium (Es): einsteinium
Electrode : electrode
Electrolyse: életrolysis
Electrolyte: électrlyte
Electron: electron
Electrophorèse: electrophoresis
Elément alcalins: alkali elements
Elueant: eluent
Emulsion: emulsion
Enantiomère: enantiomers
Energie chimique: chemical energy
Energie d'activation: activation energy
Enthalpie de combustion : enthalpy of combustion
Enthalpie de formation : enthalpy of formation
Entropie: entropy
Enzyme (catayst): catalyse enzymatique
Equation Arrehenius: Arrehenius equation
Equation bilan en toutes letters: word equation
Equation de Van der Waals: Van der Waals equation
Equation du gaz parfait: Ideal gas equation, universal gas equation
Equilibre acido-basique : acid-base equilibria
Equilibre chimique: chemical equilibrium
Erbium (Er): erbium
Espèces chimiques: chemical species
Estérification: esterification
Étain (Sn): tin
Ether: ether
Europium (Eu): europium
Exactitude des données: accuracy of data
Eyepiece: oculaire

F

Famille ou groupe de matériaux : group or materials
Fer (Fe): iron
Fermium (Fm): fermium

Fibre de glass: glass fibre
Filtrat: filtrate
Filtration: filtration
Floculation: floculation
Fluor (F): fluorine
Fonte: cast iron
Force d'un acide: acid strength
Formule brute: empirical formula
Formule dévélopée: structural formula
Formule moléculaire: molecular formula
Formule semi-développée: condensed structural formula
Formule topologique: line formula, skeletal formula
Francium (Fr): francium
Front de solvent (CCM): solvent front
Fumé: smoke
Fusion: fusion

G
Gadolinium (Gd): gadolinium
Gallium (Ga): gallium
Gants: gloves
Gaz: gas
Germanium (Ge): germanium
Givre (gelée blanche): frost (hard rime)
Gouttes: droplets
Gouttes: droplets
GPL: GLP
Graphe: graph
Groupe alkyle: alkyl group
Groupe amine: amino group
Groupe aryle: aryl group
Groupes fonctionnels: functional group identeties

H
Hafnium (Hf): hafnium

Harmonique (son): overtone
Hassium (Hs): hassium
Haut fournaux: blast furnace
Helium (He): helium
Hétérogène: heterogeneous
Holmium (Ho): holmium
Horizantale: horizontal
Horologe atomique au cesium: Cesium atomic clock
Hotte: fume hood
Hydrate: hydrate
Hydraté: hydrous
Hydrocarbones aromatique: aromatic hydrocarbons
Hydrocarbures: hydrocarbons
Hydrogène (H): hydrogen
Hydrolyse: hydrolysis
Hydrophile ou lipophobe: hydrophilic
Hydrophobe ou lipophile: hydrophobic

I
Incandescence: incandescence
Indicateur acido-basique: acid-base indicators
Indicateur coloré: universal indicator, color indicator
Indice d'octane: octane number
Inflammable: flammable
Inidium (In): inidium
Insoluble: insoluble
Iode (I): iodine
Ion: ion
Iridium (Ir): iridium
Isomère: isomer
Isotope: isotope

K
Krypton (Kr): krypton

L

Lanthane (La): lanthanum

Lawrencium (Lw): lawrencium

Liaison covalente: covalent bond

Liaison de Van der Waals: Van der Waals' bond

Liaison: bond

Ligne de dépôt (CCM): origin

Limewater : eau de chaux

Limpide: limpid

Liquéfaction: liquefaction

Liquide: liquide

Lithium (Li): lithium

Loi d'Avogadro: Avogadro's law

LPG: GPL

Lunette de protection: safety goggles

Lutécium (Li): lutetium

M

Magnésium (Mg): magnesium

Manganèse (Mn): manganese

Masque d'oxygène: oxygen mask

Masse molaire: molar mass

Masse volumique: masse density or density

Masse: mass

Matériau artificiel: synthetic compound

Matériau métallique: metallic material

Matériau minéral: mineral material

Matériau nature: natural compound

Matériau organique: organic material

Matière noire: dark matter

Mécanique quantique: quantum mechanics

Meitnerium (Mt): meitnerium

Mélange racémique: racimic mixture

Mélange: mixture

Mendélévium (Md): mendelevium

Meniscus: ménisque
Mercure (Hg): mercury
Métaux alcalino-terreux: alkaline earth metals
Métaux alcalins: alkali metals
Mettre à feu: set fire
Mild: douce
Miscible: miscible
Modèle moleculaire eclaté: ball and stick model
Mole: mole
Molécule: molecule
Molécules asymétrique: asymmetric molecules
Molybdène (Mo): molybdenium
Monoxyde de carbone: carbon monoxide
Motif, figure: pattern

N
Nanotéchnologie: nanotechnology
Néodyme (Nd): neodymium
Néon (Ne): neon
Neptunium (Np): neptunium
Nickel (Ni): nickel
Niobium (Nb): niobium
Nobélium (No): nobelium
Nocif: harmful
Nombre atomique (Z): atomic number (Z)
Nombre d'Avogadro: Avogadro's constant (number)
Nombre de nucléon: mass number (nucleon number)
Nombre quantique: quantum number
Non miscible: immiscible
Noyau: nucleus
Nuage: cloud

O
Oculaire: eyepiece
Opaque: opaque

Or (Au): gold
Osmium (Os): osmium
Osmose: osmosis
Oxydant: oxidizing agent, oxidizer
Oxydation: oxydation
Oxyde amphotère: amphoteric oxide
Oxyde d'acide
Oxyde d'acide: acidic oxide
Oxyder: oxidize
Oxygène (O): oxygen
Oxygène liquide: liquid oxygen
Oxymètre: pulse oximetry
Ozone: ozone
Ozonsphère: ozonsphere

P

Palier de temperature: temperatue dwell
Palladium (Pd): palladium
Papier de chromatographie: paper of chromatography
Papier pH: litmus paper
Période (rangée): period (row)
pH: pH
Phase mobile: mobile phase (elution)
Phase stationnaire: stationary phase
Phase: phase
Phénols: phenols
Phosphore (P): phosphorous
Photosynthèse: photosynthesis
Pile à combustible: fuel cell
Pile Daniel: Daniell cell (dry cell)
Pile galvanique: galvanic cell
Pile rechargeable: rechargeable battery
Platine (Pt): platinum
Plomb (Pb): lead
Pluie acide: acid rain

Plutonium (Pu): plutonium
Point (temperature) d'ébullition: boiling point
Point critique: critical point
Point triple (eutectique): triple point
Pollué: polluted
Pollution de l'air: air pollution
Pollution: pollution.
Polonium (Po): polonium
Polymère atactique: atactic polymer
Polymère: polymer
Polymérisation: polymerisation
Pont salin: salt bridge
Potable: drinkable
Potassium (K): potassium
Poudre: powder
Praséodyme (Pr): praseodyme
Précipitation: precipitation
Précipité: precipitate
Pression atmosphèrique: atmospheric pressure
Pression critique: critical pressure
Processus: processing
Produit chimique: chemical product
Projection de Newman: Newman projection
Promèthium (Pm): promethium
Protactinium (Pa): protactinium
Pyrolyse: pyrolysis

Q
Quantité de matière: amount of substance
Quantité vectorielle: vector quantity

R
Racémique: racemic
Radiation ultraviolet: ultraviolet radiation
Radium (Ra): radium

Radon (Rn): radon
Rapport frontal (R_f): Retention factor, retardation factor (R_f)
Rayon atomique: atomic radius
Rayonnement ionisant: ionizing radiation
Rayon-X: X-rays
Réactif: reagent
Réaction acido-basique: acid-base reactions
Réaction d'addition: addition reaction
Réaction d'addition-élimination: addition-elimination reactions
Réaction d'ordre zéro: zero order reaction
Réaction de polymérisation: addition polymerization
Réaction de substitution: substitution reaction
Réaction endothermique: endothermic reaction
Réaction exothermique: exothermic reaction
Réaction redox: redox reaction
Réagit: react
Recyclage: recycling
Réducteur: reducing agent
Réduction: reduction
Réfrigérant: condenser
Règle d'octet: octet rule
Résidu: residue
Respiration aérobique: aerobic respiration
Revêtement antiadhésif: nonstick coating
Rhénium (Re): rhenium
Rhodium (Rh): rhodium
Rosée: dew
Rouille: rust
Rubidium (Rb): rubidium
Ruthénium (Ru): ruthenium
Rutherfordium (Rf): rutherfodium

S

S'assembler: build up
Salin: saline

Samarium (Sm): samarium
Sang: blood
Saturé: saturrated
Saumure: brine
Scandium (Sc): scandium
Seaborgium (Sg): seaborgium
Sel acide: acid salt
Sélénium (Se): selenium
Silicium (Si): silicon
Sodium (Na): sodium
Solide: solid
Solidification: solidification
Solids amporphe: amorphous solids
Solute: solute
Solution aqueux: aqueous solution
Solution saline: saline solution
Solution tampon: buffer
Solution: solution
Solvant: solvent
Soude: souda
Soufre (S): sulphur
Spectre atomique: atomic spectrum
Spectre d'absorption atomique: atomic absorption spectroscopy
Spectre d'absorption: absorption spectrum
Spectre d'émission atomique: atomic emission spectroscopy
Spectroscopie moléculaire: molecular spectroscopy
Spectroscopie ultraviolet: ultraviolet spectroscopy
Stéréochimie: stereochemistry
Stéréoisomère de confirmation: conformational isomerism
Stéréoisomères: stereoisomers
Stœchiométrie: stoichiometry
Strontium (Sr): strontium
Structure: structure
Sublimation: sublimation
Surcharge: overweight

Surchauffe: overtemperature
Surface libre: Free surface
Surgeler: super-freeze
Suroscillation: overswing
Suspension: suspension
Symbole chimique: chemical Symbol
Synthèse: synthesis
Synthétiser: synthesize
T
Tableau périodique des éléments (tableau de Mendeleïev): periodic table (Mendeleïev table of elements):
Tache: spot
Tantale (Ta): tantalum
Taux d'avancement: yield calculations
Technétium (Tc): technetium
Tellure (Te): tellurium
Température critique: critical temperature
Température: temperature
Terbium (Tb): terbium
Terre rares: rare earth elements
Thallium (Ti): thallium
Théorie atomique: atomic theory
Thermodurcissable: thermoset
Thermomètre: thermometer
Thermoplastique: thermoplastic
Thorium (Th): thorium
Thulium (Tm): thulium
Titane (Ti): titanium
Titratge acido-basique: acid-base titration
Trajectoire (orbite) atomique: atomic (orbitals) trajectory
Transfert d'énergie: energy transfer
Transparent: transparent
Tube nanocarbone: carbon nanotubes
Tungestène (W): tungesten

U
UICPA: IUPAC
Unité de mesure de pollution (0.04 % = 400ppm): parts per millions (ppm)
Ununbium/Copernicium (Uub/Cn): ununbium/copernicium
Ununhexium/Livermorium (Uuh/Lv): ununhexium/livermorium
Ununnillium/Darmstadtium (Uun/Ds): ununnillium/darmstadtium
Ununoctium (Uuo): ununoctium
Ununpentium (Uup): ununpentium
Ununquadium/Flérovium Uuq/Fl): ununquadium/Flerovium
Ununseptium (Uus): Ununseptium
Ununtrium (Uut): ununtrium
Unununium/Roentegenium (Uuu/Rg): unununium/Roentegenium
Uranium (U): uranium
V
Vanadium (V): vanadium
Vapeur: steam, vapour
Vaporisation : vaporization
Variation d'enthalpie: enthalpy change
Vector quantity: quantité vectorielle
Viscoelasticité: viscoélasticity
Viscosité: viscosity
Vitesse: velocity
Volume: volume

X
Xénon (Xe): Xenon

Y
Ytterbium (Yb): ytterbium
Yttrium (Y): yttrium

Z
Zéro absolu: absolute zero
Zinc (Zn): zinc

Zirconium (Zr): zirconium
Zwitterions: zwitterions

MATHEMATIQUE - MATHEMATICS

A

Abscisse: abscissa

Absolue: absolute

Abstraction: abstraction

Accélération: acceleration

Accolade (curly-); parenthèse (round-); crochet (square-): brackets

Accolade: braces

Accroissement: increment

Addition: addition

Affine: affine (fonction)

Agrandissement: enlargement

Aigu: acute

Ainsi: thus

Aire, surface: area

Ajustement (affine): fitting

Aléatoire: random

Algebra: algebra

Algèbre de Boole (logique): Boolean algebra

Algorithme d'Euclide: Euclidean algorithm

Algorithme réparti: distributed algorithms

Algorithme: algorithm

Alignés (points): collinear

Allure, profil, forme ("mettre sous la forme..."): shape

Alphabet: alphabet

Amplitude: amplitude

Analogique: analog

Analyse: analysis

Angle aigue (inférieur à 90°): acute angle

Angle droit: right angle

Angle plat: perigon

Angle: angle

Angles adjacents: adjacent angle

Angles alternes externes: alternate exterior angles

Angles alternes internes: alternate interior angles

Angles correspondants: corresponding angles

Angstrom (unite), 10^{-15}: angstrom (unite), 10^{-15}.
Anneaux borroméens: borromean rings
Anneaux: annulus
Antecedent: antecedent.
Apex (sommet le plus élevé): apex
Appartenir: belong (to)
Approximatif, approché, grossier: rough
Approximation: approximation
Arbre (de probabilités): tree
Arc: arc
Arccot: arccotangent
Arcctg: arctangent
Arcos: arccosinus
Arête, côté: edge
Argument: argument
Arithmetique: arithematic
Arrondir par défaut (contraire de "to ceil"): floor (to)
Arrondir: rounding off
Asymptote: asymptote
Au carré: squared
Au cube: cubed
Au moins: at least
Axes: axis/axes
Axiom: axiom
Azimuthe: azimuth

B
Barre (au dessus d'une expression): vinculum
Barre (verticale, cf. vinculum), bâton (diagramme): bar
Barycentre: barycenter
Base de numération: radix, radices
Base: base
Bien défini (pour une fonction): well-defined
Bien que: though
Bijectif: bijective

Binary digit: bit
Bissectrice (U.S.): bisector
Bloc d'élement: block of elements
Borne inférieure: greatest lower bound
Borne supérieure: least upper bound
Borne: bounded
Boulier: abacus
Branch d'étude des fonctions: calculus

C

C.q.f.d. (ce qu'il falait démontrer) : Q.e.d. (quod erat demonstrandum)
Calculer: calculate, compute (to)
Canonique: canonical
Caractère alphanumérique: alphanumeric
Cardinal: cardinality
Carrée magique: Magic square
Cent: hundred
Centième partie d'un nombre: hundredth part of a number
Centre de gravité: gravity centre (centroid)
Centre du cercle circonscrit à un triangle: circumcenter of a triangle
Centre du cercle inscrit à un triangle: incenter of a triangle
Changer de sens (pour une inégalité): reversed (to be)
Chapeau (^): roof
Chercher: seek (to)
Chiffre significatif: significant digit
Chiffre, zéro: cipher, zero
Chiffres Arabe: Arabic numerals
Chiffres: numerals, digits
Coeffient binomial: binomial coefficient
Comatrice: adjugate matrix
Combinaison: combination
Compas: dividers (plur.)
Complexe: complex
Compter: count

Concerne le cercle circonscrit(e): circum (circumcirc)
Concerne le cercle ou la sphère inscrit(e): in (incercle, insphere, in-center, inradius)
Concourantes: convergent
Condition nécessaire: Necessary condition
Condition suffisante: sufficient condition
Conditions aux limites: boundary value problem
Confondu: coincident
Conjecture: conjecture
Conjugaison: conjugation
Conjugué: conjugate
Construire (une perpendiculaire): erect (to)
Continu par morceaux: piecewise continuous
Continue (fonction): continous (fucntion)
Contre-exemple: counterexample
Coordonnées cartésien: cartisian coordinates
Coordonnées polaires: polar coordinates
Coordonnées sphériques: sphérical coordinates
Coordonnées: coordinates
Corps, solide: body
Cosinus: cosine.
Côté (polygone), face (polyèdre): side
Côté de l'angle droit (dans un triangle rectangle), branche (d'un compas) (jambe dans le civil): leg
Côtés (d'un angle), côtés de l'angle droit (d'un triangle rectangle): arms
Couple: ordered pair
Courbe: curve
Cours: lecture
Crible (d'Eratosthène): sieve
Critère: test
Croisé (polygone), rentrant (angle): reflex
Cube: cube

D

Dans le sens contraire du des aiguilles d'une montre (U.S.): counter-clockwise
Dans le sens des aiguilles d'une montre: clockwise
De plus: Moreover
Dé(s): die, dice
Décimale: decimal
Déduire (calcul): deduct (to)
Déduire (raisonnement): deduce (to)
Définie: definite
Degré: degree
Dénominateur: denominator
Dérivé: derivative
Déterminant: determinant
Développement: expansion
Développer (un calcul), compléter (une base): expand (to)
Diagramme à bâton: bar chart, stick digram
Diagramme circulaire: pie chart
Diagramme en boîte: boxplot
Diagramme: diagram
Diamètre: diameter
Différence des ordonnées (de deux points): rise
Dimension: dimension.
Discret: discrete
Disque: disk
Distributivité: distributivity
Diviser: divide
Diviseur: divisor
Division: division
Domaine, portée: range
Donc: hence
Données: data
Droit (angle), rectangle (triangle): right
Droite d'Euler: Euler line
Droite: line

E

Ecart-type: standard deviation

Echanger: swap (to)

Echantillon: sample

Echantillonage: sampling

Echelle: scale

Effectuer (des simplifications par exemple): perform (to)

Elever à la puissance n: raise to the power n

Elever au carré: square (to)

Elever au cube: cube (to)

Elimination, simplification: cancellation

Eliminer, simplifier par: cancel (to)

Ellipse: ellipse

Ensemble: set

Entier (relatif) (entier naturel, natural number: integer (nom)

Entier: integral (adj.)

Equation biquadratique: biquadtratic equation

Equation caractéristique: auxiliary equation

Equation de Bernoulli: Bernoulli equation

Équerre: angle-hook

Equerre: straightedge

Equilatérale: equilateral

Espérance: expacted value

Evénements indépendants: Mutually independet events

Exact (calcul, décimales): correct

Exacte (décimale): valid

Exponentiel: exponential

Exposant (écrire en exposant): superscript

Exposant: exponent

Extrapoler: extrapolate

Extrémité: tip

F

Facteur de (dans a(b+c)), divisé par (dans a : b): into

Facteur, diviseur: factor

Factoriser, décomposer: factor (to)
Faire passer (un terme d'un membre d'une équation dans un autre), décaler: shift (to)
Fois: time
Fonction algèbrique: algebraic function
Formule: formula
Foyer: focus
Fraction: fraction
Frise: frieze

G
Géométrie analytique: analytic geometry
Graduation (sur les axes): label
Graduation: tick mark
Groupe abélien: abelian group

H
Hauteur (triangle): altitude
Hauteur: height
Histogramme: histogram
Hyperbole: hyperbola
Hypoténuse: hypotenuse
Hypothèse: hypothesis

I
Impair: odd:
Indice (base 100 par exemple): index
Indice (écrire en indice): subscript
Inégal: unequal
Inégalité: inequality
Inexact: inaccurate
Infinité: infinity
Intersection: intersection.
Intervalle: interval
Inverse (d'un nombre): reciprocal :

Inversement proportionnellement à: inversely as
Isosceles: isoceles

K
Kilogramme: kilogram
Kilomètre: kilometer

L
Largeur: width
Limite spérieure: Upper bound
Linéaire: linear
Loi d'absorption: absorption laws
Loi des associations: associative laws
Longueur: length
Losange: diamond
Losange: rhombus

M
Matrice: matrix
Médiane d'un triangle ou d'une série statistique: Median
Médiatrice: perpendicular bisector
Méthode de dichotomie: bisection method
Milliard: billion
Moindre, (le) plus petit: least
Moins: Minus
Motif (d'un pavage), patron (d'un polyèdre): pattern
Moyenne: Aaverage
Moyenne: Mean

N
Négatif ou nul: Non-positive
Noeud (unité): knot (speed unit)
Nombre abondant: abundant numbers
Nombre amiable: amicable numbers
Nombre cardinale: cardinal number

Nombre d'or: golden ratio
Nombre, chiffres (statistiques): figure(s)
Nombres réels: real numbers
Norme (vecteur): Magnitude (vector)
Noter, appeler, représenter: denote (to)
Numérateu: numerator
Numération Aztèque: Aztec numeration
Numeration binaire: binary numeration

O
Obtus (angle supérieur à 90°): obtuse
Oppose: opposite
Ordinogramme: flow chart
Ordonnée: ordinate

P
P.g.c.d. (plus grand commun diviseur): h.c.d. (highest common divisor)
P.p.c.m.: l.c.m. (least common multiple)
Pair (nombre): even (number)
Palier: bearings
Par conséquent: therefore
Par ex. (exempli gratia): e.g.
Parabole: parabola
Paradoxe du barbier: Barber paradox
Parallélépipède rectangle: cuboid
Paramètre: parameter
Partie entière (sol dans le civil): floor
Pavage (tile, tuile): tiling
Pi: Archimedes' constant
Pie (π): pi $\pi = 3.1415$
Pile ou face: heads or tails
Plan: plane
Plus grand que, supérieur à: greater than (higher than)
Plus petit que, inférieur à: less than (lower than)

Point d'inflexion: turning point (inflection point)
Point: dot
Pointillé : dotted
Polyédre: polyhedron
Positif ou nul: Non-negative
Positif: positive
Précision: accuracy
Premier quartile: first quartile
Premiers entre eux: relatively prime
Prime (′), tiret: dash
Probabilité: probability
Produit: product
Projection cylindrique équidistante: equirectangular projection
Prouver: proof
Puisque: since
Puissance: power
Pyramide: pyramid

Q
Quadrilatérale: quadrilateral
Quadrilatère qui n'est pas un trapèze (U.K.), trapèze (U.S.): trapezoid
Quartier d'un cercle: quadrant
Quotient, rapport: ratio
Quotient: quotient

R
Racine (racine carrée): root (square root)
Racine carée de deux: Pythagoras' constant
Racine carré de: squar mean root
Rang: rank
Rapporteur: protractor
Rayon (d'un cercle): radius
Rayon, demi-droite: ray
Rectangle: rectangle

Rectiligne: rectilinear
Règle (instrument): ruler
Règle de trois: golden rule
Règle, loi: rule
Régulier: regular
Repère: frame
Résoudre: resolve
Résoudre: settle (to)
Résoudre: solve
Reste (d'une division): remainder
Retenir (= faire une retenue) (emprunter dans le civil): borrow (to)
Rhomboïde: rhomboid
Rotation: revolve

S
S'annuler: vanish (to)
Saillant (angle), anguleux (point): salient
Sécante: secant
Seconde (") : double dash
Section droite: cross section
Segment droit: line segment
Segment: segment
Sens contraire d'une aiguille de montre: anticlockwise
Série de Fibonacci: Fibonacci sequence
Signe: sign
Sinus: sine
Somme des chiffres (d'un entier): cross-sum
Somme: sum
Sommet(s) (en géométrie plane): vertex, vertices
Sommet(s) (pour un volume): apex, apices
Soustraction: substraction
Statistique: statistics
Strictement moins de: fewer than
Strictement négatif: Negative
Suite: sequence

Supplimentaire: supplementary
Supposer, prendre (une valeur): Assume (to)
Sur (dans a/b): Upon
Sur (pour la lecture d'une note, 15/20 par ex.): out of
Système sexagésimal Babylonien: Babylonian sexagesimal system

T
Tangent: tangent.
Taux d'accroissement: difference quotient
Term of (in): en fonction de.
Terme: addend
Tesselation: pavage.
Théorème de Thalès: intercept theorem
Théorème: theorem
Tierce ('''): triple dash
Traçer (point par point): plot (to)
Trajectoire: trajectory
Transformation laissant invariant(e) (une figure): symmetry transformation (of a figure)
Translation: shift
Trapèze (U.K.), quadrilatère qui n'est pas un trapèze (U.S.): trapezium
Triangle: triangle.
Trier, ordonner: sort (to)
Trigonométrie: trigonemetry
Tripler: treble (to)
Troisième quartile: third quartile
Tronc (de cône): frustrum
Trunqué: truncated

U
Un quart: quarter
Unité: unity

V

Valeur absolue: absolute value
Valeur moyenne: Mean value
Valuer: value
Variable: variable
Vecteur: vector
Vérifier (un calcul): check (to)
Vers la droite (rotation), direct (repère), rermante (parenthèse): right hand (ed)
Vers la gauche (rotation), rétrograde (repère), ouvrante (paren thèse): left-hand(ed)
Verticale: vertical
Virgule: comma
Volume: volume
Vue de dessous: view from underneath
Vue de dessus: view from above

Z
Zéro: nought, nil
Zéro: zero

INFORMATIQUE - COMPUTEUR

A

Absent: away

Accès à distance: remoting

Accès administrateur: administrator access

Accro de l'internet: infoaddict

Accueil: home

Administrateur de courrier électronique: postmaster

Administrateur Web: webmaster

Adresse résolue: address resolved

Affichage: display

Affichage: view

Afficher: echo

Ajout: append

Aléatoire, au hazard: random

Alimentation électrique: power supply

Aller à: go to

Aller au début: go top

Amassé: gathered

Analyse générale d'opération: outline process

Annuaire: directory

Anomalie: abnormal

Architecture réseau: ethernet

Architecture: design

Argent électronique: E-cash

Arret prématuré: abortion

Arrêt: stop

Arrêter, empêcher: preclude

Arrêter: interrupt

Assemblage partagé: shared assembly

Assembleur: assembler

Attente: wait

Au début: topping

Au point: in focus

Authoriser: allow

B

Balayage: scanning

Balise, marqueur: markup

Bandeau publicitaire: banner

Barre de suivi: trackbar

Barrier de sécurité: firewall

Basculer en ou hors fonction: toggle on and off

Bavarder: chatter

Bit 0 ou 1: bit

Bit binaire: binary digit
blow out: se planter

Boite: box

Bouton bascule: toggle

Brochage: pin out

Broche des circuits intégrés: pins of integrated circuits

Byte, un mot constitué de 0 et de 1: byte

C

Cable alimentation: power cable

Cable d'alimentation: feeder line

Cable fibre optique: fiber-optic cable

Cache mémoire (mémoire tampon): cache

Cache mémoire: cash memory

Calendrier mensuel: monthcalendar

Caméra internet: live cam

Camera web: webcam

Capacité: storage

Caractère unique: uniqueness

Caractère: character

Carte graphique: graphic card

Carte mère: mother board

Carte réseau: network adapter card

Carte son: sound card

Carte vidéo: video card:

Carte virtuelle: virtual card

Carte: card
Cartouche d’encre: ink cartridge
Cartouche: cartridge
Chaine de caractères: string
Chemin d’accès complet: full path
Chemin d’accès: pathway
Cheval de Troie (virus): torjan
Choisi: select
Circuits intégrés: integrated circuits, silicon chips or micrchips
Circuits microcontrôleurs: microcontroller circuits
Citation: quoting
Claire: friendly
Clavier: keyboard
Clé d’accès: acces key
Clé d’enregistrement: keylogger
Clé électronique: electronic key
Cocher une case: check
Codé: encrypted
Coder: cipher
Coeur (connecteur): core
Coller: paste
Commande: order
Commerce électronique: E-business
Commerce électronique: E-commerce
Commutateur: switch
Compacter, comprimer, paquet: pack
Composant d’interface graphique: widget
Composant de l'ordinateur qui exécute les programmes: informatiques: Central processing unit (CPU)
Composants électroniques: electronic components
Compte internet: account
Compte internet: internet account
Compteur: counter
Confidentialité: privacy
Connecteur audio: DIN audio

Connexion parallèle: centronics
Consommation: consumption
Contactez-nous: feeback
Contenu: content
Contrôle utilisateur: use control
Copie de fichier: copyfile
Copier vers un fichier: copy to
Correspondence de type: mapping
Corriger: fix
Coupure: break
Couverture: jacket
Création d'un tableau: create table
Cryptage: encoding
Curseur: slider

D

Date de dernière modification d'un fichier: date last modified
Débordement, dépassement: overrun
Décalage: shift
Découper: split
Défaut: bug
Défenseur: defender
Définit une constante: define
Dégagement de responsabilité: disclaimer
Dégâts: damage
Dépanner, corriger: debug
Dépanner: debugging
Dépassement de capacité: overflow
Désactiveé: disabled
Détenteurs de puce: chip holders
Détruire: zap
Développeur: developer
Diaporama Web: web slide show
Disc dur: disk
Disc dur: hard disc

Disponible, activé: enable
Disque compacte: compact disc CD
Disque de démarrage: boot disk
Disquette: floppy disk
Données analysées: parsed
Données: data (singulier)
Double cœur: dual core
Drapeau: flag
DVD (disque): DVD

E

Éclairage: highlight
Ecran plat: flat monitor
Ecran: monitor
Ecran: screen
Ecrire une ligne: writeline
Egal à égal: peer to peer
Egal à: equal to
Elargissez: broaden
Eliminer, simplifier par: cancel (to)
Empiler, tas, pile: stack
Emplacement: placeholder
Empty: vide
En ligne: online
Encoche: notch
Enregistrement en ligne: lineage
En-tête: heading
Entrer: enter
Espace de travail: workspace
Espion: spyware
Essais: attempt
Etat d'affichage: view state:
Etiquette de formulaire: form label
Etiquette: Lbx
Evaluation: rating

Examiner: examine
Exemple: example

F

Faire suivre: readdress
Fait, terminé: done
Faraîchir: rebrush
Faux, truqué: fake
Favoris: bookmark
Favourie: favorite
Fenetre window: command window
Fermer: close
Fiche: plug
Fiches de données: data sheets
Fichier de témoins, programme mouchard: cookie
File d'attente: queue
Fin, terminé: completion
Flèche droite: right arrow
Flot: stream
Flottante: floating
Foirnisseur: content provider
Fonctionnalité: feature
Fond de panier: card cage
Forcer: force
Formatage: format
Founiseur: helpprovider
Fournisseur d'accès à internet: provider
Fragment: snippet
Fréquence: frequency

G

Gestion: handling
Glacé: glossy
Graveur: rewriter

H

Hachage: hash

Hamçennage: phishing

Hébergement Web: web hosting

Hébergement: hosting

Héritage: inherit

Heure actuelle: current time

Hors connexion: offline

Hôte: host

I

Identificateur: handle

Identificateur: identifier

Ignorer: bypass

Image interactive: imagemap

Imbriquer: nest

Impression en cours: printing

Imprimante: printer

Inclure: include

Incorporé: embedded

Index: cursor

Informatique: computer science

Instruction: directive

Intelligent: smart

Intercalaire, tablette: tray

Interdit: forbidden

Interligne: line feed

Internaute novice: dummy

Interréteur de commande: shell

Interrupteur à bascule: toggle switch

Interrupteur: switch

Intervalle, gamme: range

J

Jeu de composants: chipset

Joindre: join
Journal: logger

K
Kit de connexion: starter pack

L
Laisser un intervalle: space
Lancer: launch
Lecteur de carte: card reader
Lecteur de disquette: floppy
Lecture d'une ligne: readline
Liaison numérique asymétriques: Asymmetric Digital Subscriber Line (ADSL)
Libre: free
Lien entrant: blacklink
Lien: link
Livre d'or: guestbook
Logiciel malveillant: malware
Longueur de champ: field length

M
Magazine Web: webzine
Maison ou habitat passive : passive house
Materiel: hardware
Mégahertz: megahertz
Mémoire morte effaçable électriquement et programmable: Electrically-Erasable Programmable Read-Only Memory (EEPROM)
Mémoire morte reprogrammable: Erasable Programmable Read Only Memory (EPROM)
Mémoire morte: Programmable Read Only Memory (PROM)
Mémoire non volatile: Read-Only Memory (ROM)
Mémoire non volatile: Ultra Violet Programmable Read Only Memory (UVPROM)
Mémoire vive, mémoire système ou mémoire volatile: random-

Access memory (RAM)
Mettre en forme une page Web: format a web page
Micropresesseur: microprocessor
Mode natural: native
Modèle: pattern
Modem: modem
Modifier la structure: modify structure
Module d'extension: plug-in
Mondial: worldwide
Mot clé: keyword
Moteur de recherché: google

N
Navigateur hors connexion: offline browser
Naviguer sur le Web: browser
Naviguer: browse
Nœud: node
Nom d'emprunt: alias
Nom de famille: last name
Nom de fichier: file name
Nom de l'hote ou l'hébergeur: host name
Non analysé: unparsed
Non disponible: unavailable
Non géré: unmanaged
Notifier: notify
Numéro d'identification: ID
Numéro de thread: ID thread
Numérotation du modem: dialing modem

O
Obligatoire: required
Onglet: tab
Ordinateur de bureau: desktop
Ordinateur de poche: palmtop
Ordinateur portable: laptop

Ordinateur: computer
Ordinatuer de bureau: office computer
Ordinogramme: flow chart
Organisateur d'idées: outline processor
Ouverture d'un fichier: file open

P

Page d'accueil: home page
Page précédente: back
Page similaire: related
Panneau d'accès: door (access panel)
Paquetage: package
Paramètre fictif: placeholder
Passé système: pass-through
Pavé numérique: keypad
PC portable: notebook
Percer: crack
Perceur des programmes informatiques: cracker
Périphérique: device
Péritel: euroconector
Permettre: let
Personnalisation: customizing
Perte: leakage
Pirate du net: hacker
Pirate du réseau téléphonique: pirate telephone network
Pirate informatique: black hat
Pirater: hack
Pirates informatiques qui détruisent pour le plaisir: crasher
Pixel: pixel
Plus petit que: Less than
Point d'accès: port
Porte monnaie électronique: digital wallet
Poussoir: knob
Prénom: First name
Prêt: ready

Prime (´), tiret: dash
Prise: jack
Processeur: processor
Processeurs informatiques: computer processors CPU
Produit additionnel: add-on
Programmer, programmation: programming
Programmes informatique: computeur programs
Publicité en ligne: online advertising
Publier: publish
Puce: bullets
Puissance: power

Q
Quadrillage: grid
Quarantine: quarantaine
Qui apparaît à l'écran: pop-up
Quitter: leave

R
Raccordement: patch
Raccourci: shortcut
Rang, classer, grade: rank
Recherche d'image: image research
Recherche en ligne: look online
Redémarrer: reboot, restart
Redimensionner: resize
Régènérer, reconstruire: rebuild
Réglage: setting
Réintialiser: reset
Relecture, reproduction: playback
Remplacement, suppelanter: override
Renvoi: tag
Répertoire des fichiers temporaire: temporary Internet File
Report: carry

Requête d'écriture: (WRQ) write request
Reroidisseur: cooleur
Réseau de sentiers: trails system
Réseau informatique: computer network
Réseau local: local area network
Résolution: resolution
Résoudre: solving
Restaurer: restore
Robot: spider
Rôder: lurk
Routeur: router
Ruban: ribbon

S
Saisie d'écran: screen shot
Saisie: entry
Salon de bavardage: chat room
Sans disc: diskless
Sans fil: cordless, wireless
Saturé: flooding
Saut: jump
Sauter: skip
Scanneur, numériseur de document: scanner
Schèma: outline
Se connecter: connect
Se mettre en ligne: align
Secret: backdoor
Séparateur: splitter
Serveur d'impression: print server
Service de discussion internet: internet relay chat
Sigle: acronym
Signal d'entrée: input
Siteweb: website
Sortir: exit
Source d'information altenative: blogstream

Souriard (binette) : smiley
Souris: mouse
Sous fenetre: window pane
Sous-classe: deriver class
Sous-fenêtrage: panner
Sous-jacent: underlying
Sous-routine: gosub
Sous-système: subsystem
Station d'accueil: docking station
Stocker dans la mémoire: caching
Stopper le processus: kill
Superposition: overlay
Supprimer des fichiers: deletefile
Supprimer: delete
Surcharge: overload
Sûreté: safety
Surnom: nickname
Surveiller: guarding
Système binaire: binary number

T
Tableau: array
Tandis que: while
Taux de clic: click rate
Taxe: fee
Téléchargements des données: uploading data
Télécharger: download
Télécommande: remote control
Télécopieur: fax
Tête d'impression: printhead
Titre d'un tableau: caption
Titre, intitulé: title
Touche de raccourci: keyboard shortcut
Touche de verrouillage numérique: num lock
Touche: key

Tourner: spin
Tous droits réservés: all rights reserved
Traçage: tracing
Trace: track
Traceur: plotter
Traitement de données: data processing
Traitement: processing
Traiter: treat
Transfère le lien hypertexte: forward hyperlink
Trou: pit
Trouver: locate, found

U
Unité centrale: computeur unit
Utiliser: use

V
Valider: valid
Ventilateur: fan
Virus-vers: worm
Visual: visual

W
Web diffusion: webcast

Z
Zone de groupe: groupbox
Zone: area
Zoom avant, agrandire: zoom-in

DEVELOPPEMENT DURABLE – SUSTAINABLE DEVELOPMENT

A
Améliorer: improve
Ampoule: bulb

B
Bail foncier: land lease
Barrages des marées: tidal barrages
Bec: nozzle
Biocarburant: biofuels
Bioénergie: bioenergy
Biomasse: biomass
Boite de carton: containerboard
Boîte de vitesses: gear box

C
Canaux dérivés: tailraces
Caoutchouc: natural rubber
Carrosserie: bodywork
Carton ondulé: corrugated fiberboard
Carton: cardboard
Centrale électrique: power station
Centrale solaire photovoltaïque: photovoltaic system
Centrale solaire: solar power
Cerf-volant: flying kite
Chemin de rivière: riverbed
Cliquet, crochet, gachette, arretoir: pawl
Conception assisté par ordinateur: computer-aided design
Conduite pour Controller l'écoulement: penstock
Consommateur: consumer
Coucher de soleil: sun set
Crépuscule: twilight
Creuset: crucible

D
Développment durable (DD): sustainable development (SD)

Double vitrage: double glazing

E

Eau potable: drinking water
Echangeur de chaleur: heat exchanger
Ecluses, vannes: sluice gates
Eco-conception: ecodesign
Effet de Serre: Greenhouse effect
Emballage: packaging
Embarder, dévier la route, giration: yaw
Empiéter: impinging
Encoche, entaille, brèche: notch
Energie des vagues: wave power
Energie du vent: wind power
Énergie géothermique: geothermal energy
Energie hydroélectrique: hydroélectricity
Energie marémotrice: tidal power
Energie renouvelable: renewable energy
Energie thermique: thermal energy
Eolienne: wind turbine
Etang: ponds
Evaluation: assessment
Exploiter: harness

F

Four solaire (cuiseur solaire): solar cooker (oven)
Four solaire: solar furnace
Fournir de l'électricité en vrac: provide bulk power
Freins: brake
Fusion: molten

G

Gaz à effet de Serre: Greenhouse gas
Grande échelle: large scale

Guichet: wicket

H

Héliostat: heliostat

Hors538cote: off shore

Hors plate-forme: off-shelf

Hors réseau: off-grid

I

Impulsions électriques: electrical impulses

Inégale: unequal

Installation de retenu: impoundement facility

J

Jetable: disposable

K

Kilowatt-heure: kilowatt-hours (kWh)

L

Laine de verre: loft insulation

Lame ou pale: blade

Lever de soleil: sun rise

M

Machine à vapeur: steam engine

Marée descendante: outgoing tide

Marée montante: incoming tide

Marée sortante: ingoing tide

Marée: tide

Matériaux légers: light weight materials

Minerai de fer: iron ore

Mis en arrêt: shelved

Modèles d'écoulement du vent: wind flow patterns

Moudre: grinding

Moulin à eau: watermill

Moulin à vent: windmill

N

Norme et resources: technical standard and resouces

O

Objectif: purpose

Ozone: ozone

P

Panneaux photovoltaiques: solar cells

Panneaux solaire: solar panels

Pierre de moulin de forme cylindrique: mill stone

Pignon, roue dentée: sprocket

Précipiter: rushing

Proche de littoral: offshore

Propulseur: propellers

Puissance: power

Puits: wells

R

Rayonnement solaire: sunlight

Remuer: stir

Réseaux d'Electricité National: National Electricity Grid

Réservoir, citerne: tank

Ressources renouvelables: renewable resources

Rotor (moteur): rotor (motor)

Roué à eau: water wheel

Roue libre: freewheel

Rouleau: scroll

S

S'enflammer: ignite

S'éteint: shuts off

Scellée: sealed

Serre: Greenhouse (glasshouse)
Stator (moteur): stator (motor)
Surgir: sprang up

T
Tâche: task
Tour solaire: solar power tower, solar furnace
Tourner verticalement: spin vertically
Treillis d'acier: steel lattice
Tubes en serpentin: coil of pipes
Tubes traités: draft tubes

V
Vaisseaux marines à voiles: sail vessels
Ventilateur: fan
Verser: pour
Villages reculés: remote villages

Z
Zone costale: coastal area

Oussama Sayadi is a Physics and Chemistry teacher in France, former lecturer at the Catholic Medecine University, Lille Engineering School ICAM and the Physiotherapy Institute IKPO in Lille, an examiner and also an author of several books concerning the history of sciences.

Oussama Sayadi est professeur de sciences physiques en France. Il a enseigné à l'Univerité Catholique de Médecine et à l'ICAM de Lille. Il est également auteur de plusieurs livres d'histoire des sciences.

This dictionary is a guide, defining key terms of scientific subjects in English and French. Each entry begins with a clear, one sentence definition and is followed by explanation and examples. All entries are carefully cross-referenced and the dictionary format makes it exceptionally easy to use.

This dictionary has been deliberately designed to be valuable at every stage of Physics, Chemistry, Mathematics, Sustainable Development and Computer Science courses:

For students - everything you need is in the dictionary, making it the ideal exam revision companion.

For everyone else - basic ideas and concepts are introduced and simply explained and followed by straightforward explanation and illustrations to widen your understanding of the subject.

Achevé d'imprimer en août 2013 par LEN S.A.S. – 92150 Suresnes
Dépôt légal : août 2013
Imprimé en France